Interpreting the Constitution

◇

Interpreting the Constitution

The Debate over Original Intent

◇

EDITED BY

Jack N. Rakove

Northeastern University Press

BOSTON

Northeastern University Press

Copyright 1990 by Jack N. Rakove

Library of Congress Cataloging-in-Publication Data

Interpreting the Constitution : the debate over original intent /
edited by Jack N. Rakove.
p.   cm.
Includes bibliographical references.
ISBN 1-55553-079-6 (alk. paper)
ISBN 1-55553-081-8 (pbk. : alk. paper)
1. United States—Constitutional law—Interpretation and
construction.   2. United States—Constitutional history.
I. Rakove, Jack N., 1947–
KF4550.I58   1990
342.73′029—dc20
[347.30229]   90-34549
CIP

Designed by Catherine Johnson

This book was composed in Janson by Coghill Composition, Richmond, Virginia. It was printed and bound by McNaughton & Gunn, Inc., in Saline, Michigan. The paper is Glatfelter Offset, an acid-free sheet.

MANUFACTURED IN THE UNITED STATES OF AMERICA
94 93 92 91 90   5 4 3 2 1

For Robert and Daniel
originals of their own

Contents

◆

═══
═══

◆

◆

PART ONE

The Public Debate

◆

PART TWO

Historical Perspectives

·

PART THREE

Normative Issues

Acknowledgments

◆
———
———
———
◆

The idea for this project can be traced to my friend Gordon Wood, whom I hope one day to repay in an appropriate way, and to Bill Frohlich of Northeastern University Press, a most persuasive editor. With his usual good cheer, my Stanford colleague Thomas Gery offered advice about the selection of readings as well as the introduction. Karen Dunn-Haley of the Department of History at Stanford aided in the preparation of the bibliography. This book was prepared for publication through the use of the Kurzweil optical scanner, into whose mysteries and idiosyncrasies I was initiated by Felix Limcaoco of the Academic Information Resources office at Stanford. I am also grateful to Dee Marquez and Gloria Escobar of the Stanford Humanities Center.

I gratefully acknowledge the following:

William J. Brennan, Jr., for permission to reprint "The Constitution of the United States: Contemporary Ratification," which was first presented as a speech to the Text and Teaching Symposium at Georgetown University on October 12, 1985. Copyright © 1985 by William J. Brennan.

Paul Brest, for permission to reprint "The Misconceived Quest for the Original Understanding," which first appeared in *Boston University Law Review* v. 60, 1980. Copyright © 1980 by Paul Brest.

Lino A. Graglia, for permission to reprint "How the Constitution Disappeared," which first appeared in *Commentary* v. 81, February 1986. Copyright © 1986 by Lino A. Graglia.

The Harvard Law Review Association, for permission to reprint "The Original Understanding of Original Intent" by H. Jefferson Powell, which first appeared in *Harvard Law Review*, v. 98, March 1985. Copyright © 1985 by the Harvard Law Review Association.

James H. Hutson, for permission to reprint "The Creation of the Constitution: The Integrity of the Documentary Record," which first appeared in the *Texas Law Review* v. 65, November 1986. Copyright © 1986 by James H. Hutson.

J. Morgan Kousser and *Constitutional Commentary*, for permission to reprint "Expert Witnesses, Rational Choice, and the Search for Intent," which first appeared in *Constitutional Commentary* v. 5, Summer 1988. Copyright © 1988 by J. Morgan Kousser and *Constitutional Commentary*.

Charles A. Lofgren and *Constitutional Commentary*, for permission to reprint "The Original Understanding of Original Intent?" which first appeared in *Constitutional Commentary* v. 5, Winter 1988. Copyright © 1988 by Charles A. Lofgren and *Constitutional Commentary*.

Henry Paul Monaghan, for permission to reprint "Stare Decisis and Constitutional Adjudication," which first appeared in *Columbia Law Review* v. 88, May 1988. Copyright © 1988 by Henry Paul Monaghan.

The Society for the Advancement of Education, for permission to reprint "Interpreting the Constitution" by Edwin Meese III. Reprinted from *USA Today Magazine*, October 1986. Copyright © 1986 by the Society for the Advancement of Education.

The Trustees of Indiana University and Fred B. Rothman & Co., for permission to reprint "Neutral Principles and Some First Amendment Problems" by Robert H. Bork, which first appeared in the *Indiana Law Journal* v. 47, 1971. Copyright © 1971 by the Trustees of Indiana University and Fred B. Rothman & Co.

"Mr. Meese, Meet Mr. Madison" first appeared in *The Atlantic*, December 1986. Copyright © 1986 by Jack N. Rakove.

Interpreting the Constitution

Introduction

⁍

IN A WIDELY noticed speech to the American Bar Association in July 1985, Attorney General Edwin Meese III declared his support for "a jurisprudence of original intention" and thereby sparked—or rather rekindled—a debate about the proper norms of constitutional interpretation. "The original meaning of constitutional provisions and statutes," Meese argued, provided "the only reliable guide for judgment." A return to this standard of jurisprudence, he further suggested, would help to confine the federal judiciary—especially the Supreme Court—within its true and proper role. Judges would once again decide cases not on the basis of their views of "sound public policy" or their "ideological predilections," but rather with a principled restraint that recognized the importance of judicial deference to the political branches at both the national and state levels of government.[1]

Three months later, in a paper prepared for the Text and Teaching Symposium at Georgetown University, Associate Justice William J. Brennan restated and defended exactly the notions of constitutional interpretation that the attorney general and his conservative supporters were so eager to criticize. Without responding to Meese directly by name, Justice Brennan dismissed the idea of limiting interpretation to the recovery of original intention as both impractical and inadequate. The doctrine of original intent, he declared, "feigns self-effacing deference to the specific judgments of those who forged our original social compact. But in truth it is little more than arrogance cloaked as humility." Part of the problem, Brennan observed, lay in the difficulty of ascertaining original intent. But he devoted the heart of his address to repudiating the narrow definition of judicial responsibility that the attorney general favored and in effect to defending the path-breaking decisions to which he had contributed so much during his three decades on the Court. In Brennan's view, the Constitution was nothing less than "a sublime oration on the dignity of man," "a sparkling vision of the supremacy of the human dignity of every individual." And the proper duty of the judiciary, the senior member of the Court made clear, was to interpret the text of the Constitution in ways that would extend and amplify that vision.

Critics of the conflicting positions that Attorney General Meese and Justice Brennan represented quickly seized on these addresses as proof of everything that was wrong with their opponents' theories of jurisprudence. Liberal commentators such as the historian Arthur Schlesinger, Jr., Anthony Lewis of the *New York Times*, and Professor Laurence Tribe of the Harvard Law School denounced Meese's appeal for a "jurisprudence of original intention" as a transparent effort to provide a rationale for overturning many of the crucial decisions of the Warren and Burger courts. For their part, conservatives who joined Meese in excoriating "the radical egalitarianism and expansive civil libertarianism of the Warren Court" treated Brennan's airy generalities as a tacit confession that he was indeed disposed to elevate his own values above the explicit language of the Constitution.

The context in which these two addresses became the subject of numerous op-ed pieces and magazine essays was at least as important as anything Meese or Brennan had said. Rolling back the "judicial activism" of recent decades was a major goal of "the Reagan Revolution," and its attainment, it was widely agreed, depended on the number of nominations that President Ronald Reagan would be able to make to an aging Supreme Court. The growing public debate about the idea of a jurisprudence of original intention must be seen in that light. For many conservatives, the appeal to original intent served to legitimate the criteria that the administration could apply to its judicial appointments. Liberals who feared the erosion of the legacy of the Warren and Burger courts naturally interpreted the claims made for "originalism" in correspondingly sinister terms.

This public debate about the jurisprudence of original intention came to something of a climax in the bicentennial summer of 1987, when President Reagan nominated Judge Robert Bork to the seat vacated by the retirement of Justice Lewis Powell. A well-known critic of the Warren Court, Judge Bork was also the author of an important article, "Neutral Principles and Some First Amendment Problems," that helped prepare the way for the resurgence of originalist thought in the 1980s. There and elsewhere, Bork faulted the Supreme Court for creating or legitimating claims of rights that could not be explicitly found in the Constitution—that is, for acting as legislators prepared to range well beyond the original and limited meaning of the text. In this sense, the rejection of Bork's nomination might in part be seen as a repudiation of the theory of interpretation with which he was associated.

These events gave the issue of original intent a celebrity that general questions of constitutional interpretation—as opposed to specific interpretations of the Constitution—rarely enjoy. But in fact the debate over the importance that judges (and other officials) should ascribe to the "original meaning" of the Constitution or the "original intentions" of its framers and ratifiers has a long history. In its earliest form, a version of originalism can be traced back almost (if not quite) to the adoption of the Constitution in 1787–88. More recently, appeals to the original meaning of specific provisions of the Constitution figured prominently in many of the legal and political controversies that roiled American public life after the midpoint of the twentieth century. Probably the most important questions concerned the original meaning of the Fourteenth Amendment, which provided the central textual authority not only for the attack on segregation that gained decisive momentum with the landmark ruling in *Brown* v. *Board of Education* (1954), but also for a host of decisions extending the specific protections of the Bill of Rights to areas of state governance ranging from the rights of the criminally accused to reapportionment. Other issues also proved impossible to discuss without attempting to reconstruct the considerations that had led to the adoption of relevant clauses of the Constitution. Contentious disputes about school prayer and public aid to religious schools, for example, naturally inspired searching examination of the original meaning of the establishment clause of the First Amendment.

Nor were disputes about the original meaning of the Constitution confined to the realm of the courts and questions of individual and minority rights. Mounting congressional regret over the course and conduct of the American military intervention in Indochina, culminating in the adoption (over a presidential veto) of the War Powers Act of 1973, was accompanied by historical inquiries into the original allocation of constitutional authority over war and foreign affairs. So, too, the domestic political scandal that eventually led to the resignation of President Richard M. Nixon in August 1974 also brought originalist efforts to define the "high crimes and misdemeanors" for which impeachment was the constitutional remedy.

The merits and defects of the various forays in originalism that all these disputes launched encouraged some scholars to consider the problem of original intent in a more abstract light well before the tacit exchange between Attorney General Meese and Justice Brennan brought the issue into the public arena. Although neither Meese nor Brennan could add much of substance to the issues that scholars had already been considering, their remarks gave a new impetus and importance to an ongoing debate, and in conjunction with the bicentennial of the Constitution, they encouraged a number of legal scholars and historians to examine the issue of originalism more closely. Many of the most acute assessments of originalism have come from those who reject it on both practical and normative grounds—that is, as both a problem of historical reconstruction and a theory of constitutional interpretation. Yet by doing so, they also suggest that the idea of a jurisprudence of original intention may have a durable life of its own.

This collection of essays surveys that debate in a way that attempts to balance not only the contending claims and arguments but also the complementary concerns of history and law.

By way of introduction, Part One reprints three leading statements of the basic "conservative" and "liberal" positions: an address presenting Edwin Meese's essential views, originally delivered before his appointment as attorney general but revised after the public debate was well under way; Justice Brennan's talk at Georgetown University; and the rather slashing criticism Brennan's paper in turn received from Professor Lino A. Graglia in his article "How the Constitution Disappeared," published, appropriately enough, in the neoconservative magazine *Commentary*.

Part Two asks how well a jurisprudence of original intent can be squared with our historical knowledge of American constitutional and legal theory during the crucial period of the 1780s, when the Constitution was adopted, and the 1790s, when the first disputes over its interpretation led to the formation of the first political party system of Federalists and Democratic-Republicans. In one way or another, all four essays in this section ask whether or to what extent the idea that original intentions or understandings should inform later interpretations of the Constitution was itself part of the original meaning of the Constitution.

In their respective essays on "The Original Understanding of Original Intent," H. Jefferson Powell of the Duke University School of Law and Charles A. Lofgren of Claremont McKenna College examine the theories of legal interpretation that were available to the framers, ratifiers, and first interpreters of the Constitution. Powell argues that modern notions of intent, defined in terms of the subjective and collective purposes of legislators (or constitution writers), had not yet become part of the interpretative arsenal upon which judges and other officials could draw to resolve ambiguities in the meaning of legal texts. The intention of a statute or, by implication, a constitution, was to be discovered in the text itself, as its meaning was clarified through a common-law process of interpretation and application. Legislative history and the political and intellectual context within which the act or constitution was adopted were not considered relevant.

Lofgren accepts important parts of Powell's argument but challenges its essential conclusion on two grounds. First, he disputes Powell's reading of particular pieces of the historical evidence that best reveal how Americans after 1787 conceived of the process of constitutional interpretation. Second, and more important, he reads much of this same evidence to support the proposition that one version of originalism *did* attain authority at an early point. By the mid-1790s, some Americans did believe that "ratifier intent"—

the understanding of the Constitution prevailing at the moment of its adoption—could indeed constrain the scope and reach of subsequent interpretation. Where Powell concludes that Americans simply applied previous rules of interpretation to the task of constitutional decision making, Lofgren argues that the radical act of organizing government under a written constitution evoked a new theory of interpretation. The Constitution could not be regarded as an ordinary act of legislation. Because its authority was derived from the extraordinary act of a sovereign people, *their* understanding of the document to which they were consenting should be regarded as consequential.

In this disagreement over particular pieces of historical evidence, and especially over the ideas of James Madison, Powell and Lofgren lay the groundwork for the two remaining essays that round out Part Two. Since all appeals to original intent are appeals to the records of history, a jurisprudence of original intent requires a high degree of confidence in the quality of our documentary sources and in the capacity of judges (and other concerned parties) to read them intelligently. In "The Creation of the Constitution: The Integrity of the Documentary Record," James H. Hutson of the Library of Congress surveys the adequacy of the surviving journals and notes of debates from the Constitutional Convention of 1787 and the state ratification conventions of 1787–88. Hutson affirms the essential reliability of the notes Madison took at Philadelphia but emphasizes that they remain at best only a partial record of the great Convention. Yet even at that, Madison's notes are far superior to any of the records from the state convention—which for legal purposes are arguably (following Lofgren) the more important. The surviving documentary evidence, rich as it may be for the historian, may thus fall short of what a jurisprudence of original intent would optimally require.

The nuances of historical evidence are also the subject of my essay, "Mr. Meese, Meet Mr. Madison." Much of the prevailing modern interpretation of the political theory of the Constitution takes the form of an elaborate commentary on the ideas and writings of Madison—especially in his capacity as coauthor of *The Federalist*. Yet Madison was a subtle and complex thinker, and appeals to his original intentions at the 1787 Convention or his original understandings of the Constitution cannot be reduced to a few choice quotations from *Federalist* No. 10 and No. 51. On one point in particular, his most profound assessments of the potential "vices" of republican government are not easily reconciled with the logic of the current appeal to original intent. For where the current criticism of federal judicial activism is designed to enlarge the ability of state and local governments to reassert control over sensitive areas of social policy, Madison's deepest concern in 1787 was to prevent democratic majorities in the states from violating individual and minority rights.

All four of these essays, then, consider how well the claims for originalist jurisprudence can be justified from the vantage point of late eighteenth-century American constitutional thought. Yet the ongoing dispute about originalism obviously involves norms of legal decision making and constitutional interpretation that far transcend whatever can be gleaned from the evidence of history. Part Three of this volume accordingly includes three of the most significant contributions that legal scholars have made to the debate over originalism, as well as a final historically grounded essay of particular relevance to contemporary issues flowing from recent applications of the Fourteenth Amendment.

No one has exerted greater influence over the development of the conservative appeal to original intent than Robert Bork. Although his 1971 essay "Neutral Principles and Some First Amendment Problems" seems to say little about originalism per se, its argument is essential to the current originalist brief in at least two ways. First, Bork's criticism of the modern Supreme Court rests on the claim that too many of its modern decisions violate the original "Madisonian" constitutional design insofar as they reflect only the willful preferences of the justices, thereby usurping powers that properly belong to democratic majorities acting through their elected representatives. Second, in his objections to both the famous *Griswold* v. *Connecticut* decision (1965) enunciating a constitutional right of privacy and to expansive readings of the First Amendment's protection of free speech, Bork clearly expresses the central originalist contention that judges have no warrant for creating or legitimating new rights not explicitly mentioned in the Constitution.

In his 1980 essay "The Misconceived Quest for the Original Understanding," Dean Paul Brest of the Stanford Law School developed many of the arguments that have since been deployed to challenge the idea of originalism. Although Brest takes seriously the claims of a "moderate originalism" which recognizes that the Constitution is both "authoritative" and "open-textured," he identifies a number of reasons, from the practical to the epistemological, for doubting whether the appeal to original intent can ever provide either a desirable or a feasible rule of judicial decision making. How, for example, Brest asks, can later interpreters know how the original adopters of an act (or for that matter, the Constitution) meant their language to be interpreted? Moreover, Brest candidly defends the virtues of a "nonoriginalist" model of adjudication in all those areas where "changing public views" provide powerful grounds for preferring the judgments of the present to the authority of the past.

Professor Henry Monaghan of the Columbia University School of Law can hardly be described as a friend of the nonoriginalism that Brest is bold enough to avow. Yet in his essay, "Stare Decisis and Constitutional Adjudication," Monaghan in many ways affirms the force of the objections that originalism would have to overcome to offer a serious or feasible model of judicial decision making. Foremost among these is the substantial upheaval it would require in the prevailing constitutional and political order, whole provinces of which, Monaghan emphasizes, have departed from anything remotely resembling a historically plausible reconstruction of the original understanding. In theory, constitutional adjudication is the one area of law where the doctrine of stare decisis may exert the weakest claim against the appeal to the superior authority of the original understanding. Yet even here, Monaghan concludes, the force of settled precedent demands respect, especially when we cannot know how the original adopters of the Constitution would deal with "transformative changes" that had undeniably and conclusively altered the constitutional order.

The final essay in Part Three focuses on what might be called the methodological problem of determining the intentions of institutions whose procedures and rules of voting can mask both the motives on which they act and the array of individual purposes and expectations that enter into any collective decision. In "Expert Witnesses, Rational Choice, and the Search for Intent," Professor J. Morgan Kousser, a political historian at the California Institute of Technology, considers practical problems of determining intention in three areas: cases involving claims of discriminatory treatment based on statistical analysis; voting rights legislation; and the Fourteenth Amendment (whose meaning and interpretation are, of course, the crucial source of many of the constitutional controversies that have fueled the recent resurgence of the originalist appeal). Recognizing that questions of intent necessarily figure prominently in cases involving claims of discrimination or denial of equal protection, Kousser provides useful lessons about the practical problems that have to be overcome to make sense of the historical evidence.

The essays collected in this book hardly exhaust the range of questions and positions that the issue of original intent has generated. Yet they do represent something of the spectrum of debate and, more than that, they also demonstrate why the problem of originalism cannot be reduced either to diatribes against activist judges or to grand claims that "the Founders" drafted so vaguely worded a Constitution because they foresaw the need of later generations to interpret it expansively. (It is, after all, entirely possible that the framers and ratifiers of 1787–88 or 1865–68 would have sought to bind our hands—or the pens of our judges—could they only have anticipated the uses to which the power of judicial review could be put.) For better or worse, whether misconceived or not, appeals to the original meaning of the Constitution or the intentions of its framers or the understandings of its ratifiers do seem to be part of the American political order. The force of this appeal is not constant, but it is recurrent—and at different points in our history, it has been tapped by liberals and conservatives alike. But like other forces, the phenomenon of originalism may be easier to observe than to describe or direct. As a matter both of historical reconstruction and constitutional adjudication, the theory of originalist jurisprudence, to be taken seriously, has to encounter the range of problems identified in these essays.

The essays in this volume have been reprinted as they originally appeared, although a few obvious errors of spelling, grammar, and the like have been silently corrected. For the sake of uniformity, some changes have also been made in capitalization and in the style used for endnotes. Where individual authors refer either to other passages in their own contributions to this volume, or to other essays reprinted here, I have altered the page citations in the notes accordingly, so that they identify pages in this book rather than the original locus of publication.

Note

1. Edwin Meese III, Address before the American Bar Association, Washington, D.C., July 9, 1985.

The Public Debate

Interpreting the Constitution

◆

━━━━
━━━━

◆

EDWIN MEESE III

A LARGE PART of American history has been the history of constitutional debate. From the Federalists and the Anti-Federalists, to Webster and Calhoun, to Lincoln and Douglas, we find many examples. Now, as we approach the bicentennial of the framing of the Constitution, we are witnessing another debate concerning our fundamental law. It is not simply a ceremonial debate, but one that promises to have a profound effect on the future of our Republic.

The current debate is a sign of a healthy nation. Unlike people of many other countries, we are free both to discover the defects of our laws and our government through open discussion and to correct them through our political system.

This debate on the Constitution involves great and fundamental issues. It invites the participation of the best minds the bar, academia, and the bench have to offer. Recently, there have been important new contributions to this debate from some of the most distinguished scholars and jurists in the land. Representatives of the three branches of the federal government have entered the debate, as have journalistic commentators.

A great deal has already been said, much of it of merit and on point, but occasionally there has been confusion and in some cases even distortion. Caricatures and straw men, as one customarily finds even in the greatest debates, have made appearances. I've been surprised at some of the hysterical shrillness that we've seen in editorials and other commentary. Perhaps this response is explained by the fact that what we've said defies liberal dogma. Still, whatever the differences, most participants are agreed about the same high objective—fidelity to our fundamental law.

In this article, I would like to discuss further the meaning of constitutional fidelity. In particular, I would like to describe in more detail this Administration's approach. Before doing so, I would like to make a few commonplace observations about the original document itself.

It is easy to forget what a young country America really is. The bicentennial of our independence was just a few years ago, that of the Constitution still two years off.

The period surrounding the creation of the Constitution is not a dark and mythical realm. The young America of the 1780s and 1790s was a vibrant place, alive with pamphlets, newspapers, and books chronicling and commenting upon the great issues of the day. We know how the Founding Fathers lived, and much of what they read, thought, and believed. The disputes and compromises of the Constitutional Convention were carefully recorded. The minutes of the Convention are a matter of public record. Several of the most important participants—including James Madison, the "father" of the Constitution—wrote comprehensive accounts of the Convention. Others, Federalists and Anti-Federalists alike, committed their arguments for and against ratification, as well as their understandings of the Constitution, to paper, so that their ideas and conclusions could be widely circulated, read, and understood.

In short, the Constitution is not buried in the mists of time. We know a tremendous amount of the history of its genesis. The bicentennial is encouraging even more scholarship about its origins. We know who did what, when, and many times why. One can talk intelligently about a "founding generation."

With these thoughts in mind, I would like to discuss the Administration's approach to constitutional interpretation which has been led by President Reagan and which we at the Department of Justice and my colleagues in other agencies have advanced. To begin, it may be useful to say what it is not.

Our approach does not view the Constitution as some kind of super municipal code, designed to address merely the problems of a particular era— whether those of 1787, 1789, or 1868. There is no question that the Constitutional Convention grew out of widespread dissatisfaction with the Articles of Confederation. However, the delegates at Philadelphia moved beyond the job of patching that document to write a *Constitution*. Their intention was to write a document not just for their times, but for posterity.

The language they employed clearly reflects this. For example, they addressed *commerce*, not simply shipping or barter. Later, the Bill of Rights spoke, through the Fourth Amendment, of "unreasonable searches and seizures," not merely the regulation of specific law enforcement practices of 1789. Still later, the framers of the Fourteenth Amendment were concerned not simply about the rights of black citizens to personal security, but also about the equal protection of the law for all persons within the states.

The Constitution is not a legislative code bound to the time in which it was written. Neither, however, is it a mirror that simply reflects the thoughts and ideas of those who stand before it.

A Written Document

OUR APPROACH TO constitutional interpretation begins with the document itself. The plain fact is, it exists. It is something that has been written down. Walter Berns of the American Enterprise Institute has noted that the central object of American constitutionalism was "the effort" of the Founders "to express fundamental governmental arrangements in a legal document—to 'get it in writing.' "

Indeed, judicial review has been grounded in the fact that the Constitution is a written, as opposed to an unwritten, document. In *Marbury* v. *Madison*, Supreme Court Chief Justice John Marshall rested his rationale for judicial review on the fact that we have a written Constitution with meaning that is binding upon judges. "It is apparent," he wrote, "that the framers of the constitution contemplated that instrument as a rule for the government of *courts*, as well as of the legislature. Why otherwise does it direct the judges to take an oath to support it?"

The presumption of a written document is that it conveys meaning. As Thomas Grey of the Stanford Law School has said, it makes "relatively definite and explicit what otherwise would be relatively indefinite and tacit."

We know that those who framed the Constitution chose their words carefully. They debated at great length the most minute points. The language they chose meant something. They proposed, substituted, edited, and carefully revised. Their words were studied with equal care by the state ratifying conventions.

This is not to suggest that there was unanimity among the framers and ratifiers on all points. The Constitution and the Bill of Rights, and some of the subsequent amendments, emerged after protracted debate. Nobody got everything he wanted. What is more, the framers were not clairvoyants—they could not foresee every issue that would be submitted for judicial review. Nor could they predict how all foreseeable disputes would be resolved under the Constitution. The point is, however, that the meaning of the Constitution can be known.

What does this written Constitution mean? In places, it is exactingly specific. Where it says that Presidents of the United States must be at least thirty-five years of age, it means exactly that. (I have not heard of any claim that thirty-five means thirty or twenty-five or twenty.) Where it specifies how the House and Senate are to be organized, it means what it says.

The Constitution, including its twenty-six amendments, also expresses particular principles. One is the right to be free of an unreasonable search or seizure. Another concerns religious liberty. Another is the right to equal protection of the laws. Those who framed these principles meant something by them, and the meaning can be found, understood, and applied.

The Constitution itself is also an expression of certain general principles. These principles reflect the deepest purpose of the Constitution—that of establishing a political system through which Americans can best govern themselves consistent with the goal of securing liberty.

The text and structure of the Constitution are instructive. It contains very little in the way of specific political solutions. It speaks volumes on how problems should be approached, and by *whom*. For example, the first three articles set out clearly the scope and limits of three distinct branches of national government, the powers of each being carefully and specifically enumerated. In this scheme, it is no accident to find the legislative branch described first, as the framers had fought and sacrificed to secure the right of democratic self-governance. Naturally, this faith in republicanism was not unbounded, as the next two articles make clear.

Yet, the Constitution remains a document of powers and principles. Its undergirding premise remains that democratic self-government is subject only to the limits of certain constitutional principles. This respect for the political process was made explicit early on. When John Marshall upheld the act of Congress chartering a national bank in *McCulloch* v. *Maryland*, he wrote: "The Constitution [was] intended to endure for ages to come, and, consequently, to be adapted to the various crises of human affairs." However, to use *McCulloch*, as some have tried, as support for the idea that the Constitution is a protean, changeable thing is to stand history on its head. Marshall was keeping faith with the original intention that Congress be free to elaborate and apply constitutional powers and principles. He was not saying that the Court must invent some new constitutional value in order to keep pace with the times. In Walter Berns' words, "Marshall's meaning is not that the Constitution may be adapted to the 'various crises of human affairs,' but that the legislative powers granted by the Constitution are adaptable to meet these crises."

The approach this Administration advocates is rooted in the text of the Constitution as illuminated by those who drafted, proposed, and ratified it. In his famous *Commentaries on the Constitution of the United States*, Justice Joseph Story explained that, "The first and fundamental rule in the interpretation of all instruments is, to construe them according to the sense of the terms, and the intention of the parties."

Our approach understands the significance of a written document and seeks to discern the particular and general principles it expresses. It recognizes that there may be debate at times over the application of these principles, but it does not mean these principles can not be identified.

Constitutional adjudication is obviously not a mechanical process. It requires an appeal to reason and discretion. The text and intention of the Constitution must be understood to constitute the banks within which constitutional interpretation must flow. As James Madison said, if "the sense in which the Constitution was accepted and ratified by the nation . . . be not the guide in expounding it, there can be no security for a consistent and stable, more than for a faithful exercise of its powers."

Thomas Jefferson, so often cited incorrectly as a framer of the Constitution, in fact shared Madison's view: "Our peculiar security is in the possession of a written Constitution. Let us not make it a blank paper by construction." Jefferson was even more explicit in his personal correspondence: "On every question of construction we should carry ourselves back to the time, when the Constitution was adopted; recollect the spirit manifested in the debates; and instead of trying [to find], what meaning may be squeezed out of the text, or invented against it, conform to the probable one, in which it was passed."

In the main, a jurisprudence that seeks to be faithful to our Constitution—a jurisprudence of original intention, as I have called it—is not difficult to describe. Where the language of the Constitution is specific, it must be obeyed. Where there is a demonstrable consensus among the framers and ratifiers as to a principle stated or implied by the Constitution, it should be followed as well. Where there is ambiguity as to the precise meaning or reach of a constitutional provision, it should be interpreted and applied in a manner so as to at least not contradict the text of the Constitution itself.

The Misuse of History

SADLY, while almost everyone participating in the current constitutional debate would give assent to these propositions, the techniques and conclusions of some of the debaters do violence to them. What is the source of this violence? In large part, I believe that it is the misuse of history stemming from the neglect of the ideal of a written constitution.

There is a frank proclamation by some judges and commentators that what matters most about the Constitution is not its words, but its so-called "spirit." These individuals focus less on the language of specific provisions than on what they describe as the "vision" or "concepts of human dignity" they find embodied in the Constitution. This approach to jurisprudence has led to some remarkable and tragic conclusions.

In the 1850s, the Supreme Court under Chief Justice Roger B. Taney read blacks out of the Constitution in order to invalidate Congress's attempt to limit the spread of slavery. The *Dred Scott* decision, famously described as a judicial "self-inflicted wound," helped bring on Civil War. There is a lesson in such history. There is danger in seeing the Constitution as an empty vessel into which each generation may pour its passion and prejudice.

Our own time has its own fashions and passions. In recent decades, many have come to view the Constitution—more accurately, part of the Constitution, provisions of the Bill of Rights, and the Fourteenth Amendment—as a charter for judicial activism on behalf of various constituencies. Those who hold this view often have lacked demonstrable textual or historical support for their conclusions. Instead, they have "grounded" their rulings in appeals to social theories, to moral philosophies or personal notions of human dignity, or to "penumbras," somehow emanating ghostlike from various provisions—identified and not identified—in the Bill of Rights. The problem with this approach, as John Hart Ely, dean of the Stanford Law School, has observed with respect to one such decision, is not that it is bad constitutional law, but that it is not constitutional law in any meaningful sense at all.

Despite this fact, the perceived popularity of some results in particular cases has encouraged some observers to believe that any critique of the methodology of those decisions is an attack on the results. This perception is sufficiently widespread that it deserves an answer. My answer is to look at history.

When the Supreme Court, in *Brown* v. *Board of Education of Topeka*, sounded the death knell for official segregation in this nation, it earned all the plaudits it received. However, the Supreme Court in that case was not giving new life to old words, or adapting a "living," "flexible" Constitution to new reality; it was restoring the original principle of the Constitution to constitutional law. The *Brown* Court was correcting the damage done fifty years earlier, when in *Plessy* v. *Ferguson* an earlier Supreme Court had disregarded the clear intent of the framers of the Civil War amendments to eliminate the legal degradation of blacks, and had contrived a theory of the Constitution to support the charade of "separate but equal" discrimination.

It is amazing how so much of what passes for social and political progress is really the undoing of old judicial mistakes. Mistakes occur when the principles of specific constitutional provisions—such as those contained in the Bill of Rights—are taken by some as invitations to read into the Constitution values that contradict the clear language of other provisions.

Acceptances to this illusory invitation have proliferated in recent decades. One Supreme Court Justice identified the proper judicial standard as asking "what's best for this country?" Another said it is important to "keep the Court out in front" of the general society. Various academic commentators have poured rhetorical gasoline on this judicial fire, suggesting that constitutional interpretation appropriately be guided by such standards as whether a public policy "personifies justice," or "comports with the notion of moral evolution," or confers "an identity" upon our society, or was consistent with "natural ethical law," or was consistent with some "right of equal citizenship." These amorphous concepts, as opposed to the written Constitution, form a very poor base for judicial interpretation.

Unfortunately, as I've noted, navigation by such lodestars has in the past given us questionable economics, governmental disorder, and racism—all in the guise of constitutional law. Recently, one of the distinguished judges of one of our federal appeals courts got it about right when he wrote: "The truth is that the judge who looks outside the Constitution always looks inside himself and nowhere else." Or, as we recently put it before the Supreme Court in an important brief, "The further afield interpretation travels from its point of departure in the text, the greater the danger that constitutional adjudication will be like a picnic to which the framers bring the words and the judges the meaning."

In the *Osborne* v. *Bank of United States* decision twenty-five years after *Marbury*, Chief Justice Marshall further elaborated his view of the relationship between the judge and the law, be it statutory or constitutional: "Judicial power, as contradistinguished from the power of the laws, has no existence. Courts are the mere instruments of the law, and can will nothing. When they are said to exercise a discretion, it is a mere legal discretion, a discretion to be exercised in discerning the course prescribed by law; and, when that is discerned, it is the duty of the Court to follow it."

Any true approach to constitutional interpretation must respect the document in all its parts and be faithful to the Constitution in its entirety.

What must be remembered in the current debate is that interpretation does not imply results. The framers were not trying to anticipate every answer. They were trying to create a tripartite national government, within a federal system, that would have the flexibility to adapt to face new exigencies—as it did, for example, in chartering a national bank. Their great interest was in the distribution of power and responsibility in order to secure the great goal of liberty for all.

A jurisprudence that seeks fidelity to the Constitution—a jurisprudence of original intention—is not a jurisprudence of political results. It is very much concerned with process, and it is a jurisprudence that in our day seeks to depoliticize the law. The great genius of the constitutional blueprint is found in its creation and respect for spheres of authority and the limits it places on governmental power. In this scheme, the framers did not see the courts as the exclusive custodians of the Constitution. Indeed, because the document posits so few conclusions, it leaves to the more political branches the matter of adapting and vivifying its principles in each generation. It also leaves to the people of the states, in the Tenth Amendment, those responsibilities and rights not committed to federal care. The power to declare acts of Congress and laws of the states null and void is truly awesome. This power must be used when the Constitution clearly speaks. It should not be used when the Constitution does not.

In *Marbury* v. *Madison*, at the same time he vindicated the concept of judicial review, Marshall wrote that the "principles" of the Constitution "are deemed fundamental and permanent" and, except for formal amendment, "unchangeable." If we want a change in our Constitution or in our laws, we must seek it through the formal mechanisms presented in that organizing document of our government.

What Is at Issue

IN SUMMARY, I would emphasize that what is at issue here is not an agenda of issues or a menu of results. At issue is a way of government. A jurisprudence based on first principles is neither conservative nor liberal, neither right nor left. It is a jurisprudence that cares about committing and limiting to each organ of government the proper ambit of its responsibilities. It is a jurisprudence faithful to our Constitution.

By the same token, an activist jurisprudence, one which anchors the Constitution only in the consciences of jurists, is a chameleon jurisprudence, changing color and form in each era. The same activism hailed today may threaten the capacity for decision through democratic consensus tomorrow, as it has in many yesterdays. Ultimately, as the early democrats wrote into the Massachusetts state constitution, the best defense of our liberties is a government of laws and not men.

On this point, it is helpful to recall the words of the late Justice Felix Frankfurter: "There is not under our Constitution a judicial remedy for every political mischief, for every undesirable exercise of legislative power. The Framers carefully and with deliberate forethought refused so to enthrone the judiciary. In this situation, as in others of like nature, appeal for relief does not belong here. Appeal must be to an informed, civically militant electorate."

I close, unsurprisingly, by returning a last time to the period of the Constitution's birth. As students of the Constitution are aware, the struggle for ratification was protracted and bitter. Essential to the success of the campaign was the outcome of the debate in the two most significant states, Virginia and New York. In New York, the battle between Federalist and Anti-Federalist forces was particularly hard. Both sides eagerly awaited the outcome in Virginia, which was sure to have a profound effect on the struggle in the Empire State. When news that Virginia had voted to ratify came, it was a particularly bitter blow to the Anti-Federalist side. Yet, on the evening the message reached New York, an event took place that speaks volumes about the character of early America. The losing side, instead of grousing, feted the Federalist leaders in the taverns and inns of the city. There followed a night of good fellowship and mutual toasting. When the effects of the good cheer wore off, the two sides returned to their inkwells and presses, and the debate resumed.

There is a great temptation among those who view this debate from the outside to see in it a clash of personalities, a bitter exchange, but you and I, and I hope the other participants in this dialogue, know better. We and our distinguished opponents carry on the old tradition of free, uninhibited, and vigorous debate. Out of such arguments come no losers, only truth. It's the American way, and the Founding Fathers wouldn't want it any other way.

The Constitution of the United States: Contemporary Ratification

WILLIAM J. BRENNAN, JR.

I AM DEEPLY grateful for the invitation to participate in the "Text and Teaching" symposium. This rare opportunity to explore classic texts with participants of such wisdom, acumen and insight as those who have preceded and will follow me to this podium is indeed exhilarating. But it is also humbling. Even to approximate the standards of excellence of these vigorous and graceful intellects is a daunting task. I am honored that you have afforded me this opportunity to try.

It will perhaps not surprise you that the text I have chosen for exploration is the amended Constitution of the United States, which, of course, entrenches the Bill of Rights and the Civil War amendments, and draws sustenance from the bedrock principles of another great text, the Magna Carta. So fashioned, the Constitution embodies the aspiration to social justice, brotherhood and human dignity that brought this nation into being. The Declaration of Independence, the Constitution and the Bill of Rights solemnly committed the United States to be a country where the dignity and rights of all persons were equal before all authority. In all candor we must concede that part of this egalitarianism in America has been more pretension than realized fact. But we are an aspiring people, a people with faith in progress. Our amended Constitution is the lodestar for our aspirations. Like every text worth reading, it is not crystalline. The phrasing is broad and the limitations of its provisions are not clearly marked. Its majestic generalities and ennobling pronouncements are both luminous and obscure. This ambiguity of course calls forth interpretation, the interaction of reader and text. The encounter with the Constitutional text has been, in many senses, my life's work.

My approach to this text may differ from the approach of other participants in this symposium to their texts. Yet such differences may themselves stimulate reflection about what it is we do when we "interpret" a text. Thus

I will attempt to elucidate my approach to the text as well as my substantive interpretation.

Perhaps the foremost difference is the fact that my encounters with the constitutional text are not purely or even primarily introspective; the Constitution cannot be for me simply a contemplative haven for private moral reflection. My relation to this great text is inescapably public. That is not to say that my reading of the text is not a personal reading, only that the personal reading perforce occurs in a public context, and is open to critical scrutiny from all quarters.

The Constitution is fundamentally a public text—the monumental charter of a government and a people—and a Justice of the Supreme Court must apply it to resolve public controversies. For, from our beginnings, a most important consequence of the constitutionally created separation of powers has been the American habit, extraordinary to other democracies, of casting social, economic, philosophical and political questions in the form of law suits, in an attempt to secure ultimate resolution by the Supreme Court. In this way, important aspects of the most fundamental issues confronting our democracy may finally arrive in the Supreme Court for judicial determination. Not infrequently, these are the issues upon which contemporary society is most deeply divided. They arouse our deepest emotions. The main burden of my twenty-nine Terms on the Supreme Court has thus been to wrestle with the Constitution in this heightened public context, to draw meaning from the text in order to resolve public controversies.

Two other aspects of my relation to this text warrant mention. First, constitutional interpretation for a federal judge is, for the most part, obligatory. When litigants approach the bar of court to adjudicate a constitutional dispute, they may justifiably demand an answer. Judges cannot avoid a definitive interpretation because they feel unable to, or would prefer not to, penetrate to the full meaning of the Constitution's provisions. Unlike literary critics, judges cannot merely savor the tensions or revel in the ambiguities inhering in the text—judges must resolve them.

Second, consequences flow from a Justice's interpretation in a direct and immediate way. A judicial decision respecting the incompatibility of Jim Crow with a constitutional guarantee of equality is not simply a contemplative exercise in defining the shape of a just society. It is an order—supported by the full coercive power of the State—that the present society change in a fundamental aspect. Under such circumstances the process of deciding can be a lonely, troubling experience for fallible human beings conscious that their best may not be adequate to the challenge. We Justices are certainly aware that we are not final because we are infallible; we know that we are infallible only because we are final. One does not forget how much may depend on the decision. More than the litigants may be affected. The course of vital social, economic and political currents may be directed.

These three deflating characteristics of my relation to the constitutional text—its public nature, obligatory character, and consequentialist aspect—cannot help but influence the way I read that text. When Justices interpret the Constitution they speak for their community, not for themselves alone. The act of interpretation must be undertaken with full consciousness that it is, in a very real sense, the community's interpretation that is sought. Justices are not platonic guardians appointed to wield authority according to their personal moral predilections. Precisely because coercive force must attend any judicial decision to countermand the will of a contemporary majority, the Justices must render constitutional interpretations that are received as legitimate. The source of legitimacy is, of course, a wellspring of controversy in legal and political circles. At the core of the debate is what the late Yale Law School professor Alexander Bickel labeled "the counter-majoritarian difficulty." Our commitment to self-governance in a representative democracy must be reconciled with vesting in electorally unaccountable Justices the power to invalidate the expressed desires of representative bodies on the ground of inconsistency with higher law. Because judicial power resides in the authority to give meaning to the Constitution, the debate is really a debate about how to read the text, about constraints on what is legitimate interpretation.

There are those who find legitimacy in fidelity to what they call "the intentions of the Framers." In its most doctrinaire incarnation, this view demands that Justices discern exactly what the Framers thought about the question under consideration and simply follow that intention in resolving the case before them. It is a view that feigns self-effacing deference to the specific judgments of those who forged our original social compact. But in truth it is little more than arrogance cloaked as humility. It is arrogant to pretend that from our vantage we can gauge accurately the intent of the Framers on application of principle to specific, contemporary questions. All too often, sources of potential enlightenment such as records of the ratification debates provide sparse or ambiguous evidence of the original intention. Typically, all that can be gleaned is that the Framers themselves did not agree about the application or meaning of particular constitutional provisions, and hid their differences in cloaks of generality. Indeed, it is far from clear whose intention is relevant—that of the drafters, the congressional disputants, or the ratifiers in the states?—or even whether the idea of an original intention is a coherent way of thinking about a jointly drafted document drawing its authority from a general assent of the states. And apart from the problematic nature of the sources, our distance of two centuries cannot but work as a prism refracting all we perceive. One cannot help but speculate that the chorus of lamentations calling for interpretation faithful to "original intention"—and proposing nullification of interpretations that fail this quick litmus test—must come from persons who have no familiarity with the historical record.

Perhaps most importantly, while proponents of this facile historicism justify it as a depoliticization of the judiciary, the political underpinnings of such a choice should not escape notice. A position that upholds constitutional claims only if they were within the specific contemplation of the Framers in effect establishes a presumption of resolving textual ambiguities against the claim of constitutional right. It is far from clear what justifies such a presumption against claims of right. Nothing intrinsic in the nature of interpretation—if there is such a thing as the "nature" of interpretation—commands such a passive approach to ambiguity. This is a choice no less political than any other; it expresses antipathy to claims of the minority to rights against the majority. Those who would restrict claims of right to the values of 1789 specifically articulated in the Constitution turn a blind eye to social progress and eschew adaptation of overarching principles to changes of social circumstance.

Another, perhaps more sophisticated, response to the potent power of judicial interpretation stresses democratic theory: because ours is a government of the people's elected representatives, substantive value choices should by and large be left to them. This view emphasizes not the transcendent historical authority of the framers but the predominant contemporary authority of the elected branches of government. Yet it has similar consequences for the nature of proper judicial interpretation. Faith in the majoritarian process counsels restraint. Even under more expansive formulations of this approach, judicial review is appropriate only to the extent of ensuring that our democratic process functions smoothly. Thus, for example, we would protect freedom of speech merely to ensure that the people are heard by their representatives, rather than as a separate, substantive value. When, by contrast, society tosses up to the Supreme Court a dispute that would require invalidation of a legislature's substantive policy choice, the Court generally would stay its hand because the Constitution was meant as a plan of government and not as an embodiment of fundamental substantive values.

The view that all matters of substantive policy should be resolved through the majoritarian process has appeal under some circumstances, but I think it ultimately will not do. Unabashed enshrinement of majority will would permit the imposition of a social caste system or wholesale confiscation of property so long as a majority of the authorized legislative body, fairly elected, approved. Our Constitution could not abide such a situation. It is the very purpose of a Constitution—and particularly of the Bill of Rights—to declare certain values transcendent, beyond the reach of temporary political majorities. The majoritarian process cannot be expected to rectify claims of minority right that arise as a response to the outcomes of that very majoritarian process. As James Madison put it: "The prescriptions in favor of liberty ought to be levelled against that quarter where the greatest danger lies, namely, that which possesses the highest prerogative of power. But this is not found in either the Executive or Legislative departments of Government, but in the body of the people, operating by the majority against the minority"[1] (1 Annals 437). Faith in democracy is one thing, blind faith quite another. Those who drafted our Constitution understood the difference. One cannot read the text without admitting that it embodies substantive value choices; it places certain values beyond the power of any legislature. Obvious are the separation of powers; the privilege of the Writ of Habeas Corpus; prohibition of Bills of Attainder and ex post facto laws; prohibition of cruel and unusual punishments; the requirement of just compensation for official taking of property; the prohibition of laws tending to establish religion or enjoining the free exercise of religion; and, since the Civil War, the banishment of slavery and official race discrimination. With respect to at least such principles, we simply have not constituted ourselves as strict utilitarians. While the Constitution may be amended, such amendments require an immense effort by the People as a whole.

To remain faithful to the content of the Constitution, therefore, an approach to interpreting the text must account for the existence of these substantive value choices, and must accept the ambiguity inherent in the effort to apply them to modern circumstances. The Framers discerned fundamental principles through struggles against particular malefactions of the Crown; the struggle shapes the particular contours of the articulated principles. But our acceptance of the fundamental principles has not and should not bind us to those precise, at times anachronistic, contours. Successive generations of Americans have continued to respect these fundamental choices and adopt them as their own guide to evaluating quite different historical practices. Each generation has the choice to overrule or add to the fundamental principles enunciated by the Framers; the Constitution can be amended or it can be ignored. Yet with respect to its fundamental principles, the text has suffered neither fate. Thus, if I may borrow the words of an esteemed predecessor, Justice Robert Jackson, the burden of judicial interpretation is to translate "the majestic generalities of the Bill of Rights, conceived as part of the pattern of liberal government in the eighteenth century, into concrete restraints on officials dealing with the problems of the twentieth century." (Barnette, 319 U. S. at 639).

We current Justices read the Constitution in the only way that we can: as Twentieth-Century Americans. We look to the history of the time of framing and to the intervening history of interpretation. But the ultimate question must be, what do the words of the text mean in our time? For the genius of the Constitution rests not in any static meaning it might have had in a world that is dead and gone, but in the adaptability of its great principles to cope with current problems and current needs. What the constitutional fundamentals meant to the wisdom of other times cannot be their measure to the vision of our time. Similarly, what those fundamentals mean for us, our descendants will learn, cannot be the measure to the vision of their time. This realization is not, I assure you, a novel one of my own creation. Permit me to quote from one of the opinions of our Court, *Weems v. United States*, 217 U.S. 349, written nearly a century ago:

> Time works changes, brings into existence new conditions and pur-
> poses. Therefore, a principle to be vital must be capable of wider
> application than the mischief which gave it birth. This is peculiarly
> true of constitutions. They are not ephemeral enactments, designed to
> meet passing occasions. They are, to use the words of Chief Justice
> John Marshall, "designed to approach immortality as nearly as human
> institutions can approach it." The future is their care and provision for
> events of good and bad tendencies of which no prophesy can be made.
> In the application of a constitution, therefore, our contemplation
> cannot be only of what has been, but of what may be.

Interpretation must account for the transformative purpose of the text. Our
Constitution was not intended to preserve a preexisting society but to make
a new one, to put in place new principles that the prior political community
had not sufficiently recognized. Thus, for example, when we interpret the
Civil War Amendments to the charter—abolishing slavery, guaranteeing
blacks equality under law, and guaranteeing blacks the right to vote—we
must remember that those who put them in place had no desire to enshrine
the status quo. Their goal was to make over their world, to eliminate all
vestige of slave caste.

Having discussed at some length how I, as a Supreme Court Justice, inter-
act with this text, I think it time to turn to the fruits of this discourse. For
the Constitution is a sublime oration on the dignity of man, a bold commitment by a people to the ideal of libertarian dignity protected through law.
Some reflection is perhaps required before this can be seen.

The Constitution on its face is, in large measure, a structuring text, a
blueprint for government. And when the text is not prescribing the form of
government it is limiting the powers of that government. The original document, before addition of any of the amendments, does not speak primarily
of the rights of man, but of the abilities and disabilities of government. When
one reflects upon the text's preoccupation with the scope of government as
well as its shape, however, one comes to understand that what this text is
about is the relationship of the individual and the state. The text marks the
metes and bounds of official authority and individual autonomy. When one
studies the boundary that the text marks out, one gets a sense of the vision
of the individual embodied in the Constitution.

As augmented by the Bill of Rights and the Civil War Amendments, this
text is a sparkling vision of the supremacy of the human dignity of every
individual. This vision is reflected in the very choice of democratic self-governance: the supreme value of a democracy is the presumed worth of each
individual. And this vision manifests itself most dramatically in the specific
prohibitions of the Bill of Rights, a term which I henceforth will apply to
describe not only the original first eight amendments, but the Civil War
amendments as well. It is a vision that has guided us as a people throughout
our history, although the precise rules by which we have protected funda-

mental human dignity have been transformed over time in response to both transformations of social condition and evolution of our concepts of human dignity.

Until the end of the nineteenth century, freedom and dignity in our country found meaningful protection in the institution of real property. In a society still largely agricultural, a piece of land provided men not just with sustenance but with the means of economic independence, a necessary precondition of political independence and expression. Not surprisingly, property relationships formed the heart of litigation and of legal practice, and lawyers and judges tended to think stable property relationships the highest aim of the law.

But the days when common law property relationships dominated litigation and legal practice are past. To a growing extent economic existence now depends on less certain relationships with government—licenses, employment, contracts, subsidies, unemployment benefits, tax exemptions, welfare and the like. Government participation in the economic existence of individuals is pervasive and deep. Administrative matters and other dealings with government are at the epicenter of the exploding law. We turn to government and to the law for controls which would never have been expected or tolerated before this century, when a man's answer to economic oppression or difficulty was to move two hundred miles west. Now hundreds of thousands of Americans live entire lives without any real prospect of the dignity and autonomy that ownership of real property could confer. Protection of the human dignity of such citizens requires a much modified view of the proper relationship of individual and state.

In general, problems of the relationship of the citizen with government have multiplied and thus have engendered some of the most important constitutional issues of the day. As government acts ever more deeply upon those areas of our lives once marked "private," there is an even greater need to see that individual rights are not curtailed or cheapened in the interest of what may temporarily appear to be the "public good." And as government continues in its role of provider for so many of our disadvantaged citizens, there is an even greater need to ensure that government act with integrity and consistency in its dealings with these citizens. To put this another way, the possibilities for collision between government activity and individual rights will increase as the power and authority of government itself expand, and this growth, in turn, heightens the need for constant vigilance at the collision points. If our free society is to endure, those who govern must recognize human dignity and accept the enforcement of constitutional limitations on their power conceived by the Framers to be necessary to preserve that dignity and the air of freedom which is our proudest heritage. Such recognition will not come from a technical understanding of the organs of government, or the new forms of wealth they administer. It requires something different, something deeper—a personal confrontation with the well-springs of our society.

Solutions of constitutional questions from that perspective have become the great challenge of the modern era. All the talk in the last half-decade about shrinking the government does not alter this reality or the challenge it imposes. The modern activist state is a concomitant of the complexity of modern society; it is inevitably with us. We must meet the challenge rather than wish it were not before us.

The challenge is essentially, of course, one to the capacity of our constitutional structure to foster and protect the freedom, the dignity, and the rights of all persons within our borders, which it is the great design of the Constitution to secure. During the time of my public service this challenge has largely taken shape within the confines of the interpretive question whether the specific guarantees of the Bill of Rights operate as restraints on the power of State government. We recognize the Bill of Rights as the primary source of express information as to what is meant by constitutional liberty. The safeguards enshrined in it are deeply etched in the foundation of America's freedoms. Each is a protection with centuries of history behind it, often dearly bought with the blood and lives of people determined to prevent oppression by their rulers. The first eight amendments, however, were added to the Constitution to operate solely against federal power. It was not until the Thirteenth and Fourteenth Amendments were added, in 1865 and 1868, in response to a demand for national protection against abuses of state power, that the Constitution could be interpreted to require application of the first eight amendments to the states.

It was in particular the Fourteenth Amendment's guarantee that no person be deprived of life, liberty or property without process of law that led us to apply many of the specific guarantees of the Bill of Rights to the States. In my judgment, Justice Cardozo best captured the reasoning that brought us to such decisions when he described what the Court has done as a process by which the guarantees "have been taken over from the earlier articles of the federal bill of rights and brought within the Fourteenth Amendment by a process of absorption . . . [that] has had its source in the belief that neither liberty nor justice would exist if [those guarantees] . . . were sacrificed." (Palko, 302 U.S., at 326). But this process of absorption was neither swift nor steady. As late as 1922 only the Fifth Amendment guarantee of just compensation for official taking of property had been given force against the states. Between then and 1956 only the First Amendment guarantees of speech and conscience and the Fourth Amendment ban of unreasonable searches and seizures had been incorporated—the latter, however, without the exclusionary rule to give it force. As late as 1961, I could stand before a distinguished assemblage of the bar at New York University's James Madison Lecture and list the following as guarantees that had not been thought to be sufficiently fundamental to the protection of human dignity so as to be enforced against the states: the prohibition of cruel and unusual punishments, the right against self-incrimination, the right to assistance of counsel in a criminal trial, the right to confront witnesses, the right to compulsory process, the right not to be placed in jeopardy of life or limb more than once upon accusation of a crime, the right not to have illegally obtained evidence introduced at a criminal trial, and the right to a jury of one's peers.

The history of the quarter century following that Madison Lecture need not be told in great detail. Suffice it to say that each of the guarantees listed above has been recognized as a fundamental aspect of ordered liberty. Of course, the above catalogue encompasses only the rights of the criminally accused, those caught, rightly or wrongly, in the maw of the criminal justice system. But it has been well said that there is no better test of a society than how it treats those accused of transgressing against it. Indeed, it is because we recognize that incarceration strips a man of his dignity that we demand strict adherence to fair procedure and proof of guilt beyond a reasonable doubt before taking such a drastic step. These requirements are, as Justice John Marshall Harlan once said, "bottomed on a fundamental value determination of our society that it is far worse to convict an innocent man than to let a guilty man go free." (Winship, 397 U.S., at 372). There is no worse injustice than wrongly to strip a man of his dignity. And our adherence to the constitutional vision of human dignity is so strict that even after convicting a person according to these stringent standards, we demand that his dignity be infringed only to the extent appropriate to the crime and never by means of wanton infliction of pain or deprivation. I interpret the Constitution plainly to embody these fundamental values.

Of course the constitutional vision of human dignity has, in this past quarter century, infused far more than our decisions about the criminal process. Recognition of the principle of "one person, one vote" as a constitutional one redeems the promise of self-governance by affirming the essential dignity of every citizen in the right to equal participation in the democratic process. Recognition of so-called "new property" rights in those receiving government entitlements affirms the essential dignity of the least fortunate among us by demanding that government treat with decency, integrity and consistency those dependent on its benefits for their very survival. After all, a legislative majority initially decides to create governmental entitlements; the Constitution's Due Process Clause merely provides protection for entitlements thought necessary by society as a whole. Such due process rights prohibit government from imposing the devil's bargain of bartering away human dignity in exchange for human sustenance. Likewise, recognition of full equality for women—equal protection of the laws—ensures that gender has no bearing on claims to human dignity.

Recognition of broad and deep rights of expression and of conscience reaffirm the vision of human dignity in many ways. They too redeem the promise of self-governance by facilitating—indeed demanding—robust, uninhibited and wide-open debate on issues of public importance. Such public debate is of course vital to the development and dissemination of political

ideas. As importantly, robust public discussion is the crucible in which personal political convictions are forged. In our democracy, such discussion is a
political duty; it is the essence of self government. The constitutional vision
of human dignity rejects the possibility of political orthodoxy imposed from
above; it respects the right of each individual to form and to expresses political judgments, however far they may deviate from the mainstream and however unsettling they might be to the powerful or the elite. Recognition of
these rights of expression and conscience also frees up the private space for
both intellectual and spiritual development free of government dominance,
either blatant or subtle. Justice Brandeis put it so well sixty years ago when
he wrote: "Those who won our independence believed that the final end of
the State was to make men free to develop their faculties; and that in its
government the deliberative forces should prevail over the arbitrary. They
valued liberty both as an end and as a means." (Whitney, 274 U.S. at 375).

I do not mean to suggest that we have in the last quarter century achieved
a comprehensive definition of the constitutional ideal of human dignity. We
are still striving toward that goal, and doubtless it will be an eternal quest.
For if the interaction of this Justice and the constitutional text over the years
confirms any single proposition, it is that the demands of human dignity will
never cease to evolve.

Indeed, I cannot in good conscience refrain from mention of one grave and
crucial respect in which we continue, in my judgment, to fall short of the
constitutional vision of human dignity. It is in our continued tolerance of
State-administered execution as a form of punishment. I make it a practice
not to comment on the constitutional issues that come before the Court, but
my position on this issue, of course, has been for some time fixed and immutable. I think I can venture some thoughts on this particular subject without transgressing my usual guideline too severely.

As I interpret the Constitution, capital punishment is under all circumstances cruel and unusual punishment prohibited by the Eighth and Fourteenth Amendments. This is a position of which I imagine you are not unaware. Much discussion of the merits of capital punishment has in recent
years focused on the potential arbitrariness that attends its administration,
and I have no doubt that such arbitrariness is a grave wrong. But for me, the
wrong of capital punishment transcends such procedural issues. As I have
said in my opinions, I view the Eighth Amendment's prohibition of cruel
and unusual punishments as embodying to a unique degree moral principles
that substantively restrain the punishments our civilized society may impose
on those persons who transgress its laws. Foremost among the moral principles recognized in our cases and inherent in the prohibition is the primary
principle that the State, even as it punishes, must treat its citizens in a manner consistent with their intrinsic worth as human beings. A punishment
must not be so severe as to be utterly and irreversibly degrading to the very
essence of human dignity. Death for whatever crime and under all circum-

stances is a truly awesome punishment. The calculated killing of a human being by the State involves, by its very nature, an absolute denial of the executed person's humanity. The most vile murder does not, in my view, release the State from constitutional restraints on the destruction of human dignity. Yet an executed person has lost the very right to have rights, now or ever. For me, then, the fatal constitutional infirmity of capital punishment is that it treats members of the human race as nonhumans, as objects to be toyed with and discarded. It is, indeed, "cruel and unusual." It is thus inconsistent with the fundamental premise of the Clause that even the most base criminal remains a human being possessed of some potential, at least, for common human dignity.

This is an interpretation to which a majority of my fellow Justices—not to mention, it would seem, a majority of my fellowcountrymen—does not subscribe. Perhaps you find my adherence to it, and my recurrent publication of it, simply contrary, tiresome, or quixotic. Or perhaps you see in it a refusal to abide by the judicial principle of stare decisis, obedience to precedent. In my judgment, however, the unique interpretive role of the Supreme Court with respect to the Constitution demands some flexibility with respect to the call of stare decisis. Because we are the last word on the meaning of the Constitution, our views must be subject to revision over time, or the Constitution falls captive, again, to the anachronistic views of long-gone generations. I mentioned earlier the judge's role in seeking out the community's interpretation of the Constitutional text. Yet, again in my judgment, when a Justice perceives an interpretation of the text to have departed so far from its essential meaning, that Justice is bound, by a larger constitutional duty to the community, to expose the departure and point toward a different path. On this issue, the death penalty, I hope to embody a community striving for human dignity for all, although perhaps not yet arrived.

You have doubtless observed that this description of my personal encounter with the constitutional text has in large portion been a discussion of public developments in constitutional doctrine over the last quarter century. That, as I suggested at the outset, is inevitable because my interpretive career has demanded a public reading of the text. This public encounter with the text, however, has been a profound source of personal inspiration. The vision of human dignity embodied there is deeply moving. It is timeless. It has inspired Americans for two centuries and it will continue to inspire as it continues to evolve. That evolutionary process is inevitable and, indeed, it is the true interpretive genius of the text.

If we are to be as a shining city upon a hill, it will be because of our ceaseless pursuit of the constitutional ideal of human dignity. For the political and legal ideals that form the foundation of much that is best in American institutions—ideals jealously preserved and guarded throughout our history—still form the vital force in creative political thought and activity within the nation today. As we adapt our institutions to the ever-changing conditions of national and international life, those ideals of human dignity—liberty and justice for all individuals—will continue to inspire and guide us because they are entrenched in our Constitution. The Constitution with its Bill of Rights thus has a bright future, as well as a glorious past, for its spirit is inherent in the aspirations of our people.

Note

1. *Annals of Congress* 437.

How the Constitution Disappeared

◆

═══
═══

◆

LINO A. GRAGLIA

ATTORNEY GENERAL EDWIN MEESE'S recent statement in a speech to the American Bar Association that judges should interpret the Constitution to mean what it was originally intended to mean probably did not strike most people as controversial. Nevertheless it brought forth immediate denunciation by a sitting Supreme Court justice as "doctrinaire," "arrogant," and the product of "facile historicism." "It is a view," Justice William J. Brennan, Jr. said in a speech at Georgetown University, "that feigns self-effacing deference to the specific judgments of those who forged our original social compact," but that "in truth . . . is little more than arrogance cloaked as humility" because it is not possible to "gauge accurately the intent of the framers on application of principle to specific, contemporary questions." The view is not only mistaken, but misguided, Justice Brennan continued, because it would require judges to "turn a blind eye to social progress and eschew adaptation of overarching principles to changes of social circumstance."

To state that judges should interpret the Constitution as intended by those who wrote and ratified it ("the Framers") is only to state the basic premise of our political-legal system that the function of judges is to apply, not to make, the law. Indeed, it would be difficult to say what interpretation of a law means if not to determine the intent of the lawmaker. Justice Brennan's angry attack on the obvious as if it were disreputable, soon joined by the attacks of his colleague Justice John Paul Stevens and a legion of media commentators, makes evident that much is at stake in this debate on a seemingly esoteric matter of constitutional interpretation. What is at stake is nothing less than the question of how the country should be governed in regard to basic issues of social policy: whether such issues should be decided by elected representatives of the people, largely on a state-by-state basis, or, as has been the case for the last three decades, primarily by a majority of the nine justices of the United States Supreme Court for the nation as a whole.

The modern era of constitutional law began with the Supreme Court's 1954 decision in *Brown* v. *Board of Education*, holding compulsory school racial segregation and, it soon appeared, all racial discrimination by government, unconstitutional. The undeniable rightness of the decision as a matter of social policy, in effect ending legally imposed second-class citizenship for blacks, and its eventual acceptance by the public and ratification by Congress and the President in the 1964 Civil Rights Act, gained for the Court a status and prestige unprecedented in our history. The moral superiority of decision-making by judges to decision-making by mere "politicians" seemed evident. The result was to enable the Court to move from its historic role as a brake on social change to a very different role as the primary engine of such change.

In the years since *Brown*, nearly every fundamental change in domestic social policy has been brought about not by the decentralized democratic (or, more accurately, republican) process contemplated by the Constitution, but simply by the Court's decree. The Court has decided, on a national basis and often in opposition to the wishes of a majority of the American people, issues literally of life and death, as in its decisions invalidating virtually all restrictions on abortion and severely restricting the use of capital punishment. It has decided issues of public security and order, as in its decisions greatly expanding the protection of the criminally accused and limiting state power to control street demonstrations and vagrancy, and issues of public morality, as in the decisions disallowing most state controls of pornography, obscenity, and nudity. The Court has both prohibited the states from making provision for prayer in the schools and disallowed most forms of aid, state or federal, to religious schools. It has required that children be excluded from their neighborhood public schools and bused to more distant schools in order to increase school racial integration; ordered the reapportionment of state and federal legislatures on a "one-man, one-vote" basis; invalidated most of the law of libel and slander; and disallowed nearly all legal distinctions on the basis of sex, illegitimacy, and alienage. The list could easily be extended, but it should be clear that in terms of the issues that determine the nature and quality of life in a society, the Supreme Court has become our most important institution of government.

Since his appointment to the Court by President Eisenhower in 1956, Justice Brennan has participated in all of the Court's major constitutional decisions, has consistently voted in favor of Court intervention in the political process, and often was a leader on the Court in reaching the decision to intervene. Indeed, he has ordinarily differed with the Court only in that he would often go even farther in disallowing political control of some issues; he would, for example, go farther than the Court has in disallowing state regulation of the distribution of pornographic material and he would prohibit capital punishment in all cases. If the Court has been our most important institution of government for the past three decades, Justice Brennan—although his name is probably unknown to the great majority of his fellow citizens—has surely been our most important government official. To argue that the Supreme Court should confine itself or be confined to interpreting the Constitution as written is to undermine the basis of this status and challenge the legitimacy of his life's work.

Constitutional law is as a practical matter the product of the exercise of the power of judicial review, the power of judges, and ultimately of Supreme Court justices, to invalidate legislation and other acts of other officials and institutions of government as inconsistent with the Constitution. The central question presented by constitutional law—the only question the great variety of matters dealt with under that rubric have in common—is how, if at all, can such a power in the hands of national officials who are unelected and effectively hold office for life be justified in a system of government supposedly republican in form and federalist in organization? The power is not explicitly provided for in the Constitution and had no precedent in English law—where Parliament, not a court, is said to be supreme—which could well be taken as reason enough to assume that no such power had been granted. Alexander Hamilton argued for the power in *Federalist* 78, however, and Chief Justice John Marshall established it in *Marbury* v. *Madison* in 1803 on the ground that it is inherent in a written constitution that declares itself to be supreme law. The argument is hardly unanswerable—other nations have written constitutions without judicial review—but judicial review limited to interpretation of the Constitution in accordance with the Framers' intent does obviate the problem of policy-making by judges.

Constitutional limitations on popular government are undoubtedly undemocratic, even if they were themselves democratically adopted by a supermajority, but the only function of judges in exercising judicial review on the basis of a written constitution with determinate meaning would be the entirely judicial one of enforcing the Constitution as they would any other law. The judges, Hamilton assured the ratifying states, would have neither "force nor will"; able to "take no active resolution whatever" in enforcing the Constitution, their power would be "next to nothing." "Judicial power," Marshall reiterated, "has no existence. Courts are mere instruments of the law, and can will nothing." The notion that a court has "power to overrule or control the action of the people's representatives," Justice Owen Roberts confirmed during the New Deal constitutional crisis, "is a misconception"; the Court's only function in a constitutional case is "to lay the article of the Constitution which is invoked beside the statute which is challenged and to decide whether the latter squares with the former."

Even Justice Brennan purports to recognize what, as he notes, Alexander Bickel called "the counter-majoritarian difficulty" presented by judicial review. "Our commitment to self-governance in a representative democracy must be reconciled," Justice Brennan concedes, "with vesting in electorally unaccountable justices the power to invalidate the expressed desires of representative bodies on the ground of inconsistency with higher law." Supreme Court Justices, he acknowledges at the beginning of his speech, echoing Judge Learned Hand, "are not platonic guardians appointed to wield authority according to their personal moral predilections." At several points he even seems to offer the standard justification for judicial review, that the judges merely interpret the written Constitution. He states, for example, that the duty of the judge is to "draw meaning from the text" and "remain faithful to the content" of the Constitution and that "the debate is really a debate about how to read the text, about constraints on what is legitimate interpretation." These statements are consistent with the remainder of his speech, however, only if reading or interpreting a document is considered indistinguishable from composing or rewriting it.

Unfortunately, however, the debate is not about how judges should read or interpret the text of the Constitution, but about whether that is what they should in fact confine themselves to doing in deciding constitutional cases. The view that the duty of judges is to read and interpret the Constitution— to attempt to determine what the Framers intended to say—is precisely the view that Justice Brennan seeks to rebut and derides as uninformed and misguided. The whole point of his speech is that judges should not be confined to that task, for so to confine them would be to give them much too limited a role in our system of government and leave us insufficiently protected from the dangers of majority rule.

Justice Brennan is far from alone today in his view of the proper role of judges in exercising judicial review and of the essential irrelevance of the Constitution to constitutional law. It is, indeed, the view taken by most contemporary constitutional-law scholars, who share the political ideology of the modern-era Supreme Court and see it as their professional duty to legitimize the fruits of that ideology. Because it has become increasingly difficult—in fact, impossible—to justify the Court's controversial decisions as the result of constitutional interpretation, the bulk of modern constitutional-law scholarship consists of the invention and elaboration of "non-interpretivist" or "non-originalist" theories of judicial review—justifications for a judicial review that is not confined to constitutional interpretation in any sense that would effectively restrain judicial choice. Because the product of this review is nonetheless always called "constitutional law" and attributed in some way to the Constitution, the result is the paradox of non-interpretivist constitutional interpretation, constitutional law without the Constitution.

That more and more constitutional scholars, and now a Supreme Court Justice, should come to recognize and acknowledge that the Supreme Court's constitutional decisions of recent decades cannot be justified on any other basis—that they are not in fact based on the Constitution—can be taken as a hopeful sign. Although the effort today in an increasing flood of books, articles, and speeches is to justify those decisions nonetheless, the inevitable failure of such efforts must, it would seem, eventually cause the enterprise to be abandoned and the fact that they cannot be justified in a system of self-government to be also generally recognized and acknowledged. Justice Brennan has performed a public service by bringing this extremely important and little understood issue to greater public attention, conveniently summarizing the standard arguments for "non-interpretivist" or "non-originalist" review—i.e., what is popularly referred to as "judicial activism"—and stating his own position with unusual, even if not total, clarity and candor.

Defenders of judicial activism face the dilemma that, on the one hand, judicial policy-making cannot be defended as such in our system—the Justices, even Justice Brennan must concede, are not authorized to enact their "personal moral predilections" into law and must therefore claim that their decisions derive somehow from the Constitution. On the other hand, it happens that the Constitution is most ill-suited as a basis for substantial judicial policy-making by frequent judicial intervention in the political process in the name of protecting individual rights from majority rule. The central difficulty is that although the Constitution does create some individual rights, they are actually rather few, fairly well-defined, and rarely violated. The first task of the defender of judicial activism, therefore, is to dispose of the Constitution as unhelpful, inadequate, or irrelevant to contemporary needs. Reasons must be found why the Constitution cannot be taken to mean what it rather clearly is known to mean—especially when read, as all writings must be, in historical context—or, even better, to have any determinate meaning at all.

After disposing of the Constitution by depriving it of its historic meaning, the next task of defenders of judicial activism is to imagine a much more expansive, elevated, and abstract constitution that, having no specific meaning, can be made to mean anything and serve therefore as simply a mandate for judges to enact their versions of the public good. In response to the objection that the very thinly veiled system of government by judges thus achieved is obviously inconsistent with democracy, the argument is made that the value of democracy is easily overrated and its dangers many. The "very purpose of a Constitution," as Justice Brennan states the standard argument, is to limit democracy by declaring "certain values transcendent, beyond the reach of temporary political majorities." In any event, no real inconsistency with democracy is involved, the argument concludes, because the judges, though unrestrained by the actual text of the Constitution, will continue to be restrained by its principles, the adaptation of which to changing circum-

stances is the true and indispensable function of judges. Justice Brennan's
speech can serve as a textbook illustration of each of these moves.

Justice Brennan's attack on the notion of a constitution with a determinable
historic meaning could hardly be more thorough. First of all, he finds that
the Court's "sources of potential enlightenment" as to the intended meaning
are often "sparse or ambiguous." Even more serious, the search for meaning
is likely to be futile in any event because even the Framers, he believes, usually did not know what they meant: "Typically, all that can be gleaned is
that the Framers themselves did not agree about the application or meaning
of particular constitutional provisions, and hid their differences in cloaks of
generality." Then there is the question of "whose intention is relevant—that
of the drafters, the congressional disputants, or the ratifiers in the states?"
Indeed, there is the most basic question of all, whether the very notion of
intent makes sense, "whether the idea of an original intention is a coherent
way of thinking about a jointly drafted document drawing its authority from
a general assent of the states." It is almost as if the Constitution and its various provisions might have been drafted and adopted with no purpose at all.
Finally, there is the problem that "our distance of two centuries cannot but
work as a prism refracting all we perceive." For all these reasons, the idea
that judicial review is legitimate only if faithful to the intent of the Framers
can be held only by "persons who have no familiarity with the historical
record."

Justice Brennan has still another, although it would seem unnecessary, nail
to put in the coffin of the now demolished Constitution. Should any shred of
constitutional meaning somehow survive the many obstacles he sees to finding it, he would accord it little or no value. The world of the Framers is "dead
and gone," and it would not do, he believes, to hold the Constitution captive
to the "anachronistic views of long-gone generations." "Any static meaning"
the Constitution "might have had" in that dead world must, therefore, be of
dubious relevance today. In any event, "the genius of the Constitution rests,"
in his view, not in any such meaning but in "the adaptability of its great
principles to cope with current problems and current needs," strange as it
may seem that a writing can be great apart from its meaning and solely by
reason of its supposed ability to mean anything.

Most of Justice Brennan's objections regarding the difficulties of constitutional interpretation have some basis, but they could also be made in regard
to interpretation of almost any law. For example, one can almost always wish
for a clearer or more detailed legislative history, and it is always true that
legislators cannot foresee and agree on every possible application of a law. If
these difficulties made the effort to determine legislative intent futile, a system of written law would hardly be possible. In any event, from the premise
of an unknowable or irrelevant Constitution, the conclusion should follow
that judges have no basis or justification for declaring laws unconstitutional,

not that they are therefore free to invalidate laws on some other basis and still claim to be interpreting the Constitution.

Most important, whatever the difficulties of legal interpretation, they have little or no relevance to actual constitutional decision-making by the Supreme Court because no issue of interpretation, no real dispute about the intended meaning of the Constitution, is ordinarily involved. For example, the Constitution contains no provision mentioning or apparently in any way referring to the authority of the states to regulate the practice of abortion. However one might undertake to defend the Court's abortion decisions, it does not seem possible to argue that they are the result of constitutional interpretation in any non-fanciful sense. As another example, although the Constitution does mention religion, no process that could be called interpretation permits one to go from the Constitution's protection of religious freedom from federal interference to the proposition that the states may not provide for prayer in the schools.

A constitution so devoid of ascertainable meaning or contemporary relevance would seem quite useless as a guide to the solution of any contemporary problem and certainly as a written law enforceable by judges. The judges might as well be told to enforce a document written in an unknown language or, more in keeping with Justice Brennan's view, in disappearing ink. Having effectively eliminated the actual Constitution, however, Justice Brennan proceeds to remedy the loss—judicial activism cannot proceed with no constitution at all—by imagining and substituting a much more impressive, inspiring, and usefully uncertain one.

The constitution of Justice Brennan's vision is undoubtedly a wonderful thing, one of "great" and "overarching" principles and "majestic generalities and ennobling pronouncements [that] are both luminous and obscure." It is nothing less grand than the embodiment of "the aspiration to social justice, brotherhood, and human dignity that brought this nation into being," "a sublime oration on the dignity of man," and "a sparkling vision of the supremacy of the human dignity of every individual." Justice Brennan accurately reflects current constitutional-law scholarship, here as throughout his speech, by seeing the Constitution as simply "the lodestar for our aspirations." It is a source of constant wonderment that scholars and judges of otherwise the most secular and rationalist turn of mind can grow mystical when discussing the Constitution.

The temptation is strong, of course, to dismiss Justice Brennan's rapturous statements as mere heights of poetic fancy or utopian ecstasy, obviously not meant as serious descriptions or explanations of the Constitution. The fact remains, however, that this view of the Constitution is the only justification offered by him, or other contemporary defenders of judicial activism, for the Court's assumption and exercise of enormous government power. Fanciful as it may seem, a constitution that is simply the embodiment of "our," or at least his, aspirations accurately describes the constitution he has been enforcing for nearly three decades to override the will of the people of this country on issue after issue. It cannot be too strongly emphasized, therefore, that the Constitution we actually have bears almost no relation to, and is often clearly irreconcilable with, the constitution of Justice Brennan's vision. No more is necessary to rebut all contemporary defenses of judicial activism than that a copy of the Constitution be kept close at hand to demonstrate that the defenders of judicial activism are invariably relying on something else.

Although it may come as something of a disappointment to some, an "aspiration for social justice, brotherhood, and human dignity" happens not to have been what brought this nation, or at least the government founded on the Constitution, into being. The convention to revise the Articles of Confederation was called and the Constitution was drafted and ratified not to provide additional protections for human rights—on the contrary, the stronger national government created by the Constitution was correctly seen as a potential danger to human rights—but almost entirely for commercial purposes. The primary motivating force for the creation of a stronger national government was the felt need of a central authority to remove state-imposed obstacles to interstate trade. How little the Constitution had to do with aspirations for brotherhood or human dignity is perhaps most clearly seen in its several provisions regarding slavery. It provides, for example, that a slave was to be counted as three-fifths of a free person for purposes of representation and that slaves escaping to free states were nonetheless to be returned to their masters. It is not, as Justice Brennan would explain this, that part of the "egalitarianism in America has been more pretension than realized fact," but that there was at the time the Constitution was adopted very little pretension to egalitarianism, as is illustrated by, for example, the widespread use of property qualifications for voting.

Given the original Constitution's limited and mundane purposes, it is not surprising that it provides judges with little to work with for the purpose of advancing their personal notions of social Justice. The Constitution is, first of all, a very short document—easily printed, with all twenty-seven Amendments and repealed matter, on fewer than twenty pages—and apparently quite simple and straightforward, not at all like a recondite tome in which many things may be found with sufficient study. The original Constitution is almost entirely devoted to outlining the structure of the national government and setting forth the sometimes complicated methods of selection, and the responsibilities, of members of the House of Representatives, Senators, the President, and Supreme Court Justices. It contains few provisions protecting individual rights from the national government—federalism, i.e., limited national power and a high degree of local autonomy, was considered the principal protection—and even fewer restrictions on the exercise of state power. As to the national government, criminal trials are to be by jury, treason is narrowly defined, the writ of habeas corpus is protected, and bills of attainder and ex-post-facto laws are prohibited. The prohibition of bills of attainder and ex-post-facto laws is repeated as to the states, which are also prohibited from discriminating against citizens of other states. Finally and by far the most important in terms of actual challenges to state laws, the Framers, nicely illustrating their lack of egalitarian pretension, undertook to protect creditors from debtor-relief legislation by prohibiting the states from impairing contract rights.

The first eight of the first ten Amendments to the Constitution, the Bill of Rights adopted in 1791, provide additional protections of individual rights, but only against the federal government, not the states, and these, too, are fewer than seems to be generally imagined and certainly fewer than is typical of later declarations of rights, such as in the United Nations Charter. In terms of substantive rights, the First Amendment prohibits Congress from establishing or restricting the free exercise of religion—the main purpose of which was to leave matters of religion to the states—and from abridging the freedom of speech, press, or assembly. In addition, a clause of the Fifth Amendment prohibits the taking of private property without just compensation; the Second Amendment, rarely mentioned by rights enthusiasts, grants a right to bear arms; and the Third Amendment, of little apparent contemporary significance, protects against the forced quartering of troops in private homes. The Seventh Amendment, requiring jury trials in civil cases involving more than twenty dollars, is hard to see today as other than an unnecessary inconvenience. The remaining provisions (search and seizure, grand-jury indictment, double jeopardy, privilege against self-incrimination, due process, jury trial, right to counsel and to confront adverse witnesses, and cruel and unusual punishment) are related to criminal procedure.

Additional protections of individual rights are provided by the post–Civil War Amendments. The Thirteenth Amendment prohibits slavery and the Fifteenth prohibits denial of the right to vote on grounds of race. The great bulk of constitutional litigation concerns state law and nearly all of that litigation purports to be based on a single sentence of the Fourteenth Amendment and, indeed, on one or the other of two pairs of words, "due process" and "equal protection." If the Constitution is the embodiment of our aspirations, it must have become so very largely because of those four words. The clear historic purpose of the Fourteenth Amendment, however, was to provide federal protection against certain state discriminations on the basis of race, historically our uniquely intractable problem, but not otherwise to change fundamentally the constitutional scheme. Finally, the Nineteenth Amendment protects the right to vote from denial on grounds of sex, and the Twenty-seventh from denial on grounds of age for persons over eighteen.

The Constitution's protections of individual rights are not only few but also, when read in historical context, fairly clear and definite. State and federal legislators, all of whom are American citizens living in America and generally at least as devoted as judges to American values, have, therefore, little occasion or desire to violate the Constitution. The result is that the enactment of a clearly unconstitutional law is an extremely rare occurrence; the clearest example in our history perhaps is a 1933 Minnesota debtor-relief statute plainly prohibited by the contract clause, although, as it happens, the Supreme Court upheld it by a five-to-four decision. If judicial review were actually confined to enforcing the Constitution as written, it would be a much less potent force than the judicial review argued for and practiced by Justice Brennan.

The Constitution is undoubtedly a great document, the foundation of one of the freest and most prosperous nations in history. It does not detract from that greatness to point out that it is not, however, what Justice Brennan would make of it, a compendium of majestic generalities and ennobling pronouncements luminous and obscure; indeed, its greatness and durability surely derive in large part from the fact that the Framers' aims were much more specific and limited. Far from intending to compose an oration to human dignity, the Framers would have considered that they had failed in their effort to specify and limit the power of the national government if the effect of the Constitution should be to transfer the focus of human-rights concerns from the state to the national level. The Framers' solution to the problem of protecting human freedom and dignity was to preserve as much as possible, consistent with national commerce and defense requirements, a system of decentralized democratic decision-making, with the regulation of social conditions and personal relations left to the states. Justice Brennan's solution, virtually unlimited Supreme Court power to decide basic social issues for the nation as a whole, effectively disenfranchising the people of each state as to those issues, is directly contrary to the constitutional scheme.

Judicial review on the basis of a constitution divorced from historical meaning and viewed, instead, as simply "the lodestar for our aspirations" is obviously a prescription for policy-making by judges. It should therefore be defended, if at all, as such, free of obfuscating references to "interpretation" of the Constitution. The only real question it presents is, why should the American people prefer to have important social-policy issues decided for the whole nation by the Supreme Court—a committee of nine lawyers unelected to and essentially unremovable from office—rather than by the decentralized democratic process? Justice Brennan's answer to this question is, in essence, why not? The argument that judicial interpretation of the Constitution in accordance with the Framers' intent is essential for "depoliticization of the judiciary," he points out, has its own "political underpinnings"; it "in effect establishes a presumption of resolving textual ambiguities against the claim of constitutional right," which involves "a choice no less political than any other."

Justice Brennan is certainly correct that the presumption of constitutionality accorded to challenged acts of government officials has a political basis, but it is surprising that he should find "far from clear what justifies such a presumption." What justifies it is the basic premise of democratic government that public-policy issues are ordinarily to be decided through the electoral process, not by unelected judges; that constitutional restrictions on representative government—even if, unlike judge-made restrictions, they were once democratically adopted—are the exception, not the rule. To refuse to assume the validity of the acts of the electorally responsible officials and institutions of government is to refuse to assume the validity of representative self-government. It has, therefore, from the beginning been considered the bedrock of constitutional litigation that one who would have a court invalidate an act of the political branches must assume the burden of showing its inconsistency with the Constitution, ordinarily a most difficult task. By reversing the presumption of constitutionality, Justice Brennan would simply reject political decision-making as the norm and require elected representatives to justify their policy choices to the satisfaction of Supreme Court Justices, presumably by showing that those choices contribute to the Justices' notion of social progress.

Justice Brennan would justify the judicial supremacy he favors on the not entirely consistent grounds that, on the one hand, the Justices are the true voice of the people and, on the other, that the people are in any event not always to be trusted. "When Justices interpret the Constitution," Justice Brennan assures us, "they speak for their community, not for themselves alone" and "with full consciousness that it is, in a very real sense, the community's interpretation that is sought." Apart from the fact that no question of constitutional interpretation is in fact involved in most "constitutional" cases—the judges do not really decide cases by studying the words "due process" or "equal protection"—the community is, of course, fully capable of speaking for itself through the representatives it elects and maintains in office for that purpose. Justice Brennan does not explain why he thinks the community needs or wants unelected judges to speak for it instead or why the judges can be expected better to reflect or express the community's views.

The actual effect of most judicial rulings of unconstitutionality is, of course, not to implement, but to frustrate the community's views. For example, Justice Brennan would disallow capital punishment as constitutionally prohibited despite not only the fact that it is repeatedly provided for in the Constitution, but also the fact that it is favored by a large majority of the American people. In some cases, however, he explains, a Justice may perceive the community's "interpretation of the text to have departed so far from its essential meaning" that he "is bound, by a larger constitutional duty to the community, to expose the departure and point toward a different path." On capital punishment, Justice Brennan hopes to "embody a community striving for human dignity for all, although perhaps not yet arrived." Interpreting an aspirational constitution apparently requires prescience as well as a high degree of self-confidence.

The foundation of all defenses of judicial activism, however, is not any fanciful notion that the judges are the true voice of the people, but on the contrary, the conviction that the people, and their elected representatives, should not be permitted to have the last word. Rarely has this conviction, common among our intellectual elite, been expressed with more certainty than in Justice Brennan's speech. Judicial acceptance of the "predominant contemporary authority of the elected branches of government" must be rejected, he argues, for the same reason he rejects judicial acceptance of the "transcendent historical authority of the Framers." That reason, it now appears, is not so much that original intent is unknowable or irrelevant or that its acceptance as authoritative would be inconsistent with his notion of "proper judicial interpretation" of the Constitution because it would leave judges with too little to do. "Faith in the majoritarian process," like fidelity to original intent, is objectionable, he is frank to admit, simply because it "counsels restraint." It would, he points out, lead the Court generally to "stay its hand" where "invalidation of a legislature's substantive policy choice" is involved. Justice Brennan's confidence that his university audience shared his suspicion of democracy and distrust of his fellow citizens was such as to put beyond need of argument the unacceptability of a counsel of restraint by Supreme Court Justices in deciding basic issues of social policy.

Legislative supremacy in policy-making is derided by Justice Brennan as the "unabashed enshrinement of majority will." "Faith in democracy is one thing," he warns, but "blind faith quite another." "The view that all matters of substantive policy should be resolved through the majoritarian process has appeal," he concedes, but only "under some circumstances," and even as so qualified "it ultimately will not do." It will not do because the majority is simply not to be trusted: to accept the mere approval of "a majority of the legislative body, fairly elected," as dispositive of public-policy issues would be to "permit the imposition of a social-caste system or wholesale confiscation of property," a situation "our Constitution could not abide." How a people so bereft of good sense, toleration, and foresight as to adopt such policies could have adopted the Constitution in the first place is not explained. Justice Brennan seems to forget that if the Constitution prohibits such things—indeed, if it is an oration to human dignity, as he maintains—it must be because the American people have made it so and therefore, it would seem, can be trusted. It cannot be Justice Brennan's position that political wisdom died with the Framers and that we are therefore fortunate to have their policy judgments to restrain us; he rejects those judgments as unknowable or irrelevant. Like other defenders of judicial activism, however, he seems to view the Constitution not as an actual document produced by actual people but as a metaphysical entity from an extraterrestrial source of greater authority than the mere wishes of a majority of the American people, which source, fortunately, is in effective communication with Supreme Court Justices.

The social-caste system feared by Justice Brennan would probably be prohibited by the post–Civil War Amendments, without undue stretching, and confiscation of property by the national government—though not by the states—would be prohibited by the just-compensation clause of the Fifth Amendment. (These constitutional provisions, it may be noted in passing, would operate as impediments to such policies, providing grounds for opposing arguments, even if they were not judicially enforceable.) The real protection against such fears, however—and columnist Anthony Lewis's similar fear that without activist judicial review Oregon might establish the Reverend Sun Myung Moon's Unification Church as the official state religion—is simply the good sense of the American people. No extraordinary degree of confidence in that good sense is necessary in order to believe that these and similarly outrageous policies that are invariably offered as providing an unanswerable justification for judicial activism are so unlikely to be adopted as not to be a matter of serious concern. If they should be a matter of concern nonetheless—if, for example, it is truly feared that the people of some state might establish a church and believed that no state should be free to do so— the appropriate response would be the adoption of a constitutional amendment further limiting self-government in the relevant respects. To grant judges an unlimited power to rewrite the Constitution, Justice Brennan's recommended response, would be to avoid largely imaginary dangers of democratic misgovernment by creating a certainty of judicial misgovernment.

Judicial activism is not necessary to protect us from state-established churches, favored by almost no one, but it does operate to deprive the people of each state of the right to decide for themselves such real issues as whether provision should be made for prayer in the public schools. In any event, the issue presented by contemporary judicial activism is not whether majority rule is entirely trustworthy—all government power is obviously dangerous— or even whether certain specific constitutional limitations on majority rule might not be justifiable; the issue is whether freewheeling policy-making by Supreme Court Justices, totally centralized and undemocratic, is more trustworthy than majority rule.

Defenders of judicial activism invariably match their skepticism about democratic policy-making with a firm belief in the possibility and desirability of policy-making on the basis of principle. To free judicial review from the constraint of a constitution with a determinate meaning is not to permit unrestrained judicial policy-making in constitutional cases, it is argued, for the judges will continue to be constrained by the Constitution's principles, which, like the smile of the Cheshire cat, somehow survive the disappearance of the Constitution's text. According to this argument, judicial activism amounts to nothing more than the adaptation and application of these basic principles to changing circumstances, a necessary task if the Constitution is to remain a "living document" and a contributor rather than an obstacle to the national welfare. Thus, judicial activism is necessary, in Justice Brennan's view, as already noted, if we are not to "turn a blind eye to social progress and eschew adaptation of overarching principles to changes of social circumstance" and because the genius of the Constitution rests not in what, if anything, the Framers actually intended to provide, but in the "adaptability of its great principles to cope with current problems and current needs."

The argument that judges are constrained by constitutional principles, even though not by the constitutional text, bears no relation to reality. In the first place, it is not possible to formulate useful constitutional principles apart from or beyond the Constitution's actual provisions. The Constitution protects certain interests to a certain extent, from which fact the only principle to be derived is that the Constitution does just that. An even more basic fallacy is the argument's assumption that the solution of social problems lies in the discovery, adaptation, and application of pre-existing principles to new situations. Difficult problems of social choice arise, however, not because of some failure to discern or adapt an applicable principle, but only because we have many principles, many interests we regard as legitimate, and they inevitably come into conflict. Some interests have to be sacrificed or compromised if other interests are to be protected—for example, public demonstrations will have to be regulated at some point in the interest of maintaining public order—and there is no authoritatively established principle, rule, or generality that resolves the conflict. If there were such a principle, the conflict would not present a serious problem, but would be a matter that has already been decided or that anyone can decide who can read and reason. Value judgments have to be made to solve real policy issues, and the meaning of self-government is that they are to be made in accordance with the collective judgment of those who will have to live with the results.

There is also very little basis for Justice Brennan's apparent belief that judicial review confined to the Constitution as written would somehow be incompatible with social progress—unless social progress is simply defined as the enactment of his views. The Constitution does contain several provisions that we would probably be better off without, for example, the Seventh Amendment's requirement of a jury trial in federal civil cases involving more than twenty dollars and the Twenty-second Amendment's limitation of Presidents to two terms. Apart from the fact, however, that the Constitution, of course, provides procedures for its amendment—it can be updated if necessary without the Court's help—judicial activism has not generally served to alleviate the undesirable effects of such provisions. In any event, the Constitution's restrictions on self-government are, as already noted, relatively few and rarely such as a legislature might seek to avoid. Rarely if ever will adaptation of the Constitution's overarching principles, if any, be necessary in order to permit a legislature to implement its views of social progress.

Indeed, on the basis of our actual constitutional history—which includes the Supreme Court's disastrous decision that Congress could not prohibit the extension of slavery and, after the Civil War that decision helped bring on, the decision that Congress could not prohibit racial segregation in public places—it is possible to believe that social progress might go more smoothly without the Court's supposed adaptations of principles. If the Constitution can be said to have an overarching principle, the principle of federalism, of decision-making on most social-policy issues at the state level, is surely the best candidate, and that principle is not adapted or updated but violated by the Court's assertion of power to decide such issues. Far from keeping the Constitution a "living document," judicial activism threatens its demise.

Whatever merit Justice Brennan's justifications for judicial activism might have in theory, they do not seem relevant to the judicial activism actually practiced by the Supreme Court for the past three decades. It would be very difficult to justify the Court's major constitutional decisions during this period, and particularly its most controversial decisions, on any of the grounds Justice Brennan suggests. It would not seem possible to argue, for example, that the Justices spoke for the community, not for themselves, in reaching their decisions on abortion, busing, criminal procedure, and prayer in the schools. Nor does it seem that any of those decisions can be justified as providing a needed protection from a possible excess of democracy, as merely delaying effectuation of the aberrational enthusiasms of "temporary political majorities" until they could return to their senses. Judicial review may, as Chief Justice Harlan Fiske Stone put this standard rationalization, provide the people with an opportunity for a "sober second thought," but no amount of thought or experience is likely to change the view of the vast majority of the American people that, for example, their children should not be excluded from their neighborhood public schools because of their race or that no new protections of the criminally accused should be invented with the effect of preventing the conviction and punishment of the clearly guilty.

Finally, the contribution of most of the Court's constitutional decisions of recent decades to social progress—for example, its decision that California may not prohibit the parading of vulgarity in its courthouses or that Oklahoma may not impose a higher minimum drinking age on men than on women—is at best debatable. Very few of these decisions, it seems, could be used to illustrate the adaptation of overarching constitutional principles or transcendent constitutional values to changing circumstances. They could probably more easily be used to illustrate that, rather than helping us to cope with current problems and current needs, the Court's constitutional decisions have often been the cause of those problems and needs.

Whatever the merits of the Supreme Court's constitutional decisions of the past three decades, they have as to the issues decided deprived us of perhaps the most essential element of the human dignity Justice Brennan is concerned to protect, the right of self-government, which necessarily includes the right to make what others might consider mistakes. It is not the critics of judicial activism but the activist judges who can more properly be charged with being doctrinaire and arrogant, for it is they who presume to know the answers to difficult questions of social policy and to believe that they provide a needed protection from government by the misguided or ignorant. An opponent of judicial activism need not claim to know the answer to so difficult a question of social policy as, say, the extent, if any, to which abortion should be restricted to know that it is shameful in a supposedly democratic country that such a question should be answered for all of us by unelected and unaccountable government officials who have no special competence to do so.

Historical Perspectives

The Original Understanding of Original Intent

H. JEFFERSON POWELL

I. Introduction

*The world must construe according to its wits. The Courts must construe according
to the law.[1] — Sir Thomas More*

CONTEMPORARY DISCUSSION of the theory and methodology of constitutional interpretation exhibits no general agreement on the proper role either of history in general, or of the history of the Constitution's framing and
ratification in particular. A few scholars argue that the latter is essentially
irrelevant to the task of establishing constitutional norms;[2] a more common
position is to recognize an obligation to avoid direct contradiction of the intentions and expectations of the Constitution's framers.[3] Finally, a minority
of legal scholars,[4] and a substantial and influential group of judges,[5] maintain
that the historically demonstrable intentions of the framers should be binding
on contemporary interpreters of the Constitution. This last group not only
invokes history ("the original understanding at Philadelphia"[6]) as a normative
guide to the Constitution's meaning, but also claims historical warrant for
this interpretive strategy.[7] Raoul Berger, for example, has assured us that
"current indifference to the 'original intention' . . . is a relatively recent phenomenon."[8] The Constitution, according to Berger and others, "was written
against a background of interpretive presuppositions"—chiefly, that the goal
of future interpreters would be to carry out the framers' intent.[9] As a consequence, Berger argues, the intention of the framers should control interpre-

tation, because it is only by examining their "original intent" that the interpreter can discover the normative meaning of the Constitution. In modern
discussions, this view of constitutional decision-making has acquired a number of different labels; I shall call it "intentionalism."

The purpose of this Article is to examine the historical validity of the claim
that the "interpretive intention"[10] informing the Constitution was an expectation that future interpreters would seek the instrument's meaning in the
intentions of the delegates to the 1787 Constitutional Convention in Philadelphia. I am not concerned, then, with the historical question of what we
would say early interpreters actually did in construing the Constitution, but
with what they said they and others should do. I am also unconcerned in this
Article with what contemporary interpreters should do, although my conclusions obviously have normative implications for strict intentionalists, who
presumably regard the framers' interpretive intentions as binding for the
same reasons they believe the framers' substantive opinions should control.

The Article first explores the various cultural resources available to late
eighteenth-century Americans seeking to conceptualize the unprecedented
task of interpreting a written constitution.[11] The cultural influences of Enlightenment rationalism and British Protestantism combined in an unlikely
alliance to engender a suspicion of any sort of interpretation at all. The rich
interpretive tradition of the English common law, in contrast, offered a plethora of hermeneutical suggestions, sometimes conflicting with one another
and usually peculiar to the specific instrument being construed. Turning to
the views on constitutional interpretation expressed during and immediately
after the ratification process, I conclude that there was a tension during this
period between a global rejection of any and all methods of constitutional
construction and a willingness to interpret the constitutional text in accordance with the common law principles that had been used to construe statutes.[12]

A consensus on the proper approach to construing the Constitution later
emerged out of the political struggle between Federalists and Republicans
during the administration of John Adams. To the embattled Republicans,
conceiving the Constitution as a compact of sovereign states not only had an
intellectual appeal, but also seemed a politically expedient means to challenge
the activities of the Federalist-controlled national government. This substantive conception of the Constitution's nature was justified by, and in turn
entailed, resort to an extratextual source: the "original intent" underlying the
Constitution. The Republican constitutional theory swiftly became the common property of almost all American constitutionalists after the Republicans'
electoral triumph in 1800.

Contemporary intentionalists are correct, therefore, in claiming that resort
to "original intent" is an interpretive strategy of great antiquity in American
constitutional discourse. Despite verbal similarities, however, modern intentionalism cannot be equated with the early Republican theory. As under-

stood by its late eighteenth- and early nineteenth-century proponents, the original intent relevant to discourse was not that of the Philadelphia framers, but rather that of the parties to the constitutional compact—the states as political entities. This original "original intent" was determined not by historical inquiry into the expectations of the individuals involved in framing and ratifying the Constitution, but by consideration of what rights and powers sovereign polities could delegate to a common agent without destroying their own essential autonomy. Thus, the original intentionalism was in fact a form of structural interpretation.[13] To the extent that constitutional interpreters considered historical evidence to have any interpretive value, what they deemed relevant was evidence of the proceedings of the state ratifying conventions, not of the intent of the framers. Only later, during the breakdown of the Republican consensus, did the attention of constitutional interpreters gradually shift from the "intention" of the sovereign states to the personal intentions of individual historical actors.

II. Hermeneutical Traditions in 1787

There is more ado to interpret interpretations than to interpret things.[14]
— *Michel Montaigne*

WE CANNOT APPRECIATE how the task of interpreting the Constitution was originally understood unless we first know something about the intellectual tools that were available.[15] The Americans who wrote, debated, denounced, and ratified the Constitution of 1787 were thoroughly familiar with argument over the meaning and implications of "constitutions"; the "patriots" of the previous decade had understood the Revolution itself, in part, as the final, violent phase of a sustained effort to vindicate the true meaning of the ancient English constitution.[16] But pre-Revolutionary constitutional discourse differed in one obvious and vitally important manner from the constitutional task that independent America set for itself: the new federal Constitution, like those of the individual states, consisted not of a Burkean tradition of historical custom and political principle, but of a written document. As a result, constitutional argument in the new republics naturally and necessarily assumed the form of dispute over the proper interpretation of the constitutional texts. But Americans did not approach this novel task of constitutional interpretation free of all presuppositions about the appropriate method for construing a written instrument. They instead drew overtly on the various approaches to interpretation embedded in their cultural heritage.[17] The two most obvious sources of hermeneutical wisdom were the anti-interpretive tradition of Anglo-American Protestantism and the accumulated interpretive techniques of the common law.

A. *The Cultural Rejection of Interpretation*

One of the central themes of the Protestant Reformation of the sixteenth century was summed up in the Reformers' slogan, *"sola Scriptura"* (Scripture only).[18] In Britain, *sola Scriptura* became even more important than on the continent as a unifying principle for Protestants: the role of the English translation of the Bible in the spread of Protestantism in Britain, and Anglicanism's de-emphasis of substantive doctrine, made a professed adherence to biblical authority the main point of agreement for British Protestants.[19] In the name of obedience to the Bible, Protestants rejected the rich medieval tradition of interpretation, according to which literal exposition of the text was only one (and by no means necessarily the most important) methodology; likewise, they spurned the medieval acceptance of Pope and council as authoritative interpreters.[20] In the eyes of the British Protestants, the only authoritative, and indeed the only safe, interpreter of Scripture was Scripture itself.[21] Any exposition of the text that went beyond the text was, of necessity, a "human invention,"[22] "which a discreet Man may do well; but 'tis his Scripture, not the Holy Ghost['s]."[23]

From this position it was but a short step, already taken with respect to medieval and contemporary Catholic interpretation, to the conclusion that such "human invention" is, necessarily and always, a corruption of the text's meaning.[24] For example, the Scots Confession of 1560, discussing the authority of general councils, granted that conciliar decrees might be accepted when confirmed "by the plain Word of God." But this did not mean that a council could develop doctrines beyond the letter of Scripture, "or even [offer] the true interpretation of it, which was not expressed previously by his holy will in his Word."[25] The distinction between a decree confirmable by a text and "the true interpretation" of that text is subtle, and from a modern viewpoint perhaps vacuous. The fact remains, however, that British Protestants fervently believed that such a distinction could and should be drawn, and that their own version of Christianity could be described truthfully as a presentation of the plain Word rather than as an interpretation—even a "true interpretation"—of Scripture. British Protestant writers in the post-Reformation era delighted in contrasting their own chaste literalism to the delusive and unscriptural interpretations of their theological opponents.[26]

Attacks on the legitimacy of scriptural interpretation spilled over easily into the political sphere.[27] Reform of the law emerged as a major theme of seventeenth-century Puritan politics both in the American colonies and in interregnum England, and reformers saw the elimination of confusion and complexity in the law as a primary goal.[28] To the Puritans, the Bible could govern theological discourse because its meaning was lucid to the ordinary reader. Legal texts, in contrast, were usually obscure, and thus no explanation of their meaning could simply be "confirmed" by reference to their plain words. As a result, the Puritans argued, these supposedly authoritative texts could not in fact constrain judicial interpretation, and the elaborate interpretive techniques of the common law served only to justify judges' imposition of their personal views. Puritan lawyer William Sheppard was both prominent among and typical of the reformers. In 1656 Sheppard published a program for law reform entitled *England's Balme*.[29] The centerpiece of his criticism of the existing statutory and common law was the claim that the law was so obscure that "it is not to be understood, when it is read," and was therefore "incertain," because not even judges could agree on its proper interpretation. Sheppard advocated a kind of codification that would make the law "cleer and certain" and would require judges to disavow traditional modes of interpretation and to pledge to follow the code's wording henceforth as "the setled law."[30]

The Puritan attack on traditional legal hermeneutics was largely unsuccessful in the mother country, but in the following century its main themes were absorbed into an ideology of opposition (the "Country" ideology) that served as an important intellectual foundation for both the American revolutionaries of the 1760s and 1770s and the Jeffersonian Republicans of the 1790s.[31] For the "Country" writers, clarity and simplicity were necessary if law was to serve rather than smother liberty,[32] but these advantages of a known and written law would be lost if the law's meaning could be twisted by means of judicial construction. Furthermore, just as the Pope had usurped the authority of God by claiming the power to interpret His Word, so the judiciary could undermine the legislative prerogatives of the people's representatives by engaging in the corruptive process of interpreting legislative texts.

For cosmopolitan Americans, the influence of the *philosophes*[33]—the rationalist intellectuals and social critics of the Enlightenment era—reinforced the anti-interpretive tradition of British Protestantism. The *philosophes*, sometimes borrowing from earlier intellectual movements such as sixteenth-century humanism,[34] perceived traditional interpretation of Scripture as one of the chief props supporting the theological absurdities and religious oppression perpetrated by the established churches, and saw the niggling interpretation of complicated or obscure laws as a relic of feudal misrule and political tyranny.[35] In addition, they condemned judicial interpretation of statutes as a violation of the separation of governmental powers many believed necessary to a rational and free polity.[36] In his enormously influential essay on criminal law, the Italian jurist Cesare Beccaria wrote that judges in criminal cases must not be allowed the authority to interpret the laws because that would make them de facto legislators.[37] Beccaria contrasted "the constant fixed voice of the law" with "the erring instability of interpretation," and his firm conclusion—"the interpretation of laws is an evil"—expressed a view widely shared by educated and "progressive" individuals in the late eighteenth century.[38]

Either British biblicism or Enlightenment rationalism or both formed part of the mental furniture of virtually all literate Americans in the half-century from the Declaration of Independence through the presidency of John Quincy Adams.[39] It is therefore unsurprising that one can often discern the anti-interpretive biases of those traditions in American discussions of grand political issues,[40] as well as of private legal affairs.[41] For example, the Essex County convention, in rejecting the proposed Massachusetts constitution of 1778, explained that the document provided inadequate safeguards against "artful constructions" of the laws, with potentially tragic results.[42] The county's solution was a rigid separation-of-powers scheme that would enable each branch of government to check the others.[43] Such cultural reluctance to admit the legitimacy of significant interpretation of written documents strongly influenced Americans in their conceptualization of the task of interpreting their new Constitution. Yet despite this reluctance, the necessity of judicial construction had already engendered a second—and conflicting—source of influence: the rich common law traditions of legal interpretation.

B. Interpretation and the Common Law

Although they lacked a significant tradition of interpreting written constitutions, the newly independent Americans possessed almost an embarrassment of hermeneutical riches in the common law's centuries of dealing with wills, deeds, contracts, and statutes. By 1787, the English legal system had produced a wealth of reflection on the process of construing normative documents.[44] Moreover, the common law considered these canons of interpretation to be themselves a part of the law, and to be equally binding on the maker and the interpreter of a document.[45] The concept central to the common law's hermeneutic, and to later American discussion of constitutional interpretation, was the notion of the "intention" or "intent" underlying a text.[46] "[A]s touching construction of words," Chief Justice Fleming of the Court of King's Bench explained in 1611, "they shall be taken according to the . . . intent of parties."[47] This simple principle, however, concealed a significant ambiguity, because its salient term—intent—was by no means unequivocal in meaning.[48] The English nouns "intention" and "intent" were derived from the Latin *intentio*, which in medieval usage could refer either to individual, subjective purpose or to what an external observer would regard as the purpose of the individual's actions.[49] The English derivatives of *intentio* inherited a similar ambiguity: the "intent" or "intention" of a document could denote either the meaning that the drafters wished to communicate or the meaning the reader was warranted in deriving from the text. The two might or might not be identical. Thus, to understand the import of the common law's focus on "intent," we must determine in what sense the word itself was used.

The use of "intent" in common law interpretive discourse is well illustrated in the *Table-Talk* of seventeenth-century jurist and parliamentary hero John Selden.[50] Although Selden insisted that the "one true sense" of a document is that which "the Author meant when he [wrote] it" (the modern intention-alist's definition of "intent"), he also asserted that the court determines "the intention of the King" solely on the basis of the words of the law, and not by investigating any other source of information about the lawgiver's purposes.[51] A century and a half later, John Joseph Powell's treatise on contract law displayed the same usage of "intent." According to Powell, "the law always regards the intention of the parties" to an agreement. But it does so, he immediately continued, by applying the parties' words "to that which, in common presumption, may be taken to be their intent."[52] The law of contracts is not concerned with anyone's "internal sentiments," Powell wrote, but only with their "external expression."[53] At common law, then, the "intent" of the maker of a legal document and the "intent" of the document itself were one and the same; "intent" did not depend upon the subjective purposes of the author.[54] The late eighteenth-century common lawyer conceived an instrument's "intent"—and therefore its meaning—not as what the drafters meant by their words but rather as what judges, employing the "artificial reason and judgment of law,"[55] understood "the reasonable and legal meaning" of those words to be.[56]

Although the common law tradition identified the purpose of interpreting any document as the determination of that document's "intent," it also insisted that the proper means of carrying out this task varied according to the type of instrument to be construed. By the late eighteenth century, statutes, wills, deeds, and contracts had become the objects of what seemed at least superficially to be increasingly different interpretive methodologies. Courts treated statutes and wills similarly by purporting to pay particular attention to the subjective intentions of their drafters.[57] This concern for the drafters' purposes was, however, largely illusory. Blackstone's description of the proper approach to the construction of a will is typical: "the construction [should] be favorable, and as near the minds and apparent intents of the parties, as the rules of law will admit."[58] But Blackstone did not mean that in interpreting what lay in the testator's mind a court was free to disregard the rule of law governing the "apparent intent" of the testator's words: "the construction must also be reasonable, and agreeable to common understanding."[59] Blackstone was cautioning against hypercritical readings of the words of unlearned laypersons, not endorsing an extratextual search for the purposes underlying those words.

The courts likewise looked to "rules of law" and to "common understanding" when interpreting statutes. The modern practice of interpreting a law by reference to its legislative history was almost wholly nonexistent, and English judges professed themselves bound to honor the true import of the "express words" of Parliament.[60] The "intent of the act" and the "intent of the legislature" were interchangeable terms; neither term implied that the interpreter looked at any evidence concerning that "intent" other than the words of the text and the common law background of the statute.[61] Political and legal scholars in both Britain and the American colonies viewed strict judicial adherence to the legislature's language as a constitutional necessity, because the "known, fixed laws" could be properly established or altered only by "the whole legislature," which spoke only through its enactments.[62]

The common law tradition did admit the propriety of looking beyond the statute's wording where the text was defective on its face. In such situations judges were free to substitute coherence for gibberish.[63] A more serious interpretive problem occurred when the statute's wording was ambiguous, rather than clear but in conflict with its apparent intent. It was generally agreed that such *ambiguitas patens* could not be resolved by extrinsic evidence as to Parliament's purpose; in Francis Bacon's classic formulation, ambiguity "shall bee holpen by construction . . . but never by averrement" of the purposes of the members of Parliament.[64] This did not mean, however, that "construction" was viewed as an unstructured exercise of judicial choice. Instead, courts were bound to read acts of Parliament against the background of the common law. The Barons of the Exchequer resolved in *Heydon's Case*[65] that all statutes concerned a "mischief and defect for which the common law did not provide," and for which Parliament had ordained a remedy.[66] Therefore, "the office of all the Judges is always to make such construction as shall suppress the mischief, and advance the remedy."[67] In the performance of this office, the courts might consult the statute's preamble, which, although not an operative provision of the act, was the "key" to the purposes of its makers.[68] In seeking a statute's proper construction, courts would also admit the practical exposition of the statute supplied by usage under it.[69] But judicial precedent served as the most important source of information about an act's meaning beyond its actual text.[70] This followed almost by definition from the basic notion of "intent" as a product of the interpretive process rather than something locked into the text by its author. A prior construction of a statute provided certainty as to the meaning because, in Lord Coke's words, it was not the "private interpretation" of an individual, but rather the authoritative "resolution of judges in Courts of Justice."[71]

Whereas the common law tradition at least purported to implement the desires of the drafters in interpreting wills and statutes, the common law approach to the interpretation of contracts was blatantly unconcerned with the subjective purposes of the parties. With minor exceptions,[72] contracting parties were conclusively presumed to have meant what their words said,[73] and to have been aware of the law's canons of interpretation.[74] The view of contract prevalent before the American Revolution, a view that emphasized considerations of equity and substantive justice over contractual freedom and the will of the parties,[75] went hand in hand with the courts' lack of concern with subjective intention. Judges generally construed agreements in light of the ordinary meaning of the terms and with an eye toward the nature of the contract and the identity of the parties to it.[76]

During the same period in which Americans were drawing on these common law traditions to respond to the novel challenges posed by constitutional interpretation, certain changes were occurring within the traditional branches of the common law. A new self-consciousness about the process of interpretation developed toward the end of the eighteenth century, and the sixty years following 1800 saw a remarkable outpouring of scholarly discussion of hermeneutical issues in both Great Britain and America.[77] Judicial opinions also reflected ostensible shifts in emphasis. Statutory interpretation became even more frankly literalistic.[78] A judicial opinion of New York Senator John Young in 1835 captures the spirit of the age: "To understand the statute, it is only necessary to know the meaning of the words which are used."[79] Rather than take advantage of the increasing availability of legislative history in the form of committee reports and legislative journals, courts emphatically rejected any consideration of such "extrinsic evidence."[80]

On the surface, the interpretation of contracts took the opposite course. The will theory of contracts gained ascendancy in the early nineteenth century, and the courts accepted as their task the simple enforcement of whatever bargain the parties had made.[81] Ironically, though, the rise of the will theory was accompanied by an increasingly "objective" approach to the discovery of the parties' intent.[82] Thus, the ideology of freedom of contract did not entail any essential modification of the law's traditional hermeneutic.

Despite the anti-interpretive influences of British Protestantism and Enlightenment rationalism, the sheer necessity of judicial construction gave rise to a substantial common law tradition of legal interpretation by the end of the eighteenth century.[83] Most of the Americans influential in the framing, ratification, and early interpretation of the federal Constitution were intimately familiar with the common law[84] and they gleaned from it not only a general approach to constitutional interpretation—one centering on a search for the Constitution's "intention"—but also a variety of specific interpretive techniques. The common law, however, did not yield ready responses to a number of preliminary questions that required answers before constitutional interpretation could be assimilated to the familiar patterns of legal construction. What kind of document was the Constitution—a statute, a contract, an instrument *sui generis*? Who were its makers—the Philadelphia framers, the state conventions, the states, "We the People"? What, if any, extrinsic evidence of its meaning would be admissible in case of uncertainty—records of the federal and state conventions, statements made by its supporters, general principles of political philosophy? Without answers to these and other inquiries, the common law's hermeneutical tradition could contribute only chaos to American constitutional discourse.

III. Early Views on Interpreting the Constitution

Friend: You have given us a good Constitution.
Gouverneur Morris: That depends upon how it is construed.[85] — A. Mason

A. *The Framers and the Battle for Ratification*

Constitutional debate was not the invention of Revolutionary America, and the invocation of written documents was a wholly traditional move in English high political controversy.[86] America's innovation was to identify "the Constitution" with a single normative document instead of a historical tradition, and thus to create the possibility of treating constitutional interpretation as an exercise in the traditional legal activity of construing a written instrument.[87] The proceedings of the Philadelphia convention reflect the delegates' awareness of this innovation and their desire to craft a document that would be understood, at least in part, through the traditional processes of legal interpretation.

The Philadelphia framers' primary expectation regarding constitutional interpretation was that the Constitution, like any other legal document, would be interpreted in accord with its express language. This expectation is evident in the framers' numerous attempts to refine the wording of the text, either to eliminate vagueness[88] or to allay fears that overprecise language would be taken literally and that the aim of a given provision would thus be defeated.[89] Debates over the language of the document were abundant,[90] yet in none of them did any delegate suggest that future interpreters could avoid misconstruing the text by consulting evidence of the intentions articulated at the convention. Although the Philadelphia framers certainly wished to embody in the text the most "distinctive form of collecting the mind" of the convention,[91] there is no indication that they expected or intended future interpreters to refer to any extratextual intentions revealed in the convention's secretly conducted debates.[92] The framers shared the traditional common law view—so foreign to much hermeneutical thought in more recent years—that the import of the document they were framing would be determined by reference to the intrinsic meaning of its words or through the usual judicial process of case-by-case interpretation.[93]

In accepting the common law's objective approach to discerning the meaning of a document, the framers did not endorse strict literalism as the proper stance of future interpreters. The framers were aware that unforeseen situations would arise, and they accepted the inevitability and propriety of construction.[94] When a motion was made to extend the jurisdiction of the Supreme Court to cases arising under "this Constitution" as well as under "the laws of the United States," James Madison expressed concern that this would extend the Court's power to matters not properly within judicial cognizance:

> Mr. Madison doubted whether it was not going too far, to extend the jurisdiction of the Court generally to cases arising under the Constitution, and whether it ought not to be limited to cases of a judicial nature. The right of expounding the Constitution, in cases not of this nature, ought not to be given to that department.
> The motion of Docr. Johnson [to extend the Court's jurisdiction]

was agreed to, *nem. con.* [without dissent], it being generally supposed, that the jurisdiction given was constructively limited to cases of a judiciary nature.[95]

Although the Philadelphia framers did not discuss in detail how they intended their end product to be interpreted, they clearly assumed that future interpreters would adhere to then-prevalent methods of statutory construction.

The political struggle over the ratification of the Constitution elicited, both in print and on state convention floors, a considerable body of commentary on the Constitution's "intent," and on the means that future interpreters would use to determine that "intent." Americans generally agreed that the Articles of Confederation were a compact among the several states.[96] The Federalist proponents of the Constitution identified the contractual basis of the articles as one of their chief weaknesses.[97] One of the Constitution's virtues, in the Federalists' view, lay in its rejection of a contractual model for the polity of the United States.[98] The Federalists analogized the ratification process to the passage by a legislature (the people) of a statute (the Constitution) drafted by a committee (the Philadelphia convention). Without the people's approval, the convention's work would remain a mere proposal lacking any intrinsic authority.[99] This analogy led many Federalists to assume or assert that the Constitution would be construed in accord with the same basic principles that the common law had developed for statutory interpretation.[100] Perhaps for their own polemical purposes, the Anti-Federalists usually agreed with the statutory analogy for the proposed Constitution, and with the corollary analogy between constitutional and statutory interpretation.[101] Their complaint was that this methodology, applied to the sweeping language of the Constitution, would lead inexorably to the effective consolidation of the states into a single body politic with a single, omnipotent government.[102]

Once the Constitution was proposed to the states, a central element of the campaign to prevent ratification was the charge that the Constitution would be the object of interpretation and that judges and legislators would read into it doctrines present only "constructively" and not textually.[103] All of the anti-hermeneutic resources of Protestant biblicism and Enlightenment rationalism were enlisted in an effort to show that the Constitution was an open invitation to political corruption and oligarchic usurpation. The Constitution was ambiguous by design, the Anti-Federalists claimed, and thereby invited construction.[104] Through such construction the new federal rulers would gradually extend their power and so finally subvert American liberties.[105] The Supreme Court's power to interpret the Constitution would make the Court, not the people or their representatives, the true lawgiver.[106] Disputes over the scope of the Constitution's grants of power, the Anti-Federalists argued, showed that no one could predict how the instrument would be interpreted once adopted.[107] The good intentions of the Philadelphia delegates, or of the proponents of the Constitution in the state conventions, were irrelevant, because the *Constitution's* intention was expressed "so loosely . . . [and] inaccurately" that misconstructions were certain to occur.[108] The Protestant tradition taught that God's Word is its own interpreter, and the *philosophes* had warned against the dangers of any law not plainly comprehensible on its face; the proposed Constitution, however, contained no acceptable internal criteria to guide its interpreters.[109] Some Anti-Federalists viewed the document in an even darker light: to them it revealed a conscious desire on the part of the Philadelphia delegates, who had clothed their proceedings in a veil of secrecy, to overthrow the free and republican constitutions of the states and substitute for them a centralized despotism.[110]

The Federalist supporters of ratification offered a variety of responses to the barrage of criticism leveled against the Constitution and its alleged susceptibility to corrupting interpretation. First, to those who questioned the good faith of the Philadelphia delegates, the Federalists responded by invoking not only the great names of Washington and Franklin, but also the common law's understanding of "intent." The Anti-Federalists' fears were misguided, they asserted, because whatever the private sentiments of the Philadelphia delegates had been, those sentiments would not be the legally significant "intent" of the Constitution.[111] The members of the federal convention had been mere scriveners or attorneys appointed to draw up an instrument; the instrument's true makers were the people of the United States assembled in state conventions.[112] It was thus the people's unquestionably republican intention, evinced in the plain, obvious meaning of the text, that would control future interpretations. The Federalists additionally denied allegations that they were already corrupting the meaning of the Constitution. It was not they but their opponents, the Federalists claimed, who were engaged in lawyers' quibbles over the language of an instrument that the common sense of the people found perfectly clear.[113] As John Jay explained, Federalist statements of the document's meaning were not products of a suspect hermeneutical process; they involved "no sophistry; no construction; no false glosses, but simple inferences from the obvious operation of things."[114] Finally, Federalists argued that the Anti-Federalist attack on the Constitution's indeterminacy ignored the limits of human communicative powers: "no compositions which men can pen, could be formed, but wh[ich] would be liable to the same charge [of ambiguity]."[115] When interpretation was necessary, it would take place in accord with the rules of "universal jurisprudence," subject to correction by the amendment process provided for in Article V.[116]

A series of essays published in the *New York Journal* from October 1787 through April 1788 under the byline "Brutus" constituted by far the most powerful and sustained attack on the Constitution from an anti-hermeneutical perspective.[117] "Brutus" read the first sentence of the second section of Article III ("The judicial power shall extend to all cases, in law and equity, arising under this Constitution. . . .") to authorize the federal courts to give the Constitution both "a legal construction" and an interpretation "according to the reasoning spirit of it, without being confined to the words or letter."[118] Courts frequently would employ the latter "mode of construction" out of necessity, because the Constitution's grants of authority were "conceived in general and indefinite terms, which are either equivocal, ambiguous, or which require long definitions to unfold the extent of their meaning."[119] The courts' exercises in construction "according to the reasoning spirit," therefore, would necessarily amount to the creation of constitutional norms by judges themselves.[120]

"Brutus" felt that the courts' interpretations "according to the rules laid down for construing a law"[121] would be just as unfortunate. The common law tradition of statutory interpretation, he pointed out, permitted and even required the court to take the end or purpose of the statute into account.[122] Like many statutes, the Constitution declared its purpose in a Preamble, the wording of which made it "obvious," to "Brutus," that the Constitution "has in view every object which is embraced by any government," leaving no separate sphere of responsibility for the state authorities and reducing the present confederation to a single, consolidated nation.[123] Most horrifying of all to "Brutus" was the realization, gathered from the Preamble, from the grants of power to Congress,[124] and from the interpretive authority entrusted to the federal judiciary, that the Constitution identified the separate existence and autonomy of the states as the mischief and defect it was to cure.[125] "Brutus" insisted that the most disinterested judge, interpreting the Constitution with strict regard for the proprieties of common law statutory construction, would agree that the document "was calculated to abolish entirely the state governments, and to melt down the states into one entire government."[126] And of course, he argued, judges would not in fact be disinterested. Electorally irresponsible, endowed with that absolute authority to interpret against which English religious and political tradition warned, the federal judges would be from the beginning the final lawgivers of the system, and in the end its absolute rulers.[127]

"Brutus" therefore saw the Constitution as flawed at a deeper level than that reached by criticisms of its ambiguities or of its broad grants of power to the federal legislature. Its basic evil was its framers' misconception, deliberate or not, of the nature of fundamental law in a free society. The Philadelphia convention had devised a constitution patterned after a statute, a command issued by a legal superior and subject to technical interpretation in accord with the traditional rules of construction. But for "Brutus," a constitution should be a contract, "a compact of a people with their rulers," framed in simple and nontechnical language and enforced by the people's right to remove those rulers "at the period when the rulers are to be elected."[128] A constitution, for "Brutus," should articulate in plain terms the agreement of the community on the rightful powers of government, not establish a superior authority to determine what those powers are. Under such a political com-

pact there could be no danger of effective usurpation by the rulers, save by
force, for the compact's meaning would be clear to all and would be interpreted by the equal parties to the compact, not by a legal superior. The
Philadelphia framers, unfortunately, had followed a different model. Their
proposed constitution did not express consensus; it issued commands— mandates at once so complicated and so obscure that it would be impossible to
give them meaning without resort by the federal political bodies to the artificial techniques of traditional legal hermeneutics. By drafting an instrument
requiring such interpretation, the Philadelphia framers had ensured that future authority over the parameters of American political society would ultimately be transferred from the ordinary people to a small coterie of legal
quibblers.

Commentators have suggested that Alexander Hamilton's discussion of Article III in *Federalist* Nos. 75 through 83, which appeared in late May 1788,
was written as a direct response to the essays of "Brutus."[129] Whether or not
intended as such, those papers in fact offered the most coherent Federalist
rebuttal of the arguments of "Brutus." Hamilton had already observed in
Federalist No. 22 that one of the defects of the Articles of Confederation was
their failure to establish an effective federal judiciary.[130] In addition, in *Federalist* No. 37 James Madison had launched a devastating counterattack on the
standard Anti-Federalist charge of ambiguity.[131] Madison stressed the ines-
capable fallibility and tentativeness of all human acts of discrimination—sen-
sory, mental, or experiential—and responded to the religious overtones in
the Anti-Federalist critique with the observation that the meaning even of
God's Word "is rendered dim and doubtful, by the cloudy medium through
which it is communicated" when He "condescends to address mankind in
their own language."[132] Mortals' efforts at the framing of law obviously could
not be hoped to better those of Omnipotence; Madison thus concluded that
"all new laws, though penned with the greatest technical skill, and passed on
the fullest and most mature deliberation, are considered as more or less obscure and equivocal, until their meaning be liquidated and ascertained by a
series of particular discussions and adjudications."[133] Madison's argument,
which Hamilton had anticipated in *Federalist* No. 22,[134] was of course a restatement in somewhat abstract terms of the old common law assumption,
shared by the Philadelphia framers, that the "intent" of any legal document
is the product of the interpretive process and not some fixed meaning that
the author locks into the document's text at the outset. In his essays "Brutus"
underscored this confession that the Constitution would be subject to judicial
construction whose results were not completely foreseeable at present, and
he labored with considerable success to demonstrate that the necessary consequence was judicial tyranny.

In *Federalist* Nos. 78 through 83, Hamilton returned his attention to the
legal character of the Constitution and its provisions for a federal judiciary.
He steadfastly reiterated the *Federalist*'s earlier claims that it was appropriate

and necessary for the courts to "liquidate and fix [the] meaning and operation" of laws, including the Constitution.[135] Hamilton rejected the inference
that the future federal courts would find in the Constitution anything shock-
ing or surprising to the ordinary reader: "The rules of legal interpretation are
rules of *common sense*, adopted by the courts in the construction of the laws.
. . . In relation to such a subject [a constitution of government], the natural
and obvious sense of its provisions, apart from any technical rules, is the true
criterion of construction."[136]

Faced with the argument of "Brutus" that the courts' powers of constitutional interpretation and judicial review of legislative acts would inexorably
result in uncontrollable and ultimately despotic oligarchy, Hamilton countered by suggesting that "Brutus" had not taken the statutory analogy seriously enough. Both agreed, Hamilton approvingly and "Brutus" disapprov-
ingly, that the Constitution was to be viewed as a quasi-statute, a command
from a legal superior to those under its authority. According to this view,
Hamilton argued, the legal superior issuing the command must be considered
the ultimate repository of sovereignty in a republic: the people. But "the
nature and reason of the thing," Hamilton wrote, "teach us that the prior act
of a superior ought to be preferred to the subsequent act of an inferior and
subordinate authority; and that, accordingly, whenever a particular statute
contravenes the constitution, it will be the duty of the judicial tribunals to
adhere to the latter, and disregard the former."[137] Far from exalting the judiciary over all, the doctrine of judicial review based on the courts' construction
of the Constitution simply safeguarded the authority of the people, who had
"ordained and established" the Constitution in the first place.[138]

Hamilton and "Brutus" therefore disagreed primarily over the nature of
legal interpretation. "Brutus" feared that interpretation would inevitably
convert the Constitution's open-textured language into a license for omnipotent federal government. Hamilton countered that legal interpretation was
simply the application of common sense to text. Because the people can exercise common sense, they could tell for themselves what the Constitution
meant—and no sensible reader would take it to be a charter for tyranny.
Hamilton scornfully dismissed the notion that judges could exploit their interpretive authority to make themselves despots: lacking influence "over either the sword or the purse,"[139] he remarked, courts would possess "neither
Force nor Will, but merely judgment."[140] The insulation of judges from electoral accountability was not a threat to liberty, but rather an essential condition to the judiciary's role as independent guardian of the Constitution's
limitations on power.[141] In reality, as Hamilton had argued earlier,[142] the
seeds of tyranny lurked not within the statutory analogy proposed by the
Federalists, but within the contract analogy favored by "Brutus." A government with no justification other than a contractual meeting of the minds
could not long endure without resorting to force to resolve the disagreements
that would inevitably splinter society. The debate between Hamilton and

"Brutus" was ultimately irresolvable, for they started from different premises that paralleled the conflicting hermeneutical perspectives discussed above in Part II. "Brutus" assumed the validity of the anti-interpretive tradition's equation of construction and corruption. In sharp contrast, Hamilton accepted the validity of the common law's hermeneutical techniques as means to discovering a document's "intent."

The public debate over the adoption of the Constitution thus revealed that Americans of all political opinions accepted the applicability to constitutional interpretation of hermeneutical views developed in relation to quite different documents—the Bible, parliamentary statutes, and private contracts. But there were sharp disagreements over which interpretive approach was acceptable.[143] An important element in the Anti-Federalists' critique was their implicit appeal to the distrust of interpretation cultivated by the British Protestant tradition and Enlightenment thought. The Federalists, on the other hand, treated the availability of common law hermeneutics as a positive good: precisely because there was a developed tradition of legal interpretation, they argued, the people could predict with confidence the results of future constitutional construction.

B. The Beginnings of Constitutional Interpretation

Upon convening in the spring of 1789 to inaugurate the new government created by the ratification of the Constitution, the First Congress found itself engaged almost at once in the task of explaining the Constitution's ambiguities. The Congress's most famous exercise in constitutional interpretation was the formulation and proposal to the states of a federal bill of rights, embodied in twelve proposed amendments to the 1787 text.[144] But almost every significant issue considered by the Congress (and some arguably not so significant[145]) required some excursion into the fields of constitutional construction. The establishment of the executive departments, the debates over a protective tariff and a national bank, the consideration of a memorial against the slave trade and of the proper means of handling the public debt—all involved the resolution of issues of constitutional authority not plainly answered on the face of the document.[146] Despite their almost constant involvement with the reality of constitutional interpretation, however, many members of Congress attacked the theoretical propriety of such construction and insisted that they were merely applying the Constitution's terms. Representative Elias Boudinot of New Jersey declared: "For my part, I shall certainly attend to the terms of the Constitution in making a decision [on whether the President's removal power could be exercised constitutionally only with the concurrence of the Senate]; indeed, I never wish to see them departed from or construed, if the Government can possibly be carried into effect in any other manner."[147] Representative Elbridge Gerry of Massachusetts was dogmatic: "all construction of the meaning of the Constitution, is dangerous or unnatural, and therefore ought to be avoided."[148] Other prominent members joined in the repetition of the old anti-hermeneutical arguments.[149] More realistic about what Congress actually was doing, and concerned only that Congress should interpret well, were men like James Madison. Rising to address the scope of the President's removal power, Madison stressed the far-reaching consequences of Congress's decision on the question. "The decision that is at this time made," he declared, "will become the permanent exposition of the Constitution."[150]

The passage by the First Congress of a bill to establish a national bank,[151] drafted by Secretary of the Treasury Hamilton, provoked an elaborate debate over constitutional interpretation within the executive branch. President Washington, troubled by doubts over the constitutionality of the measure, requested formal opinions on its validity from Hamilton, Attorney General Edmund Randolph, and Secretary of State Thomas Jefferson. The opinions of Hamilton and Jefferson became classic statements of the expansive and restrictive views, respectively, of the constitutional scope of congressional power.

Both Hamilton and Jefferson purported to rely on "the usual & established rules of construction."[152] Their opposing conclusions and radically different approaches to the problem, however, demonstrated that the two men held incompatible views about the nature of the Constitution and consequently about the proper application to it of the "usual" rules of construction. Hamilton clearly remained committed to the statutory analogy he had adopted in *The Federalist*. He insisted, in good common law fashion, that the Constitution's text was to be given its "grammatical" and "popular" meaning:

> [W]hatever may have been the nature of the proposition or the reasons for rejecting it concludes nothing in respect to the real merits of the question. The Secretary of State will not deny, that whatever may have been the intention of the framers of a constitution, or of a law, that intention is to be sought for in the instrument itself, according to the usual & established rules of construction. Nothing is more common than for laws to *express* and *effect*, more or less than was intended. If then a power to erect a corporation, in any case, be deducible by fair inference from the whole or any part of the numerous provisions of the constitution of the United States, arguments drawn from extrinsic circumstances, regarding the intention of the convention, must be rejected.[153]

This absolute rejection of what modern intentionalists would regard as evidence of "intent" was perfectly consistent with language prescient of modern intentionalism. A few pages earlier, Hamilton had referred to "the intent of the [Philadelphia] convention."[154] Such locutions were common.[155] They did not in any way indicate that the writer was rejecting the traditional common law understanding of "intent" as the apparent "meaning of the text" in favor of more modern, subjective notions. Indeed, in the passage last quoted from Hamilton, the context makes it plain that he derived his knowledge of "the intent of the convention" from the "obvious & popular sense" of the constitutional expression under consideration ("necessary and proper") and from the "whole turn of the clause containing it."[156]

Just as a statute is to be construed so as to advance the remedy proposed by the legislature and revealed in the statute's preamble and provisions, so the Constitution, Hamilton wrote, must be interpreted in accord with the expansive purposes outlined in its Preamble.[157] The Constitution plainly intended to create a government capable of the "advancement of the public good."[158] The "sound maxim of construction" required, therefore, that the Constitution's grants of power be "construed liberally."[159] This conclusion from the general principles of legal interpretation was confirmed, Hamilton added, by the text itself, in the necessary and proper clause:[160] "The whole turn of the clause containing [the phrase 'necessary and proper'], indicates, it was the intent of the convention, by that clause to give a liberal latitude to the exercise of the specified powers."[161]

Jefferson, too, treated the task of constitutional construction as analogous to common law interpretation of statutes and as requiring a determination of the document's "intent." He began, however, from a different point within the tradition—from the maxim that a statute is to be construed as changing the substance of the common law only to the extent that that conclusion is plainly required.[162] Jefferson's opinion began with a list of the preexisting rules of state law that he believed the establishment of a national bank would abrogate.[163] He returned to this theme toward the end of his paper:

> Can it be thought that the Constitution intended that for a shade or
> two of *convenience*, more or less, Congress should be authorised to
> break down the most ancient and fundamental laws of the several
> States; such as those against Mortmain, the laws of Alienage, the rules
> of descent, the acts of distribution, the laws of escheat and forfeiture,
> the laws of monopoly?[164]

Jefferson's opening point was wholly traditional, but, as the quoted sentence indicates, his argument subtly shifted ground during the course of his opinion. The aberrant positions of Lord Coke and a few others to one side,[165] the common law presumption against change was only that—a commonsense assumption that legislatures do not transform whole areas of legal custom by implication.[166] But Jefferson wanted to establish a more radical interpretive principle: that the presumption in constitutional construction was against any change, not only in particular substantive laws but also in spheres of legislative competence.[167] Here Jefferson's argument left behind traditional common law notions of statutory interpretation.[168]

Jefferson implicitly accepted Hamilton's statutory analogy for constitutional interpretation yet provided no real justification for departing from the familiar patterns of statutory interpretation that Hamilton manipulated so well. Jefferson asserted that the Constitution was based on the principle embodied in the Tenth Amendment: that powers "not delegated" to the federal government are "reserved to the States respectively, or to the people."[169] He did not explain, however, how that amendment's denial to Congress of any undelegated powers necessarily carried with it an attitude of strict construction toward the powers that were delegated. Hamilton, by contrast, presented a clear picture of what the Constitution was and how it should be construed, a picture that fit easily into the traditional interpretive wisdom of the common law.

The most sustained early congressional discussion of constitutional hermeneutics arose out of the controversial treaty with Great Britain negotiated by Chief Justice John Jay. To enable the House of Representatives fully to consider the treaty's expediency and constitutionality, the powerful Republican opposition in the fourth Congress proposed a resolution calling on President Washington to transmit to the House the executive branch's files concerning Jay's negotiations. Federalist opponents of the resolution initially attacked it as unnecessary.

> I will admit, that if the President has assumed powers not delegated to
> him by the people in making and proclaiming in his Treaty, it is void
> in itself; but to what use can those papers be to us in determining that
> question? Are we to explain the Treaty by private and confidential
> papers, or by anything extraneous to the instrument itself? I conclude
> not. . .
> [I]f the articles of the instrument be constitutional, can the prepara-
> tory steps make them not so?[170]

The debate soon moved, however, to a heated discussion of the House's role in considering or implementing treaties, with the Federalists arguing that the resolution would be an unconstitutional intrusion upon the exclusive treaty powers of the President and Senate. During the debate, a number of Representatives (most but not all of them opponents of the resolution) referred to or quoted from the discussions of the Constitution's meaning that had taken place during the framing and ratification period, and thus provoked a subsidiary debate on the question of constitutional hermeneutics. Asserting that the Constitution itself "must be our sole guide," William Smith of South Carolina argued that "the general sense of the whole nation at the time the Constitution was formed" could be consulted when "the words" of the text were being construed.[171]

This use of history was related but not identical to that of modern intentionalism. The "contemporaneous expositions" on which Smith and others relied were not confined to the debates at Philadelphia, or at the state conventions, but included the defenses of the Constitution published by its proponents and even the critical interpretations of its opponents.[172] In addition, those who cited evidence from the ratification period almost invariably linked it with other expressions of constitutional opinion.[173] Typical of the caution with which these Representatives advanced historical materials as evidence of the Constitution's meaning was the tack taken by Uriah Tracy of Connecticut. Tracy began his attack on the resolution by observing that the House's present decision would probably fix the course of constitutional interpretation in future cases; he consequently urged caution on his colleagues.[174] After setting forth an elaborate analysis of the constitutional text and of American practice under the Articles of Confederation, Tracy quoted from the Virginia ratification convention debates as an illustration of the "almost unanimous understanding of the members of the different [state] Conventions."[175] Tracy "acknowledged, that, from such debates, the real state of men's minds or opinions may not always be collected with accuracy," and explained that he relied on the state proceedings not to prove an affirmative assertion, but only to show that "no one took such extensive ground as is now contended for by some of the supporters of the resolution under consideration."[176]

Although Tracy and others placed only modest weight on materials from the framing and ratification process, they were vigorously attacked by the resolution's supporters for "conjur[ing] up" such "extraneous sources."[177] Their opponents contended that the proper method of interpretation was "to attend to and compare"[178] the text's various provisions in accordance with the "ancient" rules for "the interpretation and construction of laws or Constitutions."[179] In the view of Republican spokesmen, the suggestion that the correct interpretation of the Constitution must conform to "the opinion which prevailed when the Constitution was adopted"[180] misconstrued both the nature of interpretation and the value of the available evidence. Edward Livingston of New York, who introduced the resolution, said that a construction based on history cannot be "conclusive . . . because . . . we [are] now as capable at least of determining the true meaning of that instrument as the Conventions were: they were called in haste, they were heated by party, and many adopted [the Constitution] from expediency."[181] The House, it was argued, must seek "the intrinsic meaning of the Constitution . . . from the words of it,"[182] while recognizing that the text was unavoidably ambiguous on many issues and that its framers had anticipated that those questions would "be settled by practice or by amendments."[183]

Resort to materials from the ratification era as one species of evidence as to the Constitution's context was in fact only mildly innovative, although proponents of the House resolution strove to make it appear a flagrant violation of the established canons of construction. One congressman, however, seems to have come much closer to modern intentionalism. Maryland's William Vans Murray, speaking late in the three-week-long debate, expressed surprise that those privy to information about the Philadelphia convention (especially James Madison) had not shared with the House the understanding prevalent at that convention. Vans Murray regarded the Constitution as, on the whole, so "explicit" that the text itself left no room for arguments of "expediency or sophistry."[184] But the existence, so soon after the Constitution's adoption, of "doubts upon some of its plainest passages" made it the duty of a man "known to have been in the illustrious body that framed the instrument [to] clear up difficulties by [communicating] his contemporaneous knowledge."[185] Vans Murray himself made no attempt to locate or use such information and expressed doubt about the propriety of consulting the official journal of the Philadelphia convention.[186]

On the following, final day of the debate, one of the leading Republicans in the House, Albert Gallatin of Pennsylvania, recapitulated the argument for the resolution. Its opponents had turned to extraneous evidence of various types, Gallatin said, only when they had recognized that "the letter and spirit of our Constitution" were against them.[187] Even so, Gallatin stated that he "little expected to have heard such an appeal as was made yesterday" by Vans Murray, an appeal he described as the doctrine that "the opinions and constructions of those persons who had framed and proposed the Constitution, opinions given in private, constructions unknown to the people when they adopted the instrument, should, after a lapse of eight years, be appealed to."[188] Even if it were proper to use the views expressed in the debates of a legislative body in interpreting that body's acts—a proposition Gallatin doubted—the opinions of the Philadelphia framers were as irrelevant as those of the legislative clerk who penned a statute. Gallatin conceded that the proceedings of the state conventions might serve as a source of corroborative evidence, but insisted that the House could and should resolve the question of its role with respect to treaties "by the letter of the instrument alone."[189]

The *Annals of Congress* record only one voice raised in (at least partial) support of Vans Murray, that of George Washington.[190] The resolution passed by a lopsided majority (62 to 37) and was presented to President Washington; after a few days' deliberation, Washington declined to carry out the Representatives' request. He explained in a written message to the House that delivery of the administration's files on the treaty would intrude on the confidentiality necessary to the President's successful exercise of his diplomatic responsibilities. Washington went on to reject the argument that the execution of at least some treaties demanded the concurrence of the House. He based this position on his own knowledge of the Philadelphia convention's views, on the practice of the government from 1789 to 1796, on the "plain letter" of the Constitution, and on the convention's rejection of a motion to require all treaties to be confirmed by statute—a rejection recorded in the convention's official journal.[191] The backers of the House resolution criticized Washington's conclusion and his interpretive methodology, and secured the passage of another resolution reaffirming their position.[192] During the debate over the resolution, James Madison took issue with the invocation of the Philadelphia convention by Vans Murray and Washington. Vans Murray's speech had caused Madison "some surprise, which was much increased by the pe-

culiar stress laid on the information expected," and Madison's amazement
had reawakened when Washington too appealed to the Philadelphia proceedings "as a clue to the meaning of the Constitution."[193] Personal impressions
of "the intention of the whole body," whether his own or Washington's, were
of little value according to Madison, and were likely in any case to conflict.[194]
Madison dismissed Washington's citation of the convention's journal as an
attempt to draw an affirmative conclusion from an unexplained, negative, and
"abstract vote."[195] Madison stated that he "did not believe a single instance
could be cited in which the sense of the Convention had been required or
admitted as material [to] any Constitutional question" discussed either in
Congress or in the Supreme Court.[196]

C. The Constitution and the New Supreme Court

While the members of the executive and legislative branches were busily engaged in the process of constitutional interpretation during the Constitution's
first decade, the Supreme Court found relatively few opportunities to address
constitutional issues. But in its first great case, *Chisholm* v. *Georgia*,[197] the
Court signaled its approval of a traditional statutory approach to construing
the nation's fundamental law. *Chisholm* was an action in assumpsit against the
state of Georgia, brought under the Court's original diversity jurisdiction.
Georgia denied the Court's authority to hear the case and refused to enter an
appearance.[198] Plaintiff's counsel Edmund Randolph argued that both "the
letter" and the "genuine and necessary interpretation" of the Constitution
sustained the Court's jurisdiction.[199] His argument as to the Constitution's
proper "interpretation" disavowed reliance on the "history" of the instrument
or on its Preamble, resting instead on two distinct pillars: the existence in the
Constitution of various prohibitions on state action, and the American experience of a "government of supplication" under the "deceased" Articles of
Confederation.[200] Randolph's argument was thus wholly traditional: he
sought the intent of the document by examining the text in the light of the
evil it was meant to correct.

The question of state amenability to suit in federal court had been raised
repeatedly during the ratification campaign, and the virtually unanimous
Federalist response had been to deny that the Constitution would affect the
states' sovereign immunity.[201] If the Court had regarded itself as bound by
the expectations of the Constitution's framers and supporters, a decision in
Georgia's favor obviously would have been warranted. A majority of the
Justices, however, agreed with Randolph that a "genuine interpretation" was
not to be based on such external evidence,[202] but rather was to be reached by
use of the "ordinary rules for construction."[203] These rules required that the
intent of the Constitution's maker, "the people of the United States,"[204] be
sought in the people's own, authoritative words: the constitutional text.[205]
The majority believed that these rules of construction, when applied to the

Constitution, indicated that the document was intended to allow the action against the state. The proposal and ratification of the Eleventh Amendment[206] swiftly overturned the holding of *Chisholm*, but the majority's highly traditional and strikingly nationalistic approach to constitutional interpretation foreshadowed the jurisprudence of John Marshall.

Although most Americans in public life in the 1780s accepted the propriety of a statutory analogy for constitutional construction, disagreements over substantive constitutional doctrine became more glaring as opposing political parties coalesced during the later years of Washington's administration. Constitutional issues, and in particular the split between Hamilton and Jefferson over liberal versus strict construction, played an important role in the parties' efforts to define themselves.[207] Federalists like Hamilton, applying the traditional tools of statutory construction to the Constitution's sweeping generalities, found in the text the basis for an expansive view of federal power. The Republicans, in contrast, took up the cudgels of the religious and philosophical opposition to interpretation and warned that the "wiles of construction"[208] could be controlled only by a narrow reading of the Constitution's expansive language.[209] It was in the course of their political guerrilla warfare against the dominant Federalists during the administration of Washington's successor, John Adams, that the two greatest Republican leaders, Jefferson and Madison,[210] formulated the theory of the Constitution, and of its proper interpretation, that became the basis of consensus for a quarter-century of constitutional discourse. In addition, the constitutional hermeneutic they proposed became, remotely and rhetorically, the precursor of modern intentionalism.

IV. Sovereign States and Later Theories of Constitutional Intent

A system like ours, of divided powers, must necessarily give great importance to a proper system of construction.[211] — John C. Calhoun

IN 1798, the Federalist-controlled Congress, alarmed by the radical and increasingly hostile behavior of revolutionary France and fearful of subversion by a fifth column composed of foreign immigrants and Francophile Republicans,[212] enacted the series of measures known collectively as the Alien and Sedition Acts.[213] Congress passed the Sedition Act on July 14, 1798, and federal prosecutors swiftly pressed it into action against critics of the government; at least twenty-five arrests, in most cases of editors of Republican journals, were made under either the Act or the federal common law crime of seditious libel. The government eventually succeeded in procuring several convictions and permanently shutting down a number of opposition presses.[214]

The Alien and Sedition Acts alarmed the Republican leadership on both theoretical and practical grounds. They regarded passage of the Acts as a patent transgression of both the principle of limited federal government and the liberties guaranteed by the Bill of Rights, as well as proof that the process of corruption their ideology led them to expect in any government was proceeding at an alarming rate in the United States.[215] On a practical, political level, the federal suppression of criticism was an obvious and potentially effective attempt to perpetuate Federalist control of the Presidency and Congress. The Republicans saw that a vigorous response was necessary, but the appropriate means were not obvious. Attacking the Acts through the Republican press was likely to prove self-defeating by bringing down upon the newspaper the rigor of the Sedition Act itself. Petitioning Congress for redress of grievances clearly would be futile. Public statements by prominent Republicans would put the speakers at risk—even before the Acts were passed, a Federalist-dominated grand jury had indicted a Republican congressman for communicating to his own constituents his negative evaluation of administration policies.[216] The vigor of the Federalist attempt to choke off dissent, and the Republican commitment to decentralization of power in the Union,[217] drove the Republicans to the only sphere of political power still somewhat insulated from federal retribution: the Republican-controlled legislatures of the Southern states.

In utter secrecy, Jefferson and Madison prepared two sets of resolutions denouncing the Alien and Sedition Acts as tyrannical and unconstitutional. Jefferson's draft, originally intended for submission to the North Carolina legislature, was instead proposed to the Kentucky legislature by John Breckinridge and, with certain changes, was passed by that body in November 1795.[218] Republican legislator John Taylor[219] introduced Madison's draft in the Virginia General Assembly, which approved it in late December 1798.

The initial response to the "Virginia and Kentucky Resolutions" disappointed the Republican leadership. No other state endorsed them, and several Federalist legislatures replied with strongly nationalist resolutions denying the right of state assemblies to pass on the validity of federal statutes.[220] The Kentucky legislature replied to the criticisms in 1799 by adopting a second, briefer set of resolutions reiterating the constitutional views expressed in its original resolutions.[221] The Virginia General Assembly followed suit in January 1800 by adopting a resolution approving a report, written by Madison, that reaffirmed the views expressed in its own 1798 resolutions.[222]

The Virginia and Kentucky Resolutions and Madison's Report of 1800[223] did not achieve their immediate goal of mobilizing opposition to the "reign of witches."[224] In the longer term, however, the Resolutions proved to be among the most influential extraconstitutional, nonjudicial texts in American constitutional history. They presented a vision of the United States as a league of sovereign states, a vision that in many respects was closer to the position of the Anti-Federalists than to the view espoused by the Constitution's supporters.[225] They created a vocabulary with which to express that vision.[226] And they proposed, in justification of their substantive constitutional doctrines, an interpretive strategy centered on a search for the Constitution's underlying and original "intent." The detailed implications of this strategy were spelled out over the next several decades by Madison, and were criticized by the United States Supreme Court under the leadership of Federalist Chief Justice John Marshall. Even the final passage into history of the Federalist-Republican controversies did not end the Resolutions' influence. The rhetoric of "original intent" has endured, and indeed flourished, long after the universal rejection of most of its accompanying complex of ideas.

A. The "Doctrines of '98"[227]

The Virginia and Kentucky Resolutions defined the Constitution in contractual terms, as a "compact" to which "each State acceded as a State, and is an integral party; its co-States forming, as to itself, the other party."[228] This constitutional contract did not affect the "sovereign and independent" character of the parties to it.[229] Before the Revolution the colonies and Great Britain had been de jure equal and "coordinate members . . . of an empire united by a common executive sovereign, but not united by any common legislative sovereign."[230] Therefore, upon rejecting the royal executive the states became discrete bodies politic, united only to the extent that they had delegated certain powers to a common agent, the federal government. The political society created by the Constitution was a purely artificial product of the states' compact, and the federal government was a creature of the states with absolutely no powers except those "resulting from the Compact."[231] As in other cases of international compacts among independent nations, each state was necessarily an equal and final judge over constitutional disputes because there was no legal authority superior to the states to which such disputes could be referred. The federal instrumentalities of the compact obviously could not serve as umpire, at least with respect to disputes concerning the line between federal and state power, because to allow them to do so would be to permit the agent, rather than the principal, to determine the agent's duties.[232]

The constitutional vision expressed in the Resolutions was by no means original, but the first application of that vision was not to the Constitution but to the Articles of Confederation. With the exception of a few ultranationalist Federalists,[233] all the participants in the dispute over the Constitution's ratification in the previous decade had regarded the articles as a compact among the states as independent sovereigns, and the Confederation Congress as the agent, not the superior, of the states. The Anti-Federalist charge that the Constitution plainly was intended to replace that existing league (based on a compact) with a "consolidated" government had been a central point of dispute in the ratification campaign.[234] Although the Federalist response had taken several different tacks,[235] in the end the supporters of the Constitution could not, and did not wish to, deny the noncontractual character of the instrument.[236] As James Wilson observed at the Pennsylvania convention, the Constitution was not a contract, poorly drafted or otherwise. "I cannot discover the least trace of a compact in that system. . . . This, Mr. President, is not a government founded upon compact; it is founded upon the power of the people. They express in their name and their authority, '*We the people do ordain and establish*,' &c. from their ratification alone, it is to take its constitutional authenticity; without that it is no more than *tabula rasa*. . . . I have already shewn, that this system is not a compact or contract; the system itself tells you what it is; it is an·ordinance and establishment of the people."[237] The Resolutions simply ignored the recent and well-known debates over the Constitution's character, as well as the absence within its text of references to a compact or to the states as sovereign contracting parties.[238] Jefferson and Madison offered instead a coherent reading of the Constitution based on the contractual imagery still familiar from the Confederation era. The force of the authors' styles, together with the infancy of the Constitution and the lingering memories of the Confederation, enabled the Resolutions to overcome these historical and textual obstacles and gain political acceptance.

The Resolutions explained that their substantive constitutional doctrines were legitimated by an inquiry into "the plain intent and meaning in which [the compact] was understood and acceded to by the several parties,"[239] and "the plain sense and intention of the instrument constituting that compact."[240] Because the Constitution is a contract, they argued, it is to be interpreted according to the "intent" of the contracting parties. But, as discussed above, in late eighteenth-century Anglo-American legal discourse, references to the "intent of a legal instrument" and to the "intent of its makers" were interchangeable, and in neither case did the term refer to the subjective purposes of the human authors. One construed a contract's "intent" not by embarking on a historical inquiry into what the parties actually wished to accomplish, but by applying legal norms to the contract's terms—that is, by construing the contract in accordance with the common understanding[241] of its terms, and in light of its nature and the character of the contracting parties.[242]

When the Resolutions announced that the Constitution, like an ordinary contract, should be construed according to its original and "plain intent," they were not proposing that interpreters investigate the proceedings of the Philadelphia framers. They were instead arguing for an interpretive strategy whereby the Constitution would be read against the background of eighteenth-century notions about sovereignty and the behavior of sovereign entities. As explained by St. George Tucker a few years later, the justification for giving the Constitution's grants of power to federal instrumentalities "the most strict construction that the instrument will bear"[243] was not that such an approach would conform to the general expectation of the individual delegates to Philadelphia or even those in the state conventions. Rather, strict construction was justified by reference to the "maxim of political law" that a sovereign can be deprived of any of its powers only by its express consent narrowly construed.[244] The intentionalism of the Resolutions was therefore a form of structural interpretation carried out largely by inference from the nature both of compacts and of sovereignty.[245] It was the "intent" of the states as political entities that the Resolutions deemed normative for purposes of constitutional interpretation.[246]

The Resolutions' reliance on the common law method of interpreting contracts was for the most part traditional, but in one respect Jefferson and Madison broke new ground. By emphasizing that the Constitution's proper meaning was that understood and acceded to by the states during a particular period of time in the past, the Resolutions suggested the possibility that some extratextual historical evidence might be relevant to constitutional interpretation. Indeed, the Resolutions explicitly recognized a form of direct "evidence" of the intent of the states: the proposed amendments and declarations of reserved rights that accompanied several of the states' ratification resolutions.[247] For instance, the Virginia convention's recommendation of an amendment safeguarding freedom of religion and of the press was cited in the Virginia Resolutions as an express declaration, made at the time Virginia assented to the contract, that the state did not intend to delegate authority over those subjects to the federal government.[248] Consistent with the contractual model of the Constitution, the Resolutions treated these accompanying documents as conditions attached to the state's subscription to the federal compact. By accepting Virginia's expressly conditioned ratification, the other states necessarily agreed to those conditions.[249] This use of historical evidence in constitutional interpretation is therefore not identical to modern intentionalism: it directs attention not to evidence concerning discussions preceding the framing or adoption of the text, but rather to recommendations that were themselves part of the official document constituting Virginia's ratification of the constitutional compact. Nevertheless, by focusing attention on a past historical event Jefferson and Madison raised the possibility that other historical documents might be relevant to determining the state's original intent.

In Republican hands, the intentionalist hermeneutic of the Resolutions became a powerful tool in the fight against the expansive, "liberal" construction of the Constitution favored by the Federalists. As a form of the traditional approach to contract interpretation, that intentionalism was even more familiar than Hamilton's use of common law techniques of statutory interpretation: for Hamilton, the Constitution could at most be regarded as analogous to a statute; but for Jefferson and Madison, it actually was a contract.[250] Furthermore, the interpretive strategy suggested by the Resolutions enabled the

Republicans to wield the anti-hermeneutic tradition against Federalist "construction" of the Constitution even as they insisted that their own equally extratextual interpretation involved mere adherence to the "obvious and real intention" of the compact.[251] As Madison wrote in the Report of 1800, it did "not seem possible that any just objection [could] lie against" the Virginia Resolutions' invocation of intent because that invocation "amounts merely to a declaration that the compact ought to have the interpretation plainly intended by the parties to it."[252]

The Republicans insisted that the Resolutions' version of intentionalism called simply for the application of the "acknowledged rule[s] of construction"[253] to the Constitution in order to expound that contract "according to the true sense in which it was adopted by the States, that in which it was advocated by its friends, and not that which its enemies apprehended."[254] The "friends" of the Constitution during the ratification era, however, had denied that the instrument was contractual and that the new federal government would be subordinate to the states.[255] The striking dissimilarity between this view and the one advanced by Jefferson and Madison in 1798—that the Constitution was a compact among the states and that the states possessed final authority under it—demonstrates that the Resolutions' brand of intentionalism did not in fact lead to a historically valid reconstruction of the views of the original proponents of ratification. Moreover, the interpretive strategy employed in the Resolutions was an integral part of the substantive constitutional doctrine it was designed to justify. To agree that proper constitutional interpretation involves an examination of the intent of sovereign states forming a compact, we must first agree that this is what the Constitution truly is—a contract among sovereigns. The Resolutions rested on a circularity, justifying substance by a mode of interpretation justified only by that same substance.

Circular or not, the Resolutions were triumphantly vindicated, at least in Republican eyes, by the results of the election of 1800, in which the Republicans seized control of both Congress and the Presidency from the Federalists. The victors viewed the "revolution of 1800"[256] as the people's endorsement of the approach to constitutional interpretation embodied in the "doctrines of '98." The champions of "the Republican Ascendancy" were quick to paint themselves as the heirs to a line of apostolic succession extending back to the heroes of the colonial struggles against British tyranny.[257]

With remarkable speed, the constitutional theory of the Virginia and Kentucky Resolutions established itself as American political orthodoxy. Even the state legislatures that had denounced the Resolutions in the strongest terms and decried the Virginia and Kentucky assemblies as improper arbiters of federal constitutional questions were, within a decade, preaching the pure Republican doctrines. The General Assembly of Rhode Island, for example, had replied to the Virginia Resolutions in 1799 by describing them as an "infraction of the Constitution of the United States, expressed in plain terms"[258] By 1809, however, the Rhode Island legislature was of a different mind, resolving "that the people of this State, as one of the parties to the Federal compact, have a right to express their sense of any violation of its provisions and that it is the duty of this General Assembly as the organ of their sentiments and the depository of their authority, to interpose for the purpose of protecting them from the ruinous inflictions of usurped and unconstitutional power."[259]

Acceptance of the compact theory (and of its accompanying intentionalism) spread throughout the country and, beyond the confines of John Marshall's Supreme Court, stood virtually unquestioned until the nullification crisis of 1828 through 1832.[260] Even if it were not actually coeval with the Constitution, the rhetoric of that document's original "intent" acquired an aura of age and self-evident truth all its own.

B. *James Madison's Theory of Constitutional Interpretation*

Although the Virginia and Kentucky Resolutions expressed an approach to constitutional construction that soon achieved canonical status in American politics, they did not themselves set forth a detailed interpretive methodology. That task remained for James Madison. As one of the prime movers in the Philadelphia convention of 1787 and in the Virginia ratifying convention the following year, as one of the authors of *The Federalist*, and as the draftsman of both the Virginia Resolutions of 1798 and the Report of 1800, Madison played a critical role both in the process of framing and ratifying the Constitution and in the formulation of a consensus about its meaning. Although he would have been quick to distinguish his personal opinions from the public meaning of the Constitution, the coherent interpretive theory Madison expressed in speeches and letters over many years has special value for anyone seeking to discern the "interpretive intent" underlying the Constitution.

Madison's interpretive theory rested primarily on the distinction he drew between the public meaning or intent of a state paper, a law, or a constitution, and the personal opinions of the individuals who had written or adopted it. The distinction was implicit in the common law's treatment of the concept of "intent," but Madison made it explicit and thereby illuminated its implications and underlying rationale. Madison's reliance on the basic hermeneutical premise is evident in his correspondence with Secretary of State Martin Van Buren in 1830. Responding to President Andrew Jackson's citation of a veto message Madison had sent Congress in 1817, Madison wrote that Jackson's use of his message had misconceived his personal views. But Madison conceded that Jackson might have correctly interpreted the public meaning of the message: "On the subject of the discrepancy between the construction put by the Message of the President [Jackson] on the veto of 1817 and the intention of its author, the President will of course consult his own view of the case. For myself, I am aware that the document must speak for itself, and that that intention cannot be substituted for [the intention derived through] the established rules of interpretation."[261]

Madison applied the same distinction between public meaning and private intent to statutes,[262] to the Report of 1800,[263] and to the Constitution. With respect to the Constitution, Madison described his knowledge of the views actually held by the delegates to the Philadelphia and Virginia conventions as a possible source of "bias" in his constitutional interpretations,[264] and cautioned a correspondent against an uncritical use of *The Federalist*, because "it is fair to keep in mind that the authors might be sometimes influenced by the zeal of advocates."[265] He explained that he had decided to delay publication of his notes of the Philadelphia convention until after his death "or, at least . . . till the Constitution should be well settled by practice, and till a knowledge of the controversial part of the proceedings of its framers could be turned to no improper account. . . . As a guide in expounding and applying the provisions of the Constitution, the debates and incidental decisions of the Convention can have no authoritative character."[266]

Madison employed the distinction between public meaning and private intent to differentiate the relative value of the various sources of information to which constitutional interpreters might turn for evidence on "the intention of the States."[267] The text itself, of course, was the primary source from which that intention was to be gathered, but Madison's awareness of the imperfect nature of human communication[268] led him to concede that the text's import would frequently be unclear.[269] Madison thought it proper to engage in structural inference in the classic contractual mode of the Virginia and Kentucky Resolutions, and to consult the direct expressions of state intention available in the resolutions of the ratifying conventions.[270] He regarded the debates in those conventions to be of real yet limited value for the interpreter: evidentiary problems with the surviving records[271] and Madison's insistence on distinguishing the binding public intention of the state from the private opinions of any individual or group of individuals, including those gathered at a state convention, led him to conclude that the state debates could bear no more than indirect and corroborative witness to the meaning of the Constitution.[272] Madison allowed that contemporaneous expositions of the document by its supporters were of some value, but he cautioned that such statements were to be regarded strictly as private opinions, useful chiefly in shedding light upon the meaning of words and phrases that the fluidity of language might gradually change over time.[273] Last and least in value were the records of the Philadelphia convention. Once again, there were significant evidentiary problems,[274] but Madison's objection to treating the framers' views as authoritative was based chiefly on theoretical grounds:

> Mr. [Madison] said, he did not believe a single instance could be cited
> in which the sense of the Convention had been required or admitted as
> material in any Constitutional question. . . .

But, after all, whatever veneration might be entertained for the body of men who formed our Constitution, the sense of that body could never be regarded as the Oracular guide in expounding the Constitution. As the instrument came from them, it was nothing more than the draft of a plan, nothing but a dead letter, until life and validity were breathed into it by the voice of the people, speaking through the several State Conventions.[275]

Madison was quite insistent that a distinction must be drawn between the "true meaning" of the Constitution and "whatever might have been the opinions entertained in forming the Constitution."[276] The distinction did not imply a refusal to recognize the purposive character of the instrument;[277] it simply denied that the framers' subjective intent was the purpose that mattered.[278]

The dichotomy between public meaning and private intent also informed Madison's view of constitutional precedent. He consistently thought that "*usus*,"[279] the exposition of the Constitution provided by actual governmental practice and judicial precedents,[280] could "settle its meaning and the intention of its authors."[281] Here, too, he was building on a traditional foundation: the common law had regarded usage as valid evidence of the meaning of ancient instruments, and had regarded judicial determinations of that meaning even more highly.[282] Applying this view of interpretation to the Constitution, Madison felt himself compelled to change his position on the controversial issue of Congress's constitutional power to incorporate a national bank.[283] In the First Congress, Representative Madison opposed on constitutional grounds the bill establishing the First Bank of the United States;[284] as President, Madison twenty years later signed into law the act creating the Second Bank.[285] "But even here the inconsistency," Madison assured a correspondent, "is apparent only, not real." His own "abstract opinion of the text" remained unchanged: the words of the Constitution did not authorize Congress to establish the bank.[286] Nevertheless, he recognized that Congress, the President, the Supreme Court, and (most important, by failing to use their amending power) the American people had for two decades accepted the existence and made use of the services of the First Bank, and he viewed this widespread acceptance as "a construction put on the Constitution by the nation, which, having made it, had the supreme right to declare its meaning."[287] He had signed the Second Bank bill, Madison declared, in accordance with his "early and unchanged opinion" that such a construction by usage and precedent should override the intellectual scruples of the individual,[288] and he explained to his friend the Marquis de LaFayette that "I did not feel myself, as a public man, at liberty to sacrifice all these public considerations to my private opinion."[289] In Madison's eyes, precedents—at least those derived from "authoritative, deliberate, and continued decisions"—served to "fix the interpretation of a law."[290] Furthermore, Madison claimed, this view represented not just his opinion, but the general expectation—the "interpretive intention"[291]—that prevailed at the time of the Constitution's framing and ratification: "It could not but happen, and was foreseen at the birth of the Constitution, that difficulties and differences of opinion might occasionally arise in expounding terms and phrases necessarily used in such a charter . . . and that it might require a regular course of practice to liquidate and settle the meaning of some of them."[292]

The public character of long-settled precedent was for Madison the key to reconciling his acceptance of views inconsistent with his "abstract opinion" of the bare text and his commitment to the Republican version of the old anti-interpretive tradition. To the end of his life, Madison warned his fellow citizens against expansive innovations in constitutional interpretation, "new principles and new constructions, that may remove the landmarks of power."[293] But however strongly he might have fought constitutional error when it first appeared, for Madison there could be no return to the unadorned text from interpretations that had received the approbation of the people.[294] The Constitution is a public document, and its interpretation, for Madison, was in the end a public process.

C. The Marshall Court and Constitutional Construction

The "revolution of 1800" that swept away Federalist nationalism and vindicated the "doctrines of '98" left one pocket of resistance to Jeffersonian Republicanism intact: the Supreme Court and its newly appointed Federalist Chief Justice, John Marshall. Over the three and a half decades of Marshall's tenure, his rhetorically moderate[295] yet staunchly nationalistic views prevailed on a Court increasingly populated by Republican Justices.[296] Marshall and his learned Republican friend, Justice Joseph Story, regarded the state-sovereignty and constitutional-compact themes of Republican constitutional thought as strands of wild-eyed political theory, "the cobwebs of sophistry and metaphysics."[297] Instead of searching for the intent of sovereign contracting parties, the Marshall Court followed the path, staked out in the Constitution's first years, of applying traditional methods of statutory construction to that instrument.

Marshall's conventional view of statutory construction is illustrated by his opinion in *United States* v. *Fisher*,[298] a case involving the interpretation of a federal act giving the United States priority over general creditors in bankruptcy proceedings.[299] Marshall noted the difficulties attendant upon construing an ambiguous statutory provision, and he stressed the need to cast a wide net in seeking evidence as to "the intention of the legislature": "Where the mind labors to discover the design of the legislature, it seizes every thing from which aid can be derived."[300] Although in this case Marshall perceived clarity where the defendants had seen confusion, he agreed that in interpreting ambiguous terms the Court might properly use "all the means recommended by the counsel for the defendants."[301] Cranch's report of the arguments shows that the suggested means included consultation of the act's title, preamble, and "general scope and design,"[302] and consideration of the methodology prescribed in *Heydon's Case*,[303] of other federal statutes,[304] and of the consequences of taking the act literally.[305] Although Marshall considered all of these means legitimate, he placed the most weight on a close analysis of the wording and structure of the statute's text.[306] Neither the attorneys nor the Chief Justice suggested an investigation of the congressional debates. In light of Marshall's traditional view of statutory construction and his acceptance of a statutory analogy for the Constitution, there appears to have been no inconsistency between his insistence that "the great duty of a judge who construes an instrument, is to find the intention of its makers,"[307] and his belief that a construction "within the words" of a constitutional provision is legitimate regardless of whether the framers foresaw or intended it.[308]

The Marshall Court's response to constitutional arguments based on invocations of the extratextual "intent" of the states was a renewed emphasis on the supremacy of the text, read in light of the Constitution's purposes as set forth in its Preamble: "The enlightened patriots who framed our Constitution, and the people who adopted it, must be understood to have employed words in their natural sense, and to have intended what they have said. . . . We know of no rule for construing [the Constitution] other than is given by the language of the instrument . . . taken in connection with the purposes for which [federal powers] were conferred."[309] The Marshall Court's approach to constitutional interpretation was strikingly similar to Madison's, despite their different starting points. Both Marshall and Madison accepted the common law understanding that the intent of a document is, at least in part, the product of the interpretive process; both accepted the authority of practice and precedent;[310] and neither regarded historical evidence of the framers' personal intentions as a definitive or even particularly valuable guide to constitutional construction.

D. Aftermath

The constitutional consensus created by the "doctrines of '98" and the "revolution of 1800" endured at least until the nullification crisis of Andrew Jackson's first term,[311] but cracks in its facade began to appear in the 1820s. New England Federalists' resistance to the foreign policies of Presidents Jefferson and Madison culminated in the Hartford convention of 1815, which was widely seen as a first step toward secession.[312] However politically divisive, the convention signaled that the heirs of Hamilton had accepted a key constitutional dogma of his enemies: it served notice that if the grievances voiced were not redressed, New England Federalists were prepared to invoke state sovereignty against the assertion of federal power.[313] Despite this general acceptance of the Republican account of the Constitution's nature and origin, constitutional argument continued: the political debates in the 1810s and 1820s over federal tariff policy and over congressional power to further internal improvements prompted proponents of federal power to search for means of altering the anti-nationalist legacy of the Virginia and Kentucky Resolutions. From the other end of the political spectrum, the devotees of an extreme states' rights constitutionalism criticized the more moderate policies of Madison and his successor, James Monroe, as apostasy from the Republican faith.[314]

Faced with a political need to develop new modes of constitutional interpretation to supplement or supplant the eroding Republican consensus, interpreters of the Constitution redefined the central hermeneutical concept of that consensus, the Constitution's "intent." As employed in the Virginia and Kentucky Resolutions, that term was an invitation to structural, not historical,[315] interpretation: witness how thoroughly Madison, one of the greatest of the Republican thinkers, excluded from his understanding of normative constitutional intent any trace of the historically ascertainable purposes and expectations of the Philadelphia framers. But this traditional, Republican understanding of "intent" was gradually replaced by the modern, subjective use of the word. In other areas of law, "intent" increasingly meant the historical intentions of *someone*, however much evidentiary rules might be used to frustrate a genuine search for those intentions.[316] A similar change became evident in constitutional discourse. With the growing availability of original materials revealing the actions and opinions of the individual actors who played roles in the Constitution's framing and adoption, popular and legal interest in that episode of history markedly increased.[317]

The watershed in the history of constitutional interpretation was the crisis provoked by South Carolina's strident response to the passage of a protective tariff by Congress in May 1828. Although the so-called "tariff of abominations" was extremely unpopular throughout most of the South, the reaction to it was exceptionally vigorous in South Carolina. A state convention assembled in November 1832 and passed an ordinance "nullifying" the federal act.[318] President Jackson responded with a vigorous assertion of federal supremacy and his resolve to uphold the tariff—and a potentially violent collision between federal authority and states' rights was averted only narrowly.[319] Two conflicting approaches to constitutional interpretation emerged as the intellectual product of the crisis. The nationalist school of constitutional thought, with Daniel Webster leading the way in the Senate and Justice Joseph Story serving as scholar and consultant,[320] explicitly rejected the definition of the Constitution as a compact among sovereign states. The nationalists identified the text, as construed by precedent, as the authoritative source of constitutional meaning and regarded the Supreme Court as the final and authoritative interpreter of the Constitution.[321] The states' rights school, with John C. Calhoun playing the roles of both Webster and Story, subscribed to an extreme version of the compact theory and insisted that final interpretive authority rested with the states.[322] Adherents of both camps increasingly expressed their views as explications of the "original intent" of the framers,[323] and earlier scruples against the use of "extrinsic evidence" in constitutional interpretation gradually lost their force.

The new use of the rhetoric of constitutional intention is illustrated by Judge Abel Parker Upshur's *A Brief Enquiry into the True Nature and Character of our Federal Government*,[324] published in 1840. Upshur, a distinguished Virginia jurist and states' rights politician, wrote the *Brief Inquiry* as a "review" of Story's treatise on constitutional law; the result was a closely argued critique of Story's nationalism and a reformulation of states' rights constitutionalism in light of Story's argument.[325] Although Upshur accepted and employed the interpretive tools made familiar by the Virginia and Kentucky Resolutions, he did not characterize his inferences from structure and from the political theory of sovereignty as evidence of the "intent" of the Constitution.[326] Upshur, instead, was an intentionalist in the modern sense: "The strict construction for which I contend applies to the intention of the framers of the Constitution; and this may or may not require a strict construction of their words."[327] Upshur thought that the determination of that intention was an essay in historical reconstruction, to be carried out by investigating the proceedings and opinions of the Philadelphia framers.[328]

By the outbreak of the Civil War, intentionalism in the modern sense reigned supreme in the rhetoric of constitutional interpretation. In his inaugural address, Jefferson Davis described the Confederate constitution as "the Constitution formed by our fathers," a document that differed from the older instrument's text only "insofar as it is explanatory of their well known intent."[329] Senator Charles Sumner of Massachusetts, one of the most radically nationalist members of the Union Congress, stated: "Every Constitution embodies the principles of its framers. It is a transcript of their minds. If its meaning in any place is open to doubt . . . we cannot err if we turn to the framers."[330] The implicit repudiation of the original understanding of "original intent" was complete.

V. Conclusion

IT IS COMMONLY assumed that the "interpretive intention" of the Constitution's framers was that the Constitution would be construed in accordance with what future interpreters could gather of the framers' own purposes, expectations, and intentions. Inquiry shows that assumption to be incorrect. Of the numerous hermeneutical options that were available in the framers' day—among them, the renunciation of construction altogether—none corresponds to the modern notion of intentionalism. Early interpreters usually applied standard techniques of statutory construction to the Constitution. When a consensus eventually emerged on a proper theory of constitutional interpretation, it indeed centered on "original intent." But at the time, that term referred to the "intentions" of the sovereign parties to the constitutional compact, as evidenced in the Constitution's language and discerned through structural methods of interpretation; it did not refer to the personal intentions of the framers or of anyone else. The relationship of modern intentionalism to this early interpretive theory is purely rhetorical.[331]

In defending their claim that the "original understanding at Philadelphia" should control constitutional interpretation, modern intentionalists usually argue that other interpretive strategies undermine or even deny the possibility of objectivity and consistency in constitutional law. Critics of this position typically respond with a battery of practical and theoretical objections to the attempt to construe the nation's fundamental law in accord with the historical reconstructions of the purposes of the framers. There may well be grounds to support either of these positions. This debate cannot be resolved, however, and should not be affected, by the claim or assumption that modern intentionalism was the original presupposition of American constitutional discourse. Such a claim is historically mistaken.

Notes

1. R. Bolt, *A Man for All Seasons* 152 (1962) (speech of Sir Thomas More at his trial).

2. See, e.g., Sandalow, Constitutional Interpretation, 79 *Mich. L. Rev.* 1033 (1981) (arguing that historical evidence of the framers' intent cannot constrain modern interpretation). Michael Perry admits the theoretical legitimacy of judicial enforcement of the framers' intentions, but argues that in practice modern constitutional decisionmaking does not, and need not, depend on historical argument. See M. Perry, *The Constitution, the Courts, and Human Rights* 19, 75 (1982).

3. See, e.g., J. Choper, *Judicial Review and the National Political Process* xvii–xviii (1980).

4. See, e.g., 3 W. Crosskey and W. Jeffrey, *Politics and the Constitution in the History of the United States* (1980); B. Siegan, *Economic Liberties and the Constitution* 11–14 (1980).

5. See Bork, Neutral Principles and Some First Amendment Problems, 47 *Ind. L. J.* 1 (1971) reprinted in this volume; Rehnquist, The Notion of a Living Constitution, 54 *Texas L. Rev.* 693 (1976).

6. Trimble v. Gordon, 430 U.S. 762, 778 (1977) (Rehnquist, J., dissenting).

7. See Monaghan, Our Perfect Constitution, 56 *N.Y.U. L. Rev.* 353, 375–76 (1981).

8. R. Berger, *Government by Judiciary* 363 (1977).

9. Id. at 365–66. Modern intentionalists, of course, do not claim that the legislators' personal motives, as distinguished from their intentions as lawmakers, are relevant. See Palmer v. Thompson, 403 U.S. 217, 224–25 (1971); cf. Fletcher v. Peck, 10 U.S. (6 Cranch) 87 (1810) (first Supreme Court case rejecting inquiry into legislators' motives).

10. On the concept of "interpretive intention," see Brest, The Misconceived Quest for the Original Understanding, 60 *Boston U. L. Rev.* 235–36 (1980), reprinted in this volume.

11. Pre-Revolutionary constitutional discourse frequently referred to colonial charters and parliamentary documents, such as Magna Carta and the 1688 Bill of Rights, as evidence of the meaning of the English constitution. See G. Wood, *The Creation of the American Republic, 1776–1787*, at 259–73 (1969). The use of constitutions as written fundamental laws subject to judicial interpretation and enforcement, however, was an essentially new creation of the American revolutionary period. See id. at 291. The practice, as applied to the state constitutions, was still in the embryonic stage in 1787.

12. Eighteenth-century criticism of traditional hermeneutical methods usually described what was being criticized as "construction" rather than "interpretation" of the text, perhaps because even the most literal and text-bound approach is still an interpretation. This distinction in usage, however, is not absolute. See, e.g., infra note 34; see also S. Johnson, *A Dictionary of the English Language* (London 1755) (entries for "construction" and "interpretation") (indicating that the two words can be used synonymously).

13. For a discussion of the concept of structural interpretation, see C. Black, *Structure and Relationship in Constitutional Law* (1969) (arguing that constitutional rules may be inferred from the structural relationships the Constitution ordains among government institutions).

14. M. Montaigne, Of Experience (1588), reprinted in *The Essays of Michel Eyquem de Montaigne* III.13, at 518 (W. Hazlitt ed., C. Cotton trans. 1952).

15. But see P. Bobbitt, *Constitutional Fate* 10 (1982) (contemporaneous British canons of construction are "largely beside the point"). To whatever extent Professor Bobbitt is making the historical assertion that late eighteenth-century Americans regarded contemporaneous canons of construction as "beside the point," the abundant evidence to the contrary, see infra pp. 61–75, suggests that he is mistaken.

16. See generally B. Bailyn, *The Ideological Origins of the American Revolution* (1967) (arguing that American resistance to Britain was often justified by the claim that Americans were defending English liberties and the ancient constitution); P. Maier, *From Resistance to Revolution* (1972) (same).

17. See, e.g., F. Dwarris, *A General Treatise on Statutes* *646 (in United States, interpretation of a constitution "requires the exercise of the same legal discretion as the interpretation or construction of a law"); *Federalist* No. 78 (A. Hamilton) (courts, in construing the Constitution, will follow the familiar rules of interpretation).

18. See R. Brown, *The Spirit of Protestantism* 67 (1965).

19. See A. Dickens, *The English Reformation* 189–93 (rev. ed. 1971). Instead of a detailed examination of the ordinand's Protestant orthodoxy, the Anglican Book of Common Prayer asked of men about to be made priests whether they were resolved to teach as doctrine nothing "but that you shalbe perswaded may he concluded, and proued by the scripture?" *First Book of Common Prayer of Edward VI*, Ordinal 309 (Everyman's Library ed. 1968) (1st ed. London 1549).

20. See R. Grant, *A Short History of the Interpretation of the Bible* 92–109 (rev. ed. 1984).

21. See e.g., Westminster Confession of Faith I.9 (1647), reprinted in *United Presbyterian Church in the United States of America, Book of Confessions* 6.009 (2d ed. 1970) (hereafter cited as *Book of Confessions*).

22. J. Selden, *Table-Talk: Being the Discourses of John Selden Esq.* 25 (London, 1699). A seventeenth-century jurist and member of Parliament, Selden participated in the parliamentary resistance to Charles I; this role gave him a place in the pantheon of whig defenders of liberty whom the American revolutionaries regarded as constitutional authorities. See B. Bailyn, supra note 16, at 315; P. Maier, supra note 16, at 48.

23. J. Selden, supra note 22, at 45.

24. "If I give any exposition but what is express'd in the Text, that is my invention: if you give another Exposition, that is your invention, and both are Human." Id. at 25. Protestant insistence that interpretation is corruption was linked with the rejection of the "multiple sense" approach of medieval exegesis. See Westminster Confession of Faith I.9 (1647), reprinted in *Book of Confessions*, supra note 22, at 48.

25. Scots Confession ch. XX (1560), reprinted in *Book of Confessions*, supra note 21, at 3.20.

26. See e.g. Owen, Book Review (c. 1650), reprinted in *Introduction to Puritan Theology: A Reader* 141 (E. Hindson ed. 1976) (criticizing Thomas More's 1643 work, *The Universality of God's Free Grace*). John Owen concludes his own elaborate interpretation of the Bible's teaching on the scope of divine grace with an attack on More for presenting "allegations and interpretations of Scripture" instead of the plainly revealed "mind and will of God." Id. at 170.

Critiques such as this by Protestant theologians planted the seeds of the deconstruction of Protestant orthodoxy undertaken by religious "liberals" in the late seventeenth and eighteenth centuries. Orthodox and liberal alike agreed with John Locke's claim that the sober and unprejudiced reader would find little need to interpret Scripture because such a reader would have no difficulty in understanding the plain meaning of the text. See J. Locke, Essay for the Understanding of St. Paul's Epistles, reprinted in 8 *Works of John Locke* at iii (11th ed. London 1812). Contemporary deistic and rationalistic critics of Protestant dogma thus could draw on the deeply ingrained literalism of British Protestantism in order to "demonstrate" the absurdities of traditional Christianity. See generally, H. Frei, *The Eclipse of Biblical Narrative* 51–54, 66–85 (1974) (discussing the use of literalism by deists and others to attack Protestant orthodoxy). This type of British religious radicalism was influential in the thinking of many eighteenth-century Americans. See D. Boorstin, *The Lost World of Thomas Jefferson* 151–66 (1948).

27. See generally C. Hill, *The World Turned Upside Down* (2d ed. 1974) (discussing relationship between religious radicalism and political and social criticism in seventeenth-century England).

28. See E. Dumbauld, *Thomas Jefferson and the Law* 146–55 (1978).

29. See id. at 146.

30. See id. at 148.

31. This school of thought, which modern historians usually label the "Court" ideology, emerged in England in the early eighteenth century in reaction to the policies of the dominant Court whigs. The Court leadership favored executive dominance in an increasingly powerful and centralized government. It supported a permanent military establishment and the encouragement of commerce through the Bank of England, and maintained a docile parliamentary majority through the use of patronage. Opposition leaders, both Tories and "Real Whigs" (who regarded the Court whigs as apostates from the whig heritage of 1688), developed an ideology of opposition based on suspicion of government in general and of a strong national executive in particular. The Country spokesmen identified the Court's manipulation of patronage and of the national debt as a process of "corrupting" English society that would culminate in the replacement of traditional free government by despotism on a continental model. Following 1760, Country thought became increasingly influential among the American colonists, both as an explanation for London's apparent drift toward tyranny and as a justification for resistance. Having victoriously expelled the Court from America by the Revolution, American Country thinkers like Thomas Jefferson were horrified to see it reemerge in the Federalist policies of the Washington and Adams administrations. Once again, the Country themes of localism and opposition to "energetic" government seemed relevant. See Murrin, The Great Inversion, or Court versus Country.: A Comparison of the Revolution Settlements in England (1688–1721) and America (1776–1816), in *Three British Revolutions: 1641, 1688, 1776*, at 368, 379–83, 397–401, 404–11 (J. Pocock ed. 1980); L. Banning, *The Jeffersonian Persuasion* (1978) (tracing the development of Jeffersonian Republicanism from Country ideology).

32. See L. Friedman, *A History of American Law* 79 (1973); P. Miller, *The Life of the Mind in America* 99–109, 239–49 (1965).

33. The use of a single term such as *philosophes* for the predominantly French propagandists of the eighteenth-century Enlightenment is misleading to the extent that it obscures the real disagreements—political, philosophical, and theological—among such figures as Voltaire, Diderot, Condorcet, and Rousseau. It suggests accurately enough the American tendency to treat the views of those sages as a collective body of "enlightened" (we would say "progressive") opinion and to select specific intellectual positions from them in an eclectic manner.

34. One example of this humanist thought is Sir Thomas More's *Utopia*. More's Utopians considered the "simple and apparent sense of the law" the correct interpretation since it is "open to everyone." T. More, *Utopia* 69 (R. Adams trans. 1975) (1st ed. Louvain 1516). The *philosophes* were also influenced by the opposition to legal interpretation exhibited by English political thought. See, e.g., J. Gray, *The Nature and Sources of the Law* 172 (2d ed. 1921) (quoting Whig controversialist Benjamin Hoadley, who warned George I of the dangers inherent in interpretation in a sermon delivered before the King in 1717: "Whoever hath an *absolute authority* to *interpret* any written or spoken laws, it is *he* who is truly the *Law giver* to all intents and purposes, and not the person who first wrote or spoke them."

35. See, e.g., Voltaire, *Philosophical Dictionary* 289 (T. Besterman trans. 1971) (1st ed. Geneva 1764) (entry for "Civil and Ecclesiastical laws") ("to interpret" the law "is nearly always to corrupt it").

36. See, e.g., Montesquieu, *The Spirit of the Laws* VI.3, at 34–35 (T. Nugent and J. Prichard trans. 1952) (1st ed. Geneva 1748) (in a republican polity the very nature of the constitution requires judges to follow the letter of the law).

37. C. Beccaria, *On Crimes and Punishments* 14–18 (H. Paolucci trans. 1963) (1st ed. Livorno 1764).

38. See id.; also G. Wood, supra note 11, at 301–2 (discussing American objections to judicial interpretation).

39. Cf. G. Wood, supra note 11, at 17 (noting influence of Puritan theology and Enlightenment rationalism on Revolutionary thought).

40. "Our peculiar security is in the possession of a written Constitution. Let us not make it a blank paper by construction." Thomas Jefferson to Wilson C. Nicholas (September 7, 1803), reprinted in *The Political Writings of Thomas Jefferson* 144 (E. Dumbauld ed. 1955) (hereafter cited as *Political Writings*). Many Americans during this period believed that the great political desideratum was a means of protecting the Constitution from what Edmund Pendleton called "the wiles of construction," Pendleton, The Danger Not Over, *Richmond Examiner*, October 20, 1801, quoted in L. Banning, supra note 31, at 282.

41. George Washington's final will exemplified the fear of construction. The will included an elaborate arbitration provision designed, in the event of a dispute over the will's terms, to allow a determination of Washington's (subjective) intentions "unfettered by law or legal constructions." 4 *Annals of America* 115, 119 (1968). Criticizing the Virginia Court of Appeals for a decision involving the interpretation of a will, Washington's fellow Virginian George Wythe analogized the evils of testamentary construction to the confusion scriptural interpretation had wrought on the understanding of the Bible. Aylett v. Minnis, Wythe 219, 234 n. l (Va. Ch. 1793), rev'd. 1 Va. (1 Wash.) 300 (1795); see infra p. 59 and note 59.

42. Essex Result, reprinted in *Massachusetts, Colony to Commonwealth* 73, 79–80 (R. Taylor ed. 1961).

43. See id. at 80–89.

44. Besides being familiar with common law traditions, some Americans were also conversant with the work done on questions of legal interpretation in the Continental international law tradition, especially that of Hugo Grotius, see H. Grotius, *De Iure Belli ac Pacis* (Paris 1625), Emerich de Vattel, see E. de Vattel, *Le Droit des Gens* (London 1758), and Jean Jacques Burlamaqui, see J. Burlamaqui, *Principes du Droit Naturel et Politique* (Geneva 1748). See B. Bailyn, supra note 16, at 26–29 (noting American reliance on these authors for the laws of nations and of nature).

45. See 2 T. Jarman, *A Treatise on Wills* *738 (citing eighteenth-century cases); Porter, Book

Review, 27 *N. Am. Rev.* 167, 179 (1828) reprinted in *The Legal Mind in America* 161, 167 (P. Miller ed. 1962) (the common law supplies "the principles of interpretation" used in "every branch and department of jurisprudence").

46. In an 1819 newspaper essay, John Marshall remarked that he could cite from the common law "the most complete evidence that the *intention* is the most sacred rule of interpretation." Marshall, A Friend of the Constitution, *Alexandria Gazette,* July 2, 1819, reprinted in *John Marshall's Defense of McCulloch v. Maryland* 155, 167 (G. Gunther ed. 1969) (hereafter cited as *John Marshall's Defense*). In applying "intention" language to constitutional interpretation, Marshall explicitly drew on the traditional hermeneutic of the common law. Charles Miller's observation that "intention" properly applies only to people whereas "intent" may refer to both people and documents, see C. Miller, *The Supreme Court and the Uses of History* 154 n. 12 (1969), correctly states current usage, but is inaccurate as applied to eighteenth- and early nineteenth-century authors, who used the terms interchangeably, see, e.g., S. Johnson, supra note 12 (entries for "intent" and "intention" [second definition]).

47. Hewet v. Painter, 1 Bulstrode 174, 175, 80 Eng. Rep. 864, 865 (1611).

48. Indeed, Chief Justice Fleming went on to explain that "this intention and construction of words shall be taken, according to the vulgar and usual sense, phrase and manner of speech of these words," not according to any particular meaning the parties may have intended. Id. at 175–76, 80 Eng. Rep. at 865.

49. See, e.g., Langton, Fragments on the Morality of Human Acts (c. 1200), reprinted in *A Scholastic Miscellany: Anselm to Ockham* 355–56 (E. Fairweather ed. 1956). The ambiguity of *intentio* is likely to have continued to affect the use of its English derivatives in legal discourse because virtually all lawyers were familiar with Latin.

50. J. Selden, supra note 22.

51. Id. at 4, 44.

52. 1 J. Powell, *Essay upon the Law of Contracts and Agreements* 244 (London 1790).

53. Id. at 372–73.

54. "[A]lthough it is the duty of the Court to ascertain and carry into effect the intention of the party, yet there are, in many cases, fixed and settled rules by which that intention is determined; and to such rules the wisest judges have thought proper to adhere, in opposition to their own private opinions as to the probable intention of the party." H. Broom, *A Selection of Legal Maxims* *427 (rev. ed. London 1848) (1st ed. London 1845).

Some modern students of hermeneutics attack non-author-based interpretation as an abstract and ultimately hopeless search for a text's meaning apart from any human context or usage. See, e.g., J. Bruner, *In Search of Mind* 165–66 (1983) (any message must be interpreted in terms of the intent of its originators; it is a "nice question as to whether any save linguists, logicians, lawyers and pedants ever possessed a locution for its 'timeless meaning'"); E. Hirsch, *Validity in Interpretation* 12–14 (1967) (attacking non-author-based interpretive methodologies as incoherent). Eighteenth-century common lawyers did not hold precisely the view of interpretation that Bruner and Hirsch assail. They did not deny the existence of authors, personal intentions, nor did they argue that a text can be said to have a "meaning" in itself apart from any human act of expression or understanding. Rather, they believed that the meaning *relevant* to *legal* analysis of an instrument is that understood by its interpreters, not that entertained by its drafters.

55. See Prohibitions del Roy, 12 Co. Rep. 63, 65, 77 Eng. Rep. 1342, 1343 (1608).

56. Talbot *qui tam* v. Commanders and Owners of three Brigs, 1 Dall. 95, 100 (Pa. 1784). The court went on to explain that on the basis of the words' "legal meaning" the judges could reach a "construction, by which positive words may be properly and justly modified." Id. Eighteenth-century lawyers were aware, of course, that the words of a text mean something (subjectively) to the text's framers. Yet the eighteenth-century usage of "intent(ion)" melded semantic nuances that modern usage segregates much more cleanly; it thereby blurred for eighteenth-century English speakers differences of meaning that we regard as clear. Failure to recognize the difference between modern and circa–1800 usage undermines Raoul Berger's attempt to ground his form of intentionalism in the generally accepted "interpretive intention" of the constitutional era. See supra pp. 53–54. Berger cites James Madison and Joseph Story in support of his contention, see R. Berger, supra note 8, at 364–66, but this citation reflects a striking misinterpretation of the two men's views. Although Madison did refer at times to "the intention of the framers," he made it clear on numerous occasions that he was not an "intentionalist" in Berger's sense. See infra pp. 81–84. Story's attack on the practical possibility and theoretical propriety of intentionalism was equally thorough. See 1 J. Story, *Commentaries on the Constitution of the United States* 388–92 (Boston 1833); infra pp. 84–85 and note 325; see also Powell, Joseph Story's Commentaries on the Constitution.: A Belated Review, 94 *Yale L. J.* 1285 (1985) (discussing Story's theory of constitutional interpretation).

57. See F. Dwarris, supra note 17, at *688–90.

58. 2 W. Blackstone, *Commentaries* *379 (emphasis omitted).

59. Id. (emphasis omitted). Wills were to receive special treatment because the law assumed them to be the creations of ignorant testators at death's door. See Throckmerton v. Tracy, 1 Howden 145, 162, 75 Eng. Rep. 222, 251 (C.P. 1555). The case of Aylett v. Minnis, Wythe 219 (Va. Ch. 1793), rev'd, 1 Va. (1 Wash.) 300 (1795), illustrates the limits on the common law's willingness to seek the testator's subjective purposes, in his will, the testator left his son Philip, the plaintiff, "all [his] lands in King William [County]," id. at 220 (emphasis omitted), and directed the equal division of the residuary estate among the testator's widow and children. The testator, at death, owned certain lands in the named county in fee simple and was engaged in legal action to secure possession of other property to which he held a 999-year lease. After his father's executors obtained possession, Philip laid claim to the land under lease. The defendants relied on an old English case with similar facts, Rose v. Bartlett, Croke Car. 292, 79 Eng. Rep. 856 (K.B. 1631), in which the court had interpreted a will's language to cover only lands held in fee simple. Chancellor George Wythe refused to follow the English precedent on the grounds that the reasoning of the justices was unpersuasive and that, in light of the Aylett will as a whole, the testator clearly had meant to leave Philip all of his real property, of whatever legal character, in King William County. Wythe cautioned, however, that his interpretation was not based on extratextual considerations, but rather "exactly corresponded with the meaning of William Aylett's words . . . [because the Court was] convinced that they only ought to be consulted for discovering it." *Aylett*, Wythe at 233–34. Finding Wythe's opinion too daring a departure from traditional legal hermeneutics, the Virginia Court of Appeals subsequently reversed and held that, on this issue, the legal meaning of Aylett's 1780 will was fixed by the 1631 English decision. See 1 Va. (1 Wash.) 300 (1975). A few years later Wythe, admitting that he was flouting legal tradition, launched a direct and thoroughgoing attack on the use of judicial precedents in discerning the intention of wills. See Wilkins v. Taylor, Wythe 338, 347–54 (Va. Ch. 1799) rev'd, 9 Va. (5 Call.) 150 (1804).

60. "And the judges said they ought not to make any construction against the express letter of the statute; for nothing can so express the meaning of the makers of the Act, as their own direct words, for *index animi sermo* ['the word is the sign or indicator of the soul']." Edrich's Case, 5 Co. Rep. 118a, 118b, 77 Eng. Rep. 238, 239 (C.P. 1603). During the great debate in the Fourth Congress over the House of Representatives' right of access to the executive branch's diplomatic files, Nathaniel Smith observed that proper statutory interpretation did not involve reference to anything other than the text of the act: "This was the universal practice of the Courts of Law, who, when called on to expound an act of the Legislature, never resorted to the debates which preceded it—to the opinions of members about its signification—but inspected the act itself, and decided by its own evidence." 5 *Annals of Cong.* 462 (1796); *accord* id. at 441 (remarks of Rep. William Smith) (in construing a federal act, the Supreme Court does not "call for the

journals of the two Houses, or the report of the Committee of Ways and Means, in which the law originated, or the debates of the House on passing the law"). Discussing statutory construction in the 1820s, Massachusetts legal scholar Nathan Dane wrote that "such a construction ought to be put on a statute, as may best answer the intention which the maker of it had in view"; he added, somewhat ironically, that "the only difficulty is in finding this intention," and listed the means available for discovering the legislators' intent. "Legislative history" was not on his, or anyone else's, list at the time. 6 N. Dane, *General Abridgment and Digest of American Law* 600 (Boston 1824).

61. "So the judge speaks of the King's Proclamation, this is the intention of the King, not that the King had declared his intention any other way to the judge, but the judge examining the Contents of the Proclamation, gathers by the Purport of the words, the King's intention, and then for shortness of expression says, this is the King's intention." J. Selden, supra note 22, at 44.

62. L. Leder, *Liberty and Authority* 86–87 (1968) (quoting charge to Philadelphia grand jury in 1723 case).

63. See H. Broom, supra note 54, at *534–36 (citing authorities); cf. 6 N. Dane, supra note 60, at 596 (noting that only "where the *meaning of a statute is doubtful* . . . can courts of law look to consequences in construing it"). In cases of defective wording, English judges followed the policy of upholding the validity of written instruments, see H. Broom, supra note 54, at *413 (citing Lord Coke), by searching for the general purpose of the document as a guide to construction. See, e.g., The Earl of Clanrickard's Case, Hobart 273, 277, 80 Eng. Rep. 418, 423 (C.P. 1613) (expressing approval of judges "that are curious and almost subtil . . . to invent reasons and means to make Acts, according to the just intent of the parties"); see also, F. Dwarris, supra note 17, at *689–90 (arguing that in the construction of deeds, "such exposition should, if possible, be made, as is most agreeable to the intention of the grantor," and citing The Earl of Clanrickard's Case approvingly). But the curiosity and subtlety of the judges were tempered by their abhorrence of making "exposition against express words." Id. at *706 (quoting Lord Coke).

64. F. Bacon, Containing a Collection of Some Principall Rules and Maximes of the Common Law, in *The Elements of the Common Laws of England* 1, 92 (London 1630).

65. 3 Co. Rep. 7a, 76 Eng. Rep. 637 (1584).

66. Id. at 7b, 76 Eng. Rep. at 638.

67. Id. According to Professor Lon Fuller, "mischief" in this case meant something like "repugnancy" or "inconvenience." See L. Fuller, *The Morality of Law* 83 n. 38 (rev. ed. 1969). The formula in Heydon's Case, as reported by Coke, has been extremely influential. See 1 W. Blackstone, supra note 58, at *87; 6 N. Dane, supra note 60, at 600; F. Dwarris, supra note 17, at *694–95; L. Fuller, supra, at 82–83; J. Hurst, *Dealing with Statutes* 41 (1982); T. Sedgwick, *A Treatise on the Rules Which Govern the Interpretation and Application of Statutory and Constitutional Laws* 235–37 (New York 1857).

68. Sir James Dyer, a sixteenth-century chief justice of the Court of Common Pleas, asserted, in an oft-repeated passage, that the preamble of a statute is "a key to open the minds of the makers of the act, and the mischiefs which they intended to redress." H. Broom, supra note 54, at *439. A supplementary guide to the construction of a statute was provided by its classification as public and remedial rather than private or penal, a matter often noticed in the preamble. Statutes "concerning the public good," as opposed to private and penal acts, were to he construed "liberally; that is . . . in an enlarged manner." 6 N. Dane, supra note 60, at 599 (citing cases).

69. See H. Broom, supra note 54, at *719 (citing Lord Coke); 6 N. Dane, supra note 60, at 596.

70. See Thomas Jefferson to Skelton Jones (July 28, 1809), quoted in D. Malone, *Jefferson the Virginian* 261–62 (1948) (meaning of statutes is "in the air" until "settled by decisions").

71. E. Coke, *Proeme* to *Second Part of the Institutes of the Laws of England* (London 1642); *accord* Kamper v. Hawkins, 3 Va. (1 Va. Cas.) 20, 93 (Gen. Ct. 1793) (Tucker, J.) (decisions of Virginia Supreme Court of Appeals by definition expound Virginia's constitutions and laws "in their truest sense"); see also 6 N. Dane, supra note 60, at 597 (commonly used expressions "by being often used in states, and so construed, have acquired their meaning").

72. See 1 J. Powell, supra note 52, at 387 ("ordinary import of words may be restrained" where there is "an original defect in the will of the speaker, so that it is not co-extensive with his words," or where there is "some collateral accident inconsistent with the speaker's design").

73. See id. at 372–73. Chief Justice Popham's observations in The Countess of Rutland's Case, 5 Co. Rep. 25b, 77 Eng. Rep. 89 (K.B. 1604), became proverbial, and others generalized them to include written documents of a noncontractual nature. Coke reported Chief Justice Popham to have stated that parol evidence was not admissible to vary or add to a writing because "every contract or agreement ought to be dissolved by matter of as high a nature as the first deed. . . . Also it would be inconvenient, that matter in writing made by advice and on consideration, and which finally import the certain truth of the agreement of the parties should be controlled by averment of the parties, to be proved by the uncertain testimony of slippery memory." Id. at 26a, 77 Eng. Rep. at 90. It is clear that the evaluation of extrinsic evidence of intent, both in the contractual and in the statutory areas, rested on a substantive view of what (legally significant) "intent" is. See 1 W. Blackstone, supra note 58, at *62; 1 J. Powell, supra note 52, at 372–73.

74. See Throckmerton v. Tracy, 1 Plowden 145, 162, 75 Eng. Rep. 222, 251 (C.P. 1555).

75. See P. Atiyah, *The Rise and Fall of Freedom of Contract* 169–77 (1979); M. Horwitz, *The Transformation of American Law, 1780–1860*, at 161–73 (1977); W. Nelson, *Americanization of the Common Law* 54–63 (1975).

76. See 2. J. Powell, supra note 52, at 40–41; N. Dane, supra note 60, at 574–75.

77. Good examples are H. Broom, supra note 54; F. Dwarris, supra note 17; 1–4 J. Kent, *Commentaries on American Law* (New York 1826–1830); F. Lieber, *Legal and Political Hermeneutics* (Boston 1839); T. Sedgwick, supra note 67; 1 J. Story, supra note 56, at 383–443; Hawkins, On the Principles of Legal Interpretation, 2 *Jurid. Soc'y Papers* 298 (1860).

78. Broom summarized the trend toward literalism thus: in construing a statute "to ascertain and carry out the intention of the legislature . . . the judges will bend and conform their legal reason to the words of the act, and will rather construe them literally, than strain their meaning beyond the obvious intention of Parliament." H. Broom, supra note 54, at *117; see also F. Dwarris, supra note 17, at *708 (noting that "recently" English judges had manifested an intention "to adhere more closely . . . to the words of the act of Parliament"); T. Sedgwick, supra note 67, at 382–83 (arguing that the "only safe rule" is to trace the legislative intent "as expressed *by the words which the legislature has used*").

79. Coster v. Lorillard, 14 Wend. 265, 375 (N.Y. 1835); O.W. Holmes, The Theory of Legal Interpretation, in *Collected Legal Papers* 203, 207 (1920) ("we do not inquire what the legislature meant; we ask only what the statute means"). The legitimacy of resort to legislative history was only imperfectly established in Holmes's period, see, e.g., Davis v. Pringle, 268 U.S. 315, 318 (1925) Holmes, J., and he often resisted its use as contrary to the proper "external principle of construction." See O. W. Holmes, supra at 208; see also Frankfurter, Some Reflections on the Reading of Statutes, 47 *Colum. L. Rev.* 527, 538 (1947) (quoting letter from Holmes in which the latter recalls having said, while hearing oral argument, "I don't care what [the legislature's] intention was. I only want to know what the words mean.").

80. "The journals [of the legislature's proceedings] are not evidence of the meaning of a statute, because this must be ascertained from the language of the act itself, and the facts connected with the subject on which it is to operate." Southwark Bank v. Commonwealth, 26 Pa. 446, 450

(1856); see also T. Sedgwick, supra note 67, at 243 (noting that "the intention of the legislature is to be found in the statute itself") (emphasis omitted).

81. See, e.g., M. Horwitz, supra note 75, at 180–85.

82. See P. Atiyah, supra note 75, at 459; the triumph of the will theory and the spread of an "objective" approach to contracts did not proceed at precisely the same pace, of course. See G. Gilmore, *The Death of Contract* 39–40 (1974) (noting persistence of "subjective" approach into latter part of nineteenth century).

83. An early Delaware case, Laws v. Davis, 1 Del. Cas. 256 (1800), illustrates the strength of the cultural distrust of interpretation even within the legal profession. One of the lawyers warned against carrying the potentially "unlimited power of construction" beyond narrow limits. The interpretations of judges, he feared, threaten "the law" on which "our rights hang and society depends." Id. at 258. In another Delaware case, Brown v. Brown, 1 Del. Cas. 188 (1798), Chief Justice Richard Bassett warned that judicial restraint in the exercise of a power to construe statutes was necessary in order to protect the constitutional separation of powers. See id. at 191.

84. See, e.g., A. Hamilton, Opinion on the Constitutionality of an Act to Establish a Bank (1791), reprinted in 8 *Papers of Alexander Hamilton* 97, 111 (H. Syrett ed. 1965) (referring to "the usual and established rules of construction").

85. This exchange is quoted in A. Mason, *The States Rights Debate* 107 (2d ed. 1972).

86. See C. Bowen, *The Lion and the Throne* 452–53, 482–84, 495–99 (1957); L. Leder, supra note 62, at 95–117.

87. See H. Commager, *The Empire of Reason* 227–35 (1977); G. Wood, supra note 11, at 454–63. The Articles of Confederation were also regarded by the courts as amenable to traditional hermeneutical techniques. See Talbot *qui tam* v. Commanders and Owners of three Brigs, 1 Dall. 95, 100 (Pa. 1784). In an 1824 book review, Henry Sedgwick contrasted American constitutional discourse with its British counterpart: "[Our] written constitutions have furnished a comparatively easy and definitive test, for the resolution of doubts and decision of controversies. In England also there have been constitutional disputes, and the disputants have appealed to theoretic reasoning, vague maxims, obsolete charters, ancient usages, half forgotten statutes, concerning which it has been [a] matter of doubtful discussion, whether they were or were not in force." Sedgwick, Book Review, 19 *N. Am. Rev.* 411, 438 (1824) reprinted in *The Legal Mind in America*, supra note 45, at 135, 145.

88. See, e.g., J. Madison, *Journal of the Federal Convention* 83 (E. Scott ed. 1893) (proceedings of May 31, 1787) (provision giving Congress power in cases in which state legislatures are individually "incompetent" is criticized as vague); id. at 133 (June 8) (provision giving Congress power to negate "improper" state laws is criticized as indefinite); id. at 562 (August 20) (necessary and proper clause is criticized as too vague in respect to Congress's power to establish federal offices); id. at 614 (August 27) (provision concerning impeachment and removal of President in case of "disability" is criticized as too vague).

89. Some delegates suggested that the Committee of Detail's draft provision giving each house of Congress "in all cases . . . a negative on the other" would give the House of Representatives a veto on treaties despite the later provision giving the Senate alone power to ratify treaties. Id. at 463 (August 7). Others criticized the committee's draft of the presidential veto provision because it referred to "bills" and could thus he evaded simply by styling congressional acts as "resolutions." See id. at 536–37 (August 15). Some delegates feared that the draft provision empowering Congress "to make war" would render the President incompetent to order defensive operations in the event of a surprise attack, while others thought the proposed substitution ("to declare war") left Congress's power too narrow. See id. at 548 (August 17).

90. The debate over the provision giving Congress legislative authority over maritime crimes exemplifies the convention's concern for precision. As proposed by the Committee of Detail, the provision empowered Congress "to declare the law and punishment of piracies and felonies committed on the high seas." Id. at 454 (August 6). When the provision came up for consideration by the full convention, James Madison moved to strike the words "and punishment" as superfluous. George Mason opposed the motion because he feared that the omission would leave Congress capable only of defining maritime crimes, and not of setting penalties for them. Edmund Randolph did not regard the removal of "punishment" as significant, but expressed concern over "the efficacy" of the verb "declare." Gouverneur Morris preferred "designate" to "declare," while Madison and James Wilson debated the precision of "felonies." Only after considerable discussion was the final wording settled upon. See id. at 544–46 (August 17).

91. Id. at 173 (June 16).

92. At the convention's close, the delegates decided not to publish the journal and other papers, but rather to entrust them to convention president George Washington, subject to future action by Congress under the proposed Constitution. See id. at 748 (September 17).

93. See, e.g., id. at 625–26 (August 29) (meaning of "ex post facto law" not controlled by intentions of delegates to convention); id. at 727–28 (September 14) (same).

94. See, e.g., id. at 220 n.* (June 22) (Massachusetts concurs in deletion of phrase because its purpose would be achieved without express wording); id. at 726 (September 14) (James Wilson argues that power to create monopolies is implicit in commerce power.

95. Id. at 617 (August 27).

96. See, e.g., L. Martin, *The Genuine Information Delivered to the Legislature of the State of Maryland* (1788), reprinted in 2 *The Complete Anti-Federalist* 19, 75–76 (H. Storing ed. 1981) (hereafter cited as Storing); *Federalist* No. 15, at 70–71 (A. Hamilton) (G. Wills ed. 1982); *Federalist* No. 22, at 111 (A. Hamilton) (G. Wills ed. 1982).

97. See, e.g., *Federalist* No. 18 (J. Madison) (comparing the articles to confederations of the past).

98. See, e.g., *Federalist* No. 15 (A. Hamilton); infra pp. 77–78.

99. See, e.g., *Federalist* No. 40, at 199–200 (J. Madison) (G. Wills ed. 1982) (although Anti-Federalists attack convention as if it had sought the "establishment" of the Constitution, its powers were in fact "merely advisory and recommendatory").

100. See, e.g., *Federalist* No. 78, at 395–96 (A. Hamilton) (G. Wills ed. 1982).

101. See, e.g., Letters from the Federal Farmer No. 4 (October 12, 1787) reprinted in 2 Storing, supra note 96, at 248 (assuming analogy between statutory and constitutional interpretation); Essays by Cincinnatus No. 2 (November 8, 1787) reprinted in 6 Storing, supra note 96, at 12 (applying principles of "legal construction" to Constitution).

102. The Federalists maintained that the states' autonomy was secure because the text of the Constitution did not purport to abolish it and indeed contained only a few explicit restrictions on state power. The Anti-Federalists countered that the supremacy clause and the expansive definitions of congressional authority would reduce the states to insignificance. See 3 *The Debates Resolutions, and other Proceedings, in Convention, on the Adoption of the Federal Constitution* (J. Elliot ed. 1827, 1828 and 1830) (hereafter cited as *Elliot's Debates*) (reporting the first North Carolina convention, in which Timothy Bloodworth claimed that these provisions would "produce an abolition of the state governments"). Massachusetts Anti-Federalist Amos Singletary summarized the view of those opposed to ratification when he complained that he "wished [the Federalists] would not play round the subject with their fine stories, like a fox round a trap, but come to it," and admit that after ratification "the states will be like towns in this state. Towns . . . have a right to lay taxes to raise money, and the states possibly may have the same." 1 *Elliot's Debates*, supra, at 111.

103. See, e.g., The Address and Reasons of Dissent of the Minority of the Convention of

Pennsylvania to Their Constituents, *Pennsylvania Packet and Daily Advertiser*, December 18, 1787, reprinted in 3 Storing, supra note 96, at 145, 154–57 (criticizing Constitution for permitting Congress to assume effectively unlimited powers by construction, and intimating that the instrument would allow similar self-aggrandizement by the federal judiciary).

104. See G. Wood, supra note 11, at 538; 1 Storing, supra note 96, at 54.

105. See, e.g., Letters of Centinel No. 5 (November 30, 1787), reprinted in 2 Storing, supra note 96, at 166, 167–69.

106. See 1 Storing, supra note 96, at 50.

107. This assertion was made repeatedly by Anti-Federalists in the state conventions. See, e.g., 3 *Elliot's Debates*, supra note 102, at 57 (remarks of Timothy Bloodworth at the first North Carolina convention) ("no one can say what construction congress will put upon" Article I); id. at 156 (noting remarks of Andrew Bass at the first North Carolina convention) ("[Bass] observed that gentlemen of the law and men of learning did not concur in the explanation or meaning of this constitution. . . . From the contrariety of opinions, he thought the thing was either uncommonly difficult, or absolutely unintelligible.").

108. A. Mason, supra note 85, at 134 (quoting remarks of John Smilie at the Pennsylvania ratifying convention).

109. See id. Letters of Centinel No. 2 (1787) reprinted in 2 Storing, supra note 96, at 147 (Federalist claim that unenumerated powers are not granted to the federal government is "a speculative unascertained rule of construction" that would prove "a *poor* security for the liberties of the people"); 3 *Elliot's Debates* supra note 102, at 164 (remarks of Timothy Bloodworth at the first North Carolina convention) (Constitution is flawed because it grants "indefinite power" about which "members of Congress will differ").

110. See generally, L. Banning, supra note 31, at 105–13 (discussing Anti-Federalist arguments); 1 Storing, supra note 96, at 3–76 (same).

111. See G. Wood, supra note 11, at 524–43.

112. See, e.g., 3 *Elliot's Debates*, supra note 102, at 37 (remarks of Archibald Maclaine at the first North Carolina convention) ("The constitution is only a mere proposal. If the people approve of it, it becomes their act."); *Federalist* No. 40 (J. Madison). In asserting the Philadelphia convention's authority to propose a new constitution instead of mere amendments to the Articles of Confederation, in justifying the lack of a bill of rights, and in defending against the charge that the Constitution had bypassed the states (by beginning with "we the People" instead of "we the States"), the Federalists relied on the basic proposition that the Constitution would be, if adopted, the act of the people, not of the state governments or of the federal convention.

113. See 3 *Elliot's Debates*, supra note 102, at 71 (remarks of Archibald Maclaine at the first North Carolina convention).

114. 1 id. at 255 (remarks of John Jay at the New York convention).

115. Id. at 115 (remarks of Theophilus Parsons at the Massachusetts convention); see *Federalist* No. 37 (J. Madison).

116. See 3 *Elliot's Debates*, supra note 102, at 74 (remarks of John Steele at the first North Carolina convention) ("universal jurisprudence" and a "plain obvious" construction will be applied to the Constitution); A. Mason, supra note 85, at 160 (remarks of Edmund Randolph at the Virginia convention) (improper construction of ambiguous parts of Constitution can be remedied through amendment); cf. *Federalist* No. 44, at 230 (J. Madison) (G. Wills ed. 1982) (remedy for misconstructions by Congress is electoral).

117. See 2 Storing, supra note 96, at 358.

118. Essays of Brutus No. 11, reprinted in 2 Storing, supra note 96, at 417, 419.

119. Id. at 420–21.

120. See id. at 422 ("This power in the judicial, will enable them to mould the government, into almost any shape they please.").

121. Id. at 419.

122. See id.

123. Essays of Brutus No. 12, reprinted in 2 Storing, supra note 96, at 422, 424.

124. "Brutus" thought the "most natural and grammatical" interpretation of Article I, section 8, was that it authorized Congress to do "anything which in their judgment will tend to provide for the general welfare, and [that] this amounts to the same thing as general and unlimited powers of legislation in all cases." Id. at 425.

125. See id. at 424–25.

126. Essays of Brutus No. 15, reprinted in 2 Storing, supra note 96, at 437, 441; see Essays of Brutus No. 12, id. at 422, 424–25 (courts will be authorized to interpret the Constitution "according to its spirit," which is "to subvert and abolish" all state powers)

127. See Essays of Brutus No. 15, reprinted in 2 Storing, supra note 96, at 437–41.

128. Id. at 442. The views of "Brutus" were not unique; throughout this period American writers invoked the image of a "compact" in explaining and defending the basis of the American political order. See, e.g., Amicus Republicae, *Address to the Public* (Exeter 1786), reprinted in 2 Storing, supra note 96, at 638–40 (each state was constituted by "civil compacts"; the articles are a further "solemn covenant" between the states); Hart, *Liberty Described and Recommended: In a Sermon Preached to the Corporation of Freemen in Farmington* (Hartford 1775), reprinted in 1 *American Political Writing during the Founding Era: 1760–1805*, at 305, 308–10 (C. Hyneman and D. Lutz eds. 1983) (human society is founded on "compact or mutual agreement").

129. See, e.g., L. Levy, *Judicial Review and the Supreme Court* 6 (1967) (discussing *Federalist* No. 78). But see G. Wills, *Explaining America: The Federalist* 130–150 (1981) (suggesting alternative interpretation of Hamilton's purposes).

130. "Laws are a dead letter without courts to expound and define their true meaning and operation." *Federalist* No. 22, at 109 (A. Hamilton) (G. Wills ed. 1982).

131. *Federalist* No. 37 (J. Madison) appeared on January 11, 1788, well before the main body of the *Essays'* attack on Article III and its implications.

132. *Federalist* No. 37, at 180 (J. Madison) (G. Wills ed. 1982).

133. Id. at 179.

134. "The treaties of the United States to have any force at all, must be considered as part of the law of the land. Their true import as far as respects individuals, must, like all other laws, be ascertained by judicial determinations." *Federalist* No. 22, at 109 (A. Hamilton) (G. Wills ed. 1982).

135. *Federalist* No. 78, at 396 (A. Hamilton) (G. Wills ed. 1982).

136. *Federalist* No. 83, at 422 (A. Hamilton) (G. Wills ed. 1982).

137. *Federalist* No. 78, at 396 (A. Hamilton) (G. Wills ed. 1982).

138. See id. at 395–96 ("[W]here the will of the legislature declared in its statutes, stands in opposition to that of the people declared in the constitution, the judges ought to be governed by the latter, rather than the former").

139. Id. at 393.

140. Id. at 394.

141. See id.; *Federalist* No. 79 (A. Hamilton).

142. See *Federalist* No. 16 (A. Hamilton). At the New York convention, Hamilton argued that to "take the old confederation" and entrust it with the minimal power virtually all Anti-

Federalists conceded should be placed in federal hands "would be establishing a power which would destroy the liberties of the people" because the Confederation government, lacking the legal power to act directly on individuals, could carry out its new responsibilities only by using military force. 1 *Elliot's Debates*, supra note 102, at 210 (remarks of A. Hamilton at the New York convention).

143. The complex response evoked in many Americans by the proposed Constitution is exemplified in the behavior of Edmund Randolph of Virginia. A delegate and active participant at the Philadelphia convention, Randolph found himself unable at the end to sign the convention's finished product. After his return to Virginia, however, Randolph's fears that rejection would spell the end of the union between the states, and that disunion would lead to anarchy, overcame his misgivings about the Constitution, and he played an important role in securing Virginia's ratification. See R. Rutland, *The Birth of the Bill of Rights, 1777–1791*, at 167–68, 174 (rev. ed. 1983). At the state ratifying convention, Randolph assailed the Anti-Federalists' dire prophecies as the product of "extravagant" misconstructions of the Constitution's text. But he agreed that at certain important points the Constitution was unhappily vague, and noted his special concern with the vagueness of the necessary and proper clause in designing the scope of congressional powers: "My objection is, that the clause is ambiguous, and that that ambiguity may injure the states. My fear is, that it will by gradual accessions gather [power to Congress] to a dangerous length. I trust that the members of Congress themselves will explain the ambiguous parts: and if not, the states can combine in order to insist on amending the ambiguities. I would depend on the present actual feeling of the people of America, to introduce any amendment which may be necessary." A. Mason, supra note 85, at 160 (remarks of Edmund Randolph at the Virginia convention).

144. Leading members of Congress regarded the amendments not as modifying the 1787 text, but merely as making explicit the original instrument's solicitude for individual liberties. See, e.g., 1 *Annals of Cong.* 432 (J. Gales ed. 1789) (remarks of Rep. James Madison on June 8, 1789) (Congress ought to adopt amendments that will "expressly declare the great rights of mankind secured under this Constitution"); id. at 715 (remarks of Rep. Roger Sherman on August 13, 1789) ("The amendments reported are a declaration of rights; the people are secure in them, whether we declare them or not").

145. The premier example of the latter is the famous dispute over the appropriate address for the President. See L. Banning, supra note 31, at 117–21.

146. See 4 *Elliot's Debates*, supra note 102, pt. II, at 139–232 (collecting opinions on constitutional questions expressed by members of the first Congress).

147. 1 *Annals of Congress* 526 (J. Gales ed. 1789) (remarks of Rep. Elias Boudinot on June 18, 1789).

148. Id. at 574 (remarks of Rep. Elbridge Gerry on June 19, 1789). Early in his remarks, Gerry asserted that he was "decidedly against putting any construction whatever on the Constitution." Id. at 573. Like Edmund Randolph of Virginia, Gerry had refused to sign the Constitution at the close of the Philadelphia convention. Unlike Randolph, he opposed its ratification. See 2 Storing, supra note 96, at 4–8.

149. Roger Sherman expressed a preference "to leave the Constitution to speak for itself whenever occasion demands," rather than for Congress to "attempt to construe the Constitution." 1 *Annals of Cong.* 538 (J. Gales ed. 1789) (remarks of Rep. Roger Sherman on June 18, 1789). Abraham Baldwin, a proponent of the view that Congress could make executive officers removable by unilateral actions of the President, responded to opponents' claims that his position violated Article II, section 2 (which provides that the appointment power is exercisable "by and with the advice and consent of the Senate") with the hope that "gentlemen will change their expression, and say, we shall violate their construction of the Constitution, and not the Constitution itself." For himself, Baldwin remarked, "when gentlemen tell me that I am going to construe the Constitution . . . I am very cautious how I proceed. I do not like to construe over much." Id. at 556 (remarks of Rep. Abraham Baldwin on June 19, 1789).

150. Id. at 495 (remarks of Rep. James Madison on June 17, 1789). In defending the constitutionality of Hamilton's bank bill, Fisher Ames contrasted "the letter of the constitution" with the instrument's "meaning and intention"; the latter, he argued, was properly and necessarily to be determined by "the doctrine of implication" and the use of "a reasonable latitude of construction." 4 *Elliot's Debates*, supra note 102, at 220–23 (remarks of Fisher Ames on February 3, 1791); see also 2 *Annals of Cong.* 1903–9 (1791) (alternative version of Ames's remarks).

151. Act of February 25, 1791, ch. 10, 1 Stat. 191.

152. A. Hamilton, supra note 84, at 111. Jefferson's opinion includes a similar reference. See T. Jefferson, Opinion on the Constitutionality of a National Bank (1791), reprinted in 5 *The Writings of Thomas Jefferson* 284, 286 (P. Ford ed. 1892–1899) (hereafter cited as *Writings*). Both papers make clear use of traditional interpretive strategies.

153. A. Hamilton, supra note 84, at 111. This point was made in response to Jefferson's unusual resort to "legislative history" from the Philadelphia convention's nominally secret proceedings. Jefferson referred to the well-known fact that the convention had rejected a proposal to give Congress explicit power to charter corporations. See T. Jefferson, supra note 152, at 287.

154. A. Hamilton, supra note 84, at 103.

155. See, e.g., supra note 84, at 103.

156. A. Hamilton, supra note 84, at 102–3.

157. See id. at 105.

158. Id.

159. Id.

160. See U.S. Const. Art 1, sec. 8.

161. A. Hamilton, supra note 84, at 102–3.

162. See H. Dwarris, supra note 54, at *28.

163. See T. Jefferson, supra note 152, at 284–85.

164. Id. at 289.

165. Coke suggested in Dr. Bonham's Case, 8 Co. Rep. 107, 118, 77 Eng. Rep. 638, 652 (C.P. 1610), that "when an Act of Parliament is against common right and reason, or repugnant, or impossible to be performed, the common law will controul it, and adjudge such Act to be void." Whatever Coke may have meant by this remark, British legal opinion at the time of the American Revolution was overwhelmingly against any possibility of judicial review of Parliament's acts, in the name of the common law or otherwise. See, e.g., 1 W. Blackstone, supra note 58, at *156–57 (what Parliament does, "no authority upon earth can undo").

166. See F. Dwarris, supra note 17, at *695.

167. Jefferson wrote that he "consider[ed] the foundation of the Constitution as laid on this ground: That 'all powers not delegated to the United States, by the Constitution, nor prohibited by it to the States, are reserved to the States or to the people.' " T. Jefferson, supra note 152, at 285. Hamilton did not deny the principle on which Jefferson relied, but he viewed its significance quite differently. For Hamilton, the Tenth Amendment merely restated the first principle of republican government, that all government power is a delegation from the sovereign people. But mere acceptance of this principle did not indicate what powers the people had in fact delegated to the national government. This was the real question at issue, and Hamilton answered it with his arguments, textual and hermeneutical, for a "liberal" construction of the delegation. See A. Hamilton, supra note 84, at 99–100. For Jefferson, on the other hand, the

Tenth Amendment was not a mere truism, but expressed a genuine presumption against the legitimacy of federal power, at least in the domestic sphere. See Thomas Jefferson to Justice William Johnson (June 12, 1823), reprinted in *Political Writings*, supra note 40, at 148 ("The States supposed that by their Tenth Amendment they had secured themselves against constructive powers").

168. Jefferson's argument was paralleled, however, by the strict construction approach taken by eighteenth-century international public law in regard to cessions of power by sovereigns. See Tucker, Appendix to 1 *Blackstone's Commentaries* note D, at 143 (St. G. Tucker ed. and comm. 1803).

169. U.S. Const. Amend. X.

170. 5 *Annals of Cong.* 432 (1796) (remarks of Rep. Daniel Buck); id. at 441 (remarks of Rep. William Smith).

171. Id. at 495 (remarks of Rep. William Smith); see also id. at 519-21, 523-27 (remarks of Rep. Theodore Sedgwick); id. at 574-75 (remarks of Rep. Benjamin Bourne).

172. See id. at 495-96 (remarks of Rep. William Smith) (the relevant "general opinion of the public" is that manifested uniformly by both friend and foe of ratification); id. at 523 (remarks of Rep. Theodore Sedgwick) (same); id. at 580-81 (remarks of Rep. Richard Brent) (same).

173. See id. at 496 (remarks of Rep. William Smith) (subsequent "practice of Congress"); id. at 528 (remarks of Rep. Theodore Sedgwick) ("well understood" opinion of Supreme Court); id. at 574 (remarks of Rep. Benjamin Bourne) (resolutions of state legislatures on earlier treaties); id. at 615-16 (remarks of Rep. Uriah Tracy) (views expressed of federal powers under Articles of Confederation).

174. See id. at 612 (remarks of Rep. Uriah Tracy).

175. Id. at 616.

176. Id. at 617.

177. Id. at 727 (remarks of Rep. Albert Gallatin).

178. Id.

179. Id. at 603 (remarks of Rep. William Lyman).

180. Id. at 574 (remarks of Rep. William Lyman).

181. Id. at 635 (remarks of Rep. Edward Livingston).

182. Id. at 505 (remarks of Rep. William Branch Giles).

183. Id. at 537 (remarks of Rep. Abraham Baldwin); see also id. at 538-39 (it is no objection to a fair construction of the text that it was not anticipated in the ratification era).

184. Id. at 701 (remarks of Rep. William Vans Murray). Vans Murray noted that "contemporaneous opinions [that were] still fresh" and the contents of the Philadelphia convention's special journal could serve as additional checks on misconstruction. Id.

185. Id. at 701-2.

186. See id. at 701-2.

187. Id. at 733 (remarks of Rep. Albert Gallatin).

188. Id. at 734.

189. Id. at 738.

190. President Washington's written response to the House resolution was made part of the congressional record. See id. at 760-61.

191. See id.

192. See id. at 771–72 (reprinting the text of the resolution); id. at 782–83 (noting affirmative vote on the resolution).

193. Id. at 775 (remarks of Rep. James Madison).

194. Id.

195. Id. at 776.

196. Id.

197. 2 U.S. (2 Dall.) 419 (1793).

198. See id. at 419.

199. Randolph was Attorney General of the United States at the time, but was representing the plaintiff in his private capacity.

200. See id. at 421–25.

201. See, e.g., *Federalist* No. 81 (A. Hamilton).

202. Justice Iredell dissented on statutory grounds and indicated that he disagreed with Randolph's view of the constitutional question as well. See Chisholm v. Georgia, 2 U.S. (2 Dall.) at 429, 449–50 (Iredell, J., dissenting). Justice Iredell's constitutional disagreement with the majority was not based, however, on his acceptance of evidence about the Constitution's "history," but on the eighteenth-century public-law presumption against the delegation of sovereign power. See id. at 435–36.

Justice Iredell's acceptance of the common law approach to legal interpretation is exemplified by a grand jury charge he delivered in 1799. In addressing the constitutionality of the Alien and Sedition Act, Justice Iredell noted the Republicans' view that the Alien Act violated the "migration and importation" clause of Article I, section 9. Although some Federalists rebutted the accusation by referring to the clause's well-known connection with the importation of slaves, Justice Iredell rejected this line of defense as contrary to proper legal interpretation: "I am not satisfied, as to [the Republican] objection, that it is sufficient to overrule it, to say the words do not express the real meaning, either of those who formed the constitution, or those who established it, although I do verily believe in my own mind that the article was intended only for slaves. . . . But, though this probably is the real truth, yet, if in attempting to compromise, they have unguardedly used expressions that go beyond their meaning, and there is nothing but private history to elucidate it, I shall deem it absolutely necessary to confine myself to the written instrument." G. McRee, *Life and Correspondence of James Iredell* 551, 558 (New York 1857) (quoting charge delivered by Justice Iredell to grand jury in 1799).

203. Chisholm v. Georgia, 2 U.S. (2 Dall.) at 476 (Jay, C.J.).

204. Id. at 464 (Wilson, J.); see id. at 466–68 (Cushing, J.); id. at 470–72 (Jay, C.J.).

205. See id. at 450 (Blair, J.); id. at 466 (Wilson, J.); id. at 467 (Cushing, J.); id. at 476–77 (Jay, C.J.). Indeed, Chief Justice Jay and Justice Wilson went a step beyond Randolph by relying in part on the Preamble to illuminate the Constitution's meaning. See id. at 463 (Wilson, J.); id. at 474–75 (Jay, C.J.).

206. See U.S. Const. Amend. XI ("The judicial power of the United States shall not be construed to extend to any suit . . . commenced or prosecuted against one of the United States by Citizens of another State, or by Citizens or Subjects of any Foreign State.").

207. See L. Banning, supra note 31, at 201–2.

208. Pendleton, The Danger Not Over, *Richmond Examiner*, October 20, 1801, quoted in L. Banning, supra note 31, at 282; see also Letter from Thomas Jefferson to Wilson C. Nicholas (September 7, 1803) reprinted in *Political Writings*, supra note 40, at 144 (warning of the dangers of construction).

209. See generally L. Banning, supra note 31, at 126–245 (discussing the rise of Republican opposition to the Federalist administration).

210. Madison's emergence as a key figure in the development of the state-sovereignty theory of the Constitution in the 1790s is, on the surface, somewhat surprising in light of his nationalist sympathies in the 1780s. See G. Wood, supra note 11, at 473 (noting that by 1787, Madison was "a thorough nationalist, intent on subordinating the states as far as possible to the sovereignty of the central government"). Madison's view of federal power during his Presidency can be seen as a partial return to this pre-ratification nationalism. See Madison, Message to Congress (December 5, 1815), reprinted in *The Mind of the Founder: Sources of the Political Thought of James Madison* 297 (M. Meyers rev. ed. 1981) (hereafter cited as *Mind of the Founder*) (suggesting an expansive view of congressional power). But see Madison, Veto Message (March 3, 1817), 30 *Annals of Cong.* 1061 (vetoing internal improvements bill on ground that it exceeded powers delegated to Congress). In the final constitutional struggle of his life, the nullification crisis of 1828 to 1832, Madison forcefully repudiated the extreme state sovereignty views of the nullifiers. See, e.g., J. Madison, Notes on Nullification (1835–1836), reprinted in *Mind of the Founder* supra at 417. Madison, of course, may simply have been inconsistent; a more sympathetic interpretation is that Madison's consistency lay in his constant desire to preserve the federal republic as a just and free society. See A. Koch, *Madison's "Advice to My Country"* (1966) (developing such an interpretation).

211. J. Calhoun, South Carolina Exposition (original draft, Dec. 1828) reprinted in 6 *The Works of John C. Calhoun* 1, 40 (R. Cralle ed. 1855).

212. See generally, J. Miller, *Crisis in Freedom* 3–73 (1951) (discussing historical setting of Alien and Sedition Acts).

213. Congress raised the residency requirement for naturalization from five to fourteen years. Act of June 8, 1798, ch. 54, 1 Stat. 566; (repealed by Act of April 14, 1802, ch. 28, sect. 5, 2 Stat. 153, 155). The Alien Enemies Act, ch. 66, 1 Stat. 577 (1798) (current version at 50 U.S.C. 44 21–22 [1982]), provided for the arrest and "removal" of resident aliens in the event of hostilities between their native country and the United States. The Alien Act, ch. 58, 1 Stat. 570 (1798) (expired 1800), gave the President "virtually unlimited power over all aliens in the United States," J. Miller, supra note 212, at 52, permitting him to order their surveillance, arrest, deportation, and (if they returned) imprisonment, with little judicial supervision. The Sedition Act ch. 74, 1 Stat. 596 (1798) (expired 1801), settled doubts over the existence of a federal common law offense of seditious libel by making it a statutory crime to defame the government or incite resistance to the laws of the United States. The Act's defenders pointed to its requirement that malice be proved, its allowance of truth as a defense, and its provisions for jury trial as evidence that the statute in fact allayed the common law's rigor. The Republicans, who did not think there was rightfully any federal common law to change for better or worse, saw the Act as "an experiment on the American mind to see how far it will bear an avowed violation of the Constitution," to be followed if successful by an open repudiation of republicanism. Thomas Jefferson to Stephens Mason (October 11, 1798), reprinted in *Political Writings*, supra note 40, at 156.

214. See T. Emerson, *The System of Freedom of Expression* 100 (1970) (recounting arrests under the Act); C. Haines, *The Role of the Supreme Court in American Government and Politics: 1789–1835*, at 159–60 (1944) (discussing federal common law crime of seditious libel).

215. See L. Banning, supra note 31, at 246–70; A. Koch, *Jefferson and Madison: The Great Collaboration* 174–211 (1950). Jefferson referred to the Acts as "violations of the Constitution" because they attempted "to silence by force and not by reason the complaints or criticisms, just or unjust, of our citizens against the conduct of their agents." Thomas Jefferson to Elbridge Gerry (January 26, 1799), reprinted in *Political Writings*, supra note 40, at 47.

216. See A. Koch, supra note 215, at 182–83.

217. See e.g., Madison, Consolidation, *National Gazette*, December 5, 1791, reprinted in *Mind of the Founder*, supra, note 210, at 181; Thomas Jefferson to Gideon Granger (Aug. 13, 1800).

reprinted in *Political Writings*, supra note 40, at 96, 97 (arguing against "assumption of all the state powers into the hands of the general Government").

218. See A. Koch, supra note 215, at 186–94.

219. Taylor became in later years one of the leaders of the "Old Republicans," the extreme wing of the Jeffersonian movement whose adherents regarded Jefferson's second term as somewhat compromised and the administrations of Madison and Monroe as continual apostasy from the true principles of 1798. Of the commentaries written before Calhoun began his series of state papers in 1828, Taylor's works—especially his *New Views of the Constitution of the United States* (Washington City 1823)—represent the most powerful and sustained vindication of an uncompromising states' rights interpretation of both the Virginia and Kentucky Resolutions and the Constitution.

220. See *State Documents on Federal Relations* 16–26 (H. Ames ed. 1906) (hereafter cited as *State Documents*) (collecting the most important of the replies). Ironically, having denied the right of states to judge the constitutionality of federal laws, several Federalist legislatures went on to review the Alien and Sedition Acts and to uphold their validity. See id. at 18–20 (Massachusetts); id. at 20–22 (Pennsylvania); id. at 24–25 (New Hampshire).

221. The draftsman of the 1799 Resolutions is unknown, although the Resolutions strongly reflect the ideas of both Jefferson and Madison. See A. Koch, supra note 215, at 201.

222. Previously while circulating the 1798 Resolutions to its fellow legislatures, the General Assembly had published an "Address to the People" that justified its action as an attempt to "exhibit to the people the momentous question, whether the Constitution of the United States shall yield to a construction which defies every restraint and overwhelms the best hopes of republicanism." Address of the General Assembly to the People of the Commonwealth of Virginia (1799), reprinted in 4 *Letters and Other Writings of James Madison* 509 (Philadelphia 1865) (hereafter cited as *Madison Letters*). In the Report of 1800, Madison, who had left Congress in March 1798 and entered the Virginia legislature in December 1799, see A. Koch, supra note 215, at 172, provided a point-by-point commentary on the 1798 Resolutions and concluded with a proposed resolution that the legislature renew its protest against the Alien and Sedition Acts. The General Assembly approved both the Report and the resolution. See Report on the Virginia Resolutions, reprinted in 4 *Madison Letters* supra, at 515, 555.

223. References in the text to "the Virginia and Kentucky Resolutions" are meant to include all three sets of resolutions as well as the Report of 1800. Debates over the proper interpretation of the Resolutions, including whether the Kentucky documents present a more extreme states' rights position than do Madison's products, have raged since the Old Republicans began their critique of the official—and in their view crypto-Federalist—Republicanism of Madison and Monroe. The argument put forward in this article does not require resolution of these issues. My primary assumption has been that the interpretation placed on the Resolutions by Jefferson and Madison should be respected. Both men maintained throughout their lives that their actions in office had been consistent with the constitutional position staked out in the Resolutions and with one another's views. See J. Madison, Notes on Nullification (1835–1836), reprinted in *Mind of the Founder*, supra note 210, at 418–42 (defending continuity of his views on nullification and the doctrines of the Resolutions, and denying difference between his and Jefferson's views on federalism); Thomas Jefferson to Edward Everett (Apr. 8, 1826), reprinted in *Political Writings*, supra note 40, at 151 (federal Constitution is "a compact of independent nations subject to the rules acknowledged in similar cases"); Thomas Jefferson to James Madison (February 17, 1826), reprinted in 10 *Writings*, supra note 152, at 375, 377 (referring to the half-century of "harmony of our political principles"); James Madison to William Eustis (May 22, 1823), reprinted in 9 *The Writings of James Madison* 135, (G. Hunt ed. 1910) (denying charge that the Republican leaders had "abandoned their Cause, and gone over to the policy of their opponents").

224. Thomas Jefferson to John Taylor (June 1, 1798) reprinted in 7 *Writings*, supra note 152, at 263, 265.

225. For discussions of the Anti-Federalist views of the union, see A. Mason, supra note 85, at 69–100, and 1 Storing, supra note 96, at 24–37.

226. References to the constitutional "compact" and to the continued "sovereignty" and "independence" of the states, as well as the notions of "interposition" and "nullification," were among the Resolutions' important contributions to antebellum constitutional rhetoric.

227. In later years Republicans often referred to the constitutional theory put forward in the Resolutions as the "doctrines of '98." See, e.g., *The Virginia and Kentucky Resolutions of 1798 and 1799* at 1 (J. Elliot ed. 1832) (hereafter cited as *Resolutions*).

228. Kentucky Resolutions of 1798 (T. Jefferson draft 1798), reprinted in *Resolutions*, supra note 227, at 61.

229. Kentucky Resolutions of 1799, reprinted in *Resolutions*, supra note 227, at 19, 20.

230. Madison's Report of 1800, reprinted in *Mind of the Founder*, supra note 210, at 231, 245–46.

231. Virginia Resolutions of 1798, reprinted in *Resolutions*, supra note 227, at 5.

232. See Kentucky Resolutions of 1798, reprinted in *Resolutions*, supra note 227, at 15–16; Madison's Report of 1800, reprinted in *Mind of the Founder*, supra note 210, at 231, 237.

233. Ironically, in light of later history, ultranationalist sentiment at the time of the Constitution's ratification was especially strong in the South Carolina convention. Responding to Anti-Federalist arguments that the link between the states existed solely on the basis of the Articles of Confederation and the ad hoc military alliance that had preceded their ratification, South Carolina Chancellor John Mathews asserted that the authority of the Continental Congress from the beginning was derived from the American people and that consequently Congress's resolutions had possessed "the force of law" quite apart from and before the approval of the Articles by the state legislatures. 4 *Debates in the Several State Conventions on the Adoption of the Federal Constitution* 298 (J. Elliot 2d ed. 1836) (remarks of John Mathews at the South Carolina convention). Charles Cotesworth Pinckney, a South Carolina delegate to the Philadelphia convention, claimed that "the separate independence and individual sovereignty of the several states were never thought of by the enlightened band of patriots who framed this Declaration [of Independence]." Id. at 300, 301 (remarks of Charles Cotesworth Pinckney at the South Carolina convention). Pinckney regarded the belief that "each state is separately and individually independent, as a species of political heresy." Id. Most Federalists, however, conceded that the articles made the United States no more than a league of sovereignties; the virtue of the Constitution, in their eyes, was that it would remedy this political anomaly. See supra pp. 904–5.

234. "'We the people of the United States,' is a sentence that evidently shows the old foundation of the union is destroyed, the principle of confederation excluded, and a new and unwieldy system of consolidated empire is set up, upon the ruins of the present compact between the states. Can this he denied? No, sir: It is artfully indeed, but it is incontrovertibly designed to abolish the independence and sovereignty of the states individually." Remarks of Robert Whitehill at the Pennsylvania Ratifying Convention (1787), quoted in A. Mason, supra note 85, at 135.

235. The most conciliatory Federalist position, and the one most familiar to modern lawyers through its incorporation in *The Federalist*, held that the Constitution preserved a residuum of state sovereignty. See *Federalist* No. 32 (A. Hamilton); *Federalist* No. 39 (J. Madison). These verbally moderate Federalists pointed to equal representation in the Senate, the limitation and enumeration of federal powers, and the states' closer links with the people as significant safeguards of state autonomy. See 1 *Elliot's Debates*, supra note 102, at 225, 230–31 (remarks of Alexander Hamilton at the New York convention); id. at 281, 282–84 (same); 2 id. at 95 (remarks of James Madison at the Virginia convention); 2 id. at 197, 203–5 (same); 3 id. at 122, 123 (remarks of James Iredell at the first North Carolina convention). Other Federalists were not willing to make even these concessions. See supra note 233. But even the most conciliatory Federalist would not and could not deny that the Constitution gave final and uncontrollable authority to the people's national organs of expression. See 1 *Elliot's Debates*, supra note 102, at 319, 321 (remarks of Alexander Hamilton at the New York convention); *Federalist* No. 39 at 194 (G. Wills ed. 1982).

236. The common Federalist position of turning aside attacks on the federal convention's authority or on the language of the Preamble by describing the Constitution as a grant of authority from the sovereign people implicitly repudiated all contractual images of the Union's fundamental law. See G. Wood, supra note 11, at 532–47. Not all Federalists were completely aware of this, however, and the resolutions were to show that the document could be read from a contractual perspective.

237. 3 *Elliot's Debates*, supra note 102, at 286–88 (remarks of James Wilson at the Pennsylvania convention).

238. The only textual hook on which to hang the ideas of state sovereignty and constitutional compact was the tenth amendment: "The powers not delegated to the United States by the Constitution nor prohibited by it to the States, are reserved to the States respectively, or to the people." U.S. Const. amend. X. How little support even that provision provided a theory of state sovereignty can be seen by comparing its text to that of the second of the Articles of Confederation, which declared: "Each State retains its sovereignty, freedom and independence, and every power, jurisdiction, and right, which is not by this confederation expressly delegated to the United States, in Congress assembled." The Tenth Amendment lacks the earlier provision's positive declaration of state autonomy and its restriction of federal powers to those "expressly" delegated. Instead the amendment notes that the Constitution denies certain powers to the states, and makes ambiguous reference to powers "reserved . . . to the people." Nineteenth-century advocates of state sovereignty bridled at the possibility that this last phrase could be construed as a reference in the constitutional text to the nationalist idea of a unitary American people, rather than a citizenry comprising the separate peoples of the several states. See 1 J. Davis, *The Rise and Fall of the Confederate Government* 158 (1881). The ambiguity was resolved by the framers of the Confederate States Constitution, who rewrote the Tenth Amendment to read: "The powers not delegated to the Confederate States by the Constitution, nor prohibited by it to the States, are reserved to the States, respectively, or to the people thereof." Confederate States Const. Art. VI, sec. 6 (emphasis added); see also id. preamble ("We, the people of the Confederate States, each State acting in its sovereign and independent character . . ."); id. Art. VI, sec. 5 (rewritten version of Ninth Amendment) ("The enumeration, in the Constitution, of certain rights, shall not be construed to deny or disparage others retained by the people *of the several States*" [emphasis added]).

239. Kentucky Resolutions of 1798, reprinted in *Resolutions*, supra note 227, at 15, 18; see also Kentucky Resolutions of 1799, reprinted in *Resolutions*, supra note 227, at 19, 20 (referring to the Constitution's "obvious and real intention").

240. Virginia Resolutions of 1798, reprinted in *Resolutions*, supra note 227, at 5.

241. See supra note 52.

242. See supra pp. 894–96, 899–900.

243. Tucker, supra note 168, note D, at 154.

244. Id.

245. See Madison's Report of 1800, reprinted in *Mind of the Founder*, supra note 210, at 231, 232–35; Thomas Jefferson to Edward Everett (April 8, 1826), reprinted in *Political Writings*, supra note 40, at 151; Tucker, supra note 168, note A, at 3–6; id. note D, at 141–46, 151–56, 170–72.

246. Many years later, Jefferson prepared a protest for possible use by the Virginia legislature as a response to the nationalist policies of the administration of John Quincy Adams. In this protest Jefferson recapitulated the history of the Revolution and of the establishment of the Constitution, describing all these events as actions, decisions, and intentions of the states. See Jefferson, The solemn Declaration and Protest of the Commonwealth of Virginia on the principles of the Constitution of the United States of America and on the violation of them (1825), reprinted in *Political Writings*, supra note 40, at 167–69. Madison, too, remained faithful to the idea that the Constitution was the creation of the states acting as sovereign communities. See James Madison to Daniel Webster (March 15, 1833), reprinted in 4 *Madison Letters*, supra note 222, at 293–94.

247. The Virginia convention, for example, included in its ratification resolution a declaration that the Constitution's powers could be resumed by "the people of the United States," 4 B. Schwartz, *The Roots of the Bill of Rights* 839 (1980), and that the Constitution did not grant the federal government power to infringe certain essential rights (specifically naming "the liberty of conscience and of the press"), id. In addition, the convention formally approved, and transmitted to Congress along with the ratification resolution, a lengthy declaration of "unalienable rights of the people" and a set of proposed amendments to the Constitution. See id. at 840–46.

248. See Virginia Resolutions of 1798, reprinted in *Resolutions*, supra note 227, at 5, 6.

249. The Virginia convention's ratification of the Constitution was embodied in a document that included not only the text of the Constitution, but also Virginia's declaration of reserved rights. Resort to the latter, therefore, was not consultation of a source of evidence extrinsic to the contract. Virginia, as it were, had exercised its powers as master of its offer to make that offer conditional on acceptance of Virginia's terms. Cf. Pinnel's Case, 5 Co. Rep. 117a, 117b, 77 Eng. Rep. 237, 238 (C.P. 1602) (discussing conditions on acceptances of contract offers). Madison does not discuss the consequences of other states' insisting on contradictory conditions, perhaps because the possibility of "final" but discordant interpretations by different states did not concern him, or perhaps because neither he nor Jefferson completely explored the implications of their contractual vision of the Constitution.

During the ratification campaign, a key issue had been the Anti-Federalist demand that the Constitution either be amended before adoption or ratified conditionally. The Federalists held out for unconditioned ratification, and successfully insisted that amendment propositions be recommendatory and explanatory only. See, e.g., B. Schwartz, *The Great Rights of Mankind* 135– 38, 144–47 (1977). Madison's implicit analysis of the proposed amendments in 1798 was therefore in partial conflict with the view he took of them in 1788. But, as noted on pp. 933– 34, Jefferson and Madison were not purporting to engage in historical research, but rather in legal analysis of the "intent" of the parties to the constitutional compact.

250. The states created the federal government, according to the Kentucky Resolutions of 1798, "by compact under the style and title of a Constitution for the United States . . . each State acced[ing] as a State." Kentucky Resolutions of 1798, reprinted in *Resolutions*, supra note 227, at 15.

251. Kentucky Resolutions of 1799, reprinted in *Resolutions*, supra note 227, at 19, 20.

252. Madison's Report of 1800, reprinted in *Mind of the Founder*, supra note 210, at 231, 234.

253. Id. at 253.

254. Thomas Jefferson to Elbridge Gerry (January 26, 1799), reprinted in *Political Writings*, supra note 40, at 47.

255. See supra pp. 929–30 (Constitution not contractual); supra note 235 (final authority under Constitution lies in federal, not state, hands).

256. Thomas Jefferson to Judge Spencer Roane (September 6, 1819), reprinted in *Political Writings*, supra note 40, at 151, 152.

257. James Madison to William Eustis (May 22, 1823), reprinted in 9 *The Writings of James*

Madison, supra note 223, at 135, 136; see Elliot, Preface to Resolutions, supra note 227, at 2 (the Resolutions "embody the principles of the old Republicans of the Jeffersonian school, the genuine disciples of the whigs of '76"). This invocation of "Whiggism" by Elliot evoked even more distant but equally hallowed memories of the struggle of free Englishmen against Stuart despotism.

258. State of Rhode Island and Providence Plantations to Virginia (1799), reprinted in *Documents*, supra note 220, at 17.

259. Report and Resolutions of Rhode Island on the Embargo (1809), reprinted in *State Documents*, supra note 220, at 42, 43–44.

260. States' rights constitutionalists of a later era looked back on the first three decades of the nineteenth century as a halcyon period of consensus on basic constitutional issues, although they recognized, of course, that there had been disagreements on particulars. See, e.g., 1 J. Davis, supra note 238, at 128–29 (the heresies of the Federalists were first revived around 1830 by Webster and Story); 1 A. Stephens, *A Constitutional View of the Late War between the States* 503–5 (1868) (Tucker's state sovereignty reading of the Constitution "was not gainsayed or controverted by any writer of distinction, that I am aware of, until Chancellor Kent's Commentaries appeared in 1826, and Story's, in 1833").

261. James Madison to Martin Van Buren (July 5, 1830), reprinted in 4 *Madison Letters*, supra note 222, at 89. In an earlier letter to Van Buren on June 3, 1830, Madison had written that he believed his own present understanding of the 1817 veto message "was the general understanding" in 1817, but conceded that "whether the language employed duly conveyed the meaning of which J.M. retains the consciousness, is a question on which he does not presume to judge for others." Madison to Martin Van Buren (June 3, 1830), reprinted in 4 *Madison Letters*, supra note 222, at 88; see also Madison to N. P. Trist (June 3, 1830), reprinted in 4 *Madison Letters*, supra note 222, at 87 (Madison again speaks of the meaning of the 1817 veto "to my consciousness," while admitting that "the entire text" of the message may have conveyed that meaning faultily).

262. Madison to Edward Livingston (July 10, 1822), reprinted in *Mind of the Founder*, supra note 210, at 338–39.

263. Madison to N. P. Trist (February 15, 1830), reprinted in 4 *Madison Letters*, supra note 222, at 61 (acknowledging distinction between "the object of the member who prepared the documents in question" and their "fair import," while asserting in that particular case the identity of the two).

264. Madison to Henry St. George Tucker (December 23, 1817), reprinted in 3 *Madison Letters*, supra note 222, at 53, 54.

265. Madison to Edward Livingston (April 17, 1824), reprinted in 3 *Madison Letters*, supra note 222, at 435, 436.

266. Madison to Thomas Ritchie (September 15, 1821), reprinted in 3 *Madison Letters*, supra note 222, at 228.

267. Madison to John Davis (c. 1832) (not posted), reprinted in 4 *Madison Letters*, supra note 222, at 232, 243–44. This letter illustrates well the variety of uses Madison could make of the rhetoric of "intention" without indicating any change or uncertainty in his basic interpretive stance: within a few paragraphs, Madison refers to "the intention of those who framed, or, rather, who adopted the Constitution"; he immediately states that the interpreter "must decide that intention by the meaning attached to the terms by the '*usus*' [governmental and judicial precedent]"; he remarks that it "need scarcely to be observed that" the intention so determined "could not be overruled by any latter meaning put on the phrase, however warranted by the grammatical rules of construction"; and he finally mentions the "intention of the parties to the Constitution" and the "intention of the States." Id. at 242–43 (emphasis omitted). The apparent inconsistency of Madison's use of the term to the modern reader is due to the fact that for Madison the word still retained its traditional common law meaning. See supra pp. 58–59.

268. See *Federalist* No. 37 (J. Madison); Madison to N. P. Trist (March 2, 1827), reprinted in 3 *Madison Letters*, supra note 222, at 565.

269. See Madison to N. P. Trist (March 2, 1827), reprinted in 3 *Madison Letters*, supra note 222, at 565; Madison to Judge Spencer Roane (September 2, 1819), reprinted in 3 *Madison Letters*, supra note 222, at 143, 145; cf. Madison to Thomas Grimké (January 15, 1828), reprinted in 3 *Madison Letters*, supra note 222, at 611 (laws are "always liable, more or less, till made technical by practice, to discordant interpretations").

270. See Madison to Judge Spencer Roane (May 6, 1821), reprinted in 3 *Madison Letters*, supra note 222, at 217, 220 (advocating structural inference about the intentions of the states); Madison to Joseph Cabell (March 22, 1827), reprinted in 3 *Madison Letters*, supra note 222, at 571–72; Madison to Andrew Stevenson (November 27, 1830), reprinted in 4 *Madison Letters*, supra note 222, at 121, 129–30 (amendments proposed by state ratifying conventions are evidence of states' intentions). Madison also made reference at times to the weaknesses in the previous federal system that the Constitution was intended by the states to correct—a combination of the intentionalism of the Resolutions and the traditional common law approach to statutory interpretation. Madison to Joseph Cabell (October 30, 1828), reprinted in 3 *Madison Letters*, supra note 222, at 648, 655.

271. See Madison to Jonathan Elliot (February 14, 1827), reprinted in 3 *Madison Letters*, supra note 222, at 552.

272. See id.; Madison to Andrew Stevenson (November 27, 1830), reprinted in 3 *Madison Letters*, supra note 222, at 121, 128 (interpreter must look for the meaning given the text "by the Conventions, or rather, by the people, who, through their Conventions, accepted and ratified" the text).

273. See Madison to H. Lee (June 25, 1824), reprinted in 3 *Madison Letters*, supra note 222, at 441, 442–43 (arguing that literal meaning of text varies as language changes); Madison to Andrew Stevenson (March 25, 1826), reprinted in 3 *Madison Letters*, supra note 222, at 520, 521–22 (noting value of "contemporary expositions"); Madison to N. P. Trist (March 2 1827), reprinted in 3 *Madison Letters*, supra note 222, at 565 (Constitution affected by the imprecision and mutability of language).

274. See Madison to Robert Garnett (February 11, 1824), reprinted in 3 *Madison Letters*, supra note 222, at 367; Madison to John Davis (c. 1832) (not posted), reprinted in 4 *Madison Letters*, supra note 222, at 232, 253–54 (noting difficulties in interpreting convention's proceedings); Madison to John Tyler (1833) (not posted), reprinted in 4 *Madison Letters*, supra note 222, at 280, 288–89 (criticizing as biased and inaccurate Robert Yates's and Luther Martin's accounts of the convention). The problem of accuracy could of course have been cured, at least to Madison's satisfaction, by publication of his journal, which he regarded as "a pretty ample view of what passed in that Assembly." Madison to Thomas Ritchie (September 15, 1821), reprinted in 3 *Madison Letters*, supra note 222, at 228.

275. 5 *Annals of Cong.* 776 (1796) (remarks of Rep. James Madison).

276. See Madison to John Jackson (December 27, 1821), reprinted in 3 *Madison Letters*, supra note 222, at 243–45.

277. See *Federalist* No. 37, at 179 (G. Wills ed. 1982) ("The use of words is to express ideas").

278. "But whatever respect may be thought due to the intention of the Convention which prepared and proposed the Constitution, as presumptive evidence of the general understanding at the time of the language used, it must be kept in mind that the only authoritative intentions were those of the people of the States, as expressed through the Conventions which ratified the Constitution." Madison to M. L. Hurlbert (May 1830), reprinted in 4 *Madison Letters*, supra note 222, at 73, 74.

In 1791, in the heat of the congressional debate over Hamilton's bank bill, Madison, like other opponents of the bill, occasionally referred to the Philadelphia convention's failure to adopt a proposal giving Congress the power to charter corporations. See 2 *Annals of Cong.* 1937–60 (1791) (remarks of Rep. James Madison). Thereafter, Madison's understanding of the task of constitutional interpretation remained remarkably consistent over a period stretching from 1796 (when he was a leader of the embattled Republican opposition that was resting its hopes on the states as a counterweight to the federal government) until the early 1830s (when, as an elder statesman, he was contributing his prestige to the support of federal authority against a states' rights challenge by self-proclaimed followers of the "doctrines of '98").

279. Madison to John Davis (c. 1832) (not posted), reprinted in 4 *Madison Letters*, supra note 222, at 232, 242.

280. See Madison to Judge Spencer Roane (September 2, 1819), reprinted in 3 *Madison Letters*, supra note 222, at 143 (a constitution's meaning, "so far as it depends on judicial interpretation," is established by "a course of particular decisions"); Madison to Joseph Cabell (Sept. 7, 1829), reprinted in 4 *Madison Letters*, supra note 222, at 45, 47 ("definitive power" to settle constitutional questions on the allocation of power between federal and state governments is lodged in federal Supreme Court).

281. Madison to John Davis (c. 1832) (not posted), reprinted in 4 *Madison Letters*, supra note 222, at 232, 249.

282. Madison also referred to this legal background in *The Federalist*. See *Federalist* No. 37, at 179 (J. Madison) (G. Wills ed. 1982).

283. In later life Madison was accused by states' rights advocates of inconsistency in his constitutional opinions—a charge that he denied. See Madison to W. C. Rives (October 21 1833), reprinted in 4 *Madison Letters*, supra note 222, at 309–10. He would admit to even the *appearance* of inconsistency only in the national bank case. See Madison to N. P. Trist (December 1831), reprinted in 4 *Madison Letters*, supra note 222, at 204, 211.

284. See A. Koch, supra note 215, at 108–10.

285. See id. at 254.

286. Madison to C. F. Haynes (February 25, 1831), reprinted in 4 *Madison Letters*, supra note 222, at 164, 165.

287. Madison to Marquis de LaFayette (November 1826), reprinted in 3 *Madison Letters*, supra note 222, at 538, 542; see also Madison to Thomas Jefferson (February 17, 1825), reprinted in 3 *Madison Letters*, supra note 222, at 483 (stating that Congress, in legislating in accordance with the Constitution, will inevitably reflect the will of the people).

For Madison, the most unequivocal exercise by the people of their power "to declare [the Constitution's] meaning" was the formal procedure of amendment or constitutional convention. See, e.g., Madison, Veto Message (March 3, 1817), 30 *Annals of Cong.* 1061 (1817) (in vetoing on constitutional grounds an internal improvements bill, Madison expressed his approval of the bill's object, "cherishing the hope" that an amendment rendering the bill constitutional would be secured). But Madison feared the unsettling effects of resorting too frequently to formal constitutional revision. See Madison to Thomas Jefferson (February 4, 1790), reprinted in 1 *Madison Letters*, supra note 222, at 503, 504. In Madison's view, the ordinary and indeed preferable mode for popular declaration of the Constitution's meaning was the deliberate construction put on it by the people's organs of government and confirmed by the acquiescence of officials and voters. See Madison to C. J. Ingersoll (June 25, 1831), reprinted in 4 *Madison Letters*, supra note 222, at 183–87.

288. Madison to C. E. Haynes (February 25, 1831), reprinted in 4 *Madison Letters*, supra note 222, at 164, 165; Madison to N. P. Trist (December 1831), reprinted in 4 *Madison Letters*, supra note 222, at 204, 211.

289. Madison to Marquis de LaFayette (November 1826), reprinted in 3 *Madison Letters*, supra note 222, at 538, 542.

290. Madison to N. P. Trist (December 1831), reprinted in 4 *Madison Letters*, supra note 222, at 204, 211. The obligation of legislator or judge henceforth was to follow the meaning as construed, and not his "solitary opinions." Madison to C. J. Ingersoll (June 25, 1831), reprinted in 4 *Madison Letters*, supra note 222, at 183, 184–86.

291. See supra note 10.

292. Madison to Judge Spencer Roane (September 2, 1819), reprinted in 3 *Madison Letters*, supra note 222, at 143, 145.

293. Letters of Helvidius No. 4 (1793) reprinted in *Mind of the Founder*, supra note 210, at 209, 210; see also Madison to James Monroe (December 27, 1817), reprinted in 3 *Madison Letters*, supra note 222, at 54, 56 ("Serious danger seems to be threatened to the genuine sense of the Constitution . . . by an unwarrantable latitude of construction"); Madison to Joseph Cabell (September 18, 1828) (Published with Madison's approval in the *Washington National Intelligencer* in December 1828), reprinted in *Mind of the Founder* supra note 210, at 370, 375 (contrasting congressional power to enact a protective tariff, sanctioned by forty years' exercise, with a "novel construction however ingeniously devised"). Madison's reluctance to categorize a constitutional development as sufficiently erroneous to warrant resistance was based in part on his belief that interpretation is only partially "objective." See, e.g., 5 *Annals of Cong.* 494 (1796) (remarks of Rep. James Madison) (acknowledging that "no construction" can be "perfectly free from difficulties," but recommending his own as "subject to the least").

294. Madison's view of interpretation is exemplified in his warning to one correspondent that "some care in discussing the question of a distinction between literal and constructive meanings may be necessary in order to avoid the danger of a verbal character to the discussion." Madison to N. P. Trist (March 1, 1829), reprinted in 4 *Madison Letters*, supra note 222, at 16, 17. For Madison, the (legitimate) "constructive" meaning of the Constitution is no less that instrument's "intention" than is the "literal"; and indeed the former may be the legally appropriate "intention" in the event of a conflict. Madison did not deny that some constructions of the Constitution would so transform the nature of the federal compact that nothing less than a formal exercise of the amending power could justify them, but in his view such a case would be "of a character [so] exorbitant and ruinous" as to justify revolution. See Madison to Joseph Cabell (October 30, 1828), reprinted in *Mind of the Founder*, supra note 210, at 380, 387; J. Madison, Notes On Nullification (1835–36) id. at 417, 418. Madison himself was confident that "the barrier" against any such usurpation was now "happily too strong in the text of the Instrument, in the uniformity of official construction, and in the maturity of public opinion, to be successfully assailed." Madison to C. J. Ingersoll (November 27, 1827), reprinted in 3 *Madison Letters*, supra note 222, at 601.

295. See, e.g., Marshall, A Friend to the Union, *Philadelphia Union*, April 24, 1819, reprinted in *John Marshall's Defense*, supra note 46, at 78, 87–91 (denying difference between his views in McCulloch v. Maryland and Madison's in the Report of 1800).

296. After 1811 only two Justices (Marshall and Bushrod Washington) were Federalists.

297. Joseph Story to Stephen White (March 3, 1819), reprinted in 1 W. Story, *Life and Letters of Joseph Story* 325 (1851); cf. John Marshall to Joseph Story (July 31, 1833), reprinted in 2 W. Story, supra, at 135 (describing states' rights views as "political metaphysics").

298. 6 U.S. (2 Cranch) 358 (1805).

299. Act of April 4, 1800, ch. 19, sec. 62, 2 Stat. 19, 36.

300. Fisher, 6 U.S. (2 Cranch) at 386.

301. Id. at 389.

302. Id. at 368, 372.

303. See id. at 368, 372–73.

304. See id. at 374–75.

305. See id. at 368–69.

306. See id. at 387–89.

307. Marshall, A Friend of the Constitution, *Alexandria Gazette*, July 2, 1819, reprinted in *John Marshall's Defense*, supra note 46, at 155, 168–69. Like earlier common lawyers, and like Madison, see supra note 267, Marshall could refer to the "intention of the framers", or of "those who gave these powers," McCulloch v. Maryland, 17 U.S. (4 Wheat.) 316, 415 (1819), without thereby implying that he was relying on any extratextual evidence of that intention. Marshall shared Madison's view that the Philadelphia framers were merely drafters whose views were not binding. See id. at 403; see also 1 J. Story, supra, note 56, at 383 (assessing "intention," in the words of Blackstone, from "the words, the context, the subject-matter, the effects and consequence, or the reason and spirit of the law").

308. Trustees of Dartmouth College v. Woodward, 17 U.S. (4 Wheat.) 518, 644–45 (1819); cf. Marshall, A Friend to the Union, *Philadelphia Union*, April 28, 1819, reprinted in *John Marshall's Defense*, supra note 46, at 78, 102–3 (necessary and proper means may be unforeseeable by framers).

309. Gibbons v. Ogden, 22 U.S. (9 Wheat.) 1, 188–89 (1824) (Marshall, C.J.); cf. Martin v. Hunter's Lessee, 14 U.S. (1 Wheat.) 304, 326 (1816) (Story, J.) (Constitution should receive a "reasonable construction, according to the import of its terms"); Satterlee v. Matthewson, 27 U.S. (2 Pet.) 38, 414–16 (1829) (Johnson, J., concurring) (insisting that a literal reading of the ex post facto clause correctly construes what "the Constitution most clearly intended").

310. See 1 J. Kent, *Commentaries on American Law* 242 n. a (3d ed. New York 1836) (1st ed. New York 1826) (commending Marshall and Story for their allegiance to text and precedent); 1 J. Story, supra note 56, at 392.

311. See supra note 260.

312. Federalist delegates from the New England states convened in Hartford in December 1814 and January 1815 to discuss means of opposing the unpopular war measures of the Republican administration. Among the convention's resolutions, which were approved only by the legislatures of Massachusetts and Connecticut and were rejected by nine other states, were a series of amendments to the Constitution designed to enhance New England's influence on national affairs and check the power of the federal government. An additional resolution—that the New England states should meet again in June if their reforms were not achieved—was widely interpreted as a threat of secession, but was mooted by the news of peace. See Resolutions Adopted by the Hartford Convention (1815), reprinted in *State Documents*, supra note 220, at 83, 85; Reply of the Legislature of New Jersey (1815), reprinted id. at 86 (condemning the resolutions); Extract from the Reply of the Legislature of New York (1815), reprinted id. at 87 (same).

313. During the nullification crisis, New England nationalist Nathan Dane wrote: "*States rights* and *state sovereignty*, are expressions coined for party purposes, often by minorities, who happen to be dissatisfied with the measures of the General Government, and as they are afterwards used, they produce only state delusion. In this business each large minority has had its turn." 9 N. Dane, *General Abridgment and Digest of American Law* app. 32–33 (Boston 1829).

314. See A. Schlesinger, *The Age of Jackson* 18–29 (1946).

315. The Resolutions, to be sure, did presuppose a simple and stylized model of American history in which separate, semi-sovereign colonies threw off the British yoke to become fully sovereign republics that subsequently linked themselves in a confederation through a compact. The final stage in American constitutional development was the renegotiation of the contract in 1787 through 1790. This static picture of "history," however, did not depend on any particular historical research and was not subject to revision. It was taken as a first principle.

316. See, e.g., P. Atiyah, supra note 75, at 459.

317. See J. Higham, *History* 69 (1965).

318. See Ordinance of Nullification of South Carolina (1832), reprinted in *State Documents*, supra note 220, at 169.

319. In early 1833 Congress passed both an act empowering the President to use federal power to collect the tariff, Act of March 2, 1833, ch. 57, 4 Stat. 632, and a compromise tariff act, Act of March 2, 1833, ch. 55, 4 Stat. 629, which alleviated the South Carolinians' economic objections to the "tariff of abominations." South Carolina, in convention, then repealed its repudiation of federal tariff laws and nullified the Force Act. See South Carolina's Final Action (1833), reprinted in *State Documents*, supra note 220, at 188. Both sides having saved face, the crisis subsided. See A. Schlesinger, supra note 314, at 94–97.

320. Webster and Story were friends as well as political allies, and some believe that the latter's hand can be seen in Webster's famous speeches against the compact theory on the Senate floor. See 2 V. Parrington, *Main Currents in American Thought: The Romantic Revolution in America* 300 (1927).

321. See 1 J. Story, supra note 56, at 344–75.

322. Calhoun, although originally a nationalist, secretly authored some of the early justifications of nullification adopted by South Carolina during the crisis. An open advocate of South Carolina's position by 1830, Calhoun was quickly recognized as the most powerful thinker on the states' rights side of the dispute, and Jonathan Elliot included extracts from two of his addresses in his 1832 collection of the canon of "documents in support of the Jeffersonian Doctrines of '98." See *Resolutions*, supra note 227, at 41.

323. Interestingly both Story and Calhoun avoided the "original intention" terminology for the most part—the former because of his textualism and regard for precedent, see infra note 325, the latter because of his almost pure "intentionalism" in the original sense; see Calhoun, Fort Hill Address (1831), reprinted in 6 *The Works of John C. Calhoun*, supra note 211, at 59, 60–61.

324. A. Upshur, *A Brief Enquiry into the True Nature and Character of our Federal Government* (Petersburg 1840).

325. In his treatise, Justice Story criticized states' rights constitutionalists on substantive and hermeneutical grounds. Responding to the emergence of modern intentionalism, Story roundly attacked the notion that historical evidence from the framing and ratification process could determine the Constitution's meaning. Such evidence, he thought, can reveal only "the private interpretation of any particular man, or body of men"—an interpretation that others have no reason to accept. 1 J. Story, supra note 56, at 388. The people sanctioned not the debates of the various conventions, but the text only. See id. at 389 ("Nothing but the text itself was adopted by the people"). See also id. at 388–90 (attacking use of "legislative history in constitutional interpretation). Story contended that constitutional interpretation, like statutory construction, is a matter of construing the text "according to its fair intent and objects, as disclosed in its language," and not of arguing over the "probable meaning" of the personal intentions of historical actors. Id. at 390 n. 1.

Story's brilliant polemic against the modern form of intentionalism (which he ascribes to Jefferson) attacks it not only on evidentiary, but also on theoretical grounds (it elevates private views over the expressed will of the public). The one striking deviation from this strongly textualist approach during the Marshall years was Chief Justice Marshall's opinion in Barron v. Mayor of Baltimore, 32 U.S. (7 Pet.) 243 (1833). Barron sued the city of Baltimore for violating his Fifth Amendment right to receive just compensation for a public taking of his property. Despite the open-ended character of the amendment's text, which had led some commentators to suggest that it applied to state as well as federal action, see, e.g., W. Rawle, *A View of the Constitution* 120–21, 129–30 (1825), a unanimous Court limited the amendment's scope to federal takings, at least partly because the "universally understood . . . history of the day" showed that the amendments were not intended to apply to the states. 32 U.S. (7 Pet.) at 250.

326. See, e.g., A. Upshur, supra note 324, at 58, 71 (describing his constitutionalism as based on political theory, without referring to "intent").

327. Id. at 94. Upshur never discusses the possibility that the framers' intentions might conflict with his political theory.

328. See, e.g., id. at 51–53 (using history of the proceedings of the Philadelphia convention to establish the meaning of the Preamble).

329. Address of Jefferson Davis at Montgomery, Alabama (February 18, 1861), reprinted in 9 *Annals of America* 238, 240–41 (1968).

330. Cong. Globe, 39th Cong., 1st Sess. 677 (1866).

331. To be faithful to the interpretive intentions of the generation of the framers, the modern intentionalist would have to abandon his or her intentionalism and adopt the common law view of the "intention" of a statute, or disavow the legitimacy of any extratextual interpretation in the manner of the antihermeneutical traditions of British Protestantism and European rationalism, or accept the substantive constitutional doctrines of compact and state sovereignty that grew out of the original intentionalism of the Virginia and Kentucky Resolutions.

The Original Understanding
of Original Intent?

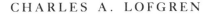

CHARLES A. LOFGREN

THE ATTORNEY GENERAL of the United States, Edwin Meese, has called for a "jurisprudence of original intention." In response, Justice William J. Brennan decries "facile historicism."[1] Whichever way the debate goes in its current phase, judges will continue to invoke original intent, legal scholars will evaluate the resulting judicial handiwork, and historians will criticize everyone's answers. But the basic issue will persist: what is the proper role for original intent in constitutional interpretation?

The issue may be considered on its own terms. This is the approach taken by Professor H. Jefferson Powell in an article that has attracted significant attention. What, Powell asks, was "the original understanding of original intent"?[2] In this article, I unabashedly appropriate Powell's central question. My purpose is to offer another reading of major chunks of the evidence that Professor Powell himself cites, although in the following pages I occasionally stray to other materials as well.

As a preliminary matter, it is important to observe that asking about the interpretive status of original intent implicates another issue: whose intent qualifies as the "original" intent? Without having systematically counted instances, I strongly sense that the disputants in the current fray overwhelmingly focus on "framer intent" to the exclusion of "ratifier intent."[3] To be sure, the emphasis is not always left unexplained. After conceding that "the intention of the ratifiers, not the Framers, is in principle decisive," Henry P. Monaghan has remarked that "the difficulties of ascertaining the intent of the ratifiers leave little choice but to accept the intent of the Framers as a fair reflection of it."[4] Sometimes, too, the label "framer" is used in a broad sense. When Justice William Rehnquist spoke in 1976 about "the framers" and about "reading the record of the Founding Fathers' debates in Philadelphia," he at least briefly mentioned the ratification debates.[5] Critics of a jurisprudence of original intention have also noted the ratifiers' role. Justice Brennan did so in order to underscore the difficulty of determining an original intent.[6] Paul Brest lumps the framers and ratifiers together under the label of "ratifiers," and then employs the collective term in the course of attacking "originalism" and "intentionalism."[7]

In truth, the questions of original intent's interpretive status and the identity of the originators are closely intertwined. Justice Brennan's remark indicates one connection: ambiguity concerning the identity of the originators lessens the force of arguments based on their understandings and expectations. Another consideration is that equating original intent exclusively or primarily with framer intent (or, alternatively, with ratifier intent), or merging framer intent and ratifier intent, may adversely affect the interpretive status of original intent, depending on whether one form of intent proves an easier target than the other. The close connection between the two issues is especially apparent when one asks about the original understanding of original intent. Who were the originators whose understandings about original intent are of interest? What might seem to be a subsidiary issue—the originators' identity—thus emerges as an integral part of the overall problem.

A second preliminary involves word usage. "Intent" is not the term that I as a historian (or, I suspect, most historians) would have chosen to use in the context of the present debate. "Understanding" or "expectation" (or the respective plurals) might better describe the subject of interest, as the title of Professor Powell's article itself suggests. But "intent" has emerged as a term of legal art, and so I use it (though not invariably) where I might not otherwise.

Finally, a preview and preemptive clarification: I argue that although the originators rejected the use of framer intent, they did not thereby envisage that constitutional interpretation would exclude consideration of original intent. Instead, they were clearly hospitable to the use of original intent in the sense of ratifier intent, which is *the* original intent in a constitutional sense.[8] In bold outline, this is not far from Professor Powell's conclusion; but in important respects he either obscures or distorts the answer.[9] In any event, as a historian dabbling in a present-day controversy I fully appreciate his disclaimer: "I am . . . unconcerned in this Article with what contemporary interpreters should do. . . ."[10] Yet, just as Professor Powell admits that his conclusions carry implications for the current debate, so perhaps do mine.

I. Framers, Ratifiers, and Framer Intent

THE MEMBERS of the Philadelphia Convention were silent about how they expected the Constitution to be interpreted. Noting the silence, Professor

Powell contends that they assumed their handiwork would be construed according to then-prevalent common-law canons of statutory interpretation. The common-law tradition, Powell demonstrates, allowed interpreters to go beyond literal words in order to clarify ambiguity, resolve apparent contradictions, cover unforeseen circumstances, and the like, all with the goal of effectuating broad purposes. With respect to statutory interpretation specifically, it permitted reference to "intent," but in a sense which was quite different from that employed by modern "intentionalists." Rather than resorting to legislative history, the common-law courts inferred intent from the text itself, taken against the statute's common-law background and its ongoing judicial application. In twentieth-century terms, common-law judges employed "objective" or "constructive" intent rather than "subjective" or "historical" intent.[11]

The extant records of the Philadelphia debates contain no explicit remarks on what may be called the framers' "interpretive intent." Professor Powell infers, however, that the framers assumed that the Constitution would be interpreted *exclusively* according to common-law canons. He relies on their attempts to refine the Constitution's language. These, he argues, reveal a realization that the instrument's precise wording would matter, just as in the case of statutes. In the course of several exchanges, the framers also recognized that interpretation could occur through construction.

Whether such evidence warrants the inference of exclusivity is problematical. For one thing, Professor Powell's reading of some of his sources is doubtful,[12] although the result, if not particularly reassuring, is not positively harmful to his argument. More telling, a desire for clarity in language is not antithetical to recognition that future interpreters might resort to subjective or historical intent to clarify any remaining obscurities. The delegates' concern about the scope of a ban on ex post facto laws indicates that they realized their own intentions would not *necessarily* control future interpretations[13] but that hardly clinches the point. Also, if I understand it correctly, a part of Professor Powell's argument has a circular quality. The framers' failure to endorse explicitly the use of subjective intent, he seems to say, shows that they accepted common-law approaches to construction, which in turn indicates that they rejected subjective intent as a guide to subsequent constitutional interpretation.[14]

Finally, a somewhat different conclusion from Powell's can be squeezed from one bit of evidence that he (like others) relies on.[15] The episode in question is the Convention's decision to keep its journals secret. Professor Powell comments that "there is no indication that [the framers] expected or intended future interpreters to refer to any extratextual intentions revealed in the convention's secretly conducted debates."[16] The only related comments in Madison's notes are these:

> Mr. King suggested that the Journals of the Convention should be
> either destroyed, or deposited in the custody of the President [of the

Convention]. He thought if suffered to be made public, a bad use
would be made of them by those who would wish to prevent the
adoption of the Constitution[.]

   Mr. Wilson prefered [sic] the second expedient. [H]e had at one
time liked the first best; but as false suggestions may be propagated it
should not be made impossible to contradict them[.]

The Convention then voted, ten states against one, to entrust the journals to
the Convention's president, George Washington, and, after a query by Washington, further resolved (unanimously) that Washington should hold the journals "subject to the order of Congress, if ever formed under the Constitution."[17]

   This episode indicates that the delegates intended that the journals not be
made public during the ratification debates. They probably feared that publication would *politically* complicate the task of gaining the requisite approval
by state conventions. (Perhaps they surmised that general knowledge of the
disagreements that emerged during the Philadelphia meeting would lead to
questions about the wisdom of various provisions.) They *may* also have feared
that knowledge of the Convention's debates (or at least of its motions and
votes, which is about all the journals contain) would influence interpretations
of the meaning of the completed document during the ratification process,
although this is not an obvious gloss on King's and Wilson's remarks.
Whether the framers thought it important to keep the journals secret from
post-ratification interpreters is even less certain from this scrap of evidence.
But grant that the debate and decision to entrust the journals to General
Washington show an intent to keep their content from entering into future
interpretations of the Constitution. This strongly hints that the delegates
feared that if the journals were published, they could affect subsequent interpretation. Put differently, the delegates understood that even if common-
law hermeneutics eschewed the use of subjective intent and legislative history
in statutory interpretation, Americans might still resort to such sources in
interpreting the Constitution.[18] It thus becomes problematic to say that the
delegates had *no* expectations that future interpreters would turn to "any
extratextual intentions revealed in the convention's secretly conducted debates."

   A solid reason nonetheless exists for concluding that the framers intended
that the Convention's proceedings *should* not enter into future interpretation.
But the reason does not run against the use of *ratifier* intent.

   The original Virginia Plan, submitted by Edmund Randolph on May 29,
provided for ratification by state conventions "expressly chosen by the people, to consider & decide" upon the Constitution.[19] This arrangement was
included in the final document in Article VII, but not without debate over
the alternative of ratification by state legislatures. In part the decision turned
on the expectation that conventions chosen specifically to consider the Con-

stitution were more likely than state legislatures to approve the document. More important, legislative ratification would give the Constitution only treaty status—that is, morally binding, but legally subject within individual states to subsequent legislative action.[20] As Madison expressed it, "the most unexceptionable form" of ratification was "by the supreme authority of the people themselves." Rufus King saw "a reference to the authority of the people expressly delegated to [state] Conventions, as the most certain means of obviating all disputes & doubts concerning the legitimacy of the new Constitution."[21]

Although the idea of a constitution drawing its legal force from the people may seem commonplace today, it was a relatively new notion in 1787. An advocate of legislative ratification, Oliver Ellsworth, "observed that a new sett [sic] of ideas seemed to have crept in since the articles of Confederation were established. Conventions of the people, or with power derived expressly from the people, were not then thought of."[22] Ratification by conventions provided a way around the shoal of indivisible sovereignty, that potent abstraction of eighteenth-century political-constitutional thought which had helped sink the first British Empire and threatened to scuttle a two-tiered governmental system in the United States. Recognition of the people as the political sovereign obviated the objection that coexisting state and central governments embodied the solecism of divided sovereignty, of *imperium in imperio*. Premised on popular sovereignty, convention ratification also comported with both the logic of the decision for independence and trends in state constitution making in the 1780s.[23]

During the Philadelphia Convention, explanations of this position did not display the fullness and clarity that they soon would. Still, the debates in Philadelphia over ratification by state conventions, when taken in the context of shifting thinking on the true nature of constitutional authority, provide the most persuasive basis for concluding that the framers themselves did not envisage framer intent as properly having a role in subsequent constitutional interpretation. Although they were the originators of the Constitution in an indubitable sense, the framers recognized that they were not the original source of the legal authority that the instrument might come to possess. Confronted with wide-ranging public opposition when the Constitution came before the state ratifying conventions, its supporters refined their explanations of the document's source. When the Antifederalists charged that the Philadelphia Convention had exceeded its powers in elaborating a dangerous new compact between rulers and the ruled, Federalists responded that the Convention had simply *proposed* a constitution. The instrument would become binding only when it received the approbation of the people. Defending the Constitution in Pennsylvania in December 1787, James Wilson explained:

> The late Convention have done nothing beyond their powers. The fact is they have exercised no power at all. And in point of validity, this

Constitution proposed by them for the government of the United
States, claims no more than a production of the same nature would
claim, flowing from a private pen. It is laid before the citizens of the
United States, unfettered by restraint; it is laid before them to be
judged by the natural, civil, and political rights of men. By their FIAT,
it will become of value and authority; without it, it will never receive
the character of authenticity and power.[24]

The following month, James Madison in *Federalist* No. 39 elaborated his
partly federal–partly national analysis of the Constitution, which diverged
from Wilson's straightforward assignment of sovereignty to the people of the
United States.[25] Yet, in *Federalist* No. 40, Madison substantially agreed with
Wilson on the place of the Philadelphia Convention itself in the constitutional
process, writing: "It is time now to recollect, that the powers [of the Conven-
tion] were merely advisory and recommendatory; that they were so meant by
the States, and so understood by the Convention; and that the latter have
accordingly planned and proposed a Constitution which is to be of no more
consequence than the paper on which it is written, unless it be stamped with
the approbation of those to whom it is addressed."[26]

In mid-1788, North Carolina Federalists illustrated the pervasiveness of the
argument. Challenged to explain how the Philadelphia Convention could appropriate the phrase "We, the People," William R. Davie, who had attended
the 1787 meeting, paraphrased Wilson: "The act of the Convention is but a
mere proposal, similar to the production of a private pen." "If the people
approve of it," added Archibald Maclaine, "it becomes their act. . . . When
that is done here, is it not the people of the state of North Carolina that do
it, joined with the people of the other states who have adopted it?"[27]

Such a defense of the Constitution again left no place for *framer* intent as
an authoritative guide to interpretation. The framers assuredly gave the document its words; they did not determine the meaning of those words as understood by the ratifiers, by those people whose views were crucial to legitimating the document as fundamental law. Indeed, even if the proceedings of
the Philadelphia Convention had been available to the ratifiers, the explanations of the Constitution's supporters regarding the Convention's role would
have precluded the founders, framers and ratifiers alike, from giving dispositive weight to the framers' intentions as an interpretive guide.

Yet the same explanations and defenses of the Constitution cast substantial
doubt on the conclusion that the founders, as they refined their thinking,
took their interpretive bearings solely from then-prevalent canons of common-law interpretation. To have done so would have required them to view
the Constitution as, or to analogize it to, a conventional legal document.
What became increasingly apparent, however, was that the Constitution
was fundamentally different; it was not a statute, but rather elaborated
a new system of government which rested crucially on the sovereignty of
the people.

Framer intent is at best a straw man in the argument over the interpretive intent of the founders. Can the same be said about ratifier intent?

II. The Ratifiers on Ratifier Intent

COMMENTS MADE DURING the ratification proceedings, both in the state conventions themselves and in the accompanying public debate, provide a less-than-direct answer to what the Constitution's proponents positively understood to be guides to constitutional interpretation. In surveying available clues, Professor Powell is, I readily concede, partly on target.

The Federalists sought to give the instrument a reasonable construction. They paid close attention to its words. They examined it in light of its purposes and the deficiencies it was designed to remedy; they analyzed its structure and harmonized its parts. Consistent with the common-law notion that meaning might flow from a series of decisions, Madison seemed to imply, in *Federalist* No. 37, that some aspects of the document's division of authority between the state and central governments would only be determined by future adjudication.[28] Drawing even more attention from Professor Powell is the attack mounted against judicial construction by the Antifederalist "Brutus," along with Alexander Hamilton's response in *Federalist* Nos. 78-83. According to Brutus, constructive interpretation of the Constitution was sure to render the judiciary supreme over the legislature, to extend national power generally, to effect "an entire subversion of the legislative, executive and judicial powers of the individual states," and to intimidate and beggar the citizenry.[29] Hamilton then "offered the most coherent Federalist rebuttal of the arguments of 'Brutus,'" as Professor Powell accurately observes. In the process, Hamilton treated the Constitution as a "quasi-statute, a command from a legal superior to those under its authority," open to interpretation through application of common sense.[30]

In the remarks of both Madison and Hamilton, Professor Powell discovers the endorsement of common-law hermeneutics. The key passage from Madison reads as follows: "All new laws, though penned with the greatest technical skill, and passed on the fullest and most mature deliberation, are considered as more or less obscure and equivocal, until their meanings be liquidated and ascertained by a series of particular discussions and adjudications."[31] Powell explains that "Madison's argument, which Hamilton had anticipated in *Federalist* No. 22, was of course a restatement in somewhat abstract terms of the old common law assumption, shared by the Philadelphia framers, that the 'intent' of any legal document is the product of the interpretive process and not some fixed meaning that the author locks into the document's text at the outset."[32]

This seems an overstatement. Madison was not yet focusing on the problem of interpreting the Constitution; instead, he was providing a transition from Publius's discussion of the weaknesses of the Confederation and the general requirements of good government, to the actual provisions of the document itself. The context of the quoted passage from Madison was a plea to Americans to realize the difficulty any drafters would face in committing to writing the proper delineation of federal and state jurisdiction. The passage itself says nothing about *how* future interpreters would give the Constitution its meaning.[33] Contrary to Professor Powell's gloss, moreover, the framers in Philadelphia had not already evinced an exclusive commitment to common-law approaches as a guide to constitutional interpretation, and in fact had given some evidence that they positively understood that Americans would resort to subjective intent if the requisite evidence were available.[34] Nor had a commitment to common-law approaches to *constitutional* interpretation appeared in *Federalist* No. 22.[35]

Regarding Hamilton, Professor Powell finds that while rejecting Brutus's portrayal of the document as a plan that was sure to lead to tyranny, he "accepted the validity of the common law's hermeneutical techniques as means to discovering a document's 'intent.'" In particular, in *Federalist* Nos. 78–83 "[h]e steadfastly reiterated *The Federalist*'s earlier claims that it was appropriate and necessary for the courts to 'liquidate and fix [the] meaning and operation' of laws, including the Constitution."[36] As explained above, however, the proposition that Publius had earlier advanced claims of this sort respecting interpretation of the Constitution needs careful qualification.

In any event, Hamilton did not specifically write in *Federalist* No. 78 that courts would have to "liquidate and fix [the] meaning and operation" of the Constitution. The quoted phrase instead appears in Hamilton's discussion of the way courts deal with conflicting statutes. If it proved impossible to harmonize them, then the judges gave effect to the most recent. "But this," wrote Hamilton, "is a mere rule of construction, not derived from any positive law, but from the nature and reason of the thing."[37] In the case of conflict between a law and a constitutional provision, however, "the nature and reason of the thing indicate the converse of that rule as proper to be followed. They teach us that the prior act of a superior ought to be preferred to the subsequent act of an inferior and subordinate authority; and that, accordingly, whenever a particular statute contravenes the constitution, it will be the duty of judicial tribunals to adhere to the latter and disregard the former." He had already provided the reason for the rule: "There is no position which depends on clearer principles, than that every act of a delegated authority, contrary to the tenor of the commission under which it is exercised, is void."[38]

In other words, Hamilton's argument in No. 78 did not address the question of *how* judges should interpret constitutional provisions, but rather stressed "that where the will of the legislature declared in its statutes, stands in opposition to that of the people declared in the constitution, the judges ought to be governed by the latter, rather than the former. They ought to regulate their decisions by the fundamental laws, rather than by those which are not fundamental."[39] Hamilton thus defended constitutional supremacy rather than judicial supremacy or judicial review. His object was to deflect Brutus's argument that the Constitution would produce judicial supremacy through constitutional construction by the courts.[40]

Hamilton did concede that the courts would necessarily have to determine the meaning of the Constitution. "The interpretation of the laws is the proper and peculiar province of the courts," he wrote. "A constitution is in fact, and must be, regarded by the judges as a fundamental law. It therefore belongs to them to ascertain its meaning as well as the meaning of any particular act proceeding from the legislative body."[41] But he deemphasized the likelihood that interpretation of the Constitution would involve intricate construction. The courts would declare void "all acts contrary to the *manifest* tenor of the constitution." "If there should happen to be an *irreconcilable* variance between the two [that is, the Constitution and a law], that which has the superior obligation and validity ought of course to be preferred."[42]

One might argue, of course, that a little interpretation is still interpretation, and that, alas, construction is construction. Hamilton nonetheless rejected exclusive use of technical common-law rules. The pertinent text is *Federalist* No. 83. There Hamilton described Antifederalist attacks on the Constitution's treatment of jury trials: "The maxims on which [the Antifederalists] rely are of this nature: 'a specification of particulars is an exclusion of generals'; or, 'the expression of one thing is the exclusion of another.' Hence, say they, as the constitution has established the trial by jury in criminal cases, and is silent in respect to civil, this silence is an implied prohibition of trial by jury in regard to the latter." Countering that "[t]he rules of legal interpretation are rules of common sense," Hamilton explained how reason and common sense ran against the Antifederalists' application of common-law rules to the jury trial issue. Then came a significant addendum: "Even if these maxims had a precise technical sense, corresponding with the ideas of those who employ them upon the present occasion, which however, is not the case, they would still be inapplicable to a constitution of government. In relation to such a subject, the natural and obvious sense of its provisions, *apart from any technical rules*, is the true criterion of construction."[43]

Hamilton undoubtedly had his private views about constitutional interpretation, but it was Hamilton as Publius who entered the public debate in the judicial numbers of *The Federalist*. That the latter Hamilton—the public Hamilton—observed a difference between techniques of constitutional interpretation and the ordinary or technical business of courts is further underscored by juxtaposing the defense in *Federalist* No. 78 of life tenure for judges with the foregoing remarks from No. 83. Judges needed to "be bound down by strict rules and precedents"; and that, combined with the "voluminous code of laws [which] is one of the inconveniences necessarily connected with the advantages of a free government," made life tenure necessary to ensure the requisite judicial experience and expertise. But elaborate education in the "artificial reason" of the law, to use Sir Edward Coke's revealing phrase, would be superfluous in constitutional interpretation, for "the natural and obvious sense of [the Constitution's] provisions, apart from any technical rules, is the true criterion of [its] construction."[44] As part of their professional training, that is, judges might imbibe the canons of statutory construction, which eschewed resort to subjective intent, as disclosed for example in legislative history; but by implication from Hamilton's expressed view, a key question in interpreting the *Constitution* becomes whether common sense and reason would direct attention to ratifier intent in order to determine the "will . . . of the people declared in the Constitution."[45]

In elaborating the ratifiers' reliance on common-law hermeneutics (including eschewal of subjective intent) in constitutional interpretation, Professor Powell arguably misreads or overextends still other pieces of evidence from the ratification controversy.[46] While it quickly becomes tedious to dissect citations, examination of several of his sources suggests the scope of the problem.

One reference is to a remark by John Jay in the New York Convention. Powell writes: "As John Jay explained, Federalist statements of the document's meaning were not products of a suspect hermeneutical process; they involved 'no sophistry; no construction; no false glosses, but simple inferences from the obvious operation of things.' "[47] In fact, in the debate in question, Jay was not discussing the Constitution's meaning or interpretation. "I argue from plain facts," he protested, and in that he was correct, for he took the Constitution to mean what surely no one contested, namely, that it established a bicameral legislature. The point in dispute was rather how the new Congress would operate, given its bicameral arrangement. Jay claimed—and this was his referent in saying, "Here is no sophistry, no construction, no false glosses, but simple inferences from the obvious operation of things"— that the two-house Congress would turn out vastly more difficult to corrupt than the Confederation Congress had proved to be.[48]

Or take this description by Professor Powell of the Federalists' interpretive intent: "When interpretation was necessary, it would take place in accord with the rules of 'universal jurisprudence,' subject to correction by the amendment process provided for in Article V."[49] Two of the citations in the accompanying footnote are particularly troublesome. One reference is to John Steele in the North Carolina Convention. Antifederalists had charged that congressional control over the manner of elections to the House of Representatives would extend to setting the qualifications of voters. Steele countered that the clause in question had to be read in light of the constitutional requirement that qualifications for electors of congressmen correspond to the qualifications for electors of the most numerous branch of the state legislature. He asked, "Is it not a maxim of universal jurisprudence, of reason and common sense, that an instrument or deed of writing shall be so construed as to give validity to all parts of it, if it can be done without involving absurdity?" He added: "By construing it [the Constitution] in the plain, obvious way I have mentioned, all parts will be valid."[50] This may indicate the influence of common-law canons of interpretation, although the reference to "universal jurisprudence" suggests a broader referent, but the comment hardly establishes a restriction running against resort to historical intent in appropriate cases.

In support of the same statement, Professor Powell also cites comments by Edmund Randolph in Virginia. Randolph, who now supported ratification after flip-flopping on the issue, allowed that Federalist reassurances regarding the necessary-and-proper clause were overly sanguine. Taken alone, the clause was an ambiguous provision that squinted toward consolidated government at the expense of the states. Yet when viewed in context, it did not subvert the principle of limited government, for otherwise the enumeration of which it was a part would be superfluous. Randolph would have preferred more careful drafting, but to disapprove the Constitution because of a few defective parts risked "the anarchy which must happen if no energetic government be established." In any event, he conceived "no danger." The vigilance of state governments in choosing senators constituted one barrier. "I trust that the members of Congress themselves will explain the ambiguous parts," he continued, "and if not, the states can combine in order to insist on amending the ambiguities. I would depend on the present actual feeling of the people of America, to introduce any amendment which may be necessary."[51]

Embedded in Randolph's remarks is a striking conclusion. To spot it, one must recognize that Randolph here looked to mechanisms other than judicial review to ensure constitutional purity. One of these was the amendment process. Through it, he argued, the Constitution guaranteed that if the ambiguities of the document were not resolved in accordance with "the present actual feeling of the people of America," then the people themselves could achieve that end. This was not a bad formulation of the idea of taking guidance from ratifier intent, considering that the phrase itself was not then a term of constitutional art. At a minimum, anyway, Randolph's comments, like Steele's in North Carolina, do not indicate endorsement of common-law hermeneutics to the exclusion of original intent in the sense of subjective ratifier intent.

Finally, there is an intriguing episode that Professor Powell does not examine. At the beginning of the ratification process, the Federalists held a clear majority in the Pennsylvania Convention. Sensing defeat and seeking ways to salvage something from the situation, their opponents tried unsuccessfully to enter their objections to various provisions into the meeting's journal. One of the Federalists speaking against the insertion of objections was Dr. Benjamin Rush, who argued that to do so would obscure and confuse the record, which was "stamped with authenticity."[52]

Like the Philadelphia Convention's decision to keep its journals at least temporarily secret, the episode is open to varying interpretations. The Federalists may have feared that to publish the Antifederalist objections in the official journal would give them greater weight in other states (a view made more realistic in light of the Pennsylvania Antifederalists' powerful critique of the Constitution). Or they may have feared a lessening of popular attachment to the new government once it went into operation. These other readings of the brief exchange are possible, but the debate suggests, I think, at least some sense on the part of the Pennsylvanians that the record of the ratification process might help to shape future understandings. As Robert Whitehill put it while arguing for inclusion of the reasons for negative votes, "the people at large will acknowledge, with thanks, the resulting information upon a subject so important to themselves and their latest posterity." Both sides were saying, in effect, that contemporary explanations would tell the people, then and later, about "the nature and tendency of the government," to quote Whitehill again. At one level the Federalists agreed; they simply did not wish the wrong explanations to "derive from [the Convention's] countenance a stamp of authenticity," to use James Wilson's variation of the phrasing.[53]

Despite the hints about ratifier intent provided by Edmund Randolph and the Pennsylvanians, it must be conceded that they remain hints. To the extent that I have examined the literature—and I cannot claim full familiarity with the outpouring of material in 1787–88, which is in the process of becoming more accessible[54]—the Federalists never explicitly and unambiguously stated that future interpreters should resort to ratifier intent. At the very least, this reticence needs attention.

Three interrelated reasons suggest themselves. First, there could be no ratifier intent until the disputants in the ratification controversy developed understandings about the instrument's meaning. Second, the pressing and primary problem was not to provide a basis for future interpretation or construction, but to explain how the Constitution would meet present and future needs. Finally, the ratifiers' endorsement of reason and common sense as guides made an explicit endorsement of ratifier intent redundant, for the former constituted a kind of proxy for the latter. Given an unchanging human nature, reason and common sense would reveal in the future what reason and common sense revealed in 1787–88. Questioned about the future status of ratifier intent, one can imagine a puzzled Federalist exclaiming, "What? Are you hinting that the Constitution will not mean in the future what it says and what its structure implies? That's a strange position. I don't understand the suggestion that we are ratifying something other than the system that common sense discloses to us. Yes, there may be a few ambiguities. Remember, though, that if the officials of the new government fail to give effect to what we ratifiers see in the document, there are correctives." Which is, of course, very nearly what some Federalists did say.

The meaning of the Constitution as it was ratified corresponded to its meaning for the people who gave the document its binding status. A truism? Perhaps. But it returns our focus to the obvious. It also reminds us that there is another issue to be addressed. What did the instrument's content—its general and specific provisions—mean to the ratifiers? This further issue can be conceived of, alternatively, as an evidentiary problem or as a problem in intellectual history. Beyond the ratification debates *per se*, it involves the accompanying public debates and the still fuller range of sources that shed light on how people in 1787–88 read those aspects of the document that the ratifiers did not explicitly address. It is a difficult practical problem, but it should not be confused with the narrower question of the interpretive intent of the ratifiers.[55]

III. Reflected Light on the Original Interpretive Intent

ADDITIONAL INSIGHT into views on constitutional interpretation in 1787–88 comes from later commentary by participants in and observers of the ratification controversy. Professor Powell surveys a number of useful sources in this regard. Receiving brief attention are the 1789 debate over the president's removal power and the conflict in 1791 among President Washington's executive officers over the constitutionality of the Bank of the United States.[56] Powell finds some participants in the removal debate denying the legitimacy of any attempt to move beyond the Constitution's words, while others accepted interpretation through construction. What passes unnoticed are comments implicating historical intent, such as the remark by Alexander White of Virginia that if the principle of enumerated powers "had not been successfully maintained by [the Constitution's] advocates in the [Virginia ratifying] convention . . . the constitution would never have been ratified."[57] Alexander Hamilton's clear rejection of framer intent in his 1791 Bank opinion gets mentioned, but not his use therein of evidence from the ratification process.[58]

Two other sources of reflected light on American understandings in 1787–88 deserve and receive fuller attention. One is the 1796 debate in the House of Representatives on how to interpret the House's role in treatymaking, "[t]he most sustained early congressional discussion of constitutional hermeneutics," writes Professor Powell.[59] The second source is James Madison, who participated in the 1796 debate and commented further in later years.

A. The House Debate of 1796

The 1796 debate occurred when House Republicans wanted access to diplomatic papers before approving appropriations to implement the Jay Treaty with England. At least some members on each side of the issue accepted the propriety of turning to the ratification controversy as a guide to constitutional interpretation in suitable cases. Professor Powell relates these comments, but contends that "this use of history was related but not identical to that of modern intentionalism. The 'contemporaneous expositions' on which . . . [the members] relied were not confined to the debates at Philadelphia, or at the state conventions, but included the defenses of the Constitution published by its proponents and even the critical interpretations of its opponents." He goes on to indicate that use of extraneous sources came under attack, but he responds that "resort to materials from the ratification era as one species of evidence as to the Constitution's context was in fact only mildly innovative, although proponents of the House resolution strove to make it appear a flagrant violation of the established canons of construction."[60] In fact, Professor Powell's exegesis of the debate in 1796 scarcely does justice to the clear evidence of acceptance of ratifier intent that the debate discloses. Again, my focus is primarily on the evidence that he himself cites.

William Smith, a South Carolina Federalist, was one of those opposing the call for papers. His argument emphasized "that the Treaty power was solely delegated to the PRESIDENT and Senate by the Constitution. . . ." To make the point, he stated, "he should not confine himself to a mere recital of the words, but he should appeal to the general sense of the whole nation at the time the constitution was formed. . . . By referring to the contemporaneous expositions of that instrument, when the subject was viewed only in relation to the abstract power, and not to a particular Treaty, we should come at the truth."[61] He then reviewed evidence purportedly showing that during ratification the Federalists defended the decision to place the treaty power with the president and the Senate, while their opponents had charged that the document unwisely excluded the House of Representatives. His evidence included remarks in the state conventions, amendments proposed in the conventions, and comments in other meetings at the time.[62] He turned, that is, to materials that reasonably might indicate the ratifiers' expectations and understandings.

With respect to Smith's comments and similar statements, however, Professor Powell claims that "those who cited evidence from the ratification period almost invariably linked it with other expressions of constitutional opinion."[63] But observe Smith's supposed qualification in this regard, as recorded by the reporter: "Having stated the general opinion of the public, as manifested by the friends as well as the enemies of the Constitution [in 1787–88], Mr. S[mith] said he would proceed to show that the practice of Congress had, from the commencement of its existence, been conformable to that opinion." Simply put, the remark does not run against or qualify use of ratifier intent, which is not surprising because Smith had just disparaged "*ex post facto* construction."[64]

Similarly, Federalist Theodore Sedgwick twitted James Madison for only recently having discovered a role for the House of Representatives in the treaty process. He noted Madison's silence on the subject during the Virginia ratification debates and inquired "how it happened that, if such was really the intention of the instrument, that such was the meaning of the people, no man had heard of it until the discovery was produced by the British [Jay] Treaty. Strange national intention, unknown for years to every individual." If the proponents of the call for diplomatic papers were "right in their construction [of the House's role], *if this was the understanding of the people at the time they deliberated on and ratified the Constitution*, the power of the PRESIDENT and Senate of making Treaties, which then created the most serious deliberation and alarming apprehensions, was the most innocent thing in nature."[65] Sedgwick went on to quote extensively from the Virginia proceedings of 1788 and then more briefly showed that interpretations by Congress and the Supreme Court provided corroboration.[66]

So, too, agreed Benjamin Bourne, who declared that "if a doubt existed as to what was the true construction of the Constitution, it ought to be conformed to the opinion which prevailed when the Constitution was adopted."[67] Professor Powell indicates that Bourne regarded subsequent interpretations by state legislatures as constitutionally authoritative, but Bourne instead turned to such legislative comments for evidence that the President and Senate had acted wisely in making the Jay Treaty. Only then did he offer the comment just quoted. In short, he maintained that the Treaty represented sound policy, and that if questions arose about constitutional powers, the understandings of 1787–88 should be dispositive.[68]

Or take the comments of Uriah Tracy, which, according to Professor Powell, typified "the caution with which these Representatives advanced historical materials as evidence of the Constitution's meaning."[69] As Powell correctly notes, Tracy explored the Constitution's text and Confederation practice. He then endorsed Benjamin Bourne's suggestion that small state jealousy contributed to the exclusion of the proportionally constituted House of Representatives from the treaty process. To clinch the point, he observed: "If any proof could be necessary, he thought the almost unanimous understanding of the members of the different Conventions in the States, who were called to discuss the Constitution for adoption, was in favor of the construction he had given," which he then summarized. He allowed, it is true, "that, from such debates, the real state of men's minds or opinions may not always be collected with accuracy,"[70] but his use of the ratification proceedings indicates that he considered them in this instance to be conclusive evidence against the Republicans' expansive interpretation of the treaty role of the House. He recognized, that is, that historical intent might not be easily reconstructed. Where it could be determined, however, it was dispositive in the resolution of textual ambiguities.[71]

In the course of the arguments surveyed in the preceding paragraphs, Federalist speakers also hypothesized what the members of the Philadelphia Convention hoped to accomplish by giving the treaty power its final form. William Vans Murray of Maryland appeared the most forthright in directing attention to the framers; in Professor Powell's view, therefore, he "seems to

have come much closer to modern intentionalism."[72] Vans Murray called on
James Madison and Abraham Baldwin, who was also a delegate to the 1787
meeting, to reveal what they surely knew about the treaty-related proceedings in Philadelphia. In making his challenge, he came close to asserting that
framer intent had a role in constitutional interpretation. But just as the other
Federalists who referred to the framers made clear that they saw the understandings of the *ratifiers* as conclusive, so Vans Murray's willingness to put
Madison and Baldwin in an embarrassing position came after he admitted
that other speakers had completely described "the opinions that were entertained at the *adoption* of the Constitution."[73] On balance, he saw the proceedings in Philadelphia as one more source of contemporaneous opinion, not
dispositive, but potentially useful as another indication of how people possessed of common understandings in 1787–88 had read the document.[74]

Republicans, it should come as no surprise, rejected Federalist conclusions
regarding the limited role of the House in the treaty process. They did so
partly by attacking the Federalists' approach to constitutional interpretation.
Professor Powell notes a number of these retorts, giving special attention to
those by Albert Gallatin and James Madison. It was Gallatin who used the
phrases that Powell quotes when he asserts that Federalist speakers "were
vigorously attacked by the resolution's supporters for 'conjur[ing] up' such
'extraneous sources.'"[75] Gallatin assuredly disparaged the opposition's "train
of arguments, drawn not from the letter or spirit of the Constitution, either
directly or by implication, but from a variety of extraneous Sources," but
assuredly, too, he accused no one of "conjur[ing] up" the sources in the sense
of inventing them or calling them into existence. Rather he argued that the
extraneous sources (which were real enough that he himself soon analyzed
them) "had been conjured up as united in ascribing to the power of making
Treaties the most unlimited and unbounded effect."[76] Saying that an improper meaning had been attributed to the sources is different from suggesting that the sources had been invented.

Particularly noteworthy is an omission by Gallatin. It came after he
charged that the Federalists, having failed to support their interpretations by
reference to the law of nations and to practice in Great Britain and under the
Articles of Confederation, "have recurred to the opinions of individuals, of
State Conventions, and finally, of the general Convention which framed the
Constitution." Taking direct aim at William Vans Murray, he then limited
his attack to the doctrine "that the opinions and constructions of those persons who had framed and proposed the Constitution, opinions given in private, constructions unknown to the people when they adopted the instrument, should, after a lapse of eight years, be appealed to."[77] Gallatin did not
condemn the retreat to ratifier intent.

Nor is the omission strange. Gallatin had already contended that recourse
to practice in Great Britain and under the Articles was appropriate in interpreting the treaty clause because those were "the two Governments which

had served as a basis and model to our present Constitution, *which were mostly contemplated by the people who adopted it.*"[78] By contrast, he caricatured the Federalists as telling the people that "[they] have had a Constitution for eight years, and have adopted it under such impressions as must have resulted from the face of the instrument; but it was the design of those who framed it, that it should have a different construction from that it naturally bears." Through analogy, he distinguished ratifier intent from framer intent: "The intention of a Legislature who pass a law may perhaps, though with caution, be resorted to, in order to explain or construe the law; but would any person recur to the intention, opinion, and private construction of the clerk who might have been employed to draft the bill?" Moving beyond analogy, he explained directly: "In the present case, the gentlemen who formed the general Convention, however respectable, entitled as they were to the thanks and gratitude of their country for their services in general, and especially on that important occasion, were not of those who made, who passed the instrument; they only drew it and proposed it. The people and the State Conventions who ratified[,] who adopted the instrument, are alone parties to it, and their intentions alone might, with any degree of propriety, be resorted to."[79]

It is true that Gallatin next questioned resort to the ratification controversy, but his concerns were evidentiary. In the debate at hand, the Federalists had referred both to Antifederalist remarks and to amendments proposed during the process. He found these to be a poor guide to pertinent understandings in 1787–88, maintaining instead that only the views of the Constitution's supporters should carry weight.[80] He then offered his own gloss on several state debates, concluding: "After such pointed contemporaneous expositions of the true meaning and spirit of the Constitution, would it still be asserted, that the opinion now expressed [by the Republicans] were a new-fangled doctrine?"[81]

Before turning to James Madison, three of Professor Powell's lesser Republican witnesses from the 1796 debate deserve mention. One unequivocally did reject ratifier intent. "As to the construction generally received when the Constitution was adopted," Edward Livingston "did not conceive it to be conclusive, even if admitted to be contrary to what now [the Republicans] contended for; because he believed we were now as capable at least of determining the true meaning of [the Constitution] as the [State] Conventions were: they were called in haste, they were heated by party, and many adopted it from expediency, without having fully debated the several article."[82]

After quoting Livingston, Professor Powell focuses on two other disputants from 1796 when he comments that "the House, it was argued, *must* seek "the intrinsic meaning of the Constitution . . . from the words of it,'[182] while recognizing that the text was unavoidably ambiguous on *many* issues and that its framers had anticipated that those questions would 'be settled by practice or by amendments.'[183]"[83] The first internal quotation, identified by Powell's footnote 182, is from a speech by William Branch Giles. What Giles actually said, at least as eventually compiled into the *Annals of Congress*, was this: "Having examined the objections to the [constitutional] construction contended for by the friends of the motion [that is, the motion that the President produce papers], drawn from collateral sources, he should turn his attention next, he said, to the intrinsic meaning of the Constitution. He would attempt to interpret the Constitution from the words of it."[84] Compare this with Professor Powell's statement, which uses a "must" and inserts an ellipsis to connect portions of two sentences. Powell's combination mangles Giles's meaning by suggesting that he rejected collateral or extrinsic sources, which he did not do.

The citation for the remainder of Powell's sentence (in footnote 183) is to a speech in which Abraham Baldwin conceded that the framers probably knew "that some objects were left a *little* ambiguous and uncertain. It was a great thing to get so many difficult subjects definitely settled at once. If they could all be agreed in, it would compact the Government. The *few* that were left *a little* unsettled might, without any great risk, be settled by practice or by amendments in the progress of Government."[85] Baldwin misjudged the Constitution's clarity, but that is slight warrant for Powell to paraphrase the congressman's "some," "a little," and "few" as "many." In fact, contrary to Powell's implication, Baldwin did not contrast (a) adjustment through practice and amendment with (b) clarification by reference to extrinsic sources from 1787–88. Instead, he soon said that "he was willing to allow due force" to "the reasons of members of the Convention, the proposed amendments of several States [during the ratification proceedings], &c," even though he detected an undue reliance on these materials in the instant debate. Such evidence, he explained, "was not of sufficient force to be a ground of absolute certainty that the thing [that is, the House's role in the treaty process] is definitely settled," particularly because the 1796 debate marked the first sustained analysis of the question, not excluding the ratification debates.[86] In sum, Baldwin carefully qualified his position.

Politics obviously shaped the debate in 1796, which may raise suspicions about conclusions drawn from it. Yet politics provides the context for most comments on constitutional issues; if all such remarks were ignored, the record would indeed be barren. (Even the confidential debates in Philadelphia were assuredly political.) The key is to evaluate the evidence while keeping context in mind. From the standpoint of deciphering the original understanding of original intent, one feature of the exchanges over the Jay Treaty is remarkable. *Both* Federalists *and* Republicans accepted use of original intent in the form of ratifier intent. More precisely, to use terms pertinent to Professor Powell's article, they accepted subjective or historical ratifier intent and sought out the actual expectations and understandings of the ratifiers.

B. James Madison's Views

And then there is James Madison. It may be partly because of the hold of framer intent on constitutional scholars and judges that Madison tops just about everyone's list of founders. Once framer intent is discounted, Madison's notes and recollections of the proceedings in Philadelphia have less importance in reconstructing the original understanding of original intent. Beyond being a leader in the Philadelphia Convention, however, Madison participated in the ratification controversy and was a careful observer of— and reflective thinker about—the entire founding period. As a result, just as Professor Powell is on solid ground in surveying the 1796 debate in Congress (if not always in the conclusions he draws from it), so he is unassailable for paying substantial attention to Madison. As he remarks, "Although [Madison] would have been quick to distinguish his personal opinions from the public meaning of the Constitution, the coherent interpretive theory Madison expressed in speeches and letters over many years has special value for anyone seeking to discern the 'interpretive intent' underlying the Constitution."[87]

Not least, Madison contributed to the 1796 debate. After the House finally resolved to request papers relating to the Jay Treaty negotiations, George Washington refused to comply. In addition to prudential reasons, the President relied on the Constitution. "Having been a member of the General Convention, and knowing the principles on which the Constitution was formed," he found that the document excluded the House from treatymaking. His view, he argued, accorded with practice and "with the opinions entertained by the State Conventions, when they were deliberating on the Constitution. . . ." "If other proofs than these, and the plain letter of the Constitution itself, be necessary to ascertain the point under consideration," he added, "they may be found in the Journals of the General Convention, which I have deposited in the office of the Department of State."[88]

Washington's foray into interpretation triggered a response from Madison, who argued along several lines.[89] One was to question the President's interpretation of the deliberations of the Philadelphia Convention. Madison concluded, though, that whatever their meaning,

> the sense of that body could never be regarded as the oracular guide in
> expounding the Constitution. As the instrument came from them it
> was nothing more than the draft of a plan, nothing but a dead letter,
> until life and validity were breathed into it by the voice of the people,
> speaking through the several State Conventions. If we were to look,
> therefore, for the meaning of the instrument beyond the face of the
> instrument, we must look for it, not in the General Convention, which
> proposed, but in the State Conventions, which accepted and ratified
> the Constitution.[90]

Professor Powell remarks that from 1796 onwards, Madison was "remark-ably consistent" in his views on interpretation,[91] and so he was.[92] In 1821, for example, he wrote Thomas Ritchie:

> As a guide in expounding and applying the provisions of the Constitu-tion, the debates and incidental decisions of the [Philadelphia] Conven-tion can have no authoritative character. However desirable it be that they should be preserved as a gratification to the laudable curiosity felt by every people to trace the origin and progress of their political institutions, & as a source perhaps of some lights on the Science of Govt.[,] the legitimate meaning of the Instrument must be derived from the text itself; or if a key is to be sought elsewhere, it must be, not in the opinions of the body which planned & proposed the Constitution, but in the sense attached to it by the people in their respective State Conventions where it recd. all the Authority which it possesses.[93]

This position accorded with Madison's earlier explanation, during the ratifi-cation controversy, of the respective roles of the Philadelphia Convention and the ratifying conventions.

Professor Powell concedes that "Madison thought it proper . . . to consult the direct expressions of state intention available in the resolutions of the ratifying conventions."[94] The force of the concession is mitigated, however, by the fact that in quoting Madison in Congress in 1796 and Madison's letter to Ritchie in 1821, Powell omits the sentences in which Madison explicitly endorsed ratifier intent.[95] In a footnote, Powell does quote a comparable en-dorsement, but merely to support his unexceptionable contention that Mad-ison rejected framer intent; he does not draw out Madison's clear meaning regarding ratifier intent.[96]

In much the same vein, Professor Powell states that Madison found the ratification debates "to be of real yet limited value" and explains that "eviden-tiary problems with the surviving records and Madison's insistence on distin-guishing the binding public intention of the state from the private opinion of any individual or group of individuals, including those gathered at a state convention, led him to conclude that the state debates could bear no more than indirect and corroborative witness to the meaning of the Constitution."[97] Again, however, the cited materials raise questions about Powell's conclu-sion. To Jonathan Elliot, Madison allowed that the extant records of the pro-ceedings might be "defective . . . in some respects & inaccurate in others," but he found them to be "highly interesting in a political as well as Historical view" and had only encouragement for Elliot's plan to publish them. In the letter, he did not conclude that the interpretive value of the ratification de-bates was only indirect and corroborative.[98]

Nor does such a conclusion reasonably flow from the cited letter to An-drew Stevenson, in which Madison discussed the meaning of the terms "common defence" and "general welfare." Here Madison demonstrated, as he did on other occasions, that he, too, could probe the journals of the Philadelphia Convention; but he put both the journals and the ratification debates in perspective when he commented: "Passing from this view of the sense in which the terms common defence & general welfare were used by the Framers of the Constitution, let us look for that in which they must have been understood by the Conventions, or rather by the people, who thro' their Conventions, accepted & ratified it."[99] At the very least, this letter does not suggest that Madison had "conclude[d] that the state debates could bear no more than indirect and corroborative witness to the meaning of the Constitution."

As for "contemporaneous expositions of the document by its supporters," the Madison described by Professor Powell accorded them "some value, but he cautioned that such statements were to be regarded strictly as private opinions, useful chiefly in shedding light upon the meaning of words and phrases that the fluidity of language might gradually change over time."[100] In fact, a letter from Madison to Henry Lee that supposedly contains or implies this qualification does not. The relevant passage reads as follows:

> I entirely concur in the propriety of resorting to the sense in which the Constitution was accepted and ratified by the nation. In that sense alone it [that is, the Constitution as construed] is the legitimate Constitution. And if that be not the guide in expounding it, there can be no security for a consistent and stable, more than for a faithful exercise of its powers. If the meaning of the text be sought in the changeable meaning of the words composing it, it is evident that the shape and attributes of the Government must partake of the changes to which the words and phrases of all living language are constantly subject.[101]

Nor does such a qualification appear in the cited letters to Andrew Stevenson and Nicholas P. Trist.[102]

Rather than resort to historical or subjective intent, Professor Powell's Madison "consistently thought that '*usus*,' the exposition of the Constitution provided by actual governmental practice and judicial precedents, could 'settle its meaning and the intention of its authors.'"[103] But Madison himself complicated his gloss on *usus* when, discussing the extent of Congress's power over foreign commerce in an unposted letter to Professor John Davis, he wrote:

> After all, we must be guided . . . by the intention of those who framed, or, rather, who adopted the Constitution; and must decide that intention by the meaning attached to the terms by the "*usus*" which is the *arbitrium*, the *jus* and the *norma loquendi*, a rule as applicable to phrases as to single words. It need scarcely to be observed that, according to this rule, the intention, if ascertained by contemporaneous interpretation and continued practice, could not be overruled by any latter [later?] meaning put on the phrase, however

warranted by the grammatical rules of construction[,] were these
at variance with it.[104]

Regarding the interpretive problem at hand—that is, the extent of the commerce power—Madison surveyed difficulties regarding foreign trade in the
1780s, as well as contemporary comment on them and the Constitution's
solutions for them. "That the power of regulating foreign commerce was expected to be given to, and used by, Congress in favour of domestic manufac-
tures," he explained, "may be seen in the debates in the Convention of Massachusetts."[105] He then quoted extensively from deliberations in the First
Congress, which he followed with the observation: "It deserves particular
attention, that the Congress which first met contained sixteen members,
eight of them in the House of Representatives, fresh from the Convention
which framed the Constitution, and a considerable number who had been
members of the State Conventions which had adopted it, taken as well from
the party which opposed as from those who had espoused its adoption."[106]

To Professor Davis, Madison also cited "a continued use of it [the commerce power as a basis for protection of domestic manufactures] for a period
of forty years, with the express sanction of the executive and judicial departments, and with the positive concurrence or manifest acquiescence of the
State authorities and of the people at large, with a very limited exception
during a few late years."[107] After reviewing several pertinent examples, Madison concluded: "If all these authoritative interpretations of the Constitution
on a particular point cannot settle its meaning and the intention of its authors, we can never have a stable and known Constitution."[108]

In his letter to Professor Davis, Madison may have partly used the term
"intention" in the sense of a meaning assigned to a document by later interpreters, as Professor Powell argues. If so, he did not conceive of the pertinent
usus as simply "the exposition of the Constitution provided by actual governmental practice and judicial precedents," as Professor Powell parenthetically
defines the word, citing, with questionable regard for context, two other
Madison letters.[109] Madison himself turned to practice and precedent only for
additional proof of the correctness of his interpretation of the foreign commerce power; and the most reasonable interpretation of his purpose in adduc-
ing such further evidence is that he saw practice and precedent as confirming
his reading of original intent. Congressmen, executive officers, and judges,
that is, had found the same intent that Madison did.

At minimum, Madison explicitly rejected modification of the Constitution's meaning through new constructions, lamenting that "some of the terms
of the Federal Constitution have already undergone perceptible deviations
from their original import." Despite "the authority of the precedents regularly continued for thirty or forty years," some still argued "that the true
character of a political system might not be disclosed even within such a
period." But he cautioned that "this would not disprove the intention of those

who made the Constitution. It would show only that it was made liable to abuses not foreseen nor soon to appear; and that it ought to be amended, but by the authority which made it, not by the authority subordinate to it."[110] In short, if the document as interpreted according to the intentions of those who made it an authoritative instrument ceased to be adequate, then formal amendment, not novel construction, was the remedy. This remedy had to be used sparingly, and only upon due consideration.[111]

Undeterred, Professor Powell finds Madison's position on the power of Congress to incorporate the Bank of the United States to be an example of his acceptance of practice and *judicial* precedent in opposition to historical intent.[112] As President, Madison signed into law the Second Bank of the United States twenty-five years after opposing the First Bank on constitutional grounds. Dodging the charge of inconsistency, he later claimed that whatever his private view of the meaning of the Constitution, it was superseded by "a course of authoritative expositions sufficiently deliberate, uniform, and settled" as to be "an evidence of the public will necessarily overruling individual opinions."[113] Of course, when he approved the Bank Bill in 1816, Madison had before him only *legislative* precedent. Later, when he questioned Andrew Jackson's veto of the rechartering of the Second B.U.S., he again focused on legislative interpretation of the Constitution. The need for stability, he explained, required that, in all but the most exceptional instances, legislators should be guided by legislative precedent in interpreting the Constitution in the same way that judges are guided by precedent in the interpretation of laws. He defended this view, using analogy and unequivocal statements, on two grounds. First, he argued that stability was essential to the rule of law; second, and arguably more fundamental, he maintained that a consistent line of legislative precedent established a presumption that the sovereign people approved the interpretation. With evident reference to the president's participation in the legislative process through the veto power, Madison thought that interposition of personal conclusions was particularly suspect "when no prospect existed of a change of construction by the public or its agents."[114]

With respect to the Bank issue, Madison conceded to Nicholas P. Trist in 1831 that "a course of authoritative, deliberate, and continued decisions" could serve to "fix the interpretation of a law," but the context of his remarks again indicates that he had legislative decisions in mind, decisions which were "an evidence of the Public Judgment, necessarily superseding individual opinions." It was fallacious, moreover, to confound "a question whether precedents could expound a Constitution, with a question whether they could alter a Const[itution]." It is significant, too, that he added: "Another error has been in ascribing to the intention of the Convention which formed the Constitution, an undue ascendancy in expounding it. Apart from the difficulty of verifying that intention[,] it is clear, that if the meaning of the Constitution is to be sought out of itself, it is not in the proceedings of the Body that proposed it, but in those of the State Conventions which gave it all the validity & authority it possesses."[115]

A comparable conclusion about the relative priority of ratifier intent emerges from an earlier letter involving the Bank issue. Writing to Judge Spencer Roane of Virginia after the decision in *McCulloch* v. *Maryland*, Madison attacked John Marshall's gratuitously broad construction of congressional authority. He admitted that words sometimes failed the founders, observing: "It could not but happen, and was foreseen at the birth of the Constitution, that difficulties and differences of opinion might occasionally arise in expounding terms & phrases necessarily used in such a charter; *more especially those which divide legislation between the General & local Governments*; and that it might require a regular course of practice to liquidate & settle the meaning of some of them." The clause italicized here, which Powell excises from his rendition of the quotation, qualifies it. This qualification, however, is less significant than the stronger qualification provided both by general context and by the two sentences that immediately followed (which Powell also omits). In them, Madison explained further: "But it was anticipated I believe by few if any of the friends of the Constitution, that a rule of construction would be introduced as broad & as pliant as what has occurred. And those who recollect, and still more those who shared in what passed in the State Conventions, thro' which the people ratified the Constitution, with respect to the extent of the powers vested in Congress, cannot easily be persuaded that the avowal of such rule would not have prevented its ratification."[116]

Overall it is difficult to find Madison conceding that the original "interpretive intent" gave construction, including construction based on *usus*, a priority over resort to ratifier intent. Instead, he invoked ratifier intent in opposition to construction: original history (as it may be labeled) put limits on adaptation. He accepted that as a private individual he lacked the authority to substitute his interpretations for the meanings accepted by the sovereign public as time passed; but that was an issue of *who* could authoritatively explain the document, not of *how* it should be done.

Writing to M. L. Hurlbert in 1830, Madison satisfactorily summarized his views on interpretation. The letter needs quoting at length:

> [T]he real measure of the powers meant to be granted to Congress by the [Philadelphia] Convention, as I understood and believe, is to be sought in the [Constitution's] specifications, to be expounded indeed not with the strictness applied to an ordinary statu[t]e by a Court of Law; nor on the other hand with a latitude that under the name of means for carrying into execution a limited Government, would transform it into a Government without limits.
>
> But whatever respect may be thought due to the intention of the Convention, which prepared & proposed the Constitution, *as presumptive evidence of the general understanding at the time of the language used*, it

must be kept in mind that the *only authoritative* intentions were those of the people of the States, as expressed thro' the Conventions which ratified the Constitution.

That in a Constitution, so new, and so complicated, there should be occasional difficulties & differences in the practical expositions of it, can surprize no one; and this must continue to be the case, as happens to new laws on complex subjects, until a course of practice of sufficient uniformity and duration to carry with it the public sanction shall settle doubtful or contested meanings.

As there are legal rules for interpreting laws, there must be analogous rules for interpreting const[itutio]ns and among the obvious and just guides to the Const[itutio]n of the U.S. may be mentioned—

1. The evils & defects for curing which the Constitution was called for & introduced.

2. The comments prevailing at the time it was adopted.

3. The early, deliberate & continued practice under the Constitution, as preferable to constructions adapted on the spur of occasions, and subject to the vicissitudes of party or personal ascendencies.[117]

This summary, along with his other remarks on the subject (including his own occasional use of the views of the *framers*), suggests a capsule restatement of Madison's views. For him, the essential guidelines to interpretation were these:

1. The text, viewed always with an eye on the dictates of limited government;

2. The deliberations in Philadelphia, insofar as they offer insight into the way contemporaries not present, and not privy to the debates, would generally have understood the final language of the text;

3. The commentaries and debates accompanying ratification, and most especially (but by no means exclusively) those within the state conventions; and

4. Early and continued practice, particularly as a check on (but not an invariable barrier to) subsequent reinterpretation.

And what might be the exceptional occasion that would warrant subsequent reinterpretation at variance with the early and continued practice embraced within the fourth guideline? Presumably such a shift might come about when there existed a widespread, sustained, and hence persuasive conviction that reinterpretation was necessary in order to adhere even more faithfully to the first three guidelines, and especially in order to observe the "authoritative intentions . . . of the people of the States, as expressed thro' the Conventions which ratified the Constitution." If practice at variance with an original understanding nonetheless continued, surviving with the long-term acquiescence of Congress, this then evidenced the will of the sovereign people.

IV. *The Original Interpretive Intent*

MADISON UNDERSTOOD the theoretical base of the new constitutional order and appreciated both the logic of the ratification process and the force of
related Federalist defenses of the Philadelphia Convention against the charge
of usurpation. He accordingly condemned resort to framer intent. So too did
most of his contemporaries when they seriously weighed its authority.
Viewed from the perspective of the founding period, framer intent is easily
dismissed—a bogus issue which is best forgotten by both "intentionalists"
and their critics. Yet it was not subjective or historical intent itself that was
troublesome to the founders. The reasons running against framer intent supported the use of ratifier intent.

The issue of the status of subjective or historical ratifier intent for the
founders should not be confounded with the question of the *extent* to which
such intent soon provided a guide to constitutional interpretation, in comparison with familiar common-law hermeneutics. In constitutional disputes
during the first years of the new government, arguments based on construction of the document eclipsed reliance on subjective intent. Thus in *Chisholm*
v. *Georgia* the Supreme Court drew on treatise writers and contextual analysis
in reading the judicial article to allow suits by individuals against states, ignoring Publius's fairly clear assurance to the contrary.[118] As another example,
both Hamilton and Jefferson emphasized construction according to common-
law rules in their exchange over the Bank of the United States.

Nonetheless, resolution of the issue of extent may be more complex. For
example, aside from the possibility that the historical intent relevant to the
Chisholm case was not so readily determined as is now commonly assumed, a
higher authority soon corrected the Court regarding the amenability of states
to suit, much in keeping with Edmund Randolph's explanation in 1788 of
the recourse available if officials lost sight of "the present actual feelings of
the people of America."[119] Then, too, Hamilton himself used ratifier intent
in his bank opinion, in a matter-of-course fashion, notwithstanding the opinion's strong condemnation of resort to framer intent.[120] And in 1796, when
the ratification debates provided arguably germane evidence on the role of
the House of Representatives in treatymaking, disputants on both sides accepted the legitimacy of turning to the debates, however much they disagreed
about what specifically qualified as evidence and about what it meant. Happily, however, the issue of extent need not be resolved here.

There is also the issue raised by Edward Livingston when he charged that
the ratifiers acted with haste and felt the goad of party.[121] As a modern student of Madison asks, "Why should we assume that those who *merely* ratified
the Constitution grasped its meaning better than those who wrote it—or
those who have since seen how it works in practice?"[122] The answer from an
"intentionalist" perspective is that whether the ratifiers better grasped the
instrument's meaning is beside the point; rather, how the ratifiers understood

the Constitution, and what they expected from it, *defines* its meaning. The act of ratifying cannot be dismissed with the adverb "merely."

The more fundamental point with respect to "the original understanding of original intent" is that by jettisoning framer intent, the founders did not throw constitutional interpretation exclusively into the grip of readily available common-law approaches, including use of constructive intent. If modern intentionalists focus on the framers, as Professor Powell alleges with considerable accuracy, they have scant theoretical or historical grounds for their history-based hermeneutics. When correctly reconstructed and understood, however, the original understanding of original intent most emphatically does not rule out a resort to the understandings and expectations of the ratifiers in 1787–88, or to the range of materials that may illuminate their views. Indeed, it is not too much to say that at least some of the founders saw the ratifiers' historical or subjective intent as a check on constructions which cut loose from the original understandings of the sovereign people.

Notes

1. E. Meese, Speech to American Bar Association, July 9, 1985, reprinted in 2 *Benchmark* 1 (1986); W. Brennan, Text and Teaching Symposium on the Constitution of the United States: Contemporary Ratification 4 (October 12, 1985) (reprinted in this volume; subsequent page references to this article are to page numbers in this volume).

2. Powell, The Original Understanding of Original Intent, 98 *Harv. L. Rev.* 25 (1985) (reprinted in this volume; subsequent page references to this article are to page numbers in this volume). On the article's reception, see, e.g., R. Dworkin, *Law's Empire* 364, 450 n.9 (1986); Dworkin, The Press on Trial, *N.Y. Rev. of Books*, February 26, 1987, at 34 n. 11.

3. Not least in reinforcing my thinking in this regard was the occasion of reviewing David Currie's encyclopedic account of the Constitution's first century in the Supreme Court. See Lofgren, Book Review, 4 *Const. Comm.* 177, 183–84 and nn. 16–18 (1987). If Currie's book exemplifies the priority given to "framer intent" within what may be called technical constitutional scholarship, Michael Kammen's sweeping survey of American constitutionalism offers at least suggestive evidence that similarly it is the framing, not the ratification, which has generally caught the nation's attention. See M. Kammen, *A Machine That Would Go of Itself: The Constitution in American Culture* (1986).

4. Monaghan, Our Perfect Constitution, 56 *N.Y.U. L. Rev.* 353, 375 n. 130 (1981).

5. See Rehnquist, The Notion of a Living Constitution, 54 *Tex. L. Rev.* 693, 694, 697, 699 (1976).

6. See W. Brennan, supra note 1, at 25. Professor Jack N. Rakove, a leading historian of the 1780s and a close student of James Madison, has used Justice Brennan's remark to reiterate the same point. On balance Rakove, too, dismisses ratifier intent. See Rakove, Mr. Meese, Meet Mr. Madison, *Atlantic Monthly*, December 1986, at 179, 181 and passim, (reprinted in this volume; subsequent page references to this article are to page numbers in this volume) which I discuss further infra, text accompanying note 122.

7. See Brest, The Misconceived Quest for the Original Understanding, 60 *B.U. L. Rev.* 234–235, and passim (1980) (reprinted in this volume; subsequent page references to this article are to page numbers in this volume).

8. Cf. Kay, The Illegality of the Constitution, 4 *Const Comm.* 57, 58–59 (1987) (discussing "preconstitutional rules").

9. In other respects, I find his discussion highly informative, in particular his explication of the major pre-existing interpretive traditions available to Americans of the late 1780s. See Powell, supra note 2, at 55–61. Powell's mistake, I believe, is to give too little weight to how the newness of the constitutional settlement of 1787–88 opened the way for and indeed called for new interpretive approaches.

10. Id. at 54.

11. Id. at 58–62. Powell also explores the differences between common-law approaches to different kinds of documents, finding resort to subjective intent acceptable in construing wills, and such resort becoming superficially acceptable regarding contracts toward the end of the eighteenth century. But the framers, he contends, "clearly assumed that future interpreters would adhere to then-prevalent methods of statutory construction." Id. at 63.

12. Regarding attempts to eliminate vagueness as indicating a commitment to common-law methods of interpretation, two of the episodes Powell cites (id. at 62 n.88) seem to me to reflect more a concern that the "vague" language in question was anything but vague in its diminution of state powers, which was precisely why some delegates supported and others opposed it. In any event, the episodes occurred while the Convention was initially reviewing the Virginia Plan—that is, at a time when everyone realized the plan was only a general statement which would need fleshing out if it proved to be the Convention's preferred approach. See 1 *The Records of the Federal Convention of 1787*, at 53–54 (M. Farrand rev. ed. 1937) (hereafter cited as *Records*) (May 31, on granting "Legislative power in all cases to which the State Legislatures were individually incompetent"); id. at 164–68 (June 8, on giving the national Legislature "authority to negative all [state] Laws which they shd. Judge to be improper"). In another instance, Powell finds the Convention debating a provision for "impeachment and removal of President in case of 'disability' " (Powell, supra note 2, at 62 n. 88), whereas the phrase in question referred to "disability to discharge the powers and duties of his office" as a phenomenon separate from impeachment and removal. See 2 *Records*, supra, at 427 (August 27, debating the section); 2 id. at 186 (Aug. 6, report of the Committee of Detail). Powell also gives more significance to the phrase "distinctive form of collecting the mind" than its context supports. Compare Powell, supra note 2, at 62, text associated with note 91, with 1 *Records*, supra, at 254–55 (June 16, remarks of Oliver Ellsworth). Here and later I cite Farrand's compilation, while Powell cites E. H. Hunt's 1893 edition of Madison's *Notes*. I have cross-checked the pertinent references.

13. See Powell, supra note 2, at 62 and n.93. Uncertain whether their wording accurately embodied their intentions, the delegates sought clarification from Blackstone's *Commentaries*. See 2 *Records*, supra note 12, at 448–49, 617 (August 29, September 14).

14. See Powell, supra note 2, at 62–63.

15. Id. at 62 (text associated with notes 91–93).

16. Id. at 62.

17. 2 *Records*, supra note 12, at 648 (September 17).

18. A comparable conclusion comes from James Madison's later comment about his own intentions in keeping secret his notes, which he knew were far more detailed than the Convention's journals. See James Madison to Thomas Ritchie (September 15, 1821), reprinted in 9 *The Writings of James Madison* 71–72 (G. Hunt ed. 1910) (hereafter cited as *Writings*).

19. 1 *Records*, supra note 12, at 22 (May 29, Virginia Plan).

20. See 1 *Records*, supra note 12, at 122–23 (June 5); 1 id. at 379 (June 22); 2 id. at 88–94 (July 23). But not everyone agreed that state conventions were more likely to ratify. See 1 id. at 335 (June 20).

21. 1 *Records*, supra note 12, at 123 (June 5, Madison); 2 id. at 92 (July 23, King).

22. 2 *Records*, supra note 12, at 91 (July 23).

23. See G. Wood, *The Creation of the American Republic, 1776–1787*, at 306–43, 524–36 (1969).

24. 2 *The Documentary History of the Ratification of the Constitution; Ratification of the Constitution by the States: Pennsylvania* 483–84 (M. Jensen ed. 1976) (hereafter cited as *Documentary History*) (Wilson's speech in the Pennsylvania Ratifying Convention, December 4, 1787).

25. Compare *Federalist* No. 39, at 253–57 (J. Madison) (J. Cooke ed. 1961) (hereafter cited as *Federalist*) with 2 *Documentary History*, supra note 24, at 348–49, 555, 558 (Wilson's speeches in the Pennsylvania Ratifying Convention, November 24, December 11, 1787). On Wilson's views, see generally Rossum, James Wilson and the Pyramid of Government, in *The American Founding: Politics, Statesmanship, and the Constitution* 62–79 (R. Rossum and G. McDowell eds. 1981).

26. *Federalist* No. 40, at 263–64 (J. Madison).

27. 4 *The Debates in the Several State Conventions on the Adoption of the Federal Constitution* 23, 25 (J. Elliot rev. ed. 1836) (hereafter cited as *Debates*). See generally 4 id. at 16–26 (debate in the North Carolina Ratifying Convention, July 24, 1788). Although the North Carolina Convention did not ratify at this time (and the State remained briefly out of the Union), its debates are a good gauge of the direction Federalist arguments had taken over the preceding months. In the episode under discussion here, if Davie echoed Wilson's earlier formulation, Maclaine's remark better mirrored Madison's more subtle view of the ratification process in *Federalist* No. 39, supra note 25.

28. See *Federalist* No. 37, at 236 (J. Madison).

29. Essays of Brutus, reprinted in 2 *The Complete Antifederalist* 420 (H. Storing ed. 1981). See id. at 417–42.

30. Powell, supra note 2, at 64–68.

31. *Federalist* No. 37, at 236.

32. Powell, supra note 2, at 66.

33. *Federalist* No. 73, at 734–37.

34. For the Philadelphia Convention's decision to keep its journals secret, see supra notes 15–18 and accompanying text.

35. While surveying the weakness of the Confederation, Hamilton in *Federalist* No. 22 explained why lack of a federal judiciary to enforce treaties created difficulties with foreign nations. In the process, he wrote: "The treaties of the United States to have any force at all, must be considered as part of the law of the land. Their true import as far as respects individuals, must, like all other laws, be ascertained by judicial determinations." Id. at 143, quoted in Powell, supra note 2, at 66 n. 134. He then argued that "one SUPREME TRIBUNAL" was necessary to avoid the problem of courts in each state rendering different interpretations of treaties. He gave no indication of what would guide the supreme tribunal in its treaty interpretations, for that was not his concern. Even less did he address the issue of how to interpret the Constitution.

36. Powell, supra note 2, at 66–67.

37. *Federalist* No. 78, at 525–26 (A. Hamilton).

38. Id. at 526.

39. Id. at 524–25.

40. For a similar reading of Hamilton's supposed defense of judicial review, see G. Wills, *Explaining America: The Federalist* 127–50 (1981).

41. *Federalist* No. 78, at 525.

42. As to what constituted a manifest contradiction, Hamilton mentioned bills of attainder, ex post facto laws, "and the like." Id. at 524.

43. *Federalist* No. 83 at 559–60 (A. Hamilton) (emphasis added).

44. See, e.g., *Federalist* No. 78, at 529–30; *Federalist* No. 83, at 560.

45. *Federalist* No. 78, at 525.

46. See Powell, supra note 2, at 64 nn. 112–16.

47. Id. at 64 (quoting in part from 2 *Debates*, supra note 27, at 285) (John Jay in the New York Ratifying Convention, June 23, 1788). For readers doing their own checking, it should be noted that Powell's citations are to the first edition of Elliot's *Debates*; I have used the more readily available second (revised) edition, which is paginated differently.

48. See 2 *Debates*, supra note 27, at 284–85.

49. Powell, supra note 2, at 64.

50. 4 *Debates*, supra note 27, at 71. Steele went on to claim that judicial invalidation of laws violating the Constitution provided a check not available under the Confederation.

51. 3 *Debates*, supra note 27, at 463–64, 470–71.

52. 2 *Documentary History*, supra note 24, at 372 (November 27, 1787). See generally id. at 370–79.

53. Id. at 377.

54. See *The Documentary History of the Ratification of the Constitution* (work of 17 or 18 vols., plus microfiche supplements, 1976–, in progress) (pub. by State Historical Society of Wisconsin).

55. Put differently, asking about the original understandings of original intent is one aspect of deciphering the understandings and expectation of 1787–88.

56. See Powell, supra note 2, at 68–70.

57. 1 *Annals of Congress* col. 535 (June 18, 1789) (J. Gales and W. Seaton eds. 1834). See also id. at cols. 474–75, 545, 547–48, 551–52 (June 16 and 18, 1789, remarks by Representatives Smith, Lee, Boudinot, and Jackson). White went on to quote the Virginia proceedings and to discuss the ratification process in North Carolina.

58. Powell quotes Hamilton's attack on Jefferson's reference to the refusal by the delegates in Philadelphia to grant Congress the power of incorporation. See Powell, supra note 2, at 69. Hamilton certainly used language at this point in his opinion that is interpretable as running against any use of historical intent, and concluded: "Nothing is more common than for laws to *express* and *effect*, more or less than was intended. If then a power to erect a corporation, in any case, be deducible by fair inference from the whole or any part of the numerous provisions of the constitution of the United States, arguments drawn from extrinsic circumstances, regarding the intention of the convention, must be rejected." Hamilton, Opinion on the Constitutionality of an Act to Establish a National Bank, February 23, 1791, reprinted in *Selected Writings and Speeches of Alexander Hamilton* 248, 258 (M. Frisch ed. 1985). Yet, in context, Hamilton closely linked his strictures against subjective intent to use of framer intent; and he himself later resorted to ratifier intent, commenting: "It is remarkable, that the State Conventions who have most, if not all of them, expressed themselves nearly thus—'Congress shall not grant monopolies, or erect any company with exclusive advantages of commerce'; thus at the same time expressing their sense, that the power to erect trading companies or corporations, was inherent in Congress, & objecting to it no further, than as to the grant of exclusive priviledges [sic]." Id. at 273.

59. Powell, supra note 2, at 71.

60. Id. at 71–73.

61. 5 *Annals of Congress* col. 495 (March 10, 1796) (History of Congress ed. 1849) (hereafter cited as *Annals of Congress*).

62. Id. at cols. 495–96.

63. Powell, supra note 2, at 71–72.

64. 5 *Annals of Congress*, supra note 61, at col. 496. Smith's full remark, which examined the implications of a proposed Antifederalist amendment in Pennsylvania that would have limited the force of treaties as internal law unless approved by the House of Representatives, ran thus: "This amendment was the most satisfactory evidence that the proposers of it did then believe that, without that amendment, such Treaty would be valid and binding, although not assented to by this House, and that they had, at that day, no idea that there existed in the Constitution the check which is now discovered by this *ex post facto* construction."

65. Id. at cols. 520, 522 (March 11, 1796) (emphasis added).

66. Id. at cols. 523–28. Sedgwick in fact came close to endorsing use of *framer* intent, which subsequently drew James Madison's ire, but his emphasis was not so much on framer intent per se as on framer intent as an especially valuable species of "contemporaneous exposition." Id. at col. 523.

67. Id. at col. 574.

68. Id. Bourne had already briefly surveyed the state convention proceedings, a survey which he concluded with the comment: "Now . . . if this was the construction of the Constitution when it was adopted in the several States, would it not be a trick on the small States [which had equal representation in the Senate] now to construe it differently?" Id. at cols. 572–73.

69. Powell, supra note 2, at 72.

70. 5 *Annals of Congress*, supra note 61, at col. 616–17 (March 17, 1796). Professor Powell quotes parts of these remarks, but does not, I think, convey their full force.

71. Powell sees Tracy's exploration of Confederation practice as further qualifying the weight he gave to the ratifiers' intent. See Powell, supra note 2, at 71–72 n.173. It is more accurate to say that Tracy argued that if the text, examined in light of pre-ratification practice, proved at all ambiguous, then the understanding of the ratifiers might settle the dispute.

72. Id. at 72.

73. 5 *Annals of Congress*, supra note 61, at col. 700 (emphasis added). His full statement, as recorded by the reporter, is instructive: "Other gentlemen, with whom he agreed in opinion, had rendered it unnecessary for him to say anything upon the opinions that were entertained at the adoption of the Constitution, upon the question now before the Committee. He believed that, from one end of America to the other, it was taken for granted that this House had nothing to do in the making of Treaties, and that this power was exclusively in the Senate and PRESIDENT. The [other] gentlemen just up . . . had placed the interests of the small States, in this construction, in so forcible and correct a point of view, that he would not say a word upon that very interesting part of the subject. But, of the contemporaneous opinions, that were supported in the Convention which framed the Constitution, he would make a remark or two." Id. Vans Murray then issued his challenge to Madison and Baldwin.

74. See id. at cols. 701–2.

75. Powell, supra note 2, at 72. Powell states in his next sentence: "Their [the Federalists'] opponents contended that the proper method of interpretation was 'to attend to and compare' the text's various provisions in accordance with the 'ancient' rules for 'the interpretation and construction of laws or Constitutions.'" The phrase "to attend to and compare" also comes from Gallatin, but Gallatin made no reference to "ancient" rules; he directly stated the rule of construction he preferred—"that construction which would give full effect to all the clauses and destroy none." 5 *Annals of Congress*, supra note 61, at col. 727 (March 24, 1796). The later quotations within Powell's sentence come from William Lyman, who eight days earlier had elaborated rules for textual construction, including *one* "maxim" that he labeled "ancient." Id. at col. 603 (March 16, 1796). Regarding his reading of the treaty power, Lyman also declared that "it had appeared, from the extracts of publications of the [ratification] period, that whatever might have been the diversity of opinion in other respects relative to the Constitution, that, in

this construction, at least, both its friends and opposers perfectly agreed." Id. at col. 604. Indeed, Lyman did not reject ratifier intent, but only read it as pointing to conclusions different from those that the Federalists now found in it.

76. Id. at col. 727 (March 24, 1796).

77. Id. at cols. 733–34.

78. Id. at col. 733 (emphasis added).

79. Id. at col. 734.

80. See id. at cols. 734–35.

81. Id. at cols. 735–37.

82. Id. at col. 635 (March 18, 1796). Livingston cautioned that if one were to look to the ratification debates, then it was the remarks of the Constitution's supporters, not its opponents, that were conclusive.

83. Powell, supra note 2, at 72 (emphasis added; the ellipsis and internal footnote numbers are Powell's).

84. *Annals of Congress*, supra note 61, at col. 505 (March 11, 1796).

85. Id. at col. 537 (March 14, 1796) (emphasis added).

86. Id. at cols. 538–39.

87. Powell, supra note 2, at 81.

88. 5 *Annals of Congress*, supra note 61, at cols. 761–62 (Washington's Message of March 30, 1796). In summarizing Washington's avowed constitutional authorities, Professor Powell omits the reference to the state ratification debates. See Powell, supra note 2, at 73.

89. 5 *Annals of Congress*, supra note 61, at cols. 774–76 (April 6, 1796).

90. Id. at col. 776.

91. Powell, supra note 2, at 83 n. 278.

92. However, to say that Madison was remarkably consistent is not to say that he was entirely consistent. In 1827, for example, he endorsed use of the journals of the Philadelphia Convention, although his wording was careful enough to allow the inference that he only meant that they would support a particular interpretation, not that they were entitled to dispositive weight. See Madison to Joseph C. Cabell (March 22, 1827), reprinted in 9 *Writings*, supra note 18, at 284, 286. For another example, see Madison to Thomas Jefferson (June 27, 1823), reprinted in 9 id. at 137, 142. So far as I have determined, the closest Madison came to directly explaining such usages was in 1830, when he described the Philadelphia Convention "as [only] presumptive evidence of the general understanding at the time of the language used." Madison to M. L. Hurlbert (May 1830), reprinted in 9 id. at 370, 372; see infra note 117 and accompanying text.

93. Madison to Ritchie (September 15, 1821), reprinted, in 9 *Writings*, supra note 18, at 71, 72. Accord, Madison to M. L. Hurlbert (May 1830), reprinted in 9 id. at 370, 372; Madison to N. P. Trist (December 1831), reprinted in 9 id. at 471, 477.

94. Powell, supra note 2, at 82.

95. See id. at 82–83, 73–74.

96. See id. at 83 n. 278 (quoting Madison to M. L. Hurlbert (May 1830), reprinted in 9 *Writings*, supra note 18, at 370, 372).

97. Powell, supra note 2, at 82.

98. Madison to Jonathan Elliot (February 14, 1827), reprinted in 9 *Writings*, supra note 18, at 270, 271.

99. Madison to Andrew Stevenson (November 27, 1830), reprinted in 9 id. at 411, 421.

100. Powell, supra note 2, at 938.

101. Madison to Henry Lee (June 25, 1824), reprinted, in 9 *Writings*, supra note 18, at 190, 191. That Madison disapproved such a change is evident in his immediately following comments. See id. at 191–92.

102. Madison commended Stevenson's "industry" in "search[ing] for a key to the sense of the Constitution, where alone the true one can be found; in the proceedings of the Convention, the cotemporary [sic] expositions, and above all in the ratifying Conventions of the States." Madison to Andrew Stevenson (March 25, 1826), reprinted in 3 *Letters and Other Writings of James Madison*, 520, 521–22 (1884) (hereafter cited as *Letters*). (If anything remarkable emerges from the letter, it is not doubts about resorting to the public expositions of 1787–88, but Madison's mention of the Philadelphia Convention.) As for the Trist letter, Powell in his parenthetical footnote elaboration correctly explains it as recognizing that the "Constitution [was] affected by the imprecision and mutability of language." Powell, supra note 2, at 84 n. 293. The letter says nothing, however, about the proper role for ratifier intent or anything else about how properly to interpret the document. To be sure, one phrase might be pulled out of context to suggest the propriety of settling word meaning through "a long course of application," but context indicates that Madison, without discussing proper interpretation, only recognized the Constitution unavoidably used some terms "the precise import of which has not been settled by a long course of application." (Reading the full sentence suggests in fact that he probably meant to write "had" rather than "has," which further underscores that he was only describing the document.) He recognized, too, that changes in word meaning had produced debates over the Constitution's meaning, a development he clearly disapproved. If anything, the reasonable inference from Madison's remarks to Trist on this occasion is that he would have welcomed clarification from the debates in 1787–88; but in its terms the letter simply does not take up the issue. See Madison to N. P. Trist (March 2, 1827), reprinted in 3 *Letters*, supra, at 565.

103. Powell, supra note 2, at 83.

104. Madison to Professor Davis (ca. 1832, not posted), reprinted in 4 *Letters*, supra note 102, at 232, 242.

105. Id. at 244.

106. Id. at 247.

107. Id. at 246–47.

108. Id. at 249.

109. Powell, supra note 2, at 83. In one of the cited letters, Madison remarked: "I have always supposed that the meaning of a law, and for a like reason, of a Constitution, *so far as it depends on Judicial interpretation*, was to result from a course of particular decisions, and not these from a previous and abstract comment on the subject." Madison to Spencer Roane (September 2, 1819), reprinted in 8 *Writings*, supra note 18, at 447 (emphasis added). The qualification here italicized indicates a more restricted view than that conveyed by Powell's phrase. Also diminishing the force of the letter to Judge Roane as authority for the phrase in question is the fact that in it Madison was arguing against aspects of a judicial precedent. In the other letter cited as support for Powell's definition of *"usus,"* Madison accepted the practical necessity of federal judicial review in federal-state disputes, which is also a rather narrow assertion. See Madison to Joseph C. Cabell (September 7, 1829), reprinted in 9 *Writings*, supra note 18, at 346. Professor Powell's footnote explanations for each letter acknowledge their restricted compass.

110. Madison to Professor Davis, reprinted in 4 *Letters*, supra note 102, at 232, 249. Madison's use herein of "made" is a little puzzling, but unless he was remarkably inconsistent with his views otherwise, he meant the term in the sense of "gave it force." Note the comment by his colleague Albert Gallatin, in 1796, that the framers "were not those who *made*, who passed the instrument; they only drew and proposed it." 5 *Annals of Congress*, supra note 61, at 734 (March 24, 1796) (emphasis added).

111. See Madison to John M. Patton (March 24, 1834), reprinted in 9 *Writings*, supra note 18, at 534, 536.

112. Powell, supra note 2, at 83–84.

113. Letter from Madison to C. E. Haynes (Feb. 25, 1831), reprinted in 9 *Writings*, supra note 18, at 442, 443. Accord, Madison to the Marquis de LaFayette (November 1826), reprinted in 3 *Letters*, supra note 102, at 538, 542; Madison to N. P. Trist (December 1831), reprinted in 9 *Writings*, supra note 18, at 471, 476–77. See also Madison to Thomas Jefferson (February 17, 1825), reprinted in 3 *Letters*, supra note 102, at 483.

114. See Madison to C. J. Ingersoll (June 25, 1831), reprinted in 4 *Letters*, supra note 102, at 183, 185.

115. Madison to N. P. Trist (December 1831), reprinted in 9 *Writings*, supra note 18, at 471, 477.

116. Madison to Spencer Roane (September 2, 1819), reprinted in 8 *Writings*, supra note 18 at 447, 450–51. Over a century later, Justice Sutherland offered a remarkably similar argument: "it is safe to say that if, when the Constitution was under consideration, it had been thought that any such danger lurked behind its plain words, it would never have been ratified." Carter v. Carter Coal Co., 298 U.S. 238, 296 (1936).

117. Madison to M. L. Hurlbert (May 1830), reprinted in 9 *Writings*, supra note 18, at 370, 371–72 (emphasis added).

118. See Chisholm v. Georgia, 2 U.S. (2 Dall.) 419 (1793), discussed in Powell, supra note 2, at 74–75; *Federalist* No. 81, supra note 25, at 548–49 (A. Hamilton). Cf. 3 *Debates*, supra note 27, at 533, 555–56 (remarks of James Madison and John Marshall in the Virginia Ratifying Convention, June 20, 1788).

119. See C. Jacobs, *The Eleventh Amendment and Sovereign Immunity* 27–40 (1972) (reviewing the state ratification debates and arguing that Antifederalists claimed and some Federalists admitted that the judicial article made the states amenable to suits by individuals); U.S. Const., Amend. XI; 3 *Debates*, supra note 27, at 471 (Randolph in the Virginia Ratifying Convention). See supra text accompanying note 51. Of course, to the extent that the ratifiers had recognized the amenability of states to suit, it becomes difficult to see the Eleventh Amendment as an attempt to restore the original intention. See generally C. Jacobs, supra, at 67–74.

120. See supra note 58 and accompanying text.

121. 5 *Annals of Congress*, supra note 61, at col. 635 (quoted supra, text accompanying note 82).

122. Rakove, supra note 6, at 183 (emphasis added).

The Creation of the Constitution:
The Integrity of
the Documentary Record

◆
═══
◆

JAMES H. HUTSON

I. Introduction

IN 1911, the Yale University Press published the *Records of the Federal Convention of 1787*, edited by Max Farrand. Farrand's edition of the *Records* was published in three volumes and, because of its comprehensive and meticulous scholarship, quickly supplanted all competing editions of Convention records. Yale reprinted the volumes in 1923, 1927, and 1934, and reissued them a final time in 1937 with the addition of a fourth, supplementary volume that contained documents discovered since the first three volumes were published in 1911. Because of the surprising number of new Convention documents that have come to light since 1937, another Farrand supplement is necessary. This Article resulted from research conducted for the preparation of such a supplement.

Some of the newly discovered documents raise questions concerning the reliability of the principal printed sources of information about the drafting and ratification of the Constitution: the Convention journal, kept by Secretary William Jackson;[1] Robert Yates's notes of debates at the Convention;[2] James Madison's notes;[3] and Jonathan Elliot's collection of debates at the state ratifying conventions.[4] The question of the integrity of the documentary record[5] is related to the current controversy about the advisability of interpreting the Constitution according to the original intention of the Framers.

───

If Convention records are not faithful accounts of what was said by the delegates in 1787, how can we know what they intended? The purpose of this Article is to issue a caveat about Convention records, to warn that there are problems with most of them and that some have been compromised—perhaps fatally—by the editorial interventions of hirelings and partisans. To recover original intent from these records may be an impossible hermeneutic assignment.

The Constitutional Convention proceedings were conducted in secrecy.[6] No publication of the speeches, resolutions, or votes of the delegates occurred until 1819, when, as the result of a joint congressional resolution of the previous year,[7] the official *Journal* of the Convention, kept by Secretary William Jackson, issued from the press. Two years later, the Convention notes of New York delegate Robert Yates appeared, covering the debates from May 25 to July 5. Jonathan Elliot began publishing his *Debates* in the state ratifying conventions in 1827. Not until 1840, more than fifty years after Washington took the presidential oath, were James Madison's notes of the debates, a full record of the Convention's proceedings, published.

How did the Supreme Court function during its first thirty years when it was compelled to construe the Constitution without the benefit of a published record that described the motives and intentions of the delegates? The answer, as Professor Powell has explained recently, is that in the early years of the Republic, written records about the gestation of the Constitution were considered irrelevant.[8] To establish its meaning, the "Philadelphia framers . . . assumed that future interpreters would adhere to the then-prevalent methods of statutory construction."[9] These methods obliged those construing statutes to effectuate the intention of the drafters, to discover their "intent" by consulting the words of the instrument and, if these were ambiguous, the common law.[10] Professor Powell finds no indication that the framers "expected or intended future interpreters to refer to any extratextual intentions revealed in the convention's secretly conducted debates."[11] The "legislative history" of the Constitution could, in short, be ignored.

At first, the Supreme Court honored this "interpretative intention" of the Framers. The Court generally eschewed the use of extrinsic aids in construing the Constitution. Summarizing their early practices, Chief Justice Marshall claimed in *Ogden* v. *Saunders*[12] that the Court had taken "frequent occasion to declare its opinion . . . that the intention of the instrument must prevail; that this intention must be collected from its words; [and] that its words are to be understood in that sense in which they are generally used by those for whom the instrument was intended."[13] But, as Professor Jacobus tenBroek has demonstrated, the Court early permitted exceptions to its rule against using extrinsic aids to construe the Constitution.[14] Because this rule was formulated in "conditions that made it only a dictum," not a "vital doctrine,"[15] the Court permitted itself to use records of the debates of the Philadelphia Convention almost as soon as they were in print. In 1854, for example, in *Carpenter* v. *Pennsylvania*,[16] the Court cited the recently published edition of Madison's notes to prove that "the debates in the federal convention upon the Constitution" demonstrated that the constitutional prohibition against ex post facto laws was restricted to criminal cases,[17] thus reversing a position Justice William Johnson had taken in 1829 in *Satterlee* v. *Matthewson*,[18] when Madison's notes were unavailable.

Professor Powell has argued that, by 1840, the "earlier scruples against the use of 'extrinsic evidence' in constitutional interpretation" had become sufficiently relaxed to allow a "modern" approach to the discovery of intent, involving "historical reconstruction" of the motives of document drafters.[19] Professor tenBroek did not assign any specific date for this transition to modernity, but, writing in 1938, he cited dozens of cases that spanned a century in which the Supreme Court employed the printed records of the debates and proceedings of the Convention to establish the Framers' intentions.[20] The "propriety of considering the proposals and debates of the Constitutional Convention," Chief Justice Frederick M. Vinson wrote in 1949, had long been a respected practice.[21] That such historical citation continues unabated is attested by recent cases like *Bowshar* v. *Synar*[22] in which Chief Justice Warren Burger cited "the debates in the Constitutional Convention" to demonstrate the "dangers of congressional usurpation of Executive Branch functions."[23]

Professor tenBroek concluded that the most frequent use by the Court of the proceedings at Philadelphia was "to affirm a conclusion which apparently, and sometimes assertedly, rests chiefly upon other grounds."[24] The perception that Convention records are used principally to "rationalize" decisions[25] and "create an illusion" that the Framers are guiding the judges,[26] has bred cynicism about them. Witness a recent article about an attorney who defends his client by citing "selected snippets from Farrand's Records of the Federal Convention of 1787,"[27] not because he subscribes to their contents, but because he knows they will impress the judge and better justify his fee;[28] the judge, described in the same article, cites Farrand, not because he grounds his decision on the intentions of the Framers, but because references to them will make his opinion sound more learned and convincing.[29] If the Convention records are no more than eye-catching, judicial wrapping paper, it is not surprising that their reliability has escaped rigorous scrutiny.

But what if the records are more than ornamental? A growing movement has called for the intentions of the Framers—presumed to be discoverable in Convention documents—to be binding on the Court. The campaign mounted in recent years by some scholars and judges, and now embraced by public officials, to convert the courts to what has been called a "Jurisprudence of Original Intention"[30] has received so much publicity that it is familiar even to readers of mass circulation newspapers.[31] Few of these readers may be aware, however, that the success of such a campaign would dictate, as Professor Michael Perry explains, that "virtually all of the constitutional doctrine regarding human rights fashioned by the Supreme Court in this century must be adjudged illegitimate."[32] Constitutional scholars to whom such a result would be repugnant have challenged the doctrine of original intent, variously called "interpretivism," "originalism," or "intentionalism,"[33] on epistemological or other grounds.[34]

An equally promising way to explore the viability of interpretivism is to scrutinize the condition of constitutional texts. Lawyers, judges, and legal scholars have been inclined to accept whatever is in print as a faithful rendition of what occurred at the Philadelphia and state ratifying conventions. Professor William W. Crosskey, it is true, in his first two volumes of *Politics and the Constitution in the History of the United States*,[35] impugned the documentary record of the Convention by charging that Madison's notes were little better than fiction.[36] But Crosskey's controversial reputation evidently has inhibited legal scholars from marshalling his arguments during the current debate, profound though their implications are for a theory of original intent. Professor John Wofford also raised serious questions about the reliability of Convention records in an article published in 1964.[37] Since then, however, little has been written about constitutional documentation. The current debate over original intent calls for a fresh examination of the historical evidence. To ascertain what weight lawyers, judges, and scholars should give to which records relating to the creation of the Constitution, this Article examines the Convention records in the chronological order in which they were published.

II. *The Accuracy and Reliability of Convention Records*

A. *The Journal of the Convention*

The Convention journal was published in 1819. Secretary William Jackson, after "burning all the loose scraps of paper which belong[ed] to the convention,"[38] handed "the Journal and other papers" generated by the Convention to George Washington on the evening of adjournment, September 17, 1787.[39] On March 19, 1796, Washington turned these documents over to the State Department. According to a receipt executed that day by Secretary of State Timothy Pickering, Washington delivered a "journal of the general or federal convention, in one hundred & fifty three pages; together with a journal of the proceedings of the Committee of the Whole House; a book exhibiting on eight pages a detail of yeas & nays on questions taken in the Convention & two loose sheets & a half sheet, containing nine pages of the like yeas and nays."[40]

In 1818, Congress passed a joint resolution ordering the Convention journal printed.[41] The task of preparing it for publication fell to Secretary of State John Quincy Adams, who found the demands of editing exasperating.

"The journals and papers were very loosely and imperfectly kept,"[42] he complained on June 2, 1818. "They were no better than the daily minutes from which the regular journal ought to have been, but never was, made out."[43]

Farrand was equally vexed by the condition of the journals and papers. He scored Jackson for "carelessly" keeping his notes[44] and excused "mistakes" in Adams's edition of the journal as "inevitable" because of the disordered materials he was using.[45] In 1964, Professor Wofford charged that the "accuracy" of the Convention journal "leaves a great deal to be desired."[46]

The inaccuracies with which Farrand and Wofford taxed the Convention journal need to be put in perspective. The journal proper—the 153-page journal of the Convention and the 28-page journal of the Committee of the Whole—was not the problem. The trouble was the seventeen-odd pages, detached from the journal, which recorded the "ayes and noes on the various questions"[47] taken in the Convention. Jackson kept these detached votes in tabular form, by delegation not individuals. In at least ninety percent of the cases, the questions on which the votes were taken were given but the dates on which the voting occurred were not. This system of recording, though nettlesome to both Adams and Farrand, posed no insuperable editorial problems because the questions for which the votes were recorded could be found by searching through the chronologically organized journal. Once the questions were found, the votes could be added at the appropriate dates. For example, Jackson's table indicated that three states voted yea, eight nay, on the question whether Congress should have power to make sumptuary laws. The journal, when examined, revealed that a motion "to make sumptuary laws" had been considered on August 20. In preparing the journal for publication, the three-to-eight vote could be matched with the August 20 motion.[48]

The real problems arose with a handful of "ayes and noes" in the detached sheets that were accompanied by no contextual information, and which Jackson had keyed to neither questions nor dates. Through considerable editorial ingenuity, Adams and Farrand succeeded in matching these votes with the appropriate motions, but the possibility that errors had been made, in a few instances, caused Farrand, ever the perfectionist, to warn that the printed edition of the journal "cannot be relied upon absolutely."[49] Another trifling problem was that, in a few instances, Jackson may have counted the votes inaccurately. Hugh Williamson, for example, noted on his copy of the Committee of Detail report that the vote on August 31 to require nine states to ratify the Constitution before it could become operative was seven-to-four; using Jackson's tables, Farrand made the vote eight-to-three.[50] It was the possibility of such inconsequential computational differences or a misattributed vote that caused Farrand to issue his warning about the accuracy of the printed journal.[51] However, the slight probability of error—and the understanding that none of it relates to what the delegates said—permits confidence in the journal, as published by John Quincy Adams or Max Farrand, as a reliable text. No such confidence is possible, however, in Yates's notes, considered next.

B. Yates's Notes

Farrand called Robert Yates's notes the source "next in importance" to Madison's notes for information about the Philadelphia Convention.[52] The frequency with which they have been cited, from the *Legal Tender Cases* in which they were curiously identified by the appellant Potter as "Yates's Minutes"[53] to more recent cases,[54] confirms the accuracy of his assessment.

The notes were published in Albany in 1821 under the title *Secret Proceedings and Debates of the Convention Assembled at Philadelphia, in the Year 1787. . . . From Notes Taken by the Late Robert Yates, Esquire, Chief Justice of New York and Copied by John Lansing, Jun., Esquire, Late Chancellor of that State, Members of that Convention.* The title page listed no editor. Washington newspapers plausibly but erroneously speculated that Lansing had seen the volume through the press.[55] The identity of the editor would have startled the country's newspaper readers, for he was none other than Citizen Genet[56]—Edmond C. Genet—the tempestuous minister of revolutionary France who convulsed American politics in 1793.[57] Fearing the guillotine, Genet refused to return to France when recalled. He married a daughter of Governor George Clinton of New York and settled on a farm in Long Island, later removing to Greenbush, near Albany. Among Clinton's political lieutenants were Yates and Lansing. They went to the Philadelphia Convention to protect the interests of New York State as the Clintonians parochially defined them. Both men withdrew on July 10 when it became apparent that they could not prevent the adoption of a strong national government. Introduced to the circle of Clinton's friends by marriage, Genet, nevertheless, was distrusted because of the tumultuous scenes he had precipitated in 1793 and because in his occasional forays into political journalism on behalf of his father-in-law, he displayed a penchant for character assassination that produced notorious libels such as one charging Rufus King, a model of probity and a pillar of the New York establishment, with robbing a widow in the settlement of an estate.[58]

Upon Yates's death in 1801, his Convention notes passed to his wife who retained them until 1808. Genet then tried to get them from Mrs. Yates to conduct a political smear campaign. Fearing for their safety in the Frenchman's hands, Lansing intervened and rescued the original manuscript from the widow, promising that she would receive a copy. Lansing completed the copy within a month, making the "transcript verbatim, without the least mutilation or other alteration."[59] Genet then extracted Lansing's copy of Yates's notes from the widow to use in promoting Clinton's political ambitions.[60]

In 1808, Clinton challenged Madison for the presidential nomination on the Jeffersonian Republican ticket.[61] Over the signature of a "Citizen of New

York," Genet wrote a polemic against Madison, entitled *A Letter to the Electors of the President and Vice President of the United States.*[62] The raw material for Genet's screed was Lansing's copy of Yates's notes, which Genet edited so drastically and tendentiously that Lansing, who had evidently anticipated just such a reckless manipulation of the sources, later congratulated himself on "getting possession of the original . . . in opposition to some ardent politicians, adverse to the election of Mr. Madison as president."[63]

In his broadside against Madison, Genet promised that the full text of Yates's notes would "soon be offered to the people,"[64] but he withheld the document for thirteen years until another set of political ends could be served by its publication. Such an opportunity presented itself on August 28, 1821, when a convention met in Albany to revise the constitution of the state of New York. Genet published what purported to be a complete version of Yates's notes—his *Secret Proceedings*, the version we now have in Farrand—shortly before the convention convened. His purpose was to influence the convention's deliberations, as he admitted in a letter, presenting his *Secret Proceedings* to President James Monroe.[65] The states "being now engaged in the revisal or foundation of their organic laws, I have," he informed the President, "thought the moment propitious to supply their Legislatures with the various opinions, views, and principles of the sages who framed the federal constitution."[66] Because of the murky nature of New York politics in the 1820s, it is not clear on whose behalf Genet produced Yates's notes. He may have been working for his father-in-law's nephew, DeWitt Clinton, who according to an older view of New York history, opposed the calling of the convention and the reforms proposed by its proponents, the Bucktail Republicans, who were suspected of scheming "to revolutionize everything."[67] Certainly, Genet's statement in his letter to Monroe that he intended Yates's notes to divulge "admonitory facts and observations that will render them less liable to be led astray by erroneous doctrines and guard them against the danger of exchanging for adventurous innovation real and substantial good,"[68] suggests that he was no friend of reform. On the other hand, recent revisionist historians who have studied the convention have portrayed the Clintonians as matching their opponents' ardor for progressive change and exceeding it in certain areas such as concern for the welfare of the black population.[69] It is conceivable, therefore, that in opposing "adventurous innovation," perhaps in race relations, Genet was cooperating with the Clintonian opposition, the Bucktail Republicans, whose power base was in Tammany Hall. We simply do not know the precise nature of his political agenda in 1821.

What is known is that, in publishing the *Secret Proceedings*, Genet took liberties with Lansing's copy of Yates's notes, liberties that appear to have exceeded those he permitted himself in the anti-Madison polemic in 1808. Lansing's copy of Yates's notes was thought to have been lost until two sheets from July 5, 1787 were discovered recently in Genet's papers at the Library of Congress.[70] By comparing the contents of those sheets—the only ones known to exist—with what Genet actually published as occurring on July 5, 1787, it can be seen that he omitted half of the material on the sheets and altered every sentence that he published.* If Genet inflicted similar depredations on the remainder of Yates's notes, those notes as now printed in the *Secret Proceedings* cannot be considered a reliable record of what occurred at the Philadelphia Convention and cannot be consulted as a source of the intentions of the Framers. When Madison read extracts from Genet's publication in August 1821, he protested its "extreme incorrectness."[71] The plaything of an unscrupulous partisan, Yates's notes as published by Genet fully deserved Madison's condemnation.

C. The Debates in the State Ratifying Conventions

Because many of the members of the Federal Convention sought seats in the ratifying conventions of their respective states to explain and defend the work done at Philadelphia, and because men like John Marshall served in these conventions, the state proceedings have always been regarded as a storehouse of information about the intentions of the Framers. Debates in the state conventions, Professor tenBroek has explained, have "frequently [been] utilized . . . in arguments before the United States Supreme Court,"[72] a fact demonstrated by Justice Byron White's use of the debates in the Pennsylvania and North Carolina ratifying conventions in his opinion in *Nixon* v. *Fitzgerald*.[73] Indeed, some recent scholars such as Professor Brest have suggested that the members of the state conventions were the true framers,[74] because it was their action in ratifying the Constitution that brought it to life and transformed it from a mere proposal to the supreme law of the land. This line of argument appears to be designed to discredit the theory of original intent by multiplying the number of framers exponentially—to a majority in each of nine ratifying conventions or, in the case of a constitutional amendment, to a majority in each of three-fourths of the state legislatures. Nevertheless, it does emphasize the importance of the state ratifying conventions as a source for ascertaining the intentions of the drafters of the Constitution.

Our information about the proceedings in the state ratifying conventions comes from a single source: Jonathan Elliot's *The Debates in the several State Conventions, on the adoption of the Federal Constitution, as recommended by the General Convention at Philadelphia, in 1787*.[75] First published in four volumes between 1827 and 1830, Elliot's work is a bibliographical brainteaser, for it was republished in at least seven more editions, in differing numbers of volumes, with the contents of individual volumes differing in many cases from edition to edition. Elliot was not a scholar. Rather, he was a Washington political

---

*[Ed. note: Photocopies and a transcript of these documents are omitted here, but may be found at pp. 14–19 of this article as originally published in 65 *Texas Law Review* (1986).]

journalist turned editor, whose press was for sale to the highest bidder. John Quincy Adams, who cancelled a government printing contract held by Elliot because he suspected price gouging, described him as "an Englishman, having no character of his own—penurious and venal—metal to receive any stamp."[76] It appears that in the 1830s, Elliot was promoting the political fortunes of John C. Calhoun, although he had opposed the South Carolinian earlier.[77] Some scholars believe that one of Elliot's purposes in preparing his *Debates* was to advance Calhoun's cause, for Elliot supplemented proceedings in the conventions with such states' rights classics as the Virginia and Kentucky Resolutions and deleted from the 1836 second edition a letter from Madison, which appeared in the first edition, attacking nullification.[78] Whether Elliot went as far as Genet and doctored the *Debates* to promote the politics of a patron is not clear, but so obvious were their shortcomings that Elliot himself apologized for them in the preface to the first edition, confessing that "the sentiments they contain may, in some instances, have been inaccurately taken down, and, in others, probably, too faintly sketched, fully to gratify the inquisitive politician."[79]

To know why the debates were "inaccurately taken down," it is necessary to know how and by whom they were recorded. Unlike the Philadelphia Convention, the state ratifying conventions were open to the public. Enterprising men recorded the debates in shorthand and then published them as commercial ventures in the newspapers and in book form. Elliot's *Debates* are a collection of these publications, generated in the first instance by shorthand reporters. And precisely here was the problem, for the technique of shorthand was in its infancy in the United States and did not provide the means of recording public discourse accurately.

Most of those stenographers who recorded the state conventions are known to us: Benjamin Russell in Massachusetts, Enoch Perkins in Connecticut, Francis Childs in New York, Thomas Lloyd in Pennsylvania and Maryland, and David Robertson in Virginia and North Carolina. Lloyd's career is better documented than those of his colleagues.[80] He claimed to have learned shorthand from the Jesuits at St. Omers, Flanders, but his system has been shown to be identical to one published by Graves and Ashton in York, England, in 1775,[81] which was in turn based on Thomas Gurney's popular method.[82] Whatever the source of Lloyd's system, like all "eighteenth-century shorthand [it] was inadequate to the task of recording speeches verbatim."[83] "Like most systems of his day," Lloyd's technique left "much to the imagination of the transcriber. There is much similarity between symbols for different letters, and there are no vowels. Lloyd omitted most articles and connectives, and used many abbreviations peculiar to him alone."[84] In short, he was technically unable to capture accurately most of what speakers said.

The other stenographers of the state conventions were in all probability even less capable of accurately conveying the proceedings than was Lloyd. By 1787, Lloyd had been dabbling in shorthand for some years. Given his inadequacies, it is hard to believe that the records of his colleagues could be considered reliable when they were mere neophytes in a technique that took at least five years to master.[85] No wonder, then, that Elliot was compelled to admit that the proceedings of the ratifying conventions were "inaccurately taken down."[86]

A survey of the records in states for which information is available shows that in some cases insufficient stenographic skills may have been the least of problems. From New Hampshire, Elliot published only a fragment of the Convention debates, the centerpiece of which was a speech by Joshua Atherton.[87] According to the historian of the New Hampshire Convention, Atherton's speech apparently was "written out from tradition, by a hand other than his own, long after the Convention."[88] In fact, it appears to have been composed by parties unknown in 1827, when it was first published as antislavery propaganda in a New Hampshire newspaper.[89]

Elliot reprinted the debates in the Massachusetts Convention from a volume published in Boston in 1788 by Benjamin Russell.[90] In a publisher's note, Russell apologized for "'some inaccuracies, and many omissions,' due to the 'inexperience' of the reporters."[91] Contemporaries testified that Russell and his colleagues inserted speeches in the published debates that they themselves had written for some of the delegates—General William Thompson of Billerica, for example, was said to have been one of the beneficiaries of their ghostwriting. "The Printers here have really mended the diction and some of the Sentiments" of the Convention delegates, a Bostonian wrote a friend on March 4, 1788.[92]

Political partisanship in Connecticut and New York, more than the shortage of stenographic expertise, compromised the quality of the record of convention debates in those states. In Connecticut, the *Connecticut Courant* and the *American Mercury*, both Federalist newspapers, hired Enoch Perkins, a young Federalist lawyer, to report the debates at Hartford. The results were egregiously partisan—only one short summary of one Anti-Federalist speech was published, and at least one Federalist speech was said to have been "particularly erroneous."[93] For New York, Elliot published Francis Childs's *Debates and Proceedings of the Convention of the State of New York* that appeared in December 1788.[94] A fledgling stenographer, Childs apologized to the delegates he recorded "for the imperfect dress in which their arguments are given to the Public. Not long accustomed to the business, he cannot pretend to as much accuracy as might be expected from a more experienced hand,—and it will easily be comprehended how difficult it must be to follow a copious and rapid Speaker, in the train of his reasoning, much more in the turn of his expression."[95] Childs further impaired his credibility by recording and publishing the debates for only two of the Convention's six weeks, and by allowing speakers to revise their remarks after the event.[96] The most damaging charge against his reliability as a reporter, however, was the accusation that he was a "partyman,"[97] a Federalist who manipulated his notes to promote factional interests.

This charge was made with more vehemence against Thomas Lloyd, the reporter of the Pennsylvania and Maryland debates. An ardent Federalist, Lloyd probably had no qualms about taking money from Pennsylvania Federalist leaders to delete all the Anti-Federalist speeches in the Convention,[98] as he in fact did in his *Debates of the Convention of the State of Pennsylvania*, published on February 7, 1788, and reprinted by Elliot.[99] In addition to suppressing the Anti-Federalists, Lloyd eliminated all Federalist speeches except those by Thomas McKean and James Wilson, the latter of which had obviously been corrected and "improved" after the Convention because they were printed with footnotes.[100] The Anti-Federalists correctly charged that Lloyd's *Debates* had been "afterwards altered, dressed and undressed by, and at the pleasure of his benefactors,"[101] and were nothing more than Federalist campaign literature. In December and January of 1787–1788, Federalist stalwarts Timothy Pickering and Tench Coxe sent prepublication excerpts from Lloyd's *Debates* to partisans in other states to furnish Federalist orators arguments for ratification.[102] Even Elliot deprecated Lloyd's notes by advising his readers that although he was publishing them, he had sought in vain to obtain better accounts of the Pennsylvania Convention.[103]

The reporter of the Virginia debates, one David Robertson, inspired little confidence in some citizens of the Old Dominion. "The Debates are not Yet published; nor is there any Cause to expect that they will be authentic; the Short Hand Man," wrote George Mason, "being a federal Partizan, [the notes] will probably be garbled, in some such Partial Manner as the Debates of the Pennsylvania Convention have been by Lloyd."[104] Robertson's *Debates and Other Proceedings of the Convention of Virginia*, published in 1788 and reprinted by Elliot,[105] shared the weaknesses of the works of his stenographic colleagues. "I find passages," wrote Madison, "some appearing to be defective, others obscure, if not unintelligible, others again which must be more or less erroneous."[106] John Marshall, whose speeches at the Virginia Convention are frequently cited in the legal literature,[107] was so distressed by Robertson's inaccuracies that he complained that "as to what is given to me . . . if my name had not been prefixed to the speaches [sic] I never should have recognized them as productions of mine."[108]

The Virginia Convention adjourned on June 27, 1788; Robertson was then hired by James Iredell and William Davie, the Federalist chieftains in North Carolina, to come to Hillsboro and record the action in the ratifying convention in the Tarheel state.[109] Apparently Robertson did not please his employers, for he refused to make a "fair copy" of his shorthand notes. This task then fell to "a little boy the son of Mr. Turnbull," who to no one's surprise, performed the work "most defectively."[110] Various Federalist speakers tinkered with the lad's work before the debates were published by Iredell and Davie. They hoped that the dissemination of the debates "would produce a salutary change in the opinions of the people,"[111] whose representatives had failed to ratify the Constitution but were scheduled to try again in 1789. Thus, the North Carolina debates as reported were designed, like those in Pennsylvania, to serve as Federalist campaign literature.

Reviewing the ratification proceedings on the floor of Congress in 1791, Elbridge Gerry asserted that "the debates of the State Conventions, as published by the short-hand writers, were generally partial and mutilated."[112] Gerry's assessment applies with equal force to Genet's edition of Yates's notes. Documents as corrupt as these cannot be relied upon to reveal the intentions of the Framers.

D. Madison's Notes

1. Their History of Controversy. Although often entreated to publish his notes on the Philadelphia Convention, James Madison never relented in his conviction that they should appear posthumously. At his death in 1836, the notes passed to his widow who sold them to the federal government, which commissioned their publication in 1840;[113] "at once," wrote Farrand, "all other records paled into insignificance."[114]

So comprehensive and convincing did the notes appear that most readers accepted them as authoritative. Partisans of Alexander Hamilton, however, challenged their veracity and an undercurrent of skepticism about their accuracy has continued ever since. Gaillard Hunt, for example, in a preface to an edition of Madison's notes published in 1920, commented on "the suspicious investigator, who thinks that Madison may have made alterations in his original record so as to suppress or distort the truth or give a coloring to the facts."[115]

The suspicious investigators found their champion three decades later in Professor William Winslow Crosskey of the University of Chicago Law School. Crosskey revealed his true feelings about Madison and his notes to his constitutional law classes. According to the reminiscence of a student, Crosskey would begin his class by slamming Farrand's *Records* on his desk and promising "to demonstrate to you that Madison was a forger—he tampered with the notes he kept of the debates at the federal constitutional convention in order to suit his own political advantage and that of his party."[116] Crosskey was more circumspect in the first two volumes of his opus, *Politics and the Constitution in the History of the United States*,[117] published in 1953, merely suggesting "the possibility that his [Madison's] testimony may have been, not inadvertently, but deliberately false and misleading."[118] Elsewhere in the volume, however, Crosskey became more explicit, declaring that Madison "presented falsely the sentiments of other men"[119] and inserted "spurious" dialogue in his notes.[120] Crosskey argued that Madison's motive in doctoring his manuscript was to play politics—to make his Convention notes support the doctrines of the Jeffersonian-Republican party that coalesced in the 1790s and that Madison helped to lead for the remainder of his career. If we accept Crosskey's account, Madison's notes, no less than Genet's and Lloyd's, were the product of political partisanship and were, on that account, corrupt.

Crosskey's volumes aroused conflicting passions. Admirers praised them enthusiastically;[121] detractors accused the author of McCarthyism on the grounds that Crosskey made unproven charges and innuendos against Madison.[122] Mixed reviews did not discourage Professor Crosskey.[123] He completed most of a third volume, published posthumously by his disciple William Jeffrey in 1980,[124] bringing his account up to the eve of the Convention. Crosskey also finished some sections on the Convention itself, including one on the ex post facto and contract clauses that was published posthumously as a law review article in 1968.[125] Crosskey characteristically charged Madison with fabricating passages in his notes and further distorting them by deliberately omitting relevant information.[126]

Although potentially a formidable weapon in the debates over the validity of attempting to discern the Framers' "original intent," Crosskey's thesis has not been wielded by legal scholars. Some historians and biographers, however, have embraced it with enthusiasm. In 1970, for example, Paul Clarkson and Samuel Jett, biographers of *Luther Martin of Maryland*,[127] charged that "scores of . . . serious (and often demonstrably inaccurate) 'corrections,' alterations, and additions, made over a period of fifty years . . . raise a serious question as to accuracy of [Madison's] record."[128] The treatment Madison's notes receive in Christopher and James Collier's 1986 monograph, *Decision in Philadelphia: The Constitutional Convention of 1787*,[129] demonstrates the persistence of Crosskey's influence.[130] The Colliers draw on the scholarship of S. Sidney Ulmer, himself an adherent of Crosskey, who in 1958 charged that Madison's "objectivity" as a reporter of the Convention debates was "corrupted beyond repair,"[131] to assert that "Charles Pinckney of South Carolina was cheated of credit for his role in modeling the Constitution" by Madison's having "suppressed" evidence of Pinckney's activities in Philadelphia.[132] And, in a passage of pure Crosskey, the Colliers charge that after 1800, Madison became interested in "controlling as much as he could the history" of the creation of the Constitution and "altered his own speeches" to accomplish his objective.[133] Madison, they conclude, "improved his own arguments and abbreviated those of his opponents."[134]

Crosskey himself was more severe with Madison, charging that Madison invented dialogue at the Convention exactly as would a writer of fiction. Thus, he argued that John Dickinson's speech on August 29, explaining Blackstone's definition of the scope of ex post facto laws, was "a later Madisonian fabrication";[135] that debates on August 21 on the imports and exports clause contained "certain spurious passages";[136] and that a colloquy between Dickinson and Gouverneur Morris on August 15 had "very much the appearance of a later interpolation."[137]

No visual evidence supports these charges—an examination of the relevant manuscript pages of Madison's notes reveals no significant alteration of the text on any of these dates. Therefore, Crosskey's allegations must be based on a theory that Madison completely rewrote his notes (or parts of them) at a later date using a fresh supply of paper and substituting the newly composed sheets for the ones he had prepared earlier. Does an examination of the paper used in Madison's manuscript support such a theory?

2. Their Accuracy Confirmed. Watermarks on the pages of Madison's manuscript notes reveal that he used British papers, predominantly those of the celebrated Kentish manufacturer James Whatman, whose family has been called the "most eminent British paper makers of the eighteenth century."[138] On all but seven days of the Convention Madison used Whatman paper, recognized by three watermarks: (1) J Whatman, (2) a crown and post horn with a pendant cursive W, or (3) a crown and post horn with a pendant GR. The only days Madison did not use Whatman paper were June 26, June 29, July 17, and July 18, when he employed paper with the watermark T French; and September 7, 15, and 17, when he used paper marked Budgen. All of this paper must have been manufactured before 1794 because none of it is dated, and a British law of 1794 required all paper to be dated to obtain a rebate on the export excise tax.[139]

A comparison of Madison's notes with letters he wrote during the Convention demonstrates that on every date such a comparison is possible, the paper used for the notes and letters is identical. For example, on July 18, Madison wrote Jefferson a letter on paper with Whatman's crown, post horn, and cursive W watermark; the July 18 pages in the notes bear the same watermark. When chain lines and laid lines are compared, using betaradiography, the letter and note sheets prove to be identical. Similar results are obtained by comparing other letters written during the summer, for example, Madison to Pendleton on May 27, to Jefferson on June 6, to Monroe on June 10, to Madison, Sr. on July 28 and September 4, to Convention notes composed on each of these days. Paper studies indicate that Madison's notes were written out, as he later claimed they were, as soon as possible after he took them on the floor of the Convention.[140]

Also militating against the theory of a later, massive adulteration of Madison's notes is the recent discovery of the "Eppes copy" of those notes. Probably in the summer of 1791, though possibly as late as 1793, John Wayles Eppes, Thomas Jefferson's nephew, who was living at the time with his uncle in Philadelphia, transcribed Madison's notes.[141] Eppes's transcription, less the pages from June 21 to July 18, has been found in the Edward Everett papers at the Massachusetts Historical Society. A comparison of the Eppes transcription with Madison's notes for August 15, 21, and 29, dates on which Professor Crosskey claimed Madison "fabricated" and "interpolated" the proceedings, demonstrates that the two documents are identical, proving no changes were made in Madison's notes (on these dates, at least) after Eppes executed his copy in 1791 or 1793. It appears, then, that Madison did not rewrite the story of the Constitutional Convention later in life.

As Farrand pointed out, however, Madison did make some changes in his notes in the years after the Convention.[142] Failing to understand Madison's purposes, Professor Wofford misjudged his alterations. There is no explanation, however, for Wofford's fabrication of the statement he attributed to Farrand, that Madison's emendations "seriously impaired the value of his notes."[143] Wofford asserted that "after the publication of the official—and inaccurate—Journal, Madison went over his notes and made numerous changes in them."[144] It has been shown above, however, that the mistakes in the Journal were so inconsequential—involving only a few computational and assignment of vote errors—that even if Madison included all of the Journal errors, he would not have significantly compromised the value of his notes. Madison, however, did not use the printed Journal as the sole source of his emendations. Unbeknownst to Wofford, Madison had a copy of Secretary William Jackson's manuscript journal years before its publication in 1819; by using it he avoided incorporating any editorial errors that John Quincy Adams may have introduced.

In taking notes at the Convention, Madison had the good sense not to try to do too much.[145] If a set speech was being delivered, in many cases he did not try to record it. Instead, he sought copies from the speakers, who usually obliged, either immediately or later in the proceedings.[146] Madison followed the same practice with motions and resolutions. Short ones he recorded on the spot; longer ones he obtained from their movers after the session. It is obvious he anticipated having access to Jackson's journal, for during the introduction of long motions such as that of August 18, which he did not at the time record, he reminded himself to "see Journal of Convention."[147] Madison thus expected that Jackson, as secretary of the Convention, would preserve in his journal all the motions and resolutions made and that after the Convention he could borrow Jackson's journal and remedy the omissions in his notes. This is precisely what happened. In 1789, Washington lent Jackson's manuscript journal to Madison and Madison made a copy.[148] Then, Madison compared his notes to his copy and inserted in the notes, on slips of paper of varying sizes, the texts of the motions and resolutions that he had not recorded in 1787. When the journal was printed in 1819, Madison compared it with his notes, as expanded by the 1789 collation, and made some additional corrections in the interest of further improving the record.[149] Thus, insofar as existing evidence permits a judgment, Madison's notes are a faithful account of what he recorded at the Convention in 1787—augmented by motions, resolutions, and votes that he believed to be, and in the vast majority of cases were, accurately recorded by Jackson and accurately printed by John Quincy Adams in 1819.

We see, then, that unlike Yates's notes and the state ratifying debates,

Madison's notes and the Convention journal do not suffer from editorial interventions by their authors or others, disqualifying them as sources of information about the Convention. But the question of how accurately these works reveal the intentions of the Framers remains, for although they are faithful accounts of what Madison and Jackson recorded in 1787, it is necessary to know if what Madison and Jackson recorded was a faithful account of what occurred on the floor of the Convention. In short, how good were they as reporters?

3. Lingering Questions. The Convention journal consists of little more than a chronological list of motions. It is, in one of Genet's few accurate statements about a constitutional document, a mere "diplomatic skeleton" that needs the discourse of delegates to "fill up . . . its vital parts."[150] Why did the journal lack debates that would explain the objectives of the delegates in making their motions, as well as the meaning they attached to such motions? Secretary Jackson did keep shorthand notes of the debates using his own idiosyncratic system. He was preparing to publish these notes in 1827 to flesh out his skeleton,[151] but no publication appeared and the notes have disappeared. The journal, therefore, reveals little about the delegates' intent.

Madison's notes, then, stand alone as the key to the Framers' intentions. If his notes on any given day are compared to the fragmentary records of debates left by other delegates that Farrand printed or that have been discovered more recently, a rough approximation between the different accounts is evident—demonstrating that Madison was not inventing dialogue, but was trying to capture what was said. Still, there is an enigma about Madison's note-taking methods. The Convention was in session from 10:00 A.M.[152] to mid-afternoon every day except Sunday—"not less than five, for a large part of the time Six and sometimes 7 hours sitting every day," Washington wrote on September 17, 1787.[153] These were full sessions of the Convention; committees, as Madison and others attested, met before or after the day's business, and there is no evidence that the Convention took breaks, although individual members must have excused themselves now and again.

If read aloud, Madison's notes for any particular day consume only a few minutes, suggesting that he may have recorded only a small part of each day's proceedings. An experiment was tried to verify this hypothesis. On April 17–19, 1986, the Council of Scholars of the Library of Congress sponsored a symposium on scholarship. A portion of the final day was devoted to a discussion of the symposium papers previously delivered. Thirty-odd people participated in the symposium, roughly the number present on any one day during the Convention. A chairman moderated exchanges about issues raised earlier in the symposium. The debates were recorded on electromagnetic tape and transcribed verbatim. One hour's discussion yielded 8,400 words. Comparing this figure to the 6,000–7,000 words used in a typical, fifty-minute undergraduate lecture[154] demonstrates its plausibility. For comparison purposes a word count was made of Madison's debates for each day the Convention was in session in June. June was chosen because it was Madison's most productive month as a recorder. The weather was cool, he was fresh, and the Convention was talking rather than incessantly voting on motions as it did in August and September. Madison averaged 2,740 words per session in June. Because sessions lasted five hours—the Convention did not go to a longer schedule until August[155]—he averaged 548 words per hour, a figure which can be rounded up to 600 words per hour to simplify calculations. At this rate Madison recorded only 600 of a possible 8,400 words per hour, or seven percent of each hour's proceedings, Even if the possible words per hour are reduced to 6,000, Madison recorded only ten percent of each hour's proceedings.

This experiment, it will be objected, is impressionistic, unscientific, and flawed. And so it is. Yet conceding every shortcoming, it demonstrates that there is a significant quantitative difference between what Madison recorded and what was said at the Convention, even if the shortfall cannot be expressed in a mathematical percentage precise enough to please the more pedantic. Because Madison's raw Convention notes—his "abbreviations and marks intelligible to myself"[156]—have not survived, it is not known if he recorded all or nearly all of each session and then severely compressed the results or if he followed stenographer Robertson's practice in the Virginia Convention of ignoring everything that seemed "desultory" or "irregular."[157] Whatever the case, much appears to be missing.

Another feature of Madison's notes is troublesome. His own remarks at the Convention occupy a considerable portion of the notes, yet they cannot have been delivered as they are now recorded in print. Madison could not speak and record at the same time. Because he did not prepare his speeches in advance— "having never written one before hand," as he reported late in life[158]—dialogue attributed to him must have been composed after the day's proceedings. After a few hours' reflection, Madison may have written a good deal more and a good deal that differed from what he said earlier. Consider his speech of June 6 that some political scientists regard as among the most important delivered at the Convention. In it, Madison presented his theory of the benefits of an expanded republic, which he elaborated in *Federalist* 10.[159] As it appears in Farrand's printed version of Madison's notes, the speech occupies approximately two pages,[160] Lansing did not report it at all; Genet-Yates and Hamilton gave it six lines;[161] Pierce five;[162] and King four.[163] The speech as delivered must have been far briefer than the one Madison inserted in his notes. Speeches written and "improved" after the event and large-scale deletions are reminiscent of Genet, Lloyd, and the shorthand reporters, however different Madison's motives may have been.

Madison's notes are not a forgery, but they are far from a verbatim record of what was said in the Convention. They omit much of what happened in

Philadelphia. The extent of their omission is the measure of the difficulty in using them to discover the delegates' intentions.

III. A Note on the Documentation of the Bill of Rights

THE FIRST CONGRESS under the new federal government, meeting from early April through the end of September 1789, sent twelve amendments to the states for ratification on September 25, 1789. The ten amendments eventually ratified are known, of course, as the Bill of Rights.

In 1789, the Senate did not permit its proceedings to be reported.[164] The documentary record of debates on the Bill of Rights consists, therefore, of deliberations in the House of Representatives. These were published in 1834 by the Washington firm of Gales & Seaton under the title, *The Debates and Proceedings in the Congress of the United States*, known to and cited by scholars as *Annals of Congress*.[165] For the first session of the First Congress, the period covering the gestation of the Bill of Rights, the *Annals of Congress* is a reprinting of a publication called the *Congressional Register*,[166] prepared by none other than Thomas Lloyd, the shorthand reporter of the debates in the Pennsylvania and Maryland ratifying conventions.

Far from improving by 1789, Lloyd's technical skills had become dulled by excessive drinking.[167] In 1940, the Library of Congress acquired the manuscript of Lloyd's shorthand notes of the debates from April 8 to May 15, 1789, and from January 19 to June 3, 1790. These notes were transcribed, insofar as they could be, by a shorthand expert, and the transcription was compared to the debates printed by Lloyd in the *Congressional Register*. It was discovered that what Lloyd published "bears only slight resemblance to the literal transcript of his own notes. Sometimes a speech is printed for which no notes or only very brief notes exist; sometimes a long speech reported in the manuscript is printed very briefly or not at all."[168] Another investigator has reported that Lloyd's reports were frequently "garbled" and that he neglected to report speeches whose texts are known to exist elsewhere.[169] Lloyd's manuscript also demonstrates a wandering mind, for it is periodically interrupted by doodling, sketches of members, horses, and landscapes, and by poetry. It is thus little wonder that on May 9, 1789, Madison condemned the *Congressional Register* as exhibiting "the strongest evidences of mutilation & perversion"[170] and that Elbridge Gerry, after accusing Lloyd of persisting in his Federalist partisanship, complained that "sometimes members were introduced as uttering arguments directly the reverse of what they had advanced."[171] The accuracy of Lloyd's reports "is not to be relied on," Madison advised a correspondent.

> The face of the debates shews that they are defective, and desultory,
> where not revised, or written out by the Speakers. In some instances,

he makes them inconsistent with themselves, by erroneous reports of their speeches at different times on the same subject. He was indolent and sometimes filled up blanks in his notes from memory or imagination. I recollect that he put into my mouth, a speech, drawn much from the latter and in its style suited rather to a youthful declaimer than to me in my situation. He finally became a votary of the bottle and perhaps made too free use of it sometimes at the period of his printed debates.[172]

Some Congressmen did not censure Lloyd quite so severely, but even his apologists admitted that his reports abounded with errors.[173]

Therefore, in seeking to ascertain the intentions of the drafters of the Bill of Rights, scholars should know that the *Annals of Congress*—the source traditionally relied upon for that purpose—is the voice of Thomas Lloyd, a voice even less reliable in 1789 than it was at the Pennsylvania ratifying convention.

IV. Conclusion

THIS ARTICLE has examined the most important documentary records surrounding the creation of the Constitution and has found them to be defective in varying degrees. In some cases recorders were incompetent. In others, documents were separated from their compilers and published by editors with partisan agendas who revised and deleted the original material. And in yet others, compilers retained control over their records but still produced alterations and omissions. There were differences in the extent of editorial alteration and in the motives of the editors. But in all cases the resulting documents are not full, reliable records of the debates at the Constitutional and ratifying conventions.

If we conclude that this array of defects has corrupted the historical documentation of the Constitution, it would appear to be impossible to rely upon the documentary record to discover the intentions of the Framers. A jurisprudence of original intention is not precluded by these findings, but it would be obliged to seek the intention of the Framers in the words of the Constitution, as the Framers themselves intended. Whether so restrictive a requirement would promote or retard the goals of the proponents of original intent is beyond the scope of this inquiry. The author will be satisfied if lawyers, judges, historians, and legal scholars are reminded, as they periodically need to be, that the mere fact that a record is in print does not make it reliable.

Notes

1. *Journal, Acts and Proceedings of the Convention, Assembled at Philadelphia, Monday, May 14, and Dissolved, September 17, 1787, which formed the Constitution of the United States* (Boston 1819) (hereafter cited as *Convention Journal*).

2. Secret Proceedings and Debates of the Convention Assembled at Philadelphia, in the Year 1787, for the Purpose of Forming the Constitution of the United States of America. From Notes Taken by the Late Robert Yates, Esquire, Chief Justice of New York, and Copied by John Lansing, Jun., Esquire, Late Chancellor of that State, Members of that Convention (Albany 1821) (hereafter cited as *Secret Proceedings*).

3. The Papers of James Madison (H. Gilpin ed. 1842).

4. The Debates in the several State Conventions, on the adoption of the Federal Constitution, as recommended by the General Convention at Philadelphia, in 1787 (J. Elliot ed. 1827, 1828 & 1830) (hereafter cited as Elliot's *Debates*.)

5. Documentary sources also exist in the form of letters written by delegates during and after the Convention and in fragmentary notes of debates, motions, and other proceedings. The delegates' letters, a few of which Farrand published, discuss personal and family matters, private business, Philadelphia society—everything but activities—on the Convention floor. The delegates' silence about the Constitution was the result of a secrecy rule, adopted by the Convention on May 29, 1787, and observed with fidelity throughout the proceedings. The fragmentary notes of debate, which also are published in Farrand, supplement Madison's and Yates's notes, but suffer the same defects as these fuller accounts, which will be described in the course of this Article. There were reports about the Convention in contemporary newspapers, but because of the delegates' self-imposed gag rule, and because the Convention was closed to the public, they were merely guesses and rumors.

6. See supra note 5.

7. 3 Stat. 475 (1818), reprinted in 3 *The Records of the Federal Convention of 1787* at 425 (M. Farrand rev. ed. 1937) (hereafter cited as M. Farrand).

8. Powell, The Original Understanding of Original Intent, 98 *Harv. L. Rev.* (1985) (reprinted in this volume; subsequent page references to this article are to page numbers in this volume). See p. 62.

9. Id. at 62–63.

10. See, e.g., Gouverneur Morris to Timothy Pickering (December 22, 1814), reprinted in 3 M. Farrand, supra note 7, at 419, 420 ("what can a history of the Constitution avail towards interpreting its provisions? This must be done by comparing the plain import of the words with the general tenor and object of the instrument").

11. Powell, supra note 8, at 62.

12. 25 U.S. (12 Wheat.) 213 (1827) (Marshall, C.J., dissenting).

13. Id. at 332.

14. tenBroek, Admissibility and Use by the United States Supreme Court of Extrinsic Aids in Constitutional Construction, (pt. 1), 26 *Calif. L. Rev.* 287, 290 (1938).

15. Id. at 307. Professor tenBroek noted: "[T]he doctrine of the United States Supreme Court that the meaning of the Constitution is to be derived from the text itself unless internal factors create a doubt survives in a great state of infirmity. Never a vital doctrine, its present weakness represents the course of its history and results from its origin, its intrinsic character, the nature of its use and the development of antithetical doctrines. Formulated in *dictum*, it never overcame the stigma of its unfortunate birth."

16. 58 U.S. (17 How.) 456 (1854).

17. Id. at 463.

18. 27 U.S. (2 Pet.) 380, 416 (1829) ("The whole of this difficulty arises out of that unhappy idea, that the phrase 'ex post facto,' in the constitution of the United States, was confined to criminal cases exclusively; a decision which leaves a large class of arbitrary legislative acts without the prohibitions of the constitution").

19. Powell, supra note 8 at 86–87.

20. tenBroek, Use by the United States Supreme Court of Extrinsic Aids in Constitutional Construction (pt. 2), 26 *Calif. L. Rev.* 437, 437–54 (1938). In this second of two articles (see tenBroek, supra note 14) Professor tenBroek analyzes such cases by dividing them into five categories—cases in which the court: (a) places primary reliance on convention debates and proceedings; (b) relies on the proceedings to support a doctrine previously established without them; (c) utilizes the debates by way of affirmation; (d) examines them to show they do not contradict a result reached; and (e) renders a decision in conflict with revealed debates and proceedings. Id. at 437.

21. National Mut. Ins. Co. v. Tidewater Transfer Co., 337 U.S. 582, 631 n.8 (1948) (Vinson, C.J., dissenting).

22. 106 S.Ct. 3181 (1986).

23. Id. at 3189 (citing Buckley v. Valeo, 424 U.S. 1 [1976]).

24. tenBroek, supra note 20 at 443.

25. Id. at 448.

26. Perry, Interpretivism, Freedom of Expression, and Equal Protection, 42 *Ohio St. L. J.* 261, 265 (1981).

27. Leedes, A Critique of Illegitimate Noninterpretivism, 8 *Dayton L. Rev.* 533, 542–43 (1983).

28. Id. at 543.

29. See id.

30. Address by Attorney General Edwin Meese III, American Bar Association Meeting (July 9, 1985, Washington, D.C.); see Meese Assails High Court for Church-state Rulings, Wash. Times, July 10, 1985, at Al, col. 4. For recent expressions of the Attorney General's views, see Meese, Toward a Jurisprudence of Original Intention, 2 *Benchmark* 1 (1986); Meese, The Attorney General's Views of the Supreme Court: Toward a Jurisprudence of Original Intention, 45 *Pub. Admin. Rev.* 701 (1985).

31. See USA Today, October 17, 1985, at 14A, col. 3.

32. M. Perry, *The Constitution, the Courts and Human Rights* 91 (1982).

33. See. e.g., J. Ely, *Democracy and Distrust: A Theory of Judicial Review* 1–11 (1980) ("interpretivism"); Brest, The Misconceived Quest for the Original Understanding, 60 *B. U. L. Rev.* 204, (1980) ("originalism") (reprinted in this volume; subsequent page references to this article are to page numbers in this volume); Grey, Do We Have an Unwritten Constitution? 27 *Stanford L. Rev.* 703, 705 (1975) (analyzing the "interpretive model"); Powell, supra note 8, at 53–54 ("intentionalism").

34. See Brest, supra note 33, at 238–41; Tushnet, Following the Rules Laid Down: A Critique of Interpretivism and Neutral Principles, 96 *Harv. L. Rev.* 781, 786–804 (1983). Both Professors Brest and Tushnet disavow the belief that the past is unknowable, but occasionally their views approach such a conclusion. "Even when the interpreter performs the more conventional historian's role, one may wonder whether the task is possible. There is a hermeneutic tradition . . . which holds that we can never understand the past in its own terms, free from our prejudices or preconceptions. We are hopelessly imprisoned in our own world-views; we can shed some preconceptions only to adopt others, with no reason to believe that they are the conceptions of the different society that we are trying to understand. One need not embrace this essentially solipsistic view of historical knowledge to appreciate the indeterminate and contingent nature of the historical understanding that an originalist historian seeks to achieve.

"None of this is to disparage doing history and other interpretive social science. It suggests, however, that the originalist constitutional historian may be questing after a chimera." Brest, supra note 33, at 241 (footnotes omitted). "The intellectual world of the framers is one that bears some resemblance, which is more than merely genetic, to ours. A hermeneutic interpretivism would force us to think about the social contents of the resemblances and dissimilarities. It would lead us not to despair over the gulf that separates the framers' world from ours, but rather to the crafting of creative links between their ideals and our own. But in recognizing the magnitude of the creative component, we inevitably lose faith in the ability of interpretivism to provide the constraints on judges that liberal constitutional theory demands." Tushnet, supra, at 803–4.

35. W. Crosskey, *Politics and the Constitution in the History of the United States* (2 vols. 1953).

36. 1 id. at 12–13; 2 id. at 1009, 1012, 1020.

37. Wofford, The Blinding Light: The Uses of History in Constitutional Interpretation, 31 *Univ. Chicago L. Rev.* 502, 503–6 (1964).

38. 3 M. Farrand, supra note 7, at 82.

39. Id.

40. Id. at 370. The manuscript journal and related documents are now at the National Archives and Records Administration, Washington, D.C., where they may be consulted by scholars.

41. 3 Stat. 475 (1818), reprinted in 3 M. Farrand, supra note 7, at 425.

42. John Quincy Adams: Memoirs (May 13–June 2, 1819), reprinted in 3 M. Farrand, supra note 7, at 430, 433.

43. Id. Farrand printed excerpts from John Quincy Adams's memoirs that traced the custodial history of the Journal. As shown there, and still commonly believed, George Washington had confidential care of the Journal papers from the Convention adjournment until March 19, 1796. Id. at 431. It has recently come to light, however, that during this time, Washington lent the Journal to Madison who copied it, and thus had the convention information long before anyone else. Such possession is a significant blow to those who argue that Madison corrupted his account of the proceedings with much later reminiscences. See infra notes 144–49 and accompanying text.

44. 1 M. Farrand, supra note 7, at xiii.

45. Id. at xii ("As Adams had nothing whatever to guide him in his work of compilation and editing, mistakes were inevitable, and not a few of these were important").

46. Wofford, supra note 37, at 504. Confidence in Wofford's judgment would be stronger had he not, some lines later, identified Washington as "president of the Congress of the Confederation," a body in which he never served. Washington served in the First and Second Continental Congresses, 1774–1775, but held no offices; the "Congress of the Confederation" began with the adoption of the Articles of Confederation in 1781.

47. 1 M. Farrand, supra note 7, at xiii.

48. As Farrand explained: "The secretary's minutes consist of the formal journal of the Convention, the journal of the Committee of the whole House and, partly on loose sheets and partly in a bound blank book, a table giving the detail of ayes and noes on the various questions. The detail of ayes and noes offers the greatest difficulty, for no dates are given and to about one tenth of the votes no questions are attached. The photograph of the first loose sheet of this table reveals the difficulties at a glance; the later pages are not as bad as the first, for the secretary evidently profited by experience, but uncertainty and confusion are by no means eliminated. For convenience of reference, in the present edition a number in square brackets is prefixed to each vote, and the editor has taken the liberty of dividing the detail of ayes and noes into what are, according to his best judgment, the sections for each day's records. The sections are retained intact, and a summary of each vote in square brackets is appended to that question in the Journal to which, in the light of all the evidence, it seems to belong." 1 M. Farrand, supra note 7, at xiii.

49. Id.

50. 2 id. at 477. Williamson's copy of the Committee of Detail report is in the Manuscript Division, Library of Congress.

51. Farrand said: "In the judgment of the editor, however, a word of warning seems necessary. With notes so carelessly kept, as were evidently those of the secretary [William Jackson], the Journal cannot be relied upon absolutely. The statement of questions is probably accurate in most cases, but the determination of those questions and in particular the votes upon them should be accepted somewhat tentatively." 1 id. at xiii–xiv.

52. 1 id. at xv.

53. Legal Tender Cases, 79 U.S. (12 Wall.) 457, 497 n.* (1870).

54. See, e.g., Goldberg v. Kelly, 397 U.S. 254, 273 (1970) (Black, J., dissenting) (citing "Yates's Minutes" for support); National Mut. Ins. Co. v. Tidewater Transfer Co., 337 U.S. 582, 634 n.13 (1948) (Vinson, C.J., dissenting) ("The sense of the Convention at this point was expressed in Yates's Notes").

55. Albany Argus, September 11, 1821 (referring to commentary in Washington newspapers).

56. 3 M. Farrand, supra note 7, at 410 n. 1.

57. In 1793, Genet fitted out privateers in American ports to sail against British shipping in violation of American neutrality. When the government protested, Genet threatened to go over Washington's head by appealing to the American people. Such actions caused even Genet's friends to distance themselves from him. For an accurate, short sketch of Genet, see 7 *Dictionary of American Biography* 207–9 (1931).

58. D. Fox, *The Decline of Aristocracy in the Politics of New York* 81 (1919).

59. John Lansing to Genet (July 6, 1821), reprinted in *Albany Argus*, August 24, 1821.

60. *Albany Argus*, September 11, 1821.

61. Morison, The First National Nominating Convention, 1808, 17 *American Historical Review* 744, 746 (1912).

62. E. Genet, *A Letter to the Electors of the President and Vice President of the United States* (1808) (available in the Rare Book and Special Collections Divisions, Library of Congress).

63. Lansing letter, supra note 59.

64. E. Genet, supra note 62 at 3–4.

65. Genet's letter, of which there are two drafts—one dated simply August, the other August 27, 1821—may be found in his papers at the Library of Congress.

66. Id.

67. See A. Kass, *Politics in New York State, 1800–1830* at 89 (1965).

68. Genet letter, supra note 65.

69. See, e.g., A. Kass, supra note 67, at 88 ("at the outset the primary raison d'etre of the [Clintonians] had been to achieve universal manhood suffrage and to abolish laws for the imprisonment of debtors.").

70. The manuscript of Yates's notes that Lansing obtained from Mrs. Yates and from which he made the copy Genet used also has disappeared.

71. James Madison to Joseph Gales (August 26, 1821), reprinted in 3 M. Farrand, supra note 7, at 446: "I thank you for your friendly letter of the 20th. inclosing an extract from notes by Judge Yates, of debates in the Convention of 1787, as published in a N.Y. Paper [*Commercial Advertizer*, August 18, 1821]. . . .

"If the extract be a fair sample, the work about to be published will not have the value claimed for it. . . . [The] intrinsic evidence alone ought to satisfy every candid reader of the extreme incorrectness of the passage in question.

"Whatever may have been the personal worth of the 2 delegates from whom the materials in this case were derived, it cannot be unknown that they represented the strong prejudices in N.Y. agst. the object of the Convention which was among other things to take from that state the important power over its commerce and that they manifested, until they withdrew from the Convention, the strongest feelings of dissatisfaction agst. the contemplated change in the federal system and as may be supposed, agst. those most active in promoting it. Besides misapprehensions of the ear therefore, the attention of the note taker wd naturally be warped, as far at least as, an upright mind could be warped, to an unfavorable understanding of what was said in opposition to the prejudices felt." Id. at 446–47.

72. tenBroek, supra note 20, at 454.

73. 457 U.S. 731, 774–75 (1981) (J. White, dissenting).

74. Brest, supra note 33, at 214–15.

75. See Elliot's *Debates*, supra note 4.

76. 6 *Dictionary of American Biography* 93 (1931).

77. Id.

78. Leonard Rapport, senior archivist at the National Archives and Records Administration, intends to illuminate the Elliot-Calhoun connection in a forthcoming article.

79. 1 Elliot's *Debates*, supra note 4, at v.

80. Tinling, Thomas Lloyd's Reports of the First Federal Congress, 18 *Wm. and Mary Q.* 519 (1961).

81. Id. at 541.

82. E. Butler, *The Story of British Shorthand* 79 (1951).

83. Tinling, supra note 80, at 530.

84. Id.

85. E. Butler, supra note 82, at 60.

86. 1 Elliot's *Debates*, supra note 4, at v.

87. 2 id. at 203–4.

88. J. Walker, *A History of the New Hampshire Convention* 4–5 (1888).

89. Id.

90. B. Russell, *Debates, Resolutions and other Proceedings of the Convention . . . Together with the Yeas and Nays on the decision of the Grand Question* (Boston 1788), reprinted in 1 Elliot's *Debates*, supra note 4, at 25–184.

91. S. Harding, *The Contest over the Ratification of the Federal Constitution in the State of Massachusetts* 177 (1896 and photo. reprint 1970) (quoting B. Russell, supra note 90).

92. David Sewell to George Thatcher (March 4, 1788), reprinted in 6 *Hist. Mag.* 343 (1869).

93. 3 *Documentary History of the Ratification of the Constitution* 336, 573 (M. Jensen ed. 1978) (hereafter cited as *Documentary History*).

94. 1 Elliot's *Debates*, supra note 4, at 185–358. Commenting on the work of Childs and other reporters of the debates in the ratifying conventions, Elliot wrote Madison that he was "fully sensible of the imperfections of many of the materials." Jonathan Elliot to Madison (August 19, 1830) (available in Madison Papers, Library of Congress).

95. 5 *The Papers of Alexander Hamilton* 12 (H. Syrett ed. 1962).

96. John Lansing to Abraham Yates and Melancton Smith (October 3, 1788) (available in Lamb Papers, New York Historical Society).

97. G. Saladino, A Guide to Sources for Studying the Ratification of the Constitution by New York State, in *The Reluctant Pillar: New York and the Adoption of the Federal Constitution* 133, 188 (S. Schecter ed. 1985).

98. On Lloyd's being "bought up by the Federalists," see *Pennsylvania and the Federal Constitution* 14–15 (J. McMaster and F. Stone eds. 1888). "Of the proceedings of the [Pennsylvania] convention no full and satisfactory record is known to exist. . . . The minutes are exceedingly meagre; but from them it appears that Thomas Lloyd applied to the convention for the place of assistant clerk. Lloyd was a shorthand writer of considerable note, and, when the convention refused his request, determined to report the debates and print them on his own account. His advertisement promised that the debates should be accurately taken in shorthand, and published in one volume octavo at the rate of one dollar the hundred pages. These fine promises, however, were never fulfilled. Only one thin volume ever came out, and that contains merely the speeches of Wilson and a few of those of Thomas M'Kean. The reason is not far to seek. He was bought up by the Federalists, and, in order to satisfy the public, was suffered to publish one volume containing nothing but the speeches made by the two federal leaders." Id.

99. T. Lloyd, *Debates of the Convention of the State of Pennsylvania on the United States Constitution, Proposed for the Government of the United States* (Philadelphia 1788), reprinted in 3 Elliot's *Debates*, supra note 4, at 221–322.

100. *Pennsylvania and the Federal Constitution*, supra note 98, at 765–85.

101. Peep Junior, *Independent Gazetteer* (Philadelphia), February 5, 1788.

102. 2 *Documentary History*, supra note 93, at 41–42.

103. This notice was contained in the preface to volume 3 of the first edition (1830) of Elliot's *Debates*; it was deleted in subsequent editions.

104. 3 *Papers of George Mason: 1725–1792*, at 1126 (R. Rutland ed. 1970).

105. D. Robertson, *Debates and Other Proceedings of the Convention of Virginia* (1788) reprinted in 2 Elliot's *Debates*, supra note 4, at 33–487.

106. Madison to Jonathan Elliot (November 1827) (available in Madison Papers, Library of Congress).

107. See, e.g., R. Berger, *Government by Judiciary: The Transformation of the Fourteenth Amendment* 304 (1977).

108. 1 *Papers of John Marshall* 256 n.7 (H. Johnson ed. 1974).

109. William Davie to James Iredell (December 19, 1788) (available in Iredell Papers, Duke University).

110. Id.

111. 2 G. McRee, *Life and Correspondence of James Iredell* 235 (1858).

112. 2 *Annals of Congress* 2005 (1791).

113. The document's history is chronicled in correspondence in 1 *The Papers of James Madison*, supra note 3, at xii–xxiv.

114. 1 M. Farrand, supra note 7, at xv.

115. *The Debates in the Federal Convention of 1787 which Framed the Constitution of the United States of America* at xxi (G. Hunt & J. Scott eds. 1920) (hereafter cited as *The Debates*).

116. Krash, William Winslow Crosskey, 35 *Univ. Chicago L. Rev.* 232 (1968).

117. W. Crosskey, supra note 35.

118. 2 id. at 1009.

119. 2 id. at 1012.

120. 1 id. at 313.

121. See, e.g., Heinmann & Kelso, Politics and the Constitution—A Dual Review (Book Review), 39 *Iowa L. Rev.* 139 (1953).

122. For the charge of McCarthyism, see Hart, Professor Crosskey and Judicial Review, 67 *Harv. L. Rev.* 1456, 1475 (1954).

123. Crosskey promised to present fully documented proof in later volumes. 2 W. Crosskey, supra note 35, at 1175.

124. 3 W. Crosskey and W. Jeffrey, *Politics and the Constitution in the History of the United States* (1980).

125. Crosskey, The Ex-Post-facto and the Contracts Clauses in the Federal Convention: A Note on the Editorial Ingenuity of James Madison, 35 *Univ. Chicago L. Rev.* 248 (1968).

126. Id. at 252–53.

127. P. Clarkson and S. Jett, *Luther Martin of Maryland* (1970).

128. Id. at 95.

129. C. Collier and J. Collier, *Decision in Philadelphia: The Constitutional Convention of 1787* (1986).

130. See id. at 69, 81. Other scholars have relied on Crosskey's work. In 1984, John Murrin praised portions of Crosskey's work. About Crosskey's attacks against Madison, however, Murrin concluded, "To this reviewer, Crosskey's accusation seems tortured and unconvincing. Madison's memorandum is hardly a 'clear' instance of falsification. . . . Crosskey's attempt to indict Madison is premised on pure speculation." Murrin, Book Review, 58 *N.Y.U. L. Rev.* 1254, 1263–64 (1983) (reviewing 3 W. Crosskey and W. Jeffrey, supra note 124).

131. Ulmer, Charles Pinckney: Father of the Constitution, 10 *S.C.L.Q.* 225, 245 (1958).

132. C. Collier and J. Collier, supra note 129, at 64, 69.

133. Id. at 66–67.

134. Id. at 81.

135. Crosskey, supra note 125, at 252.

136. 1 W. Crosskey, supra note 35, at 313.

137. 2 id. at 1021.

138. T. Balston, *James Whatman: Father and Son* 1 (1957).

139. Id. at 157.

140. 1 M. Farrand, supra note 7, at xvi. In a preface to the Debates, written before his death, Madison had explained with what care the material was gathered and written up: "I chose a seat in front of the presiding member, with the other members, on my right and left hand. In this favorable position for hearing all that passed I noted in terms legible and in abbreviations and marks intelligible to myself what was read from the Chair or spoken by the members; and losing not a moment unnecessarily between the adjournment and reassembling of the Convention I was enabled to write out my daily notes during the session or within a few finishing days after its close." Indeed Madison was evidently regarded by his fellow-delegates to the Convention as a semi-official reporter of their proceedings, for several of them took pains to see that he was supplied with copies of their speeches and motions. Id. (footnotes omitted).

141. For a discussion of Eppes's transcription, see 19 *Papers of Thomas Jefferson* 549–51 (J. Boyd ed. 1974) and 10 *Papers of James Madison* 8–9 (R. Rutland et al. eds. 1977) (hereafter cited as R. Rutland). Both Boyd and Rutland give the history behind the "Eppes copy." In what was probably the summer of 1791, Thomas Jefferson was tutoring his nephew, John Wayles Eppes, and as an exercise Jefferson had Eppes copy Madison's convention notes. R. Rutland, supra, at 7. The seriousness of the task impressed Eppes such that he later revealed that "the particular and confidential manner in which he entrusted them to me prevented my making the smallest extract from any part of them—and so careful was I of preserving sacred a document the importance of which to posterity I could not but feel, that I never suffered the papers to mix either with my own or any others entrusted to my care." 19 *Papers of Thomas Jefferson*, supra, at 549.

142. 1 M. Farrand supra note 7, at xvi–xix; see infra note 149.

143. Wofford, supra note 37, at 505 (citing 1 M. Farrand, supra note 7, at xvii). This statement does not occur in any of the editions of Farrand's *Records*.

144. Id.

145. In a letter to John Adams, Jefferson wrote: "Do you know that there exists in manuscript the ablest work of this kind ever yet executed, of the debates of the constitutional convention of Philadelphia in 1788 [sic]: The whole of everything said and done there was taken down by Mr. Madison, with a labor and exactness beyond comprehension." Thomas Jefferson to John Adams (Aug. 10, 1815), reprinted in 3 M. Farrand, supra note 7, at 421.

146. The manuscript of Madison's notes at the Library of Congress contains motions and speeches, such as Randolph's of May 29 introducing the Virginia Plan, in the handwriting of the authors who gave them to Madison to incorporate into his notes.

147. This reminder in Madison's manuscript of the notes of debates at the Library of Congress was not reprinted by Farrand.

148. On Madison's copy of the official journal and the use to which he put it, see Pierson and Keller, A New Madison Manuscript Relating to the Federal Convention of 1787, 36 *Amer. Hist. Rev.* 17–30 (1930).

149. Farrand discovered that, when Genet published his edition of Yates's notes in 1821, Madison collated it with his notes and incorporated some of Yates's material. 1 M. Farrand, supra note 7, at xviii. The amount of borrowing from Yates turns out, on examination, to be minimal. "Another extensive set of corrections is to be found in the speeches made in debate. These are generally in the form of additions to Madison's original record. Because of misquotations of his own remarks, Madison condemned Yates's notes severely, as being a 'very erroneous edition of the matter'. It is more than surprising, then, to discover that these additions were taken from Yates." Id. at xviii (footnote omitted). Hunt and Scott explain such a curious borrowing by misinformation that Madison was willing to take from Yates: "The chief source of Madison's corrections of his notes was the official Journal of the convention which was printed in 1819 and Yates's *Secret Proceedings and Debates of the Federal Convention* which appeared in 1821. Whenever Madison thought either of these records were more correct than his he changed or added to his; but he noted more frequently errors in the official Journal itself. Yates's record he regarded as having little value. Nevertheless, he derived from it a few lesser motions which had escaped him." *The Debates*, supra note 115, at xxi–xxii.

150. Proposals for Publishing the *Secret Debates of the Convention* (Albany, New York, March 30, 1821) (available in Genet Papers, Library of Congress).

151. Memorandum of Timothy Pickering (August 11, 1827) (available in Pickering Papers, Massachusetts Historical Society).

152. Max Farrand noted: "It seems to have been the practise of the Convention at the close of the day's session to adjourn until the next morning at ten o'clock. Apparently the hours were somewhat irregular, and on August 18, it was agreed to meet precisely at 10 A.M., and no motion to adjourn was to be in order until 4 P.M. On August 24, the hour of adjournment was fixed at 3 P.M." 1 M. Farrand, supra note 7, at 2 n. 1.

153. 5 *Diaries of George Washington* 185 (D. Jackson and D. Twohig eds. 1979). In a letter of

September 20, 1787, to Mrs. Jane Mecom, Benjamin Franklin confirmed that the Convention met for at least five hours per day. 3 M. Farrand, supra note 7, at 98 ("The Convention finished the 17th instant. I attended the Business of it 5 Hours in every Day from the Beginning; which is something more than four Months.").

154. Twenty typed pages, more or less, of 350–odd words.

155. On August 18, the Convention voted to begin meeting from 10:00 A.M. to 4:00 P.M. to relieve the "extreme anxiety of many members of the Convention to bring the business to an end." 2 M. Farrand, supra note 7, at 328.

156. 1 id. at xvi.

157. 11 *Papers of James Madison* 75 (R. Rutland and C. Hobson eds. 1977). "David Robertson's effort to preserve the Richmond debates in stenographic form was noble but flawed. He was absent on at least one occasion, and on others he admittedly could not hear the speaker, or he skimmed over parts of speeches which struck him as 'desultory,' or 'some irregular conversation.' " Id. Yet, Rutland and Hobson write, "with all these shortcomings, Robertson's work (despite Antifederalists' objections that he was a Federalist partisan) still provides the most comprehensive record of what occurred in any of the state ratifying conventions." Id. at 76.

158. Madison to Gales and Seaton (August 5, 1833) (available in Madison Papers, Library of Congress).

159. *Federalist* No. 10 (J. Madison).

160. 1 M. Farrand, supra note 7, at 134–36.

161. 1 id. at 141, 146.

162. 1 id. at 147.

163. 1 id. at 143–44.

164. *A National Program for the Publication of Historical Documents: A Report to the President by the National Historical Publications Commission* 93 (1954).

165. Id.

166. 12 *Papers of James Madison* 63 (R. Rutland et al. eds. 1977).

167. Tinling, supra note 80, at 537–38.

168. Id. at 530.

169. *National Program*, supra note 164, at 93–94.

170. Tinling, supra note 80, at 533 (quoting from Madison Papers, Library of Congress).

171. Tinling, supra note 80, at 532, 536.

172. Madison to Edward Everett (January 7, 1832) (available in Edward Everett Papers), quoted in Tinling, supra note 80, at 537–38.

173. Tinling, supra note 80, at 533–536.

Mr. Meese, Meet Mr. Madison

◆

═══
═══

◆

JACK N. RAKOVE

THE CONSTITUTION TURNS two hundred next year, and Americans will be asked to recall the remarkable Convention which met in Philadelphia during that famous summer of 1787. Yet in a curious way, events are conspiring to make the Constitution an object of celebration and controversy at the same time. For the past year, a flurry of op-ed pieces and other essays have debated the merits of Attorney General Edwin Meese's call for a return to a "jurisprudence of original intention." Now, however, with the retirement of Chief Justice Warren Burger, his replacement by Justice William Rehnquist, and the appointment of Judge Antonin Scalia, a Supreme Court that has often been narrowly divided on crucial questions seems on the verge of the fundamental reorientation that many conservatives have long demanded.

Whether such a change will in fact occur is another matter—especially since the same reorientation was already supposed to have resulted from the four appointments Richard Nixon enjoyed during his first term. But whatever happens, the growing influence of conservative legal scholarship, coupled with real controversy over many of the Court's most significant decisions, seemingly guarantee that the issues Mr. Meese has raised will remain the subject of public debate for some time.

What is this debate about? Taken at face value, the idea of a "jurisprudence of original intention" simply holds that a judge interpreting the Constitution or a statute should adhere as closely as he can to the expressed ideas and purposes of its framers. In this sense, original intent literally tells judges how they should read the laws they apply and enforce: narrowly and with a great sense of restraint. But in a more fundamental sense, the question that conservatives are raising is not, How do judges judge? but rather, What role should the judiciary play within the entire constitutional system? For, conservatives argue, if judges can freely ignore the intentions either of the original framers of the Constitution or of legislators, they can substitute their own preferences or values for the expressed choice of popularly elected officials. As the one branch of government least accountable to the public, the judiciary should hesitate long and carefully before imposing its opinions on the views of the political departments.

At another level, of course, conservative complaints spring from strong objections to key decisions of the past three decades—against all those controversial rulings involving abortion, mandatory busing, affirmative action, the rights of the criminally accused and convicted, school prayer, and aid to religious schools. In its rulings in these areas, conservatives argue, the Supreme Court has violated the original intent of the Constitution in three ways. First, the Court has often ignored or distorted the original meaning of the Bill of Rights and the Fourteenth Amendment, the textual sources that most clearly identify the rights the Constitution explicitly protects. Second, the Court has acted improperly by establishing new rights that the written Constitution does not even mention—most flagrantly in its rulings on abortion. Finally, by creating new rights and by imposing radical remedies (like busing) for past wrongs, the Court has undermined the constitutional principle of separation of powers. No longer content simply to decide individual cases, the federal judiciary has set itself the task of making broad social policy, a responsibility that properly belongs to the elective branches of government. A judge may properly strike down laws that promote segregation or administrative rules that confine prisoners in excessively vile conditions. But when he takes over the management of a school system (as Federal Judge W. Arthur Garrity did in Boston) or mandates the expenditure of public funds to alleviate jail overcrowding, he acts as judge, lawmaker, and administrator together—and that concentration of power, James Madison wrote in *Federalist* 47, "may justly be pronounced the very definition of tyranny."

This attack on the undemocratic nature of the judiciary turns on its head the position conservatives traditionally favored. Conservatives once relied on the courts to protect the rights of property against regulation by progressive majorities in the state legislatures and Congress. Now they hope to restrain "the unfettered and inevitably arbitrary wills of an elite few"—which is how Terry Eastland, Meese's spokesman, characterizes the Court—so that democratic majorities can presumably restore prayer to the schools, restrict abortion, suppress pornography, and fill the jails to overflowing. And since these "social issues" largely fall under the control of the states, the attack on activist judges also clothes itself in the garb of federalism.

This reversal has led many liberals to accuse Mr. Meese of rank opportunism. Anthony Lewis has argued that "what really interests the present Attorney General is not judicial philosophy but particular political results," while Arthur Schlesinger, Jr. suggests that the "shamelessly selective" way in which Mr. Meese applies his theory to actual cases proves that he is "the biggest chameleon of the lot." What respect does Meese show for original intent, they wonder, when he declares that the President need not faithfully execute a law whose constitutionality he questions? Mr. Meese's complaints about judicial activism would vanish, they suspect, if the Court struck down the War Powers Act, or if new appointments produced a reliable majority of conservative justices willing, say, to eliminate affirmative action programs root and branch.

Lewis and Schlesinger are in effect judging the meaning of Meese's remarks by their view of his intentions. In doing so, they ironically illustrate one of the key difficulties with the Attorney General's position. Establishing the intention behind any action is a tricky business—as Meese or any other attorney surely should know. It is difficult enough to gauge the intent even of a single individual—whether it be Edwin Meese in his American Bar Association address of 1985 or James Madison in 1787. The task grows geometrically more complex when we try to ascribe intent to groups of people—especially men acting two centuries ago, who have left us incomplete records of their motives and concerns, and who reached decisions through a process that fused principled debate with hard-driven bargains.

Justice Brennan had such objections in mind last fall, when he dismissed Mr. Meese's "doctrinaire" position as "arrogance cloaked as humility." In the first place, Brennan noted, our historical sources typically offer only "sparse or ambiguous evidence of the original intention" of the framers of the Constitution. (Here he echoed the late Justice Robert Jackson, who once noted that the historical records were "almost as enigmatic as the dreams Joseph was called upon to interpret for Pharaoh.") Nor is it even clear, Brennan added, whose intent deserves the greatest weight. The Constitution and the Bill of Rights were the joint work of the fifty-five delegates to the 1787 Convention and the ninety-odd members of the First Congress. But they became supreme law only after being ratified by hundreds of obscure convention delegates and legislators in the states—and arguably it is their understanding of what they were approving, and not the intentions of the actual framers, that we ought to respect.

Justice Brennan and other liberals have a different idea of the role that history should play in jurisprudence. Rather than recover the "static meaning" the Constitution had "in a world that is dead and gone," judges must trace the distance between the framers' time and our own, and then apply the great underlying principles of the Constitution to the modern problems that our litigious society asks the courts to resolve. And while judges should ordinarily defer to the expressed will of the legislature, they cannot make majority rule the only basis of decision. For within the larger scheme of our system, the great duty of the judiciary is to protect individual and minority rights against the improper actions of popular majorities.

How should an informed but reasonably impartial citizen respond to these claims? The great difficulty is that the Constitution does not tell us how to resolve disputes over its meaning. Nowhere does it explicitly endorse the idea of judicial review, the doctrine which gives the judiciary the special function of protecting the Constitution against violations by other branches of government—by Congress, the President, or the states. Nowhere does it say whether later interpreters should follow their best understanding of the original intentions of the framers and ratifiers of 1787–91 (or 1865–68, in the case of the critical Civil War amendments), as Attorney General Meese proposes, or whether they should only seek instead to apply its general principles to new realities, as Justice Brennan argues in response. Nowhere does it tell us whether we should read what scholars call the "silences" of the Constitution as freeing us to interpret it as we best see fit, or as withholding from the judiciary the broad power its detractors insist it has usurped.

In all that has been written on this subject in recent months, little has been said about the historical Constitution itself. To a historian like myself, who spends most of his waking hours in the eighteenth century, this neglect is distressing but hardly surprising. At bottom, the current controversy is not about what happened two hundred years ago at Philadelphia, but about what should happen today; and what is at stake today is, after all, too important to be left to the historians.

Yet one cannot talk intelligently about original intent without taking history far more seriously than the current disputants have so far done. That is precisely why the approach of the Bicentennial may serve an unexpectedly useful purpose. It offers a convenient occasion to turn the discussion back to its eighteenth-century roots—to ask how and why the Constitution was made, and even how its framers thought it should be interpreted. And by the same token, the existence of serious controversy over the meaning of the Constitution may prevent the bicentennial celebrations from degenerating into the kind of rituals the new patriotism otherwise promises they will become.

One proof of the dangers of allowing lawyers to meddle with history can be found in the efforts that both Attorney General Meese and Professor Laurence Tribe (a leading liberal scholar at the Harvard Law School) have already made to enlist James Madison on their side of the current controversy. In what are virtually textbook examples of "law office history," Meese and Tribe both manage to get the point half right. The Attorney General rightly notes that Madison believed that judges should interpret the Constitution according "to the sense in which [it] was accepted and ratified by the nation" in 1788, while Professor Tribe correctly observes that Madison held that the intentions of the framers "could *never* be regarded as the oracular guide in expounding the Constitution." Not surprisingly, neither cites, much less tries to resolve, the apparent contradiction in Madison's opinions.

Unlike his good friend Thomas Jefferson—who had the habit, Madison once wrote, of "expressing in strong and round terms, impressions of the moment"—Madison liked to savor his distinctions. The one he sought to develop here is among his most puzzling. And because that is the case, his attempt to explain how the Constitution should be interpreted offers a usefully ambiguous starting point for asking what an appeal to original intent means in practice.

Madison's distinction can be restated in this way: In trying to interpret the Constitution, a judge should ignore whatever he may learn of the original intentions of its authors, the delegates to the 1787 Convention; but he should defer to the popular understanding of the Constitution that prevailed at the time of its ratification. The distinction has one great advantage. It is consistent with the idea that the Constitution derives its force from the consent of the governed. (One can also ask, though, whether a consent given in 1788 expresses popular sovereignty more effectively than the "inevitably arbitrary wills of an elite few" justices can claim to do today.)

Yet if Madison's position has its logic, it creates as many problems as it solves. Why should we assume that those who merely ratified the Constitution grasped its meaning better than those who wrote it—or those who have since seen how it worked in practice? The debates of 1787–88 elicited a range of opinions about its likely effects. Some of these predictions were quite sensible, but others nicely illustrate what the late Richard Hofstadter called "the paranoid style in American politics." And how can we possibly discover what the anonymous voters and obscure local leaders who were passing judgment on the Constitution truly thought? Did they read *The Federalist* with the same insight that students of political theory now bring to it? And if we treat *The Federalist* as our best evidence of how the Constitution was understood—as so many commentators have done—do we not find ourselves again relying on the intentions of the framers, since Madison and Alexander Hamilton wrote all but a handful of its eighty-five essays?

Madison's objections to giving any weight to the intentions of the framers reveal a more serious and perhaps fatal problem with a jurisprudence of original intention. Simply put, the appeal to original intent cannot be justified on its own terms—if by intent we mean the historical motives and purposes of the actual authors of the Constitution. There is no reason to believe that the framers thought their intentions should guide later interpretations of the Constitution. They never considered publishing the journal of their deliberations, which would at least have provided a curious public with a skeletal history of the evolution of the text. Nor did Madison allow his own notes of the debates at Philadelphia to appear in his own lifetime—even though disputes over the meaning of the Constitution arose as soon as the new government was organized in 1789.

There are many ways to set about examining the current controversy from the distant vantage point of the framers. But perhaps the one that best reveals the range of possibilities, difficulties, and ironies that this quest uncovers is to view the making of the Constitution from the perspective of Madison, the one Framer who is now regarded, as Michael Kammen has noted, "as the most profound, original, and far-seeing among all his peers." He is in fact the one member of the Convention whose intentions we know best, and whose ideas now dominate our own understanding of the founding.

Madison the man hardly cut a commanding figure. He lacked the stern charisma of Washington, the restless ambition of John Adams, or the engaging charm of Jefferson. He was less cosmopolitan than Franklin, less bold than Hamilton. Thomas Paine was a far more pungent writer, and Patrick Henry a far more stirring orator. What set Madison apart and enabled him to exercise a special influence of his own was the relentlessly logical intellect that he brought to bear on all public questions. Once he was done examining an issue, even his opponents found it hard to avoid viewing it from the perspective he had fashioned.

Madison had just turned twenty-four when the Revolutionary War broke out, in April 1775. Three years had passed since the completion of his studies at the College of New Jersey (now Princeton University), but Madison remained a directionless young man with little ambition. In our own time, he would have been a natural candidate for graduate school.

The Revolution changed all that. Slowly Madison found in public life the commitment and fulfillment that the management of a plantation or a legal practice could never have provided. From the moment of his election to the Orange County Committee of Safety in late 1774 until the end of his presidency in 1817, his active involvement in politics never flagged. And even in retirement, his concern with the Republic and *res publica*—public affairs— continued unabated, until his death in 1836 marked the passing of the last of the Revolutionary patriarchs.

For a number of reasons, virtually every attempt to explain the Constitution centers on Madison. To begin with, he played the most critical role throughout the entire course of events that led to the writing, adoption, and amendment of the Constitution. From the moment he entered the Continental Congress in 1780, no one was more actively engaged in the efforts first to ratify and then to amend the Articles of Confederation, the country's original federal charter. When the delegates to the Federal Convention assembled in May 1787, the ideas that Madison incorporated in the fifteen-point Virginia Plan set their basic agenda. He quickly assumed a leading role during the debates that followed, forcing his colleagues to view the problems of republican government from the elevated heights he had scaled. And once the Constitution was ratified, Madison (now in Congress) took the lead in drafting the amendments that eventually formed the Bill of Rights.

Even more important, our own understanding of what the framers intended is largely derived from Madison: from his speeches and writings as well as from the invaluable notes of debate he kept at Philadelphia. The most profound statements of the theory of the Constitution, scholars agree, are found in his contributions to *The Federalist*, especially in *Federalist* 10 and 51, the seminal texts of American political science.

But most important, the issues that Madison struggled with were, finally, the same issues that we are being asked to consider today. Can the private rights of individuals and minorities be safely trusted to the will of democratic majorities within the states, or will they be better protected by the presumably more enlightened officials of the national government? Can any constitution enumerate all the rights and liberties that deserve protection? How much latitude may judges exercise in interpreting the Constitution, and what weight are they obliged to give to the intentions and understandings of its adopters? Madison pondered the first two of these questions in great detail in 1787–88, and the third in the years to follow, especially as he monitored the growth of judicial power that the great Chief Justice John Marshall did so much to establish—originally in the landmark 1803 *Marbury* v. *Madison* decision (the suit that most clearly established the principle of judicial review).

It is easy enough for both sides of the current controversy over constitutional interpretation to appeal to Madison's authority. Like today's liberals, Madison doubted that individual rights could be safely left to the judgment of democratic majorities. But like the conservatives, he had serious reservations about the political capacity of the judiciary. Indeed, when in 1821 he criticized the Marshall Court for "mingling with their judgments pronounced, comments & reasonings of a scope beyond them," he might just as well have been attacking Professor Ronald Dworkin's argument that judges should decide cases not according to constitutionally sanctioned rights but rather in the light of broad principles of moral philosophy.

For the historian, however, the deeper challenge is to explain the complexity and nuance of Madison's thought, and—still deeper—to recapture what was experimental, and thus tentative and uncertain, in everything he and his colleagues sought to accomplish. It is this awareness of the self-consciously experimental nature of the Convention that reveals why the search for its definitive "original intentions" is so problematic.

Madison came to Philadelphia the best prepared of any of the delegates. He had spent the preceding months diagnosing what he called the "vices of the political system of the United States," and reviewing the history of the great republican confederacies, both ancient and modern. His readings, he recalled, had failed to satisfy his curiosity about "the process, the principles, the reasons, and the anticipations"—in a word, the intentions—"which had prevailed in the formation of the most distinguished Confederacies," and this frustration led him to keep a detailed record of the debates. But what Madison also set out to preserve once a quorum appeared on May 25, 1787—eleven days late—was the fate of his own intentions. For he approached the Convention in the grip of a great intellectual passion, with the same exultation that in 1776 had led John Adams to rejoice at being "sent into life at a time when the greatest lawgivers of antiquity would have wished to live."

Three sets of major issues that Madison knew the delegates would act on should be familiar to everyone who can recall school lessons on the Constitution. First, to free the union from its "imbecilic" dependence on the good will of the states, the new government required independent power to make and execute its own laws and to raise its own revenues. It proved far easier to forge agreement on these principles than on a second set of issues, which involved balancing the conflicting interests that the delegates represented: small states and large, slave states and free, northern merchants and southern planters.

But the time and energy the prolonged maneuvers over these claims commanded might better have been devoted to a third set of issues: how to divide power among the three independent branches of the new government. Here the delegates drew their major lessons from the new constitutions that most of the states had written at the time of independence. The central feature of these constitutions—as Gordon Wood has shown in his brilliant study of *The Creation of the American Republic, 1776–1787*—was their concentration of power in the legislatures, and especially in the lower houses. How to prevent these sovereign bodies from running roughshod over both the state constitutions and the two weaker branches of government—the executive and judiciary—had emerged as the great question of American constitutionalism.

Most of the framers shared this concern with the failings of the state constitutions. What set Madison apart was the depth of his analysis of both the source of the problems and their solution. More than any of his colleagues, he believed that the time had come to rescue not only the union from the states, but the states from themselves. It was in his brilliant assessment of the problems of republican government within the states that Madison most directly challenged the position that conservatives affirm today—namely, that claims of individual and minority rights not explicitly protected in the text of the Constitution are better left to the judgment of democratic majorities within the states than to the arbitrary will of federal judges.

The simple truth, he thought, was that incompetent lawmakers were passing too many laws, and that these poorly drawn acts were in turn being revised or repealed before anyone knew how well they were working. More alarming still, the "injustice" of the laws that had been adopted since 1776 suggested that the will of the majority could no longer be regarded as "the safest guardian both of public good and private rights." Self-interested or "factious" majorities within the assemblies or among the people at large were giving free rein to their impulses, undeterred by any of the moral restraints that one might hope would check such "vicious" behavior—honor, or a sense of the public good, or even religion, whose effects on public policy Madison strongly distrusted.

What kinds of rights did Madison fear these majorities would violate? In one sense, at least, his concerns would warm the heart of today's most ardent Republican. In 1787 Madison was particularly anxious to protect the rights of property against unjust laws arising from "the lower orders" of society. Alarmed by the passage of paper money laws and by Shays's Rebellion (the uprising of debtor farmers in Massachusetts), he foresaw a day when "power will slide into the hands" of "those who will labor under all the hardships of life, and secretly sigh for a more equal distribution of its blessings"—when, in other words, citizens with little or no property would favor "agrarian" laws breaking up the great estates of Madison's own class.

Yet the rights of property hardly exhausted his fears. Madison was no less intent on protecting the rights of religious dissenters and non-believers against even the weak forms of established religion that still survived in six of the states. In 1785 he had led the opposition against a Virginia bill to levy taxes to support all "teachers of the Christian religion"—a measure that, in the context of the time, can be fairly equated with the kind of non-discriminatory aid to religion in general that many conservatives now argue that the establishment clause of the First Amendment was *not* meant to prohibit. In Madison's view, the private exercise of religion was to be entirely free from both government regulation and support.

Rights of property and conscience, as well as the body of civil liberties that had come to be recognized as part of the Anglo-American political tradition, were thus among Madison's central concerns. But what is perhaps most striking about his thinking on this subject is that he strongly resisted the idea that any constitution or bill of rights could ever fully identify the entire range of liberties that deserved protection. Bills of rights had been part of many of the state constitutions of 1776; Madison's own first notable action in public life had been to secure an amendment to the most famous of these, the Virginia Declaration of Rights. But by 1787, he and virtually every other framer of the Constitution believed that such statements, however carefully drawn, had little worth. Bills of rights were not self-enforcing; they were mere "parchment barriers" (he later wrote Jefferson) that "overbearing majorities in every state" had repeatedly violated, or that "an infinitude of legislative expedients" could always find ways to circumvent.

How to prevent majorities within both the community and the legislature from violating individual and minority rights was thus Madison's overriding concern in 1787, and it was reflected in virtually every major facet of his constitutional thought.

The great discovery that Madison carried to Philadelphia was that laws destructive of private rights were far less likely to be enacted in an extended national republic than within the smaller sphere of the states. Because a national republic would embrace so many diverse and shifting interests, the danger of the wrong kinds of coalitions forming and enduring among the community at large would be greatly reduced. And the new Congress, he predicted, would consist of legislators far more enlightened and scrupulous than the petty demagogues who controlled the state assemblies. (This, of course, was the theory that took its mature form in *Federalist* 10 and 51.)

But Madison was prepared to trust congressmen only so far. From his own experience of state government, he had concluded that "the real source of danger in the American constitutions" was "the powerful tendency in the legislature to absorb all power into its vortex." What he accordingly feared in 1787 was that both the executive and the judiciary would prove not too strong but too weak. Alone, neither could resist the legislature, the one branch of government that could claim to speak for the will of the community. To give the executive branch and the judiciary the influence and political strength they separately lacked, Madison proposed that they should be allied in a Council of Revision. This Council would "examine" every act of Congress *before* it took effect, and its "dissent" would "amount to a rejection" unless Congress overrode this veto.

This remedy would secure the national government against "the mischiefs of faction," Madison believed, but within the smaller spheres of the *states*, which would still conduct much of the ordinary business of government, majorities rooted in economic interests or religion or other passions would continue to violate private rights. To deal with this residual danger to liberty Madison formulated his most radical proposal: to make every state law subject to the "negative" (or veto) of the national government, exercised jointly by the Council of Revision and Congress (or perhaps just the Senate). Of all the intentions that Madison voiced at the Convention, this was the most original and, to his mind, crucial. Armed with such a power, the union could protect itself against the interfering laws that the states might pass. But more important, the "negative" would further enable the national government to act as a "dispassionate and disinterested umpire in disputes" within each of the states, curbing "the aggressions of interested majorities on the rights of minorities and of individuals."

It is difficult to see how Attorney General Meese can invoke the true original intentions of the "Father of the Constitution" to confirm his opinion about the proper place of the judiciary. The idea that claims of individual rights could be safely left to the judgment of majorities—especially *state* majorities—runs directly contrary to everything that Madison thought at the time the Constitution was adopted. The Madison of 1787 would also have opposed the current conservative cry that judges should simply decide cases, not make policy. Far from isolating the judiciary from the political arena, the proposed Council of Revision was intended to bring it directly into the lawmaking process as an advisory body to the legislature. Madison sought thereby to improve the quality of law at its source, so that the American legal codes would gain "the perspicuity, the conciseness, and the systematic character" they otherwise lacked. The judiciary would then actively protect "the community at large" against "those unwise and unjust measures which constituted so great a portion of our calamities." The Madison who hoped the judiciary would act "to restrain the legislature from encroaching on the other co-ordinate departments, or on the rights of the people at large; or from passing laws unwise in their principle, or incorrect in their form" was not an unqualified defender of legislative supremacy.

Nor, finally, can it be said that the principal author of the Bill of Rights believed that judges should protect only those rights that the text of the Constitution explicitly recognized. To the contrary, Madison, James Wilson, and other Federalists took seriously the argument that the constitutional recognition of particular rights would imply "that those rights which were not singled out" would be rendered "insecure." Madison in particular feared that "a positive declaration of some of the most essential rights could not be obtained in the requisite latitude." Under political pressure and at the urging of Jefferson, Madison finally (but grudgingly) admitted that a bill of rights might help, over time, to instill in the people a greater respect for "the fundamental maxims of free government." But even as he was shepherding the first amendments through Congress in 1789, he privately described them (amazingly enough) as a "nauseous project"—if not to himself, than at least to his fellow congressmen—required only for expedient reasons of politics. Doubtless, Madison would look askance at many of the specific claims of "rights" asserted in recent litigation. It is difficult to imagine him using the First Amendment to protect pornography or invalidating state prohibitions of contraception on the grounds that (in the famous words of Justice William O. Douglas) "penumbras, formed by emanations" from the Bill of Rights established "zones of privacy" into which public authority could not intrude. Equally important, Madison and many of the framers might well have been staggered by the range of remedies that the courts have devised and imposed after finding that individual and minority rights have indeed been violated. It is, after all, one thing to say that judges should simply void laws that clearly infringe upon such rights. But when judges move further and provide practical remedies for the redress of past wrongs—by mandating schemes for hiring minority workers, say, or making teacher assignments to alleviate the effects of segregation—they may act in political and administrative capacities that outrun both the boundaries of judicial competence and the notions of separation of powers to which the framers were so deeply attached.

On balance, however, Madison's larger concerns lend greater support to Justice Brennan than to Attorney General Meese. His general theory invited judges and legislators alike to be generous, not frugal in defining and defending the range of personal rights. Moreover, one can readily project many of his eighteenth-century concerns to the civil rights issues that lie at the core of the activist jurisprudence of the last three decades. What, after all, was the edifice of Jim Crow segregation that the Court struck down if not a classic example of how self-interested majorities within the states could trample upon the rights of minorities? One could easily argue, too, that Madison would have supported the "one man-one vote" decisions of the early 1960s: he had endorsed the regular reapportionment of legislative seats as early as 1785. And perhaps most strikingly, Madison would find "nauseous" the current conservative claim, backed only by the most tendentious and selective scholarship, that the First Amendment permits non-discriminatory federal support of religion.

The fact that the critical modern steps in favor of desegregation, reapportionment, and separation of Church and State originated with the judiciary would probably have surprised Madison, but only because he expected that judges would command so little influence and respect. He would not, I think, be disappointed with the results. In each of these areas, expanded rights and liberties have had to be wrenched from the control of groups whose behavior arguably confirmed his prediction that "wherever there is an interest and power to do wrong, wrong will generally be done." And for better or worse, it is the difficulty of convincing "factious majorities" to do right that suggests why judges cannot confine themselves to invalidating wrongful laws and regulations but often must also go ahead to devise the further remedies that plaintiffs seek. Doubts about the political competence of the judiciary must be weighed, in other words, against doubts about the good faith of legislators and their constituents.

Most of the framers at Philadelphia shared Madison's doubts about the value of bills of rights, and his other innovative proposals also enjoyed strong support in debate—notably from the Scottish-born James Wilson, the leading legal mind within the Convention. The fact remains that neither the Council nor the veto was adopted—and for that reason Madison left the Convention deeply disappointed with its results. Even before it adjourned, he wrote to Jefferson that the Constitution would fail to "prevent the local mischiefs which everywhere excite disgusts against the state governments." In a second letter written in late October, he provided an elaborate justification for the veto on state laws, and again predicted that without it the Constitution would prove "materially defective" because the new government would be unable to protect private rights. Only four weeks later, however, Madison published *Federalist* 10, which explained why the national government would be free of all those vices that its author privately felt (but did not say) would continue to plague the states.

For the serious student of "original intent," Madison's early disillusionment with the results of the Convention raises awkward questions. To begin with, consider how it affects our reading of *Federalist* 10. One could argue that this essay still deserves greater weight in interpreting the Constitution than Madison's earlier ideas, since *The Federalist* describes what was actually adopted, not simply proposed. But then one has to ask whether a public essay written largely to answer objections against the Constitution merits more attention than its author's private and presumably more honest assessment of the Constitution's failings.

But there are more important problems than ascertaining the status of *Federalist* 10. What weight can we assign Madison's ideas when his colleagues rejected the conclusions to which he thought they led? Can we even ask whether Madison has been overrated, if not as a thinker, then at least in terms of his final influence on the Constitution?

Yet even in defeat Madison's intentions are highly relevant to the current controversy over judicial power. For it was in rejecting the Council of Revision and the veto on state laws that the framers most clearly addressed the role of the judiciary in the constitutional system.

Until very recently the hoary question of whether the framers intended the judiciary to exercise the power of judicial review had ceased to be a subject of active scholarly interest. But at some point controversy over the scope and application of judicial review naturally raises questions about its legitimacy, and these in turn prove difficult to address without considering the evolution of judicial power since 1787. This is not a new concern, provoked only by the oratory of Attorney General Meese. In fact, it was Alexander Bickel, a leading scholar at Yale Law School, who raised most of the critical issues in his seminal book of 1962, *The Least Dangerous Branch* (a title in turn taken from Alexander Hamilton's classic defense of judicial review in *Federalist* 78).

Judicial review, one should also note, is a power with multiple uses. At the narrowest, it may simply be the means by which the judiciary defends itself against efforts by the other branches to interfere with its own particular functions. More broadly, judicial review works to protect the Constitution against improper acts by Congress or the President, and the entire federal government against interference by the states. Finally—and what has been the true source of controversy over the past three decades—judicial review has enabled the judiciary to recognize and advance claims of individual rights against the actions of both the federal government and the states.

Madison's original notion of judicial power had rested on three fundamental assumptions. First, the judiciary, by itself, would lack the political strength to resist the improper acts of either Congress or the state legislatures. Second, even if the courts did overturn wrongful laws, their rulings would often come too late to undo or remedy the injuries to private rights that would already have been committed. That was why the Council of Revision was to act before a law took effect. But third, Madison also believed that the final right to judge whether a national or state law was constitutional should belong not to the judges but to Congress. He may have hoped that Congress would rarely override the Council of Revision, but he was too much the republican to allow the least accountable branch of the government to have the final say on the Constitution.

Here at last conservatives can find in Madison's original position support for their own attacks on judicial supremacy. But ironically, it was precisely on this point that the majority of the Convention turned Madison's logic and his reservations about judicial power upside down. They believed that the influence and independence of the judiciary would be reduced, not enhanced, if it acquired the advisory functions he proposed. The fatal defect in the Council of Revision was that it would make it harder for the judiciary to check the other branches. "Judges ought to be able to expound the law as it should come before them," Rufus King argued, "free from the bias of having participated in its formation." Other delegates argued against the veto over state laws on the grounds that neither Congress nor the Council of Revision could possibly review the enormous volume of legislation the states would submit. In its place—and without debate—they put the supremacy clause, which bound the state judiciaries to enforce the federal Constitution and laws against conflicting state statutes.

By rejecting Madison's proposals, then, the delegates expressed their confidence in the capacity of the national and state judiciaries alike. But more than that, they also revealed that they expected judges to exercise the power of judicial review. "As to the constitutionality of laws, that point will come before the judges in their proper official character," Luther Martin flatly stated. "And in this character they have a negative on the laws." Martin, the original author of the supremacy clause, may have hoped that only state courts would review state laws; but his colleagues expected that appeals involving federal questions would fall to the national judiciary.

Such statements leave one wondering how anyone could ever have doubted whether judicial review was part of the original constitutional design. True, in 1787 the idea that courts could overturn laws was still a novelty, realized in only a handful of state cases to which little attention had yet been paid. Elbridge Gerry was not announcing a self-evident truth when he informed the Convention that "In some states the judges had actually set aside laws as being against the constitution." Even so, the delegates repeatedly spoke as if they simply presumed that the federal judiciary would be able to overturn both state and national laws.

Yet, remarkably, the framers never discussed judicial review systematically or even directly. Virtually all of their comments on the subject were uttered during the debate over the Council of Revision—in other words, over a proposal that was defeated, not one that was adopted. They defined neither the scope of judicial review nor the basis on which judges would test whether laws were constitutional—the issues that lie at the crux of the current controversy. Resisting the idea that the Constitution should include a comprehensive list of private rights, they never considered whether the federal courts were restricted to protecting only the handful of rights that the Constitution explicitly mentioned. The best we can say is that the delegates considered the various uses of judicial review—ranging from the simple self-protection of the judicial function to the voiding of state and federal laws—without definitively determining how or when it might be exercised.

One final point deserves emphasis. Where Madison would have explicitly given Congress the final word on constitutionality, the majority implicitly allowed it to override only presidential vetoes, not judicial decisions. Madison conceded as much in October 1788. By failing to state how disputes over "expounding" the Constitution would be resolved, he noted, the Convention by default left that judgment to the courts simply because they were the last to act and thus to determine whether a law would be executed. This result, Madison complained, "was never intended, and can never be proper"—but inadvertently or otherwise, it seemed to be part of the Constitution.

This revealing comment again reminds us that the relation between the meaning of the Constitution and the intentions of its authors can never be taken for granted. But more than that, it encourages us to ask how the framers could have treated so vital a matter as judicial review in so seemingly careless a fashion. And this in turn can lead to a more realistic, balanced, and even critical appraisal of the great work of 1787—to a view that still celebrates "the miracle at Philadelphia" but restores the framers, with all their wisdom and political skill, to the imperfect historical context in which they acted.

In theory the need to balance the legislature should have led the delegates to focus their greatest intellectual efforts on designing the two weaker departments. It should have led them to explore, for example, how the Supreme Court was to exercise its novel but potentially momentous power of judicial review, or to define the nature of "the executive power" that Article II vested in the President. But here, where they had to be most inventive, the delegates also proved most tentative. In practice they shied away from sustained discussions of the substance of executive and judicial power, perhaps because they simply felt so much more comfortable with the familiar subject of legislative power. And even when they could no longer avoid the other two branches, much of their discussion centered on issues of election, appointment, and tenure. We can plot in excruciating detail "the tedious and reiterated discussions" (as Madison described them) that led to the establishment of the electoral college; but when it comes to explaining why the Convention finally allowed the President to share the power of treatymaking with the Senate, we have to rely on scraps of debate and circumstantial evidence to account for one of the most momentous decisions the framers took.

Some scholars try to close such gaps in what the framers said by attributing to them ideas derived from what it is believed they read in the writings of the Enlightenment, or by tracing their concerns to precedents in the British constitution. Obviously, the framers did not act in an intellectual vacuum. Yet what is most apparent in their deliberations is not how much they learned from Old World sources but how little they depended on outside authorities once they had set about designing the new government. (Madison once dismissed appeals to such luminaries as Locke and Montesquieu as "a field of research which is more likely to perplex than to decide.") Only in the crudest sense did the Convention model the branches of the new government on their British counterparts. The Senate was not a House of Lords, and the President was to be neither a constitutional monarch nor a prime minister. And the idea of an independent judiciary took a distinct form in America precisely because our Constitution was to be a concise written charter, not a complex and fluid mass of statutory law, common-law precedent, royal prerogative, and custom such as together made up the British constitution.

This intense self-awareness of the originality of their achievement stands out strongly in the writings of the framers and their contemporaries, and remains compelling after two centuries. Originality is not perfection, however. Because fears of disunion and domestic turbulence did exert a powerful influence in the late 1780s, the framers and their supporters were eager to describe the Constitution as a document designed to last "for ages to come." Yet having learned so much from the experience of a mere decade of self-government, and having celebrated their ability to do so, they would, I believe, find it incredible that later generations would not improve upon their discoveries, would not indeed understand the meaning of the Constitution and the liberties they designed it to protect better than they had.

Amid all the platitudes and heroic accolades to which we will be subjected during the celebrations ahead, an awareness of the imperfections and ambiguities of the Constitution or of the limits of the framers' vision will not be easy to maintain. We can better understand what the framers accomplished by grasping the problems that they failed to resolve than by attributing to them a perfect knowledge and foresight that they never pretended to possess.

Normative Issues

Neutral Principles and Some First Amendment Problems

◆
———
═══
———
◆

ROBERT H. BORK

A PERSISTENTLY DISTURBING aspect of constitutional law is its lack of theory, a lack which is manifest not merely in the work of the courts but in the public, professional and even scholarly discussion of the topic. The result, of course, is that courts are without effective criteria and, therefore we have come to expect that the nature of the Constitution will change, often quite dramatically, as the personnel of the Supreme Court changes. In the present state of affairs that expectation is inevitable, but it is nevertheless deplorable.

The remarks that follow do not, of course, offer a general theory of constitutional law. They are more properly viewed as ranging shots, an attempt to establish the necessity for theory and to take the argument of how constitutional doctrine should be evolved by courts a step or two farther. The first section centers on the implications of Professor Herbert Wechsler's concept of "neutral principles," and the second attempts to apply those implications to some important and much-debated problems in the interpretation of the First Amendment. The style is informal since these remarks were originally lectures and I have not thought it worthwhile to convert these speculations and arguments into a heavily researched, balanced and thorough presentation, for that would result in a book.

The Supreme Court and the Demand for Principle

THE SUBJECT OF the lengthy and often acrimonious debate about the proper role of the Supreme Court under the Constitution is one that preoc-

197

cupies many people these days: when is authority legitimate? I find it convenient to discuss that question in the context of the Warren Court and its works simply because the Warren Court posed the issue in acute form. The issue did not disappear along with the era of the Warren Court majorities, however. It arises when any court either exercises or declines to exercise the power to invalidate any act of another branch of government. The Supreme Court is a major power center, and we must ask when its power should be used and when it should be withheld.

Our starting place, inevitably, is Professor Wechsler's argument that the Court must not be merely a "naked power organ," which means that its decisions must be controlled by principle.[1] "A principled decision," according to Wechsler, "is one that rests on reasons with respect to all the issues in a case, reasons that in their generality and their neutrality transcend any immediate result that is involved."[2]

Wechsler chose the term "neutral principles" to capsulate his argument, though he recognizes that the legal principle to be applied is itself never neutral because it embodies a choice of one value rather than another. Wechsler asked for the neutral application of principles, which is a requirement, as Professor Louis L. Jaffe puts it, that the judge "sincerely believe in the principle upon which he purports to rest his decision." "The judge," says Jaffe, "must believe in the validity of the reasons given for the decision at least in the sense that he is prepared to apply them to a later case which he cannot honestly distinguish."[3] He must not, that is, decide lawlessly. But is the demand for neutrality in judges merely another value choice, one that is no more principled than any other? I think not, but to prove it we must rehearse fundamentals. This is familiar terrain but important and still debated.

The requirement that the Court be principled arises from the resolution of the seeming anomaly of judicial supremacy in a democratic society. If the judiciary really is supreme, able to rule when and as it sees fit, the society is not democratic. The anomaly is dissipated, however, by the model of government embodied in the structure of the Constitution, a model upon which popular consent to limited government by the Supreme Court also rests. This model we may for convenience, though perhaps not with total accuracy, call "Madisonian."[4]

A Madisonian system is not completely democratic, if by "democratic" we mean completely majoritarian. It assumes that in wide areas of life majorities are entitled to rule for no better reason than that they are majorities. We need not pause here to examine the philosophical underpinnings of that assumption since it is a "given" in our society; nor need we worry that "majority" is a term of art meaning often no more than the shifting combinations of minorities that add up to temporary majorities in the legislature. That majorities are so constituted is inevitable. In any case, one essential premise of the Madisonian model is majoritarianism. The model has also a counter-majoritarian premise, however, for it assumes there are some areas of life a majority should not control. There are some things a majority should not do to us no matter how democratically it decides to do them. These are areas properly left to individual freedom, and coercion by the majority in these aspects of life is tyranny.

Some see the model as containing an inherent, perhaps an insoluble, dilemma.[5] Majority tyranny occurs if legislation invades the areas properly left to individual freedom. Minority tyranny occurs if the majority is prevented from ruling where its power is legitimate. Yet, quite obviously, neither the majority nor the minority can be trusted to define the freedom of the other. This dilemma is resolved in constitutional theory, and in popular understanding, by the Supreme Court's power to define both majority and minority freedom through the interpretation of the Constitution. Society consents to be ruled undemocratically within defined areas by certain enduring principles believed to be stated in, and placed beyond the reach of majorities by, the Constitution.

But this resolution of the dilemma imposes severe requirements upon the Court. For it follows that the Court's power is legitimate only if it has, and can demonstrate in reasoned opinions that it has, a valid theory, derived from the Constitution, of the respective spheres of majority and minority freedom. If it does not have such a theory but merely imposes its own value choices, or worse if it pretends to have a theory but actually follows its own predilections, the Court violates the postulates of the Madisonian model that alone justifies its power. It then necessarily abets the tyranny either of the majority or of the minority.

This argument is central to the issue of legitimate authority because the Supreme Court's power to govern rests upon popular acceptance of this model. Evidence that this is, in fact, the basis of the Court's power is to be gleaned everywhere in our culture. We need not canvass here such things as high school civics texts and newspaper commentary, for the most telling evidence may be found in the U.S. Reports. The Supreme Court regularly insists that its results, and most particularly its controversial results, do not spring from the mere will of the Justices in the majority but are supported, indeed compelled, by a proper understanding of the Constitution of the United States. Value choices are attributed to the Founding Fathers, not to the Court. The way an institution advertises tells you what it thinks its customers demand.

This is, I think, the ultimate reason the Court must be principled. If it does not have and rigorously adhere to a valid and consistent theory of majority and minority freedoms based upon the Constitution, judicial supremacy, given the axioms of our system, is, precisely to that extent, illegitimate. The root of its illegitimacy is that it opens a chasm between the reality of the Court's performance and the constitutional and popular assumptions that give it power. I do not mean to rest the argument entirely upon the popular understanding of the Court's function. Even if society generally should ultimately perceive what the Court is in fact doing and, having seen, prove content to have major policies determined by the unguided discretion of judges rather than by elected representatives, a principled judge would, I believe, continue to consider himself bound by an obligation to the document and to the structure of government that it prescribes. At least he would be bound so long as any litigant existed who demanded such adherence of him. I do not understand how, on any other theory of judicial obligation, the Court could, as it does now, protect voting rights if a large majority of the relevant constituency were willing to see some groups or individuals deprived of such rights. But even if I am wrong in that, at the very least an honest judge would owe it to the body politic to cease invoking the authority of the Constitution and to make explicit the imposition of his own will, for only then would we know whether the society understood enough of what is taking place to be said to have consented.

Judge J. Skelly Wright, in an argument resting on different premises, has severely criticized the advocates of principle. He defends the value-choosing role of the Warren Court, setting that Court in opposition to something he refers to as the "scholarly tradition," which criticizes that Court for its lack of principle.[6] A perceptive reader, sensitive to nuance, may suspect that the Judge is rather out of sympathy with that tradition from such hints as his reference to "self-appointed scholastic mandarins."[7]

The "mandarins" of the academy anger the judge because they engage in "haughty derision of the Court's powers of analysis and reasoning."[8] Yet, curiously enough, Judge Wright makes no attempt to refute the charge but rather seems to adopt the technique of confession and avoidance. He seems to be arguing that a Court engaged in choosing fundamental values for society cannot be expected to produce principled decisions at the same time. Decisions first, principles later. One wonders, however, how the Court or the rest of us are to know that the decisions are correct or what they portend for the future if they are not accompanied by the principles that explain and justify them. And it would not be amiss to point out that quite often the principles required of the Warren Court's decisions never did put in an appearance. But Judge Wright's main point appears to be that value choice is the most important function of the Supreme Court, so that if we must take one or the other, and apparently we must, we should prefer a process of selecting values to one of constructing and articulating principles. His argument, I believe, boils down to a syllogism. I. The Supreme Court should "protect our constitutional rights and liberties." II. The Supreme Court must "make fundamental value choices" in order to "protect our constitutional rights and liberties." III. Therefore, the Supreme Court should "make fundamental value choices."[9]

The argument displays an all too common confusion. If we have constitutional rights and liberties already, rights and liberties specified by the Constitution,[10] the Court need make no fundamental value choices in order to protect them, and it certainly need not have difficulty enunciating principles. If, on the other hand, "constitutional rights and liberties" are not in some real sense specified by the Constitution but are the rights and liberties the Court chooses, on the basis of its own values, to give to us, then the conclusion was contained entirely in the major premise, and the judge's syllogism is no more than an assertion of what it purported to prove.

If I am correct so far, no argument that is both coherent and respectable can be made supporting a Supreme Court that "chooses fundamental values" because a Court that makes rather than implements value choices cannot be squared with the presuppositions of a democratic society. The man who understands the issues and nevertheless insists upon the rightness of the Warren Court's performance ought also, if he is candid, to admit that he is prepared to sacrifice democratic process to his own moral views. He claims for the Supreme Court an institutionalized role as perpetrator of limited coups d'etat.

Such a man occupies an impossible philosophic position. What can he say, for instance, of a Court that does not share his politics or his morality? I can think of nothing except the assertion that he will ignore the Court whenever he can get away with it and overthrow it if he can. In his view the Court has no legitimacy, and there is no reason any of us should obey it. And, this being the case, the advocate of a value-choosing Court must answer another difficult question. Why should the Court, a committee of nine lawyers, be the sole agent of change? The man who prefers results to processes has no reason to say that the Court is more legitimate than any other institution. If the Court will not listen, why not argue the case to some other group, say the Joint Chiefs of Staff, a body with rather better means for implementing its decisions?

We are driven to the conclusion that a legitimate Court must be controlled by principles exterior to the will of the Justices. As my colleague, Professor Alexander Bickel, puts it, "The process of the coherent, analytically warranted, principled declaration of general norms alone justifies the Court's function."[11] Recognition of the need for principle is only the first step, but once that step is taken much more follows. Logic has a life of its own, and devotion to principle requires that we follow where logic leads.

Professor Bickel identifies Justice Felix Frankfurter as the leading judicial proponent of principle but concedes that even Frankfurter never found a "rigorous general accord between judicial supremacy and democratic theory."[12] Judge Wright responds, "The leading commentators of the scholarly tradition have tried ever since to succeed where the Justice failed."[13] As Judge Wright quite accurately suggests, the commentators have so far had no better luck than the justice.

One reason, I think, is clear. We have not carried the idea of neutrality far enough. We have been talking about neutrality in the *application* of principles.

If judges are to avoid imposing their own values upon the rest of us, however, they must be neutral as well in the *definition* and the *derivation* of principles.

It is easy enough to meet the requirement of neutral application by stating a principle so narrowly that no embarrassment need arise in applying it to all cases it subsumes, a tactic often urged by proponents of "judicial restraint." But that solves very little. It certainly does not protect the judge from the intrusion of his own values. The problem may be illustrated by *Griswold* v. *Connecticut*,[14] in many ways a typical decision of the Warren Court. *Griswold* struck down Connecticut's statute making it a crime, even for married couples, to use contraceptive devices. If we take the principle of the decision to be a statement that government may not interfere with any acts done in private, we need not even ask about the principle's dubious origin, for we know at once that the Court will not apply it neutrally. The Court, we may confidently predict, is not going to throw constitutional protection around heroin use or sexual acts with a consenting minor. We can gain the possibility of neutral application by reframing the principle as a statement that government may not prohibit the use of contraceptives by married couples, but that is not enough. The question of neutral definition arises: Why does the principle extend only to married couples? Why, out of all forms of sexual behavior, only to the use of contraceptives? Why, out of all forms of behavior, only to sex? The question of neutral derivation also arises: What justifies any limitation upon legislatures in this area? What is the origin of any principle one may state?

To put the matter another way, if a neutral judge must demonstrate why principle X applies to cases A and B but not to case C (which is, I believe, the requirement laid down by Professors Wechsler and Jaffe), he must, by the same token, also explain why the principle is defined as X rather than as X *minus*, which would cover A but not cases B and C, or as X *plus*, which would cover all cases, A, B and C. Similarly, he must explain why X is a proper principle of limitation on majority power at all. Why should he not choose *non-X*? If he may not choose lawlessly between cases in applying principle X, he may certainly not choose lawlessly in defining X or in choosing X, for principles are after all only organizations of cases into groups. To choose the principle and define it is to decide the cases.

It follows that the choice of "fundamental values" by the Court cannot be justified. Where constitutional materials do not clearly specify the value to be preferred, there is no principled way to prefer any claimed human value to any other. The judge must stick close to the text and the history, and their fair implications, and not construct new rights. The case just mentioned illustrates the point. The *Griswold* decision has been acclaimed by legal scholars as a major advance in constitutional law, a salutary demonstration of the Court's ability to protect fundamental human values. I regret to have to disagree, and my regret is all the more sincere because I once took the same position and did so in print.[15] In extenuation I can only say that at the time I thought, quite erroneously, that new basic rights could be derived logically by finding and extrapolating a more general principle of individual autonomy underlying the particular guarantees of the Bill of Rights.

The Court's *Griswold* opinion, by Justice Douglas, and the array of concurring opinions, by Justices Arthur Goldberg, Byron White and John Marshall Harlan, all failed to justify the derivation of any principle used to strike down the Connecticut anti-contraceptive statute or to define the scope of the principle. Justice Douglas, to whose opinion I must confine myself, began by pointing out that "specific guarantees in the Bill of Rights have penumbras, formed by emanations from those guarantees that help give them life and substance."[16] Nothing is exceptional there. In the case Justice Douglas cited, *NAACP* v. *Alabama*,[17] the State was held unable to force disclosure of membership lists because of the chilling effect upon the rights of assembly and political action of the NAACP's members. The penumbra was created solely to preserve a value central to the First Amendment, applied in this case through the Fourteenth Amendment. It had no life of its own as a right independent of the value specified by the First Amendment.

But Justice Douglas then performed a miracle of transubstantiation. He called the First Amendment's penumbra a protection of "privacy" and then asserted that other amendments create "zones of privacy."[18] He had no better reason to use the word "privacy" than that the individual is free within these zones, free to act in public as well as in private. None of these penumbral zones—from the First, Third, Fourth or Fifth Amendments, all of which he cited, along with the Ninth—covered the case before him. One more leap was required. Justice Douglas asserted that these various "zones of privacy" created an independent right of privacy,[19] a right not lying within the penumbra of any specific amendment. He did not disclose, however, how a series of specified rights combined to create a new and unspecified right.

The *Griswold* opinion fails every test of neutrality. The derivation of the principle was utterly specious, and so was its definition. In fact, we are left with no idea of what the principle really forbids. Derivation and definition are interrelated here. Justice Douglas called the amendments and their penumbras "zones of privacy," though of course they are not that at all. They protect both private and public behavior and so would more properly be labelled "zones of freedom." If we follow Justice Douglas in his next step, these zones would then add up to an independent right of freedom, which is to say, a general constitutional right to be free of legal coercion, a manifest impossibility in any imaginable society.

Griswold, then, is an unprincipled decision, both in the way in which it derives a new constitutional right and in the way it defines that right, or rather fails to define it. We are left with no idea of the sweep of the right of privacy and hence no notion of the cases to which it may or may not be applied in the future. The truth is that the Court could not reach its result in *Griswold* through principle. The reason is obvious. Every clash between a minority claiming freedom and a majority claiming power to regulate involves a choice between the gratifications of the two groups. When the Constitution has not spoken, the Court will be able to find no scale, other than its own value preferences, upon which to weigh the respective claims to pleasure. Compare the facts in *Griswold* with a hypothetical suit by an electric utility company and one of its customers to void a smoke pollution ordinance as unconstitutional. The cases are identical.

In *Griswold* a husband and wife assert that they wish to have sexual relations without fear of unwanted children. The law impairs their sexual gratifications. The State can assert, and at one stage in that litigation did assert, that the majority finds the use of contraceptives immoral. Knowledge that it takes place and that the State makes no effort to inhibit it causes the majority anguish, impairs their gratifications.

The electrical company asserts that it wishes to produce electricity at low cost in order to reach a wide market and make profits. Its customer asserts that he wants a lower cost so that prices can be held low. The smoke pollution regulation impairs his and the company's stockholders' economic gratifications. The State can assert not only that the majority prefer clean air to lower prices, but also that the absence of the regulation impairs the majority's physical and aesthetic gratifications.

Neither case is covered specifically or by obvious implication in the Constitution. Unless we can distinguish forms of gratification, the only course for a principled Court is to let the majority have its way in both cases. It is clear that the Court cannot make the necessary distinction. There is no principled way to decide that one man's gratifications are more deserving of respect than another's or that one form of gratification is more worthy than another.[20] Why is sexual gratification more worthy than moral gratification? Why is sexual gratification nobler than economic gratification? There is no way of deciding these matters other than by reference to some system of moral or ethical values that has no objective or intrinsic validity of its own and about which men can and do differ. Where the Constitution does not embody the moral or ethical choice, the judge has no basis other than his own values upon which to set aside the community judgment embodied in the statute. That, by definition, is an inadequate basis for judicial supremacy. The issue of the community's moral and ethical values, the issue of the degree of pain an activity causes, are matters concluded by the passage and enforcement of the laws in question. The judiciary has no role to play other than that of applying the statutes in a fair and impartial manner.

One of my colleagues refers to this conclusion, not without sarcasm, as the "Equal Gratification Clause." The phrase is apt, and I accept it, though not the sarcasm. Equality of human gratifications, where the document does not impose a hierarchy, is an essential part of constitutional doctrine because of the necessity that judges be principled. To be perfectly clear on the subject, I repeat that the principle is not applicable to legislatures. Legislation requires value choice and cannot be principled in the sense under discussion. Courts must accept any value choice the legislature makes unless it clearly runs contrary to a choice made in the framing of the Constitution.

It follows, of course, that broad areas of constitutional law ought to be reformulated. Most obviously, it follows that substantive due process, revived by the *Griswold* case, is and always has been an improper doctrine.

Substantive due process requires the Court to say, without guidance from the Constitution, which liberties or gratifications may be infringed by majorities and which may not. This means that *Griswold*'s antecedents were also wrongly decided, e.g., *Meyer* v. *Nebraska*,[21] which struck down a statute forbidding the teaching of subjects in any language other than English; *Pierce* v. *Society of Sisters*,[22] which set aside a statute compelling all Oregon school children to attend public schools; *Adkins* v. *Children's Hospital*,[23] which invalidated a statute of Congress authorizing a board to fix minimum wages for women and children in the District of Columbia; and *Lochner* v. *New York*,[24] which voided a statute fixing maximum hours of work for bakers. With some of these cases I am in political agreement, and perhaps *Pierce*'s result could be reached on acceptable grounds, but there is no justification for the Court's methods. In *Lochner*, Justice Rufus Peckham, defending liberty from what he conceived as a mere meddlesome interference, asked, "are we all . . . at the mercy of legislative majorities?"[25] The correct answer, where the Constitution does not speak, must be "yes."

The argument so far also indicates that most of substantive equal protection is also improper. The modern Court, we need hardly be reminded, used the equal protection clause the way the old Court used the due process clause. The only change was in the values chosen for protection and the frequency with which the Court struck down laws.

The equal protection clause has two legitimate meanings. It can require formal procedural equality, and, because of its historical origins, it does require that government not discriminate along racial lines. But much more than that cannot properly be read into the clause. The bare concept of equality provides no guide for courts. All law discriminates and thereby creates inequality. The Supreme Court has no principled way of saying which nonracial inequalities are impermissible. What it has done, therefore, is to appeal to simplistic notions of "fairness" or to what it regards as "fundamental" interests in order to demand equality in some cases but not in others, thus choosing values and producing a line of cases as improper and as intellectually empty as *Griswold* v. *Connecticut*. Any casebook lists them, and the differing results cannot be explained on any ground other than the Court's preferences for particular values: *Skinner* v. *Oklahoma*[26] (a forbidden inequality exists when a state undertakes to sterilize robbers but not embezzlers); *Kotch* v. *Board of River Port Pilot Commissioners*[27] (no right to equality is infringed when a state grants pilots' licenses only to persons related by blood to existing pilots and denies licenses to persons otherwise as well qualified); *Goesaert*

v. *Cleary*[28] (a state does not deny equality when it refuses to license women as bartenders unless they are the wives or daughters of male owners of licensed liquor establishments); *Railway Express Agency* v. *New York*[29] (a city may forbid truck owners to sell advertising space on their trucks as a distracting hazard to traffic safety though it permits owners to advertise their own business in that way); *Shapiro* v. *Thompson*[30] (a state denies equality if it pays welfare only to persons who have resided in the state for one year); *Levy* v. *Louisiana*[31] (a state may not limit actions for a parent's wrongful death to legitimate children and deny it to illegitimate children). The list could be extended, but the point is that the cases cannot be reconciled on any basis other than the Justices' personal beliefs about what interests or gratifications ought to be protected.

Professor Wechsler notes that Justice Frankfurter expressed "disquietude that the line is often very thin between the cases in which the Court felt compelled to abstain from adjudication because of their 'political' nature, and the cases that so frequently arise in applying the concepts of 'liberty' and 'equality'."[32] The line is not very thin; it is non-existent. There is no principled way in which anyone can define the spheres in which liberty is required and the spheres in which equality is required. These are matters of morality, of judgment, of prudence. They belong, therefore, to the political community. In the fullest sense, these are political questions.

We may now be in a position to discuss certain of the problems of legitimacy raised by Professor Wechsler. Central to his worries was the Supreme Court's decision in *Brown* v. *Board of Education*.[33] Wechsler said he had great difficulty framing a neutral principle to support the *Brown* decision, though he thoroughly approved of its result on moral and political grounds. It has long been obvious that the case does not rest upon the grounds advanced in Chief Justice Earl Warren's opinion, the specially harmful effects of enforced school segregation upon black children. That much, as Wechsler and others point out, is made plain by the *per curiam* decisions that followed outlawing segregated public beaches, public golf courses and the like. The principle in operation may be that government may not employ race as a classification. But the genesis of the principle is unclear.

Wechsler states that his problem with the segregation cases is not that "history does not confirm that an agreed purpose of the Fourteenth Amendment was to forbid separate schools or that there is important evidence that many thought the contrary; the words are general and leave room for expanding content as time passes and conditions change."[34] The words are general but surely that would not permit us to escape the framers' intent if it were clear. If the legislative history revealed a consensus about segregation in schooling and all the other relations in life, I do not see how the Court could escape the choices revealed and substitute its own, even though the words are general and conditions have changed. It is the fact that history does not reveal detailed choices concerning such matters that permits, indeed requires, resort to other modes of interpretation.

Wechsler notes that *Brown* has to do with freedom to associate and freedom not to associate, and he thinks that a principle must be found that solves the following dilemma:

> If the freedom of association is denied by segregation, integration forces an association upon those for whom it is unpleasant or repug-nant. Is this not the heart of the issue involved, a conflict in human claims of high dimension. . . . Given a situation where the state must practically choose between denying the association to those individuals who wish it or imposing it on those who would avoid it, is there a basis in neutral principles for holding that the Constitution demands that the claims for association should prevail? I should like to think there is, but I confess that I have not yet written the opinion. To write it is for me the challenge of the school-segregation cases.[35]

It is extremely unlikely that Professor Wechsler ever will be able to write that opinion to his own satisfaction. He has framed the issue in insoluble terms by calling it a "conflict between human claims of high dimension," which is to say that it requires a judicial choice between rival gratifications in order to find a fundamental human right. So viewed it is the same case as *Griswold* v. *Connecticut* and not susceptible of principled resolution.

A resolution that seems to me more plausible is supported rather than troubled by the need for neutrality. A court required to decide *Brown* would perceive two crucial facts about the history of the Fourteenth Amendment. First, the men who put the amendment in the Constitution intended that the Supreme Court should secure against government action some large measure of racial equality. That is certainly the core meaning of the amendment. Second, those same men were not agreed about what the concept of racial equality requires. Many or most of them had not even thought the matter through. Almost certainly, even individuals among them held such views as that blacks were entitled to purchase property from any willing seller but not to attend integrated schools, or that they were entitled to serve on juries but not to intermarry with whites, or that they were entitled to equal physical facilities but that the facilities should be separate, and so on through the endless anomalies and inconsistencies with which moral positions so frequently abound.

The Court cannot conceivably know how these long-dead men would have resolved these issues had they considered, debated and voted on each of them. Perhaps it was precisely because they could not resolve them that they took refuge in the majestic and ambiguous formula: the equal protection of the laws.

But one thing the Court does know: it was intended to enforce a core idea of black equality against governmental discrimination. And the Court, because it must be neutral, cannot pick and choose between competing gratifi- cations and, likewise, cannot write the detailed code the framers omitted, requiring equality in this case but not in another. The Court must, for that reason, choose a general principle of equality that applies to all cases. For the same reason, the Court cannot decide that physical equality is important but psychological equality is not. Thus the no-state-enforced-discrimination rule of *Brown* must overturn and replace the separate-but-equal doctrine of *Plessy* v. *Ferguson*. The same result might be reached on an alternative ground. If the Court found that it was incapable as an institution of policing the issue of the physical quality of separate facilities, the variables being insufficiently comparable and the cases too many, it might fashion a no-segregation rule as the only feasible means of assuring even physical equality.

In either case, the value choice (or, perhaps more accurately, the value impulse) of the Fourteenth Amendment is fleshed out and made into a legal rule—not by moral precept, not by a determination that claims for associa- tion prevail over claims for separation as a general matter, still less by consid- eration of psychological test results, but on purely juridical grounds.

I doubt, however, that it is possible to find neutral principles capable of supporting some of the other decisions that trouble Professor Wechsler. An example is *Shelley* v. *Kraemer*,[36] which held that the Fourteenth Amendment forbids state court enforcement of a private, racially restrictive covenant. Al- though the amendment speaks only of denials of equal protection of the laws by the state, Chief Justice Vinson's opinion said that judicial enforcement of a private person's discriminatory choice constituted the requisite state action. The decision was, of course, not neutral in that the Court was most clearly not prepared to apply the principle to cases it could not honestly distinguish. Any dispute between private persons about absolutely any aspect of life can be brought to a court by one of the parties; and, if race is involved, the rule of *Shelley* would require the court to deny the freedom of any individual to discriminate in the conduct of any part of his affairs simply because the contrary result would be state enforcement of discrimination. The principle would apply not merely to the cases hypothesized by Professor Wechsler— the inability of the state to effectuate a will that draws a racial line or to vindicate the privacy of property against a trespasser excluded because of the homeowner's racial preferences—but to any situation in which the person claiming freedom in any relationship had a racial motivation.

That much is the common objection to *Shelley* v. *Kraemer*, but the trouble with the decision goes deeper. Professor Louis Henkin has suggested that we view the case as correctly decided, accept the principle that must necessarily underline it if it is respectable law and proceed to apply that principle. "Gen- erally, the equal protection clause precludes state enforcement of private dis- crimination. There is, however, a small area of liberty favored by the Consti- tution even over claims to equality. Rights of liberty and property, of privacy and voluntary association, must be balanced in close cases, against the right not to have the state enforce discrimination against the victim. In the few instances in which the right to discriminate is protected or preferred by the Constitution, the state may enforce it."[37] This attempt to rehabilitate *Shelley* by applying its principle honestly demonstrates rather clearly why neutrality in the application of principle is not enough. Professor Henkin's proposal fails the test of the neutral derivation of principle. It converts an amendment whose text and history clearly show it to be aimed only at governmental discrimination into a sweeping prohibition of private discrimination. There is no warrant anywhere for that conversion. The judge's power to govern does not become more legitimate if he is constrained to apply his principle to all cases but is free to make up his own principles. Matters are only made worse by Professor Henkin's suggestion that the judge introduce a small number of exceptions for cases where liberty is more important than equality, for now even the possibility of neutrality in the application of principle is lost. The judge cannot find in the Fourteenth Amendment or its history any choices between equality and freedom in private affairs. The judge, if he were to undertake this task, would be choosing, as in *Griswold* v. *Connecticut*, between competing gratifications without constitutional guidance. Indeed, Professor Henkin's description of the process shows that the task he would assign is legislative:

> The balance may be struck differently at different times, reflecting
> differences in prevailing philosophy and the continuing movement
> from *laissez-faire* government toward welfare and meliorism. The
> changes in prevailing philosophy themselves may sum up the judgment
> of judges as to how the conscience of our society weighs the competing
> needs and claims of liberty and equality in time and context—the
> adequacy of progress toward equality as a result of social and eco-
> nomic forces, the effect of lack of progress on the life of the Negro
> and, perhaps, on the image of the United States, and the role of
> official state forces in advancing or retarding this progress.[38]

In short, after considering everything a legislator might consider, the judge is to write a detailed code of private race relations. Starting with an attempt to justify *Shelley* on grounds of neutral principle, the argument rather curiously arrives at a position in which neutrality in the derivation, definition and application of principle is impossible and the wrong institution is governing society.

The argument thus far claims that, cases of race discrimination aside, it is always a mistake for the Court to try to construct substantive individual rights under the due process or the equal protection clause. Such rights cannot be constructed without comparing the worth of individual gratifications, and that comparison cannot be principled. Unfortunately, the rhetoric of constitutional adjudication is increasingly a rhetoric about "fundamental" rights that inhere in humans. That focus does more than lead the Court to construct new rights without adequate guidance from constitutional materials. It also distorts the scope and definition of rights that have claim to protection.

There appear to be two proper methods of deriving rights from the Constitution. The first is to take from the document rather specific values that text or history show the framers actually to have intended and which are capable of being translated into principled rules. We may call these specified rights. The second method derives rights from governmental processes established by the Constitution. These are secondary or derived individual rights. This latter category is extraordinarily important. This method of derivation is essential to the interpretation of the First Amendment, to voting rights, to criminal procedure, and to much else.

Secondary or derivative rights are not possessed by the individual because the Constitution has made a value choice about individuals. Neither are they possessed because the Supreme Court thinks them fundamental to all humans. Rather, these rights are located in the individual for the sake of a governmental process that the Constitution outlines and that the Court should preserve. They are given to the individual because his enjoyment of them will lead him to defend them in court and thereby preserve the governmental process from legislative or executive deformation.

The distinction between rights that are inherent and rights that are derived from some other value is one that our society worked out long ago with respect to the economic marketplace, and precisely the same distinction holds and will prove an aid to clear thought with respect to the political marketplace. A right is a form of property, and our thinking about the category of constitutional property might usefully follow the progress of thought about economic property. We now regard it as thoroughly old hat, passé, and in fact downright tiresome to hear rhetoric about an inherent right to economic freedom or to economic property. We no longer believe that economic rights inhere in the individual because he is an individual. The modern intellectual argues the proper location and definition of property rights according to judgments of utility—the capacity of such rights to forward some other value. We may, for example, wish to maximize the total wealth of society and define property rights in a way we think will advance that goal by making the economic process run more efficiently. As it is with economic property rights, so it should be with constitutional rights relating to governmental processes.

The derivation of rights from governmental processes is not an easy task, and I do not suggest that a shift in focus will make anything approaching a mechanical jurisprudence possible. I do suggest that, for the reasons already argued, no guidance whatever is available to a court that approaches, say, voting rights or criminal procedures through the concept of substantive equality.

The state legislative reapportionment cases were unsatisfactory precisely because the Court attempted to apply a substantive equal protection approach. Chief Justice Warren's opinions in this series of cases are remarkable for their inability to muster a single respectable supporting argument. The principle of one man, one vote was not neutrally derived: it runs counter to the text of the Fourteenth Amendment, the history surrounding its adoption and ratification, and the political practice of Americans from colonial times up to the day the Court invented the new formula.[39] The principle was not neutrally defined: it presumably rests upon some theory of equal weight for all votes, and yet we have no explanation of why it does not call into question other devices that defeat the principle, such as the executive veto, the committee system, the filibuster, the requirement on some issues of two-thirds majorities and the practice of districting. And, as we all know now, the principle, even as stated, was not neutrally applied.[40]

To approach these cases as involving rights derived from the requirements of our form of government is, of course, to say that they involve guarantee clause claims. Justice Frankfurter opposed the Court's consideration of reapportionment precisely on the ground that the "case involves all the elements that have made the Guarantee Clause cases non-justiciable," and was a "Guarantee Clause claim masquerading under a different label."[41] Of course, his characterization was accurate, but the same could be said of many voting rights cases he was willing to decide. The guarantee clause, along with the provisions and structure of the Constitution and our political history, at least provides some guidance for a Court. The concept of the primary right of the individual in this area provides none. Whether one chooses to use the guarantee of a republican form of government of Article IV, section 4 as a peg or to proceed directly to considerations of constitutional structure and political practice probably makes little difference. Madison's writing on the republican form of government specified by the guarantee clause suggests that representative democracy may properly take many forms, so long as the forms do not become "aristocratic or monarchical."[42] That is certainly less easily translated into the rigid one person, one vote requirement, which rests on a concept of the right of the individual to equality, than into the requirement expressed by Justice Potter Stewart in *Lucas* v. *Forty-Fourth General Assembly*[43] that a legislative apportionment need only be rational and "must be such as not to permit the systematic frustration of the will of a majority of the electorate of the State."[44] The latter is a standard derived from the requirements of a democratic process rather than from the rights of individuals. The topic of governmental processes and the rights that may be derived from them is so large that it is best left at this point. It has been raised only as a reminder that there is a legitimate mode of deriving and defining constitutional rights, however difficult intellectually, that is available to replace the present unsatisfactory focus.

At the outset I warned that I did not offer a complete theory of constitutional interpretation. My concern has been to attack a few points that may be regarded as salient in order to clear the way for such a theory. I turn next to a suggestion of what neutrality, the decision of cases according to principle, may mean for certain First Amendment problems.

Some First Amendment Problems: The Search for Theory

THE LAW HAS settled upon no tenable, internally consistent theory of the scope of the constitutional guarantee of free speech. Nor have many such theories been urged upon the courts by lawyers or academicians. Professor Harry Kalven, Jr., one whose work is informed by a search for theory, has expressed wonder that we should feel the need for theory in the area of free speech when we tolerate inconsistencies in other areas of the law so calmly.[45] He answers himself: "If my puzzle as to the First Amendment is not a true puzzle, it can only be for the congenial reason that free speech is so close to the heart of democratic organization that if we do not have an appropriate theory for our law here, we feel we really do not understand the society in which we live."[46] Kalven is certainly correct in assigning the First Amendment a central place in our society, and he is also right in attributing that centrality to the importance of speech to democratic organization. Since I share this common ground with Professor Kalven, I find it interesting that my conclusions differ so widely from his.

I am led by the logic of the requirement that judges be principled to the following suggestions. Constitutional protection should be accorded only to speech that is explicitly political. There is no basis for judicial intervention to protect any other form of expression, be it scientific, literary or that variety of expression we call obscene or pornographic. Moreover, within that category of speech we ordinarily call political, there should be no constitutional obstruction to laws making criminal any speech that advocates forcible overthrow of the government or the violation of any law.

I am, of course, aware that this theory departs drastically from existing Court-made law, from the views of most academic specialists in the field, and that it may strike a chill into the hearts of some civil libertarians. But I would insist at the outset that constitutional law, viewed as the set of rules a judge may properly derive from the document and its history, is not an expression of our political sympathies or of our judgments about what expediency and prudence require. When decision making is principled it has nothing to say about the speech we like or the speech we hate; it has a great deal to say about how far democratic discretion can govern without endangering the basis of democratic government. Nothing in my argument goes to the question of what laws should be enacted. I like the freedoms of the individual as well as most, and I would be appalled by many statutes that I am compelled to think would be constitutional if enacted. But I am also persuaded that my generally libertarian commitments have nothing to do with the behavior proper to the Supreme Court.

In framing a theory of free speech, the first obstacle is the insistence of many very intelligent people that the "First Amendment is an absolute." Devotees of this position insist, with a literal respect they do not accord other parts of the Constitution, that the Framers commanded complete freedom of expression without governmental regulation of any kind. The First Amendment states: "Congress shall make no law . . . abridging the freedom of speech." Those who take that as an absolute must be reading "speech" to mean any form of verbal communication and "freedom" to mean total absence of governmental restraint.

Any such reading is, of course, impossible. Since it purports to be an absolute position we are entitled to test it with extreme hypotheticals. Is Congress forbidden to prohibit incitement to mutiny aboard a naval vessel engaged in action against an enemy, to prohibit shouted harangues from the visitors' gallery during its own deliberations, or to provide any rules for decorum in federal courtrooms? Are the states forbidden, by the incorporation of the First Amendment in the Fourteenth, to punish the shouting of obscenities in the streets?

No one, not the most obsessed absolutist, takes any such position, but if one does not, the absolute position is abandoned, revealed as a play on words. Government cannot function if anyone can say anything anywhere at any time. And so we quickly come to the conclusion that lines must be drawn, differentiations made. Nor does that in any way involve us in a conflict with the wording of the First Amendment. Laymen may perhaps be forgiven for thinking that the literal words of the amendment command complete absence of governmental inhibition upon verbal activity, but what can one say of lawyers who believe any such thing? Anyone skilled in reading language should know that the words are not necessarily absolute. "Freedom of speech" may very well be a term referring to a defined or assumed scope of liberty, and it may be this area of liberty that is not to be "abridged."

If we turn to history, we discover that our suspicions about the wording are correct, except that matters are even worse. The framers seem to have had no coherent theory of free speech and appear not to have been overly concerned with the subject. Professor Leonard Levy's work, *Legacy of Suppression*,[47] demonstrates that the men who adopted the First Amendment did not display a strong libertarian stance with respect to speech. Any such position would have been strikingly at odds with the American political tradition. Our forefathers were men accustomed to drawing a line, to us often invisible, between freedom and licentiousness. In colonial times and during and after the Revolution they displayed a determination to punish speech thought dangerous to government, much of it expression that we would think harmless and well within the bounds of legitimate discourse. Jeffersonians, threatened by the Federalist Sedition Act of 1798, undertook the first American elaboration of a libertarian position in an effort to stay out of jail. Professor Walter Berns offers evidence that even then the position was not widely held.[48] When Jefferson came to power it developed that he read the First Amendment only to limit Congress and he believed suppression to be a proper function of the state governments. He appears to have instigated state prosecutions against Federalists for seditious libel. But these later developments do not tell us what the men who adopted the First Amendment intended, and their discussions tell us very little either. The disagreements that certainly existed were not debated and resolved. The First Amendment, like the rest of the Bill of Rights, appears to have been a hastily drafted document upon which little thought was expended. One reason, as Levy shows, is that the Anti-Federalists complained of the absence of a Bill of Rights less because they cared for individual freedoms than as a tactic to defeat the Constitution. The Federalists promised to submit one in order to get the Constitution ratified. The Bill of Rights was then drafted by Federalists, who had opposed it from the beginning; the Anti-Federalists, who were really more interested in preserving the rights of state governments against federal power, had by that time lost interest in the subject.[49]

We are, then, forced to construct our own theory of the constitutional protection of speech. We cannot solve our problems simply by reference to the text or to its history. But we are not without materials for building. The First Amendment indicates that there is something special about speech. We would know that much even without a First Amendment, for the entire structure of the Constitution creates a representative democracy, a form of government that would be meaningless without freedom to discuss government and its policies. Freedom for political speech could and should be inferred even if there were no First Amendment. Further guidance can be gained from the fact that we are looking for a theory fit for enforcement by judges. The principles we seek must, therefore, be neutral in all three meanings of the word: they must be neutrally derived, defined, and applied.

The law of free speech we know today grows out of the Supreme Court decisions following World War I—*Schenck* v. *United States*,[50] *Abrams* v. *United States*,[51] *Gitlow* v. *New York*,[52] *Whitney* v. *California*[53]—not out of the majority positions but rather from the opinions, mostly dissents or concurrences that were really dissents, of Justices Oliver Wendell Holmes and Louis Brandeis. Professor Kalven remarks upon "the almost uncanny power" of these dissents. And it is uncanny, for they have prevailed despite the considerable handicap of being deficient in logic and analysis as well as in history. The great Smith Act cases of the 1950's, *Dennis* v. *United States*,[54] as modified by *Yates* v. *United States*,[55] and, more recently, in 1969, *Brandenburg* v. *Ohio*[56] (voiding the Ohio criminal syndicalism statute), mark the triumph of Holmes and Brandeis. And other cases, culminating perhaps in a modified version of *Roth* v. *United States*,[57] have pushed the protections of the First Amendment outward from political speech all the way to the fields of literature, entertainment, and what can only be called pornography. Because my concern is general theory I shall not attempt a comprehensive survey of the cases nor engage in theological disputation over current doctrinal niceties. I intend to take the position that the law should have been built on Justice Edward Sanford's majority opinions in *Gitlow* and *Whitney*. These days such an argument has at least the charm of complete novelty, but I think it has other merits as well.

Before coming to the specific issues in *Gitlow* and *Whitney*, I wish to begin the general discussion of First Amendment theory with consideration of a passage from Justice Brandeis's concurring opinion in the latter case. His *Whitney* concurrence was Brandeis's first attempt to articulate a comprehensive theory of the constitutional protection of speech, and in that attempt he laid down premises which seem to me correct. But those premises seem also to lead to conclusions which Justice Brandeis would have disowned.

As a starting point Brandeis went to fundamentals and attempted to answer the question why speech is protected at all from governmental regulation. If we overlook his highly romanticized version of history and ignore merely rhetorical flourishes, we shall find Brandeis quite provocative.

> Those who won our independence believed that the final end of the state was to make men free to develop their faculties; and that in its government the deliberative forces should prevail over the arbitrary. They valued liberty both as an end and as a means. They believed liberty to be the secret of happiness and courage to be the secret of liberty. The belief that freedom to think as you will and to speak as you think are means indispensable to the discovery and spread of political truth; that without free speech and assembly discussion would be futile; that with them, discussion affords ordinarily adequate protection against the dissemination of noxious doctrine . . . They recognized the risks to which all human institutions are subject. But they knew . . . that it is hazardous to discourage thought, hope and imagination; that fear breeds repression; that repression breeds hate; that hate menaces stable government; that the path of safety lies in the opportunity to discuss freely supposed grievances and proposed remedies; and that the fitting remedy for evil counsels is good ones.[58]

We begin to see why the dissents of Brandeis and Holmes possessed the power to which Professor Kalven referred. They were rhetoricians of extraordinary potency, and their rhetoric retains the power, almost half a century later, to swamp analysis, to persuade, almost to command assent.

But there is structure beneath the rhetoric, and Brandeis is asserting, though he attributes it all to the Founding Fathers, that there are four benefits to be derived from speech. These are:

1. The development of the faculties of the individual;
2. The happiness to be derived from engaging in the activity;

3. The provision of a safety value for society; and,

4. The discovery and spread of political truth.

We may accept these claims as true and as satisfactorily inclusive. When we come to analyze these benefits, however, we discover that in terms of constitutional law they are very different things.

The first two benefits—development of individual faculties and the achievement of pleasure—are or may be found, for both speaker and hearer, in all varieties of speech, from political discourse to shop talk to salacious literature. But the important point is that these benefits do not distinguish speech from any other human activity. An individual may develop his faculties or derive pleasure from trading on the stock market, following his profession as a river port pilot, working as a barmaid, engaging in sexual activity, playing tennis, rigging prices or in any of thousands of other endeavors. Speech with only the first two benefits can be preferred to other activities only by ranking forms of personal gratification. These functions or benefits of speech are, therefore, to the principled judge, indistinguishable from the functions or benefits of all other human activity. He cannot, on neutral grounds, choose to protect speech that has only these functions more than he protects any other claimed freedom.

The third benefit of speech mentioned by Brandeis—its safety valve function—is different from the first two. It relates not to the gratification of the individual, at least not directly, but to the welfare of society. The safety valve function raises only issues of expediency or prudence, and, therefore, raises issues to be determined solely by the legislature or, in some cases, by the executive. The legislature may decide not to repress speech advocating the forcible overthrow of the government in some classes of cases because it thinks repression would cause more trouble than it would prevent. Prosecuting attorneys, who must in any event pick and choose among cases, given their limited resources, may similarly decide that some such speech is trivial or that ignoring it would be wisest. But these decisions, involving only the issue of the expedient course, are indistinguishable from thousands of other managerial judgments governments must make daily, though in the extreme case the decision may involve the safety of the society just as surely as a decision whether or not to take a foreign policy stand that risks war. It seems plain that decisions involving only judgments of expediency are for the political branches and not for the judiciary.

This leaves the fourth function of speech—the "discovery and spread of political truth." This function of speech, its ability to deal explicitly, specifically, and directly with politics and government, is different from any other form of human activity. But the difference exists only with respect to one kind of speech: explicitly and predominantly political speech. This seems to me the only form of speech that a principled judge can prefer to other claimed freedoms. All other forms of speech raise only issues of human gratification and their protection against legislative regulation involves the judge in making decisions of the sort made in *Griswold* v. *Connecticut*.

It is here that I begin to part company with Professor Kalven. Kalven argues that no society in which seditious libel, the criticism of public officials, is a crime can call itself free and democratic.[59] I agree, even though the framers of the First Amendment probably had no clear view of that proposition. Yet they indicated a value when they said that speech in some sense was special and when they wrote a Constitution providing for representative democracy, a form of government that is meaningless without open and vigorous debate about officials and their policies. It is for this reason, the relation of speech to democratic organization, that Professor Alexander Meiklejohn seems correct when he says: "The First Amendment does not protect a 'freedom to speak.' It protects the freedom of those activities of thought and communication by which we 'govern.' It is concerned, not with a private right, but with a public power, a governmental responsibility."[60] But both Kalven and Meiklejohn go further and would extend the protection of the First Amendment beyond speech that is explicitly political. Meiklejohn argues that the amendment protects "forms of thought and expression within the range of human communications from which the voter derives the knowledge, intelligence, sensitivity to human values: the capacity for sane and objective judgment which, so far as possible, a ballot should express." He lists four such thoughts and expressions: "1. Education, in all its phases . . . 2. The achievements of philosophy and the sciences . . . 3. Literature and the arts . . . 4. Public discussions of public issues."[61]

Kalven, following a similar line, states: "[T]he invitation to follow a dialectic progression from public official to government policy to public policy to matters in the public domain, like art, seems to me to be overwhelming."[62] It is an invitation, I wish to suggest, the principled judge must decline. A dialectic progression I take to be a progression by analogy from one case to the next, an indispensable but perilous method of legal reasoning. The length to which analogy is carried defines the principle, but neutral definition requires that, in terms of the rationale in play, those cases within the principle be more like each other than they are like cases left outside. The dialectical progression must have a principled stopping point: I agree that there is an analogy between criticism of official behavior and the publication of a novel like *Ulysses*, for the latter may form attitudes that ultimately affect politics. But it is an analogy, not an identity. Other human activities and experiences also form personality, teach and create attitudes just as much as does the novel, but no one would on that account, I take it, suggest that the First Amendment strikes down regulations of economic activity, control of entry into a trade, laws about sexual behavior, marriage and the like. Yet these activities, in their capacity to create attitudes that ultimately impinge upon the political process, are more like literature and science than literature and science are like political speech. If the dialectical progression is not to become an analogical stampede, the protection of the First Amendment must be cut off when it reaches the outer limits of political speech.

Two types of problems may be supposed to arise with respect to this solution. The first is the difficulty of drawing a line between political and non-political speech. The second is that such a line will leave unprotected much speech that is essential to the life of a civilized community. Neither of these problems seems to me to raise crippling difficulties.

The category of protected speech should consist of speech concerned with governmental behavior, policy or personnel, whether the governmental unit involved is executive, legislative, judicial or administrative. Explicitly political speech is speech about how we are governed, and the category therefore includes a wide range of evaluation, criticism, electioneering and propaganda. It does not cover scientific, educational, commercial or literary expressions as such. A novel may have impact upon attitudes that affect politics, but it would not for that reason receive judicial protection. This is not anomalous, I have tried to suggest, since the rationale of the First Amendment cannot be the protection of all things or activities that influence political attitudes. Any speech may do that, and we have seen that it is impossible to leave all speech unregulated. Moreover, any conduct may affect political attitudes as much as a novel, and we cannot view the First Amendment as a broad denial of the power of government to regulate conduct. The line drawn must, therefore, lie between the explicitly political and all else. Not too much should be made of the undeniable fact that there will be hard cases. Any theory of the First Amendment that does not accord absolute protection for all verbal expression, which is to say any theory worth discussing, will require that a spectrum be cut and the location of the cut will always be, arguably, arbitrary. The question is whether the general location of the cut is justified. The existence of close cases is not a reason to refuse to draw a line and so deny majorities the power to govern in areas where their power is legitimate.

The other objection—that the political-nonpolitical distinction will leave much valuable speech without constitutional protection—is no more troublesome. The notion that all valuable types of speech must be protected by the First Amendment confuses the constitutionality of laws with their wisdom. Freedom of non-political speech rests, as does freedom for other valuable forms of behavior, upon the enlightenment of society and its elected representatives. That is hardly a terrible fate. At least a society like ours ought not to think it so.

The practical effect of confining constitutional protection to political speech would probably go no further than to introduce regulation or prohibition of pornography. The Court would be freed of the stultifying obligation to apply its self-inflicted criteria: whether "(a) the dominant theme of the material taken as a whole appeals to a prurient interest in sex; (b) the material is patently offensive because it affronts contemporary community standards relating to the description or representation of sexual matters; and (c) the material is utterly without redeeming social value."[63] To take only the last criterion, the determination of "social value" cannot be made in a principled way. Anything some people want has, to that degree, social value, but that cannot be the basis for constitutional protection since it would deny regulation of any human activity. The concept of social value necessarily incorporates a judgment about the net effect upon society. There is always the problem that what some people want some other people do not want, or wish actively to banish. A judgment about social value, whether the judges realize it or not, always involves a comparison of competing values and gratifications as well as competing predictions of the effects of the activity. Determination of "social value" is the same thing as determination of what human interests should be classed as "fundamental" and, therefore, cannot be principled or neutral.

To revert to a previous example, pornography is increasingly seen as a problem of pollution of the moral and aesthetic atmosphere precisely analogous to smoke pollution. A majority of the community may foresee that continued availability of pornography to those who want it will inevitably affect the quality of life for those who do not want it, altering, for example, attitudes toward love and sex, the tone of private and public discourse and views of social institutions such as marriage and the family. Such a majority surely has as much control over the moral and aesthetic environment as it does over the physical, for such matters may even more severely impinge upon their gratifications. That is why, constitutionally, art and pornography are on a par with industry and smoke pollution. As Professor Walter Berns says: "A thoughtful judge is likely to ask how an artistic judgment that is wholly idiosyncratic can be capable of supporting an objection to the law. The objection, 'I like it,' is sufficiently rebutted by 'we don't.' "[64]

We must now return to the core of the First Amendment, speech that is explicitly political. I mean by that criticisms of public officials and policies, proposals for the adoption or repeal of legislation or constitutional provisions and speech addressed to the conduct of any governmental unit in the country.

A qualification is required, however. Political speech is not any speech that concerns government and law, for there is a category of such speech that must be excluded. This category consists of speech advocating forcible overthrow of the government or violation of law. The reason becomes clear when we return to Brandeis's discussion of the reasons for according constitutional protection to speech.

The fourth function of speech, the one that defines and sets apart political speech, is the "discovery and spread of political truth." To understand what the Court should protect, therefore, we must define "political truth." There seem to me three possible meanings to that term:

  1. An absolute set of truths that exist independently of Constitution or statute.

  2. A set of values that are protected by constitutional provision from the reach of legislative majorities.

  3. Within that area of life which the majority is permitted to govern in accordance with the Madisonian model of representative government, whatever result the majority reaches and maintains at the moment.

The judge can have nothing to do with any absolute set of truths existing independently and depending upon God or the nature of the universe. If a judge should claim to have access to such a body of truths, to possess a volume of the annotated natural law, we would, quite justifiably, suspect that the source of the revelation was really no more exalted than the judge's viscera. In our system there is no absolute set of truths, to which the term "political truth" can refer.

Values protected by the Constitution are one type of political truth. They are, in fact, the highest type since they are placed beyond the reach of simple legislative majorities. They are primarily truths about the way government must operate, that is, procedural truths. But speech aimed at the discovery and spread of political truth is concerned with more than the desirability of constitutional provisions or the manner in which they should be interpreted.

The third meaning of "political truth" extends the category of protected speech. Truth is what the majority thinks it is at any given moment precisely because the majority is permitted to govern and to redefine its values constantly. "Political truth" in this sense must, therefore, be a term of art, a concept defined entirely from a consideration of the system of government which the judge is commissioned to operate and maintain. It has no unchanging content but refers to the temporary outcomes of the democratic process. Political truth is what the majority decides it wants today. It may be something entirely different tomorrow, as truth is rediscovered and the new concept spread.

Speech advocating forcible overthrow of the government contemplates a group less than a majority seizing control of the monopoly power of the state when it cannot gain its ends through speech and political activity. Speech advocating violent overthrow is thus not "political speech" as that term must be defined by a Madisonian system of government. It is not political speech because it violates constitutional truths about processes and because it is not aimed at a new definition of political truth by a legislative majority. Violent overthrow of government breaks the premises of our system concerning the ways in which truth is defined, and yet those premises are the only reasons for protecting political speech. It follows that there is no constitutional reason to protect speech advocating forcible overthrow.

A similar analysis suggests that advocacy of law violation does not qualify as political speech any more than advocacy of forcible overthrow of the government. Advocacy of law violation is a call to set aside the results that political speech has produced. The process of the "discovery and spread of political truth" is damaged or destroyed if the outcome is defeated by a minority that makes law enforcement, and hence the putting of political truth into practice, impossible or less effective. There should, therefore, be no constitutional protection for any speech advocating the violation of law.

I believe these are the only results that can be reached by a neutral judge who takes his values from the Constitution. If we take Brandeis's description of the benefits and functions of speech as our premise, logic and principle appear to drive us to the conclusion that Sanford rather than Brandeis or Holmes was correct in *Gitlow* and *Whitney*.

Benjamin Gitlow was convicted under New York's criminal anarchy statute which made criminal advocacy of the doctrine that organized government should be overthrown by force, violence or any unlawful means. Gitlow, a member of the Left Wing section of the Socialist party, had arranged the printing and distribution of a "Manifesto" deemed to call for violent action and revolution. "There was," Justice Sanford's opinion noted, "no evidence of any effect resulting from the publication and circulation of the manifesto."[65] Anita Whitney was convicted under California's criminal syndicalism statute, which forbade advocacy of the commission of crime, sabotage, acts of force or violence or terrorism "as a means of accomplishing a change in industrial ownership or control, or effecting any political change." Also made illegal were certain connections with groups advocating such doctrines. Miss Whitney was convicted of assisting in organizing the Communist Labor Party of California, of being a member of it and of assembling with it.[66] The evidence appears to have been meager, but our current concern is doctrinal.

Justice Sanford's opinions for the majorities in *Gitlow* and *Whitney* held essentially that the Court's function in speech cases was the limited but crucial one of determining whether the legislature had defined a category of forbidden speech which might constitutionally be suppressed.[67] The category might be defined by the nature of the speech and need not be limited in other ways. If the category was defined in a permissible way and the defendant's speech or publication fell within the definition, the Court had, it would appear, no other issues to face in order to uphold the conviction. Questions of the fairness of the trial and the sufficiency of the evidence aside, this would appear to be the correct conclusion. The legislatures had struck at speech not aimed at the discovery and spread of political truth but aimed rather at destroying the premises of our political system and the means by which we define political truth. There is no value that judges can independently give such speech in opposition to a legislative determination.

Justice Holmes's dissent in *Gitlow* and Justice Brandeis's concurrence in *Whitney* insisted the Court must also find that, as Brandeis put it, the "speech would produce, or is intended to produce, a clear and imminent danger of some substantive evil which the state constitutionally may seek to prevent."[68] Neither of them explained why the danger must be "clear and imminent" or, as Holmes had put it in *Schenck*, "clear and present"[69] before a particular instance of speech could be punished. Neither of them made any attempt to answer Justice Sanford's argument on the point:

> [T]he immediate danger [created by advocacy of overthrow of the government] is none the less real and substantial, because the effect of a given utterance cannot be accurately foreseen. The state cannot reasonably be required to measure the danger from every such utterance in the nice balance of a jeweler's scale. A single revolutionary spark may kindle a fire that, smoldering for a time, may burst into a sweeping and destructive conflagration. It cannot be said that the state is acting arbitrarily or unreasonably when in the exercise of its judgment as to the measures necessary to protect the public peace and safety, it seeks to extinguish the spark without waiting until it has enkindled the flame or blazed into conflagration. It cannot reasonably be required to defer the adoption of measures for its own peace and safety until the revolutionary utterances lead to actual disturbances of the public peace or imminent and immediate danger of its own destruction; but it may, in the exercise of its judgment, suppress the threatened danger in its incipiency.[70]

To his point that proof of the effect of speech is inherently unavailable and yet its impact may be real and dangerous, Sanford might have added that the legislature is not confined to consideration of a single instance of speech or a single speaker. It fashions a rule to dampen thousands of instances of forcible overthrow advocacy. Cumulatively these may have enormous influence, and yet it may well be impossible to show any effect from any single example. The "clear and present danger" requirement, which has had a long and uneven career in our law, is improper not, as many commentators have thought, because it provides a subjective and an inadequate safeguard against the regulation of speech, but rather because it erects a barrier to legislative rule where none should exist. The speech concerned has no political value within a republican system of government. Whether or not it is prudent to ban advocacy of forcible overthrow and law violation is a different question although [*sic*]. Because the judgment is tactical, implicating the safety of the nation, it resembles very closely the judgment that Congress and the President must make about the expediency of waging war, an issue that the Court has wisely thought not fit for judicial determination.

The legislature and the executive might find it wise to permit some rhetoric about law violation and forcible overthrow. I am certain that they would and that they should. Certain of the factors weighted in determining the constitutionality of the Smith Act prosecutions in *Dennis* would, for example, make intelligible statutory, though not constitutional, criteria: the high degree of organization of the Communist party, the rigid discipline of its members and the party's ideological affinity to foreign powers.[71]

Similar objections apply to the other restrictions Brandeis attempted to impose upon government. I will mention but one more of these restrictions. Justice Brandeis argued:

> Even imminent danger cannot justify resort to prohibition of these functions essential to effective democracy, unless the evil apprehended is relatively serious. . . . Thus, a state might, in the exercise of its police power, make any trespass upon the land of another a crime, regardless of the results or of the intent or purpose of the trespasser. It might, also, punish an attempt, a conspiracy, or an incitement to commit the trespass. But it is hardly conceivable that this court would hold constitutional a statute which punished as a felony the mere voluntary assembly with a society formed to teach that pedestrians had the moral right to cross unenclosed, unposted, waste lands and to advocate their doing so, even if there was imminent danger that advocacy would lead to a trespass. The fact that speech is likely to result in some violence or in destruction of property is not enough to justify its suppression. There must be the probability of serious injury to the state.[72]

It is difficult to see how a constitutional court could properly draw the distinction proposed. Brandeis offered no analysis to show that advocacy of law violation merited protection by the Court. Worse, the criterion he advanced is the importance, in the judge's eyes, of the law whose violation is urged.

Modern law has followed the general line and the spirit of Brandeis and Holmes rather than of Sanford, and it has become increasingly severe in its limitation of legislative power. *Brandenburg* v. *Ohio*, a 1969 *per curiam* decision by the Supreme Court, struck down the Ohio criminal syndicalism statute because it punished advocacy of violence, the opinion stating: "*Whitney* [the majority opinion] has been thoroughly discredited by later decisions . . . These later decisions have fashioned the principle that the constitutional guarantees of free speech and free press do not permit a State to forbid or proscribe advocacy of the use of force or of law violation except where such advocacy is directed to inciting or producing imminent lawless action and is likely to incite or produce such action."[73] It is certainly true that Justice Sanford's position in *Whitney* and in *Gitlow* has been completely undercut, or rather abandoned, by later cases, but it is not true that his position has been discredited, or even met, on intellectual grounds. Justice Brandeis failed to accomplish that, and later Justices have not mounted a theoretical case comparable to Brandeis's.

These remarks are intended to be tentative and exploratory. Yet at this moment I do not see how I can avoid the conclusions stated. The Supreme Court's constitutional role appears to be justified only if the Court applies principles that are neutrally derived, defined and applied. And the requirement of neutrality in turn appears to indicate the results I have sketched here.

Notes

1. H. Wechsler, Toward Neutral Principles of Constitutional Law, in *Principles, Politics, and Fundamental Law* 3, 27 (1961) (hereafter cited as Wechsler).

2. Id.

3. L. Jaffe, *English and American Judges as Lawmakers* 38 (1969).

4. R. Dahl, *A Preface to Democratic Theory* 4–33 (1956).

5. Id. at 23–24.

6. Wright, Professor Bickel, the Scholarly Tradition, and the Supreme Court, 84 *Harv. L. Rev.* 769 (1971) (hereafter cited as Wright).

7. Id. at 777.

8. Id. at 777–78.

9. This syllogism is implicit in much of Judge Wright's argument, e.g., "If it is proper for the Court to make fundamental value choices to protect our constitutional rights and liberties, then it is self-defeating to say that if the Justices cannot come up with a perfectly reasonable and perfectly general opinion *now*, they should abstain from decision altogether." Id. at 770. The first clause is the important one for present purposes; the others merely caricature the position of commentators who ask for principle.

10. Judge Wright also seems to take this position at times. "Constitutional choices are in fact different from ordinary decisions. The reason is simple: the most important value choices have already been made by the framers of the Constitution." Id. at 784. One wonders how the Judge squares this with his insistence upon the propriety of the judiciary making "fundamental value choices." The Warren Court has chosen to expand the Fourteenth Amendment's theme of equality in ways certainly not foreseen by the framers of that provision. A prior Court expanded the amendment's theme of liberty. Are both Courts to be judged innocent of having made the most important value choices on the ground that the framers mentioned both liberty and equality? If so, the framers must be held to have delegated an almost complete power to govern to the Supreme Court, and it is untrue to say that a constitutional decision is any different from an ordinary government decision. Judge Wright simply never faces up to the problem he purports to address: how free is the Court to choose values that will override the values chosen by elected representatives?

11. A. Bickel, *The Supreme Court and the Idea of Progress* 96 (1970).

12. Id. at 34.

13. Wright, supra note 6, at 775.

14. 381 U.S. 479 (1965).

15. Bork, The Supreme Court Needs a New Philosophy, *Fortune*, December 1968, at 170.

16. 381 U.S. at 484.

17. 357 U.S. 449 (1958).

18. 381 U.S. at 484.

19. Id. at 485, 486.

20. The impossibility is related to that of making interpersonal comparisons of utilities. See L.

Robbins, *The Nature and Significance of Economic Science*, ch. 4 (2d ed. 1969); P. Samuelson, *Foundations of Economic Analysis* 243–52 (1965).

21. 262 U.S. 390 (1922).

22. 268 U.S. 510 (1925).

23. 261 U.S. 525 (1923).

24. 198 U.S. 45 (1905).

25. Id. at 59.

26. 316 U.S. 535 (1942).

27. 330 U.S. 552 (1947).

28. 335 U.S. 464 (1948).

29. 336 U.S. 106 (1949).

30. 394 U.S. 618 (1969).

31. 391 U.S. 68 (1968).

32. Wechsler, supra note 1, at 11, citing Frankfurter, John Marshall and the Judicial Function, 69 *Harv. L. Rev.* 217, 227–28 (1955).

33. 347 U.S. 483 (1954).

34. Wechsler, supra note 1, at 43.

35. Id. at 47.

36. 334 U.S. 1 (1948).

37. Henkin, Shelley v. Kraemer: Notes for a Revised Opinion, 110 *U. Pa. L. Rev.* 473, 496 (1962).

38. Id. at 494.

39. See the dissents of Justice Frankfurter in Baker v. Carr, 369 U.S. 186. 266 (1966); Justice Harlan in Reynolds v. Sims, 377 U.S. 533, 589 (1964); and Justice Stewart in Lucas v. Forty-Fourth Gen. Assembly, 377 U.S. 713, 744 (1964).

40. See Fortson v. Morris, 385 U.S. 231 (1966).

41. Baker v. Carr, 369 U.S. 186, 297 (1962).

42. *Federalist* No. 43 (J. Madison).

43. 377 U.S. 713 (1964).

44. Id. at 753–54.

45. H. Kalven, *The Negro and the First Amendment* 4–5 (1966) (hereafter cited as Kalven).

46. Id. at 6.

47. L. Levy, *Legacy of Suppression* (1960) (hereafter cited as Levy).

48. Berns, Freedom of the Press and the Alien and Sedition Laws: A Reappraisal, 1970 *Sup. Ct. Rev.* 109.

49. Levy, supra note 47, at 224–33.

50. 249 U.S. 47 (1919).

51. 250 U.S. 616 (1919).

52. 268 U.S. 652 (1925).

53. 274 U.S. 357 (1927).

54. 341 U.S. 494 (1951).

55. 354 U.S. 298 (1957).

56. 395 U.S. 444 (1969).

57. 354 U.S. 476 (1957).

58. 274 U.S. at 375.

59. Kalven, supra note 45, at 16.

60. Meiklejohn, The First Amendment Is an Absolute, 1961 *Sup. Ct. Rev.* 245, 255.

61. Id. at 256–57.

62. Kalven, The New York Times Case: A Note on "The Central Meaning of the First Amendment," 1964 *Sup. Ct. Rev.* 191, 221.

63. A Book Named "John Clelend's Memoirs of a Woman of Pleasure" v. Attorney General, 383 U.S. 413, 418 (1966).

64. Berns, Pornography vs. Democracy: The Case for Censorship, *Public Interest*, winter 1971, at 23.

65. 268 U.S. at 656.

66. 274 U.S. at 372 (Brandeis, J. dissenting).

67. 268 U.S. at 668; 274 U.S. at 362–63.

68. 274 U.S. at 373.

69. 249 U.S. at 52.

70. 268 U.S. at 669.

71. 341 U.S. at 511.

72. 274 U.S. at 377–78.

73. 395 U.S. at 447.

The Misconceived Quest
for the Original Understanding

◆

━━━━
━━━━

◆

PAUL BREST

BY "ORIGINALISM" I mean the familiar approach to constitutional adjudication that accords binding authority to the text of the Constitution or the intentions of its adopters.[1] At least since *Marbury*, in which Chief Justice Marshall emphasized the significance of our Constitution's being a written document,[2] originalism in one form or another has been a major theme in the American constitutional tradition. The most widely accepted justification for originalism is simply that the Constitution is the supreme law of the land.[3] The Constitution manifests the will of the sovereign citizens of the United States—"we the people" assembled in the conventions and legislatures that ratified the Constitution and its amendments. The interpreter's task is to ascertain their will.[4] Originalism may be supported by more instrumental rationales as well: Adherence to the text and original understanding arguably constrains the discretion of decisionmakers and assures that the Constitution will be interpreted consistently over time.

The most extreme forms of originalism are "strict textualism" (or literalism) and "strict intentionalism." A strict textualist purports to construe words and phrases very narrowly and precisely. For the strict intentionalist, "the whole aim of construction, as applied to a provision of the Constitution, is . . . to ascertain and give effect to the intent of its framers and the people who adopted it."[5]

Much of American constitutional interpretation rejects strict originalism in favor of what I shall call "moderate originalism." The text of the Constitution is authoritative, but many of its provisions are treated as inherently open-textured. The original understanding is also important, but judges are more concerned with the adopters' general purposes than with their intentions in a very precise sense.

Some central doctrines of American constitutional law cannot be derived even by moderate originalist interpretation, but depend, instead, on what I shall call "nonoriginalism." The modes of nonoriginalist adjudication defended in this article accord the text and original history presumptive weight, but do not treat them as authoritative or binding. The presumption is defeasible over time in the light of changing experiences and perceptions.

This paper has two parts. The first takes originalism seriously as a theory of constitutional interpretation in order to understand its concepts, methodologies, and limitations. Part One concludes that neither strict textualism nor strict intentionalism is a tenable approach to constitutional decisionmaking, but that moderate originalism is coherent and workable. Part Two advances a normative thesis based on what I assert to be the ends of constitutional government. I argue that in resolving many constitutional disputes nonoriginalist adjudication better serves these ends than does moderate originalism.[6]

Part One: The Concepts and Methods of Originalism

PART ONE EXAMINES the three fundamental methods of originalism: interpretation of the text of the Constitution, interpretation of the intentions of its adopters, and inference from the structure and relationships of government institutions.

I. Textualism

Textualism takes the language of a legal provision as the primary or exclusive source of law (a) because of some definitional or supralegal principle that only a written text can impose constitutional obligations,[7] or (b) because the adopters intended that the Constitution be interpreted according to a textualist canon, or (c) because the text of a provision is the surest guide to the adopters' intentions. The last of these, probably the central rationale for an originalist-based textualism, is sometimes stated as a preamble to textualist canons. For example: "It is a cardinal rule in the interpretation of constitutions that the instrument must be so construed as to give effect to the intention of the people, who adopted it. This intention is to be sought in the Constitution itself, and the apparent meaning of the words employed is to be taken as expressing it, except in cases where that assumption would lead to absurdity, ambiguity, or contradiction."[8] Implicit in the preceding quotation is a canon of interpretation paradigmatic of textualism—the so-called "plain meaning rule." Chief Justice Marshall invoked this canon in *Sturges* v. *Crown-*

ingshield: "[A]lthough the spirit of an instrument, especially of a constitution, is to be respected not less than its letter, yet the spirit is to be collected chiefly from its words. . . . [I]f, in any case, the plain meaning of a provision, not contradicted by any other provision in the same instrument, is to be disregarded, because we believe the framers of that instrument, could not intend what they say, it must be one in which the absurdity and injustice of applying the provision to the case, would be so monstrous that all mankind would, without hesitation, unite in rejecting the application."[9] The plain meaning of a text is the meaning that it would have for a "normal speaker of English" under the circumstances in which it is used.[10] Two kinds of circumstances seem relevant: the linguistic and the social contexts. The linguistic context refers to vocabulary and syntax. The social context refers to a shared understanding of the purposes the provision might plausibly serve.[11]

A tenable version of the plain meaning rule must take account of both of these contexts. The alternative, of applying a provision according to the literal meanings of its component words, misconceives the conventions that govern the use of language.[12] Chief Justice Marshall argued this point eloquently and, I think, persuasively, in *McCulloch* v. *Maryland*,[13] decided the same year that he invoked the plain meaning rule in *Sturges*. The state had argued that the necessary and proper clause authorized only legislation "indispensable" to executing the enumerated powers. Marshall responded with the observation that the word "necessary," as used "in the common affairs of the world, or in approved authors, . . . frequently imports no more than that one thing is convenient, or useful, or essential to another."[14] He continued:

> Such is the character of human language, that no word conveys to the mind, in all situations, one single definite idea; and nothing is more common than to use words in a figurative sense. Almost all compositions contain words, which, taken in their rigorous sense, would convey a meaning different from that which is obviously intended. It is essential to just construction that many words which import something excessive, should be understood in a more mitigated sense—in that sense which common usage justifies. . . . This word, then, like others, is used in various senses; and, in its construction, the subject, the context, the intention of the person using them, are all to be taken into view.[15]

As Marshall implied, to attempt to read a provision without regard to its linguistic and social contexts will either yield unresolvable indeterminacies of language or just nonsense. Without taking account of the possible purposes of the provisions, an interpreter could not, for example, decide whether singing, flag-waving, flag-burning, picketing, and criminal conspiracy are within the protected ambit of the First Amendment's "freedom of speech,"[16] or whether the "writings" protected by the copyright clause include photographs, paintings, sculptures, performances, and the contents of phonograph records.[17] She would not know whether the phrase, "No person except a natural born Citizen . . . shall be eligible to the Office of President,"[18] disqualified persons born abroad or those born by caesarean section. We understand the range of plausible meanings of provisions only because we know that some interpretations respond to the kinds of concerns that the adopters' society might have while others do not.[19]

That an interpreter must read a text in the light of its social as well as linguistic context does not destroy the boundary between textualism and intentionalism. Just as the textualist is not concerned with the adopters' idiosyncratic use of language, she is not concerned with their subjective purposes. Rather, she seeks to discern the purposes that a member of the adopters' society would understand the provision to encompass.[20]

Suppose that phrases such as "commerce among the several states," or "freedom of speech," or "equal protection of the laws," have quite different meanings today than when they were adopted. An originalist would hold that, because interpretation is designed to capture the original understanding, the text must be understood in the contexts of the society that adopted it: "The meaning of the constitution is fixed when it is adopted, and it is not different at any subsequent time when a court has occasion to pass upon it."[21]

When a provision is interpreted roughly contemporaneously with its adoption, an interpreter unconsciously places the provision in its linguistic and social contexts, which she has internalized simply because she is of that society. But she cannot assume that a provision adopted one or two hundred years ago has the same meaning today as it had for the adopters' society. She must immerse herself in their society to understand the text as they understood it. Although many provisions of the Constitution may pose no serious interpretive problems in this respect, the textualist interpreter cannot be sure of this without first understanding the ordinary usage at the time of adoption. Did "commerce" include manufacture as well as trade?[22] Did the power to "regulate" commerce imply the power to prohibit it?[23] Did the power to "regulate commerce among the several states" include the power to regulate intrastate transactions which affected interstate commerce?[24] With what absoluteness did eighteenth-century Americans understand the prohibitions against "impairing" contractual obligations[25] and "abridging the freedom of speech?"[26] What did the words "privileges," "immunities," "due process," "equal protection of the laws," "citizen," and "person" mean to those who adopted the Fourteenth Amendment in 1868?[27]

Despite the differences between textualism and intentionalism, placing a constitutional provision in its original contexts calls for a historical inquiry quite similar to the intentionalist interpreter's. I shall consider these together in section IV.

II. Intentionalism

By contrast to the textualist, the intentionalist interprets a provision by ascertaining the intentions of those who adopted it. The text of the provision is often a useful guide to the adopters' intentions, but the text does not enjoy a favored status over other sources.[28] Before turning to issues of intentionalism in constitutional interpretation, it is helpful to examine the underlying concepts through a simple example.

A. The Basic Concepts

1. The Adopters' Perspective. Suppose that you are the mayor of a small town and that you alone have the power to enact ordinances. The town maintains a park through which a dirt road runs. The road has traditionally been used as a shortcut by cars going to and from an adjacent residential neighborhood. It is also used by joggers. Last week, a blue 1973 Ford bumped into a jogger on this road. You immediately enacted an ordinance providing: "No vehicles shall be permitted in the park." When you came into your office this morning you were confronted by citizens asking whether you "intended" to prohibit various vehicles and activities from the park. Does the ordinance prohibit use of the park by a white 1975 Chevy sedan, a moped, a baby carriage? Does it forbid the local distributor of a crash-proof car from dropping it into the park from a helicopter as a publicity stunt?

These proposed uses have several features in common. First, each is prohibited by some literal interpretation of the ordinance. Second, each may annoy or endanger people using the park for recreational purposes. Third, you did not advert to any of these examples when you promulgated the regulation.[29] Nonetheless, you will almost surely conclude that your intentions were not the same with respect to all of the proposed uses. Just how you know what your intentions were is not crucial for our purposes. Yet it may be useful if, without any pretensions of rigor, I mention some aspects of the process of understanding or recollecting one's intentions.

You have three sources available. First, you can recall any instances of the rule's application which passed through your mind during the process of adopting it. I will call these your subjective exemplary applications of the rule. Second, you can look to the language of the rule you drafted, which implies conventional exemplary applications—those that your language would suggest to other members of your society. Third—though I am not certain how independent this is from the first two—you can recall the undesirable consequences that you hoped to avoid by enacting the rule. These may be conceptualized on different levels of generality. Moving from the abstract to the particular, you might have hoped to protect pedestrians using the park from harm, or from injury caused by vehicles, or from being run into by cars.

In reconstructing your intent, you will compare a proposed application with both conventional and subjective examples in the light of the consequences you hoped to avoid. The more a putative application differs from these applications, the less likely it falls within your intentions. "The more it differs"— but differs in what respect? Assuming that Fiat makes baby carriages as well as automobiles, is a Fiat sports car more like a Fiat baby carriage or more like a Chevrolet sedan? The concern, of course, is with salient differences, and salience is determined by the consequences you hoped to avoid, which in turn . . .

However circular the process may seem, it often leads us somewhere. For example, you will surely conclude that you intended to prohibit the 1975 Chevy and that you intended not to prohibit the baby carriage. (Intent "to" and "not to" are mirror images, reflecting the same degree of determinacy.) What of the publicity stunt, dropping the vehicle into the park by helicopter? Of course, now that it comes to your attention, you would like to prohibit it. But it is too remote from either your subjective examples, or from society's conventional examples, to have been within your intentions when you enacted the ordinance. You did not intend the ordinance to prohibit this conduct.

And what of mopeds? Assume that you "intended not to" prohibit bicycles because you considered them among the legitimate uses of the park to be protected by the ordinance. Then mopeds probably lie on the periphery of the examples of both protected and prohibited uses: they both serve and disserve your purposes to some extent. Even if you had adverted to the issue you might not have reached a definite decision. Your intent with respect to mopeds was indeterminate.

2. The Interpreter's Perspective and the Application of Rules. Suppose that the mayor's intentions are as I have described them. The municipal court judge is an intentionalist interpreter and is therefore required to consult the mayor's intentions. How should she rule on the various constituents' requests for advisory opinions?

The decisions in the cases concerning the Chevy sedan and the baby carriage are clear-cut: the Chevy may not be driven through the park; the baby carriage may be perambulated. Assuming that the "no vehicles" regulation is the only colorably relevant law on the books, the car may be dropped from a helicopter. If this seems strange, suppose that a neighboring town has no ordinance whatever concerning vehicles in its park, and the car dealer wishes to perform the stunt there. That town's mayor would also have enacted a law prohibiting the stunt if only he had anticipated it, but of course he didn't. The only difference between that town and ours is that we have language on the books that conceivably applies. But from an intentionalist standpoint this is irrelevant, for our mayor never intended the words to deal with this situation. An intentionalist judge may no more prohibit the stunt based on what the lawmaker might have intended than a textualist may prohibit the stunt based on what a lawmaker might have written.

How should the judge decide the legality of mopeds in the park? By hypothesis the mayor's intent was indeterminate. Should the judge treat this as tantamount to a finding of no intent and therefore hold that mopeds are not prohibited by the regulation? Intentionalist theory alone does not warrant this conclusion any more than it does the opposite. Even if the judge also holds to an institutional theory that allocates "policy" decisions to nonjudicial agencies—in this case, the mayor—she would have no basis for preferring one or the other outcome, for a decision either way is equally one of policy. Thus, the judge's decision must be rooted elsewhere, perhaps in a libertarian disfavor of government regulation or an environmentalist disfavor of gas-powered vehicles. Even if these are values generally shared in the community, however, the judge's decision would not be determined by intentionalist interpretation.

3. The Adopters' Interpretive Intent. Suppose that the mayor has the legal authority not only to adopt substantive regulations, but also to stipulate the canons by which the judge shall interpret them.[30] Suppose that when the judge inquires into the mayor's intentions about how his regulations should be interpreted—his interpretive intent—she discovers that he is a literalist, or perhaps a moderate intentionalist. That is, suppose that he intends his enactments to be interpreted either by the canon: "Adhere strictly to my language regardless of my intentions" or: "Take my language and what you understand to be my objectives as general guidelines, but don't try to figure out how I would have decided any particular case."[31]

If under these circumstances the judge continues to engage in strict intentionalist interpretation, she has subordinated fidelity to the adopter's intentions to some other value.

4. Individual and Institutional Intent. Imagine, finally, a less autocratic town in which ordinances are enacted by a five-member city council. Although the council unanimously enacts the "no vehicles" ordinance, its members have contradictory intentions concerning its application. What rules determine the intent of the city council—the institutional intent of a multimember body? If we make some simplifying assumptions, the same rules that determine whether a proposed enactment is binding law also determine what intentions are binding.

Consider how intentionalist lawmakers would respond to the disquieting prediction that their laws will be interpreted by purely textualist canons. They would try to specify their intentions in the text of the provision, and the text would, ideally, articulate all and only those intentions that gain a majority vote of the city council. Suppose, for example, that a five-member city council was deliberating the proposed "no vehicle" ordinance. Two council members oppose any regulation; two favor a regulation that prohibits mopeds. The fifth member favors the prohibition of motor vehicles in general but wishes to exempt mopeds. Under these circumstances, the two other proponents might accede to language explicitly exempting mopeds from the regulation in order to assure that at least some other motor vehicles are prohibited.

Of course, the intentionalist interpreter is concerned with the adopters' intentions whether or not these are embodied in the text. In effect, she accords each participant an intention-vote, and the counting of these votes determines the reach of the provision. If a version of the "no vehicles in the park" regulation that specified "this shall prohibit mopeds" would have failed by one vote, then, whatever its language, the regulation lacks the intention-votes necessary to prohibit mopeds and the intentionalist interpreter may not prohibit them.[32]

Let me conclude this section by defending it against the charge that I have created a straw intentionalist, for few if any intentionalist interpreters actually attempt to count the intention-votes of the adopters of statutory and constitutional provisions.[33] The preceding discussion does not purport to set out a methodology of intentionalist interpretation, but rather analyzes the concepts that underlie the practice. In the real world, of course, an interpreter must rely on quite different, and much cruder, ways of determining the adopters' intentions. Nonetheless, her methodology assumes the existence of an attainable ideal which is fairly described by the metaphor of intention-votes—the intentionalist analogue to actual votes. Much of the remainder of Part One inquires to what extent the intentionalist ideal can actually be achieved.

B. Intentions in Constitutional Interpretation

The artificially simple examples of the mayor and city council have allowed us to examine some of the basic concepts implicit in intentionalism. I should like to explore these issues further in the context of constitutional interpretation.

1. Who Are the Adopters? The adopters of the Constitution of 1787 were some portion of the delegates to the Philadelphia Convention and majorities or super-majorities of the participants in the ratifying conventions in nine states.[34] For all but one amendment to the Constitution,[35] the adopters were two-thirds or more of the members of each house of Congress and at least a majority of the legislators in two-thirds of the state legislatures.

For a textual provision to become part of the Constitution, the requisite number of persons in each of these bodies must have assented to it. Likewise, an intention can only become binding— only become an institutional intention—when it is shared by at least the same number and distribution of adopters. (Hereafter, I shall refer to this number and distribution as the "adopters.")

If the only way a judge could ascertain institutional intent were to count individual intention-votes, her task would be impossible even with respect to a single multimember law-making body, and a fortiori where the assent of several such bodies were required. Therefore, an intentionalist must necessarily use circumstantial evidence to educe a collective or general intent.

Interpreters often treat the writings or statements of the framers of a provision as evidence of the adopters' intent. This is a justifiable strategy for the moderate originalist who is concerned with the framers' intent on a relatively abstract level of generality—abstract enough to permit the inference that it reflects a broad social consensus rather than notions peculiar to a handful of the adopters. It is a problematic strategy for the strict originalist.

As the process of adoption moves from the actual framers of a constitutional amendment to the members of Congress who proposed it to the state legislators who ratified it, the amount of thought given the provision surely diminishes—especially if it is relatively technical or uncontroversial, or one of several disparate provisions (e.g., the Bill of Rights) adopted simultaneously. This suggests that there may be instances where a framer had a determinate intent but other adopters had no intent or an indeterminate intent. For example, suppose that the framers of the commerce clause considered the possibility that economic transactions taking place within the confines of a state might nonetheless affect interstate commerce in such a way as to come within the clause, and that they intended the clause to cover such transactions. But suppose that most of the delegates to the ratifying conventions did not conceive of this possibility and that either they "did not intend" that the clause encompass such transactions or else their intentions were indeterminate. Under these circumstances, what is the institutional intent, i.e., the intent of the provision?

If the intent of the framers is to be attributed to the provision, it must be because the other adopters have in effect delegated their intention-votes to the framers.[36] Leaving aside the question whether the adopters-at-large had any thoughts at all concerning this issue of delegation, consider what they might have desired if they had thought about it. Would they have wanted the framers' intentions to govern without knowing what those intentions were? The answers might well differ depending on whether the adopters had "no intent" or "indeterminate intent."

A delegate to a ratifying convention might well want his absence of intention (i.e., "no-intent") regarding wholly intrastate transactions to be treated as a vote against the clause's encompassing such transactions (i.e., "intent-not"): Since no-intent is the intentionalist equivalent of no-text, to accede to the framers' unknown intentions would be tantamount to blindly delegating to them the authority to insert textual provisions in the Constitution.

Where the framers intend that the activity be covered by the clause, and the adopters' intentions are merely indeterminate, the institutional intent is ambiguous. One adopter might wish his indeterminate intent to be treated as "no intent." Another adopter might wish to delegate his intention-vote to those whose intent is determinate. Yet another might wish to delegate authority to decisionmakers charged with applying the provision in the future. Without knowing more about the mind-sets of the actual adopters of particular constitutional provisions, one would be hard-pressed to choose among these.

2. The Adopters' Interpretive Intent. The intentionalist interpreter's first task must be to determine the interpretive intentions of the adopters of the provision before her—that is the canons by which the adopters' intended their provisions to be interpreted.[37] The practice of statutory interpretation from the eighteenth through at least the mid-nineteenth century suggests that the adopters assumed—if they assumed anything at all—a mode of interpretation that was more textualist than intentionalist. The plain meaning rule was frequently invoked: judicial recourse to legislative debates was virtually unknown and generally considered improper. Even after references to extrinsic sources became common,[38] courts and commentators frequently asserted that the plain meaning of the text was the surest guide to the intent of the adopters.[39]

This poses obvious difficulties for an intentionalist whose very enterprise is premised on fidelity to the original understanding.[40]

3. The Intended Specificity of a Provision. I now turn to an issue that lies at the intersection of what I have called interpretive and substantive intent: How much discretion did an adopter intend to delegate to those charged with applying a provision? Consider, for example, the possible intentions of the adopters of the cruel and unusual punishment clause of the Eighth Amendment. They might have intended that the language serve only as a shorthand for the Stuart tortures which were their exemplary applications of the clause. Somewhat more broadly, they might have intended the clause to be understood to incorporate the principle of *ejusdem generis*—to include their exemplary applications and other punishments that they found or would have found equally repugnant.[41]

What of instances where the adopters' substantive intent was indeterminate—where even if they had adverted to a proposed application they would not have been certain how the clause should apply? Here it is plausible that—if they *had* a determinate interpretive intent—they intended to delegate to future decisionmakers the authority to apply the clause in light of the general principles underlying it. To use Ronald Dworkin's terms, the adopters would have intended future interpreters to develop their own "conceptions" of cruel and unusual punishment within the framework of the adopters' general "concept" of such punishments.[42]

What of a case where the adopters viewed a certain punishment as not cruel and unusual? This is not the same as saying that the adopters "intended not to prohibit the punishment." For even if they expected their laws to be interpreted by intentionalist canons, the adopters may have intended that their own views not always govern. Like parents who attempt to instill values in their child by both articulating and applying a moral principle, they may have accepted, or even invited, the eventuality that the principle would be applied in ways that diverge from their own views.[43] The adopters may have understood that, even as to instances to which they believe the clause ought or ought not to apply, further thought by themselves or others committed to its underlying principle might lead them to change their minds. Not believing in their own omniscience or infallibility, they delegated the decision to those charged with interpreting the provision. If such a motivation is plausible with respect to applications of the clause in the adopters' contemporary society, it is even more likely with respect to its application by future interpreters, whose understanding of the clause will be affected by changing knowledge, technology, and forms of society.

The extent to which a clause may be properly interpreted to reach outcomes different from those actually contemplated by the adopters depends on the relationship between a general principle and its exemplary applications. A principle does not exist wholly independently of its author's subjective, or his society's conventional exemplary applications,[44] and is always limited to some extent by the applications they found conceivable. Within these fairly broad limits, however, the adopters may have intended their examples to constrain more or less. To the intentionalist interpreter falls the unenviable task of ascertaining, for each provision, how much more or less.

III. Inference from Structure and Relationship

In an important lecture given in 1968, Professor Charles Black described a mode of constitutional interpretation based on "inference from the structures and relationships created by the constitution in all its parts or in some principal part."[45] Professor Black observed that in *McCulloch* v. *Maryland*,[46] "Marshall does not place principal reliance on the [necessary and proper] clause as a ground of decision. . . . [B]efore he reaches it he has already decided, on the basis of far more general implications, that Congress possesses the power, not expressly named, of establishing a bank and chartering corporations; . . . he addresses himself to the necessary and proper clause only in response to counsel's arguing its *restrictive* force."[47] Indeed, the second part of *McCulloch*, which held that the Constitution prohibited Maryland from levying a tax on the National Bank, rested exclusively on inferences from the structure of the federal system, and not at all on the text of the Constitution. Similarly, *Crandall* v. *Nevada*[48] was not premised on the privileges and immunities clause of either Article IV or the Fourteenth Amendment. Rather, the Court inferred a right of personal mobility among the states from the structure of the federal system:

> [The citizen] has the right to come to the seat of government to assert
> any claim he may have upon that government, or to transact any
> business he may have with it. To seek its protection, to share its
> offices, to engage in administering its functions. He has a right to free
> access to its sea-ports, through which all the operations of foreign
> trade and commerce are conducted, to the subtreasuries, the land
> offices, the revenue offices, and the courts of justice in the several
> States, and this right is in its nature independent of the will of any
> State over whose soil he must pass in the exercise of it.[49]

Citing examples like these, Professor Black argued that interpreters too often
have engaged in "Humpty-Dumpty textual manipulation" rather than relying
"on the sort of political inference which not only underlies the textual manipulation but is, in a well constructed opinion, usually invoked to support the
interpretation of the cryptic text."[50]

Inference from structure and relationship is no less legitimate than other
originalist modes of interpretation, nor less fraught with indeterminacy. Like
the language of many constitutional provisions, the constitutional ordering
of institutions permits alternative inferences. Contrary to Chief Justice Marshall's implication in *McCulloch*, for example, the nature of a federal constitution does not entail that the national legislative powers must be construed
expansively[51] or that state taxation of the operations of a national bank is
necessarily prohibited. Moreover, because an originalist interpreter is concerned only with the structure and relationships of institutions as of the time
they were established or restructured, she confronts the same hermeneutical
problems as the textualist and intentionalist. It is to these that I now turn.

IV. The Interpreter-Historian's Task

The interpreter's task as historian can be divided into three stages or categories. First, she must immerse herself in the world of the adopters to try to
understand constitutional concepts and values from their perspective. Second, at least the intentionalist must ascertain the adopters' interpretive intent
and the intended scope of the provision in question. Third, she must often
"translate" the adopters' concepts and intentions into our time and apply
them to situations that the adopters did not foresee.

The first stage is common to originalists of all persuasions. Although the
textualist's aim is to understand and apply the language of a constitutional
provision, she must locate the text in the linguistic and social contexts in
which it was adopted. Similarly, the originalist "structuralist" interpreter
must situate the institutions in their original contexts. The intentionalist
would ideally count the intention-votes of the individual adopters. In practice, she can at best hope to discover a consensus of the adopters as manifested in the text of the provision itself, the history surrounding its adoption,
and the ideologies and practices of the time.

The essential difficulty posed by the distance that separates the modern interpreter from the objects of her interpretation has been succinctly stated by Quentin Skinner in addressing the analogous problem facing historians of political theory:[52]

> [I]t will never in fact be possible simply to study what any given classic writer has *said* . . . without bringing to bear some of one's own expectations about what he must have been saying. . . . [T]hese models and preconceptions in terms of which we unavoidably organize and adjust our perceptions and thoughts will themselves tend to act as determinants of what we think or perceive. We must classify in order to understand, and we can only classify the unfamiliar in terms of the familiar. The perpetual danger, in our attempts to enlarge our historical understanding, is thus that our expectations about what someone must be saying or doing will themselves determine that we understand the agent to be doing something which he would not—or even could not— himself have accepted as an account of what he *was* doing.[53]

To illustrate the problem of doing original history with even a single example would consume more space than I wish to here. Instead, I suggest that a reader who wants to get a sense of the elusiveness of the original understanding study some specific areas of constitutional history, reading both works that have been well received,[54] and also the controversy surrounding some of those that have not.[55]

The intentionalist interpreter must next ascertain the adopters' interpretive intent and the intended breadth of their provisions.[56] That is, she must determine what the adopters intended future interpreters to make of their substantive views. Even if she can learn how the adopters intended contemporary interpreters to construe the Constitution, she cannot assume they intended the same canons to apply one or two hundred years later. Perhaps they wanted to bind the future as closely as possible to their own notions. Perhaps they intended a particular provision to be interpreted with increasing breadth as time went on. Or—more likely than not—the adopters may have had no intentions at all concerning these matters.[57]

For purposes of analytic clarity I have distinguished between (1) the adopters' interpretive intent and the intended scope of a provision and (2) their substantive intent concerning the application of the provision. If interpretive intent and intended scope can be ascertained at all, they may instruct the interpreter to adopt different canons of interpretation than she would prefer. Under these circumstances, the intentionalist interpreter may wish to ignore these intentions and limit her inquiry to the adopters' substantive intentions. Leaving aside the normative difficulty of such selective infidelity,[58] this is a problematic strategy: To be a coherent theory of interpretation, intentionalism must distinguish between the adopters' personal *views* about an issue and their *intentions* concerning its constitutional resolution. And it is only by reference to their interpretive intent and the intended scope of a provision that this distinction can be drawn.

The interpreter's final task is to translate the adopters' intentions into the present in order to apply them to the question at issue. Consider, for example, whether the cruel and unusual punishment clause of the Eighth Amendment prohibits the imposition of the death penalty today. The adopters of the clause apparently never doubted that the death penalty was constitutional.[59] But was death the same event for inhabitants of the American colonies in the late eighteenth century as it is two centuries later? Death was not only a much more routine and public phenomenon then, but the fear of death was more effectively contained within a system of religious belief.[60] Twentieth-century Americans have a more secular cast of mind and seem less willing to accept this dreadful, forbidden, solitary, and shameful event.[61] The interpreter must therefore determine whether we view the death penalty with the same attitude—whether of disgust or ambivalence—that the adopters viewed their core examples of cruel and unusual punishment.[62]

Intentionalist interpretation frequently requires translations of this sort. For example, to determine whether the commerce clause applies to transactions taking place wholly within the boundaries of one state, or whether the First Amendment protects the mass media, the interpreter must abstract the adopters' concepts of federalism and freedom of expression in order to find their analogue in our contemporary society with its different technology, economy, and systems of communication.[63] The alternative would be to limit the application of constitutional provisions to the particular events and transactions with which the adopters were familiar. Even if such an approach were coherent,[64] however, it would produce results that even a strict intentionalist would likely reject: Congress could not regulate any item of commerce or any mode of transportation that did not exist in 1789; the First Amendment would not protect any means of communication not then known.

However difficult the earlier stages of her work, the interpreter was only trying to understand the past. The act of translation required here is different in kind, for it involves the counterfactual and imaginary act of projecting the adopters' concepts and attitudes into a future they probably could not have envisioned. When the interpreter engages in this sort of projection, she is in a fantasy world more of her own than of the adopters' making.

Even when the interpreter performs the more conventional historian's role, one may wonder whether the task is possible. There is a hermeneutic tradition, of which Hans-Georg Gadamar is the leading modern proponent, which holds that we can never understand the past in its own terms, free from our prejudices or preconceptions.[65] We are hopelessly imprisoned in our own world-views; we can shed some preconceptions only to adopt others, with no reason to believe that they are the conceptions of the different society that we are trying to understand. One need not embrace this essentially solipsistic view of historical knowledge to appreciate the indeterminate and contingent nature of the historical understanding that an originalist historian seeks to achieve.

None of this is to disparage doing history and other interpretive social science. It suggests, however, that the originalist constitutional historian may be questing after a chimera. The defense that "We're doing the best we can" is no less available to constitutional interpreters than to anyone else. But the best is not always good enough. The interpreter's understanding of the original understanding may be so indeterminate as to undermine the rationale for originalism. Although the origins of some constitutional doctrines are almost certainly established, the historical grounding of many others is quite controversial.[66] It seems peculiar, to say the least, that the legitimacy of a current doctrine should turn on the historian's judgment that it seems "more likely than not," or even "rather likely," that the adopters intended it some one or two centuries ago.

V. Two Types of Originalism

The originalist interpreter can approach her task with different attitudes about the precision with which the object of interpretation—the text, intentions, or structure—should be understood. In this section I describe the attitudes of "strict" and "moderate" originalism—two areas, not points, on a spectrum—and briefly survey the practices of American constitutional decisionmaking in terms of them.

I have devoted very little attention to the most extreme form of strict textualism—literalism. A thorough-going literalist understands a text to encompass all those and only those instances that come within its words read without regard to its social or perhaps even its linguistic context. Because literalism poorly matches the ways in which we speak and write, it is unable to handle the ambiguity, vagueness, and figurative usage that pervade natural languages, and produces embarrassingly silly results.

Strict intentionalism requires the interpreter to determine how the adopters would have applied a provision to a given situation, and to apply it accordingly. The enterprise rests on the questionable assumption that the adopters of constitutional provisions intended them to be applied in this manner. But even if this were true, the interpreter confronts historiographic difficulties of such magnitude as to make the aim practicably unattainable.

Strict textualism and intentionalism are not synergistic, but rather mutually antagonistic approaches to interpretation. The reader need only consider the strict textualist's and intentionalist's views of the First Amendment protection of pornographic literature.[67] By contrast, moderate textualism and intentionalism closely resemble each other in methodology and results.

A moderate textualist takes account of the open-textured quality of language and reads the language of provisions in their social and linguistic contexts. A moderate intentionalist applies a provision consistent with the adopters' intent at a relatively high level of generality, consistent with what is sometimes called the "purpose of the provision."[68] Where the strict intentionalist tries to determine the adopters' actual subjective purposes, the moderate intentionalist attempts to understand what the adopters' purposes might plausibly have been,[69] an aim far more readily achieved than a precise understanding of the adopters' intentions.

Strict originalism cannot accommodate most modern decisions under the Bill of Rights and the Fourteenth Amendment, or the virtually plenary scope of congressional power under the commerce clause. Although moderate originalism is far more expansive, some major constitutional doctrines lie beyond its pale as well.

A moderate textualist would treat almost all contemporary free speech and equal protection decisions as within the permissible ambit of these clauses, though not necessarily entailed by them. Because of our uncertainty about the original understanding, it is harder to assess the legitimacy of these doctrines from the viewpoint of a moderate intentionalist. For example, the proper scope of the First Amendment depends on whether its adopters were only pursuing "representation reinforcing" goals,[70] or were more broadly concerned to promote a free marketplace of ideas or individual autonomy.[71] The level of generality on which the adopters conceived of the equal protection clause presents a similar uncertainty, but whether or not a moderate intentionalist could accept all of the "new" or "newer" equal protection,[72] she could read the clause to protect "discrete and insular minorities" besides blacks.

On the other hand, a moderate originalist, whether of textualist or intentionalist persuasion, would have serious difficulties justifying (1) the incorporation of the principle of equal protection into the Fifth Amendment,[73] (2) the incorporation of provisions of the Bill of Rights into the Fourteenth Amendment,[74] (3) the more general notion of substantive due process, including the minimal rational relationship standard,[75] and (4) the practice of judicial review of congressional legislation established by *Marbury* v. *Madison*.[76] Although these doctrines strain or go beyond the text of the Constitution, for reasons made apparent in the preceding pages, one cannot say with certainty that they are not authorized by the original understanding. For purposes of Part Two it is enough that the legitimacy of their origins cannot be established with much certainty.[77]

Part Two: The Authority of the Constitution

THROUGHOUT PART ONE we assumed that judges and other public officials were bound by the text or original understanding of the Constitution. Part

Two challenges this assumption. I begin by showing that the issue is not foreclosed by the written Constitution itself, and then offer some criteria for evaluating competing strategies of constitutional decisionmaking. I then describe a familiar alternative to originalism—(mere) adjudication. The remainder of Part Two compares the alternatives and concludes that adjudication which takes account of the text and original understanding without, however, treating them as authoritative, generally serves the ends of constitutionalism better than originalist interpretation.

I. The Authority of the Constitution and the Purposes of Constitutional Decisionmaking

What authority does the written Constitution have in our system of constitutional government? This is not an empty question. The English experience demonstrates that a constitutional democracy—a government of limited powers ultimately responsible to its citizens—need not be premised on a written document.[78] And although Article VI declares that the Constitution is the "supreme law of the land," a document cannot achieve the status of law, let alone supreme law, merely by its own assertion.

According to the political theory most deeply rooted in the American tradition, the authority of the Constitution derives from the consent of its adopters.[79] Even if the adopters freely consented to the Constitution, however, this is not an adequate basis for continuing fidelity to the founding document, for their consent cannot bind succeeding generations.[80] We did not adopt the Constitution, and those who did are dead and gone.

Given the questionable authority of the American Constitution—indeed, of any (quasi) revolutionary constitution at the moment of its inception—it is only through a history of continuing assent or acquiescence that the document could become law.[81] Our constitutional tradition, however, has not focused on the document alone, but on the decisions and practices of courts and other institutions. And this tradition has included major elements of nonoriginalism. The doctrines described in the conclusion to Part One are as well-settled parts of the constitutional landscape as most originalist-based doctrines. They are among the principal subjects that occupy professionals who "do" constitutional law—lawyers, judges, law professors and law students—and are considered part of constitutional law by the media and by the lay public. A description of the American legal system that omitted them or treated them as aberrational would be extraordinarily inaccurate. To make the point affirmatively, the practice of supplementing and derogating from the text and original understanding is itself part of our constitutional tradition.

The fact of this tradition undermines the exclusivity of the written document. It does not, however, establish the legitimacy of nonoriginalism. Acquiescence is not the same as "consent," which must be informed and knowingly and freely given. Those conditions have not in fact been met, and perhaps can never be met in a large industrial society.[82]

Actual consent is not, then, a practicable measure of the legitimacy of any system of government,[83] and a fortiori not of a particular practice or institution. Owen Fiss has suggested that it is not even an appropriate measure of institutional legitimacy: "Consent goes to the system, not the particular institution; it operates on the whole rather than on each part. The legitimacy of particular institutions, such as courts, depends not on the consent—implied or otherwise—of the people, but rather on their *competence*, on the special contribution they make to the quality of our social life. Legitimacy depends on the capacity of the institution to perform a function within the political system and its willingness to respect the limitations on that function."[84] Whether or not the practices of constitutional decisionmaking should ideally be validated by consent as well as competence, I think we must accept Professor Fiss's observation *faute de mieux*.

Having abandoned both consent and fidelity to the text and original understanding as the touchstones of constitutional decisionmaking, let me propose a designedly vague criterion: How well, compared to possible alternatives, does the practice contribute to the well-being of our society—or, more narrowly, to the ends of constitutional government? Among other things, the practice should (1) foster democratic government; (2) protect individuals against arbitrary, unfair, and intrusive official action; (3) conduce to a political order that is relatively stable but which also responds to changing conditions, values, and needs; (4) not readily lend itself to arbitrary decisions or abuses; and (5) be acceptable to the populace. The following paragraphs amplify the first two of these, and I shall discuss specific applications of all of them below.

Central to our constitutional order are the related though not always compatible concerns for individual rights and decisionmaking through democratic processes. For better or worse, the judiciary has assumed a major role in protecting both. In what has become a classic description of the special role of constitutional adjudication, Alexander Bickel wrote:

> [M]any actions of government have two aspects: their immediate,
> necessarily intended, practical effects, and their perhaps unintended
> or unappreciated bearing on values we hold to have more general and
> permanent interest. It is a premise we deduce not merely from the fact
> of a written constitution but from the history of the race, and ulti-
> mately as a moral judgment of the good society, that government
> should serve not only what we conceive from time to time to be our
> immediate material needs but also certain enduring values. . . . But
> such values do not present themselves ready-made. They have a past
> always, to be sure, but they must be continually derived, enunciated,
> and seen in relevant application.[85]

In the same spirit, Owen Fiss argues that the judiciary should give "concrete meaning and application to our constitutional values"—the values which "give our society an identity and inner coherence [and] its distinctive public morality."[86]

Thus, the practice of constitutional adjudication should enforce those, but only those, values which are fundamental to our society. Adopting this vague norm does not automatically foreclose either strict or moderate originalism. It may still be contended that the ends of constitutionalism are best served by enforcing only values embodied in the text and original understanding of the Constitution.[87] However, originalism can no longer be defended a priori but must justify itself in the face of alternative approaches to constitutional decisionmaking.

One such alternative would safeguard two of our most fundamental values—the integrity of majoritarian processes and the rights of minorities. This special judicial role was suggested in footnote 4 of Justice Harlan Fiske Stone's opinion in the *Carolene Products* case.[88] It is the thesis of John Ely's recent book, *Democracy and Distrust: A Theory of Judicial Review*. Ely argues that the judiciary properly performs these "representation-reinforcing" functions, but that courts are not competent to ascertain and apply any other "fundamental values." A broader approach, implicit in Bickel's and Fiss's more general description of the judicial function, would protect all fundamental values against official intrusion, without inquiring whether the intrusion resulted from defects of democratic processes.

Independent of any of these views of the proper *domain* of judicial intervention are a variety of notions about the amount of *deference* that a court should accord a legislative or administrative decision under review. For example, although the substantive scope of Bickel's judicial function is broad, he, like many other scholars and judges in the "fundamental values'" tradition, would accord legislation a very strong presumption of constitutionality.[89] Professor Ely, on the other hand, is less concerned with judicial deference within the more circumscribed sphere of intervention that he advocates.

The thesis of this article is not tied to Bickel's, Ely's, or any other particular nonoriginalist method. Rather, the thesis is that whether one views the appropriate realm of judicial inquiry as broad or narrow, and whether one approaches the enterprise with a deferential or interventionist bias, the aims of constitutionalism are best served by nonoriginalist adjudication which treats the text and original history as important but not necessarily authoritative.

II. Adjudication as an Alternative to Originalist Interpretation

Several features of adjudication[90] commend it as a plausible method for deriving and applying Bickel's "fundamental" values or Ely's "representation-reinforcing" values. Judges—especially federal judges—are relatively independent officials. Cases are presented through arguments based on precedent, policy, and principle, by parties who stand equally before the court. The court must justify its decisions by articulating reasons for them. The concreteness of the dispute, and the method of "testing" a result by articulating a governing principle and applying it to this and similar cases—real or hypothetical—induce the court to take responsibility for its decisions and to look beyond the circumstances of the particular dispute. And although the court gives strong presumptive weight to its precedents, the presumption is defeasible: Precedents are modified and even overruled to reflect perceived changes in social needs and values. Therefore, a doctrine that survives over a period of time has the approval of a court composed, in effect, of all the judges who have ever had occasion to consider and apply it.[91]

This is, of course, an idealized[92] description of the Anglo-American "case" or "common law" method, which derives legal principles from custom, social practices, conventional morality, and precedent. Most American constitutional doctrines have evolved through adjudication, for it is the method of moderate originalism in the many cases where original sources alone cannot resolve the controversy before the court.[93]

The only difference between moderate originalism and nonoriginalist adjudication is one of attitude toward the text and original understanding. For the moderate originalist, these sources are conclusive when they speak clearly. For the nonoriginalist, they are important but not determinative. Like an established line of precedent at common law, they create a strong presumption, but one which is defeasible in the light of changing public values. The text and original understanding exert the strongest claims when they are contemporary and thus likely to reflect current values and beliefs, or simply the expressed will of a current majority;[94] or where they specify the procedures and numbers relating to elections, appointments to government offices, and the formal validity of laws, where certainty is an important objective or inherently arbitrary lines must be drawn.[95] The presumption is most likely to be overcome in adjudication under broad clauses involving issues of equality and liberty, where legal and moral principles are closely intertwined.

III. Originalism Evaluated

A. Strict Originalism
The discussion in Part One showed that strict textualism cannot produce sensible constitutional decisions. This section attempts to show why strict intentionalism is not well suited to eliciting fundamental or "representation-reinforcing" values.

Even if the adopters were extraordinarily wise and public spirited, they were also self-interested: The Constitution reflects a pragmatic and not always principled compromise among a variety of regional, economic, and political interests. The strict intentionalist must winnow the adopters' under-lying values from these interests.[96] Besides the methodological and historiographic difficulties of this enterprise, it is prey to a normative prob-lem: The drafting, adopting, or amending of the Constitution may itself have suffered from defects of democratic process which detract from its moral claims. To take an obvious example, the interests of black Americans were not adequately represented in the adoption of the Constitution of 1787 or the Fourteenth Amendment. Whatever moral consensus the Civil War Amend-ments embodied was among white male property-holders and not the popu-lation as a whole. Similarly, the assumption that the contract clause reflected widely held norms of eighteenth-century America is weakened to the extent that creditors were well-represented and debtors underrepresented in the Philadelphia and state ratifying conventions.[97]

To characterize these as defects of democratic process may seem anachro-nistic or question-begging: Even if we regard them as defects, they may not have been so regarded by many participants at the time. Moreover, the ar-gument may prove too much, for the making of almost any law suffers from similar imperfections. But my point is not that an early nineteenth-century court should have tried to abolish slavery or guarantee full racial equality in the face of a contrary constitutional understanding. Rather, the fact that a provision was drafted by an unrepresentative and self-interested portion of the adopters' society weakens its moral claim on a different society one or two hundred years later.

Assume that the intentionalist interpreter can filter out the purely prag-matic factors and identify the moral consensus of an earlier era in American history. What is the likelihood that the same consensus exists today? Sup-pose, for example, that the prevalent public morality in 1868 did not extend beyond the limited formal racial equality mandated by a narrow reading of the Civil Rights Act of 1878.[98] Many intervening phenomena—including the achievements of blacks in the face of a century of discrimination, changes in the economy with attendant changes in migration and labor patterns, and direct evidence of attitude change—suggest that the nation's values had shifted significantly by 1954, and certainly by the mid-1960s.[99] The history of the preceding decades justifies Chief Justice Warren's comment in *Brown* that "in approaching this problem, we cannot turn the clock back to 1868 when the Amendment was adopted, or even to 1896 when *Plessy* v. *Ferguson* was written."[100]

To return to the contract clause, assuming for the sake of argument that most eighteenth-century Americans believed that contractual obligations should be absolutely inviolate, how many of our contemporaries share that belief? Consider Chief Justice Charles Evans Hughes's response in the *Min-nesota Mortgage Moratorium Case*:

> It is manifest . . . that there has been a growing appreciation of public
> needs and of the necessity of finding ground for a rational compromise

between individual rights and public welfare. The settlement and consequent contraction of the public domain, the pressure of a constantly increasing density of population, the interrelation of the activities of our people, and the complexity of our economic interests, have inevitably led to an increased use of the organization of society in order to protect the very bases of individual opportunity. . . . [T]he question is no longer merely that of one party to a contract as against another, but of the use of reasonable means to safeguard the economic structure upon which the good of all depends.[101]

Finally, strict intentionalism produces a highly unstable constitutional order. The claims of scholars like William Winslow Crosskey and Raoul Berger[102] demonstrate that a settled constitutional understanding is in perpetual jeopardy of being overturned by new light on the adopters' intent—shed by the discovery of historical documents, re-examinations of known documents, and reinterpretations of political and social history. Moreover, constitutional interpretation is not a scientific process but a subjective undertaking which vests the historian with enormous discretion in ordering and analyzing her data. Novel interpretations are due as much to changes in the interpreter's perspective as to anything extrinsic. And we have witnessed enough dramatic revisions of social and political history to be sure that the past is not about to stand still.

B. *Moderate Originalism*

Moderate originalism is a perfectly sensible strategy of constitutional decisionmaking. But its constraints are illusory and counterproductive. Contrary to the moderate originalist's faith, the text and original understanding have contributed little to the development of many doctrines she accepts as legitimate. Consider the relationship between the original understanding of the Fourteenth Amendment and current doctrines prohibiting gender-based classifications[103] and discriminations in the political process.[104] For the moderate originalist these may be legitimately premised on the equal protection clause. But to what extent have originalist sources *guided* the evolution of these doctrines? The text is wholly open-ended, and if the adopters had any intentions at all about these issues, their resolution was probably contrary to the Court's. At most, the Court can claim guidance from the general notion of equal treatment reflected in the provision. I use the word "reflected" advisedly, however, for the equal protection clause does not establish a principle of equality; it only articulates and symbolizes a principle defined by our conventional public morality. Indeed, because of its indeterminacy, the clause does not offer much guidance even in resolving particular issues of discrimination based on race.[105]

To see this from a different perspective, suppose that the equal protection clause had provided: "No State shall deny any person the equal protection of the laws *on account of race*."[106] If the Court had nonetheless expanded the requirement of equal treatment beyond racial classifications—under the aegis of, say, the due process clause—would the gender and voting decisions have been any less responsive to changing public values than they have in fact been under the actual clause? Or suppose that tomorrow it were demonstrated, as conclusively as such things ever can be, that the adopters intended to limit the clause to a narrow range of racially discriminatory practices.[107] Would many decades of moderate originalist doctrine become retroactively misguided?[108]

We need not rely on counterfactual examples to examine the importance of the text and original understanding to sound constitutional decisionmaking. I have already noted that a moderate originalist cannot easily justify the incorporation of principles of equal treatment into the due process clause of the Fifth Amendment or the incorporation of most of the Bill of Rights into the Fourteenth Amendment. But these reciprocal incorporation doctrines are relatively easy to justify on nonoriginalist grounds. They did not require inventing any new rights as such, but only demanded that the federal government respect rights that were properly—from a moderate originalist standpoint—applied to the states, and vice-versa. The main issue facing the Court was whether policies of federalism made it inapposite to impose on one government constraints that the Constitution placed on the other.

The Court incorporated the equal protection clause into the Fifth Amendment in a companion case to *Brown*, with the casual comment that "in view of our decision that the Constitution prohibits the states from maintaining racially segregated public schools, it would be unthinkable that the same Constitution would impose a lesser duty on the Federal Government."[109] I cannot think of a plausible argument against this result—other than the entirely correct originalist observation that it is not supported by even a generous reading of the Fifth Amendment.[110]

The selective incorporation of the Bill of Rights into the Fourteenth Amendment was not as easy, for it implicated venerable traditions of state diversity and autonomy. At first tentatively, then gradually with more authority, the Court proceeded to articulate a doctrine of incorporation[111] that reflected and contributed to a changing conception of federalism. I cannot prove the point, but the mature doctrine, though not necessarily every judicial gloss on particular clauses, seems responsive to current public norms.

Consider a final example. By the early 1970s it was well established that restrictions on access to the franchise violated the equal protection clause unless they served compelling state interests. In *Richardson* v. *Ramirez*[112] the Court refused to apply this doctrine to prohibit the disfranchisement of ex-felons. The Court noted that most nineteenth-century state constitutions denied the vote to ex-felons and that section 2 of the Fourteenth Amendment reduced a state's representation in Congress to the extent that it denied the vote to male citizens over twenty-one except those who had participated in rebellion "or other crime." With only two Justices dissenting on the merits, the Court concluded that "those who framed and adopted the Fourteenth Amendment could not have intended to prohibit outright in section 1 of that Amendment that which was expressly exempted from the lesser sanction of reduced representation imposed by section 2 of the Amendment."[113]

This observation seems correct but beside the point. The adopters would probably have disapproved of all of the Court's modern voting rights decisions, beginning with the *Reapportionment* and *Poll Tax Cases.*[114] But the moral and political principles on which the modern decisions depend apply with equal force to convicted felons. To adhere to the general doctrine but not require the state to justify its discrimination is arbitrary and unprincipled.[115]

In sum, if you consider the evolution of doctrines in just about any extensively adjudicated area of constitutional law—whether "under" the commerce, free speech, due process, or equal protection clauses—explicit reliance on originalist sources has played a very small role compared to the elaboration of the Court's own precedents. It is rather like having a remote ancestor who came over on the Mayflower.

IV. The Ideology of Originalism and the Role of the Written Constitution

It has been said that the written Constitution lies at the core of the American "civil religion."[116] Not only judges and other public officials, but the citizenry at large habitually invoke the Constitution to justify and criticize judicial decisions and government conduct. Belief in the continuing authority of the Document may contribute to a sense of national unity and to law-abiding behavior by officials and citizens. Thus, even though some of our most important constitutional practices are not originalist, the ideology of originalism may evoke concerns for a reader otherwise inclined to accept the practice of nonoriginalist constitutional decisionmaking.

One concern centers on informed consent and legitimacy. It is simply antidemocratic to conceal something as fundamental as the nature of constitutional decisionmaking—especially if concealment is motivated by the fear that the citizenry wouldn't stand for the practice if it knew the truth. If the Court can't admit what it is doing, then it shouldn't do it.

The premise that the government should be open about its practices seems right, as does the implication that the judiciary has not been fully candid about its decisionmaking processes: Although the Supreme Court has often disavowed strict originalism and acknowledged its moderate originalist stance,[117] it has not usually admitted that some of its decisions go still further. Yet it is not plausible that the truth about constitutional adjudication has been successfully hidden in the face of almost two centuries of continual exposés of the Court's infidelities to the original meaning of the Constitution—criticisms levied by dissenting justices, lawyers, politicians, and newspaper editors, as well as scholars. The justices have not pulled the wool over the eyes of anyone who cared to see.

A second concern focuses on the decisionmaking process itself: Even if judicial forays beyond the limits of moderate originalism are justified, perhaps they remain within proper bounds only because they occur within a pervasive originalist ethic. On this view, confining the Court to some form of originalism is rather like setting the speed limit at fifty-five miles an hour to keep cars from going faster than sixty-five.[118]

The felt need to justify decisions by invoking the authority of the Constitution may indeed constrain decisions.[119] I have argued that the constraints imposed by adjudication which treat the text and original understanding as persuasive but not authoritative better serve these ends. Until and unless the Court abandons its moderate originalist pretensions we can only rely on our hunches.

A reader inclined to acknowledge the legitimacy of nonoriginalist decision-making may nonetheless intuit a distinction between supra-constitutional and contra-constitutional decisions, and find it easier to accept decisions that supplement the Constitution than those which ignore or derogate from the document. On this view, the Court's expansive readings of the Bill of Rights and the Fourteenth Amendment are legitimate, whereas the holding in the *Minnesota Mortgage Moratorium Case*[120] may be unacceptable.

The distinction between supplementing and derogating from the Constitution does not readily fit most power-granting provisions. For example, a supra-constitutional expansion of Congress's powers under Article I would be contra-constitutional under the Tenth Amendment. The distinction probably has the most appeal when it is invoked to protect individual rights, where we hope to use the authority of the written document as a defense against the abuse of government power. But I think the hope is illusory. Many of what we have come to regard as the irreducible minima of rights are actually supra-constitutional; almost none of the others are entailed by the text or original understanding. To the extent that institutional safeguards—such as the independence of the judiciary—protect against the contraction of individual rights, they seem to do so whether the Court is engaged in originalist or nonoriginalist adjudication.

I come finally to the central problem posed for nonoriginalist adjudication by the fact of a written Constitution, adopted and amendable by supermajoritarian processes. Even if the adopters have no claim over citizens two centuries later, their Constitution remains the governing document of the United States. It establishes the national government, its branches and offices, its relationship to the states, and the states' relationships among themselves. And although the amending power has been used sparingly, it is a vital element in the constitutional scheme.

Even though nonoriginalist adjudication respects these features of the constitutional order by according presumptive weight to the text and original history,[121] the availability of the amending process specified by Article V poses two distinct challenges to my thesis. First, should not the absence of an amendment be taken as popular consent to the Constitution as written? A short but adequate answer is that if inaction can be read as tacit consent to anything—a problematic assumption in any case—it is to the Court's constitutional decisions, including its nonoriginalist doctrines.

Second, doesn't the possibility of constitutional amendment supplement originalist interpretation so that together they adequately serve the ends of constitutionalism? I think not. First, the formal process of amendment is too cumbersome to bear sole responsibility for constitutional change. The adoption of an amendment usually requires considerable mobilization and intense interest focused on a specific issue. But if constitutional adjudication is to perform the functions described earlier, its growth must proceed more incrementally. And it in fact has: If you consider the development of a line of doctrine, for example under the First Amendment or the equal protection clause, there have been few, if any, obvious focal points for an amendment—either because any particular point would lie such a short distance from antecedent judicial doctrine, or because the language already in the Constitution is capable of encompassing the change.[122]

At least equally important, the formal amendment process is poorly suited to protecting minorities against injuries currently sustained as a result of legislative action or neglect, for the initiation and adoption of an amendment depends on extraordinary action by these same institutions. Imagine, if you will, the fate of an amendment proposed in the mid-1950s to protect Communists or to require school desegregation. Consider the history of the Equal Rights Amendment since it was most recently introduced in Congress in 1970.[123] Of course, if these examples imply that the amending process inadequately protects minority interests, they also highlight a difficulty with judicial intervention. If support cannot be gained for a constitutional amendment, what assurance is there that a judicial decision to the same effect embodies "fundamental values"? But to hold that a purpose of our Constitution is to protect individual rights, whether in Bickel's or Ely's sense, is to concede that there will be times when no majority, let alone a supermajority, will adequately protect those rights.

V. Conclusion

Because moderate originalism and nonoriginalism so often produce identical results, and their practices so often seem identical, it is useful to reiterate their attitudes toward original sources. The moderate originalist acknowledges that the text and original history are often indeterminate and that the elaboration of constitutional doctrine must often proceed by adjudication based on precedent, public values, and the like. But adjudication may not proceed in the absence of authorization from some original source, and when the text or original history speaks clearly it is binding. The nonoriginalist treats the text and original history as presumptively binding and limiting, but as neither a necessary nor sufficient condition for constitutional decision-making.[124]

The argument of Part Two is addressed chiefly to those who would have the judiciary serve the ends of constitutional government by enforcing "fundamental values" or by playing a "representation-reinforcing" role. In one form or another, these alternative views of the judicial function have dominated modern American constitutional theory and practice. The burden of my argument is that nonoriginalist adjudication serves these ends better than either strict or moderate originalism. To put it bluntly, one can better protect fundamental values and the integrity of democratic processes by protecting them than by guessing how other people meant to govern a different society a hundred or more years ago.

Notes

1. John Ely uses the term "interpretivism" to describe essentially the same concept. J. H. Ely, *Democracy and Distrust: A Theory of Judicial Review*, chs. 1–2 (1980). At the cost of proliferating neologisms I have decided to stick with "originalism." Virtually all modes of constitutional decisionmaking, including those endorsed by Professor Ely, require interpretation. The differences lie in what is being interpreted, and I use the term "originalism" to describe the interpretation of text and original history as distinguished, for example, from the interpretation of precedents and social values.

2. Marbury v. Madison, 5 U.S. (1 Cranch) 137 (1803).

3. Id. at 175–80.

4. In a somewhat modified form of the theory, the sovereign people are our contemporaries, and it is their will that officials be bound by the text and original understanding. See pp. 225–26 infra.

5. Home Bldg. & Loan Assoc. v. Blaisdell, 290 U.S. 398, 453 (1934) (Sutherland, J., dissenting).

6. Throughout the article I refer to actual constitutional doctrines to illustrate points and test arguments. This should not obscure my underlying purpose, which is not to describe, explain, or justify the Supreme Court's practices, but rather to argue what the practice should be.

7. For example, on the ground that the law must be available to all citizens. Cf. L. Fuller, *The Morality of Law* 34–35, 43–44 (1964) (exploring through allegory the importance of "a published code declaring rules to be applied in future disputes" and suggesting moral and legal foundations for "formalization of the desideratum of publicity").

8. H. Black, *Handbook on the Construction and Interpretation of the Laws* 20 (1911).

9. 17 U.S. (4 Wheat.) 202–3 (1819).

10. Holmes, The Theory of Interpretation, 12 *Harv. L. Rev.* 417, 419 (1899). Holmes also noted that "the normal speaker of English is merely a special variety, a literary form, so to speak, of our old friend the prudent man. He is external to the particular writer, and a reference to him as the criterion is simply another instance of the externality of the law." Id. at 418.

11. A third circumstance—the occasion for the utterance—may also be relevant. For example, words formally promulgated by a legislature may sometimes have a different meaning than in casual conversation. This may be true of phrases that are used as legal terms of art but also have looser ordinary usages. For example, while "ex post facto law" is often used by laypersons to mean any sort of retroactive decision, a legislature might use it as a legal term of art limited to criminal retroactivity. See, e.g., Calder v. Bull, 3 U.S. (3 Dall.) 386 (1798). But see W. W. Crosskey, *Politics and the Constitution in the History of the United States* ch. XI (1953).

The mere fact that a phrase appears in a formal legal utterance, however, does not entail that it was used as a term of art. This is especially true of constitutional provisions. Although the ratifying conventions that adopted the Constitution and the legislatures that adopted the amendments included many lawyers, the vast majority of participants were laypersons, and it cannot simply be assumed that they used the phrase in its technical sense.

12. See H. L. A. Hart, *The Concept of Law* 125–26 (1961); Curtis, A Better Theory of Legal Interpretation, 3 *Vand. L. Rev.* 407 (1950); Schulman, Reason, Contract, and Law in Labor Relations, 68 *Harv. L. Rev.* 999, 1003–5 (1955).

13. 17 U.S. (4 Wheat.) 316 (1819).

14. Id. at 413.

15. Id. at 414–15.

16. See, e.g., G. Gunther, *Constitutional Law* 1234–59 (9th ed. 1975) (collecting cases); Nimmer, The Meaning of Symbolic Speech under the First Amendment, 21 *U.C.L.A. L. Rev.* 29 (1973).

17. See generally 1 M. Nimmer, *Copyright* sect. 8 (1973).

18. U.S. Const. Art. II, sect. 1, cl. 5.

19. One can imagine a society having our vocabulary and syntax, but in which these provisions would properly be understood to encompass instances which seem absurd to us. For example, the eligibility clause would have quite a different meaning in a culture which supposed that people born by caesarean section were evil, stupid, or dangerous. See P. Brest, *Processes of Constitutional Decisionmaking* 31–32 (1975) (hereafter cited as *Processes*). See generally Fuller, Positivism and Fidelity to Law—A Reply to Professor Hart, 71 *Harv. L. Rev.* 630, 662–64 (1958).

20. See pp. 234–36, 238–39 infra.

21. T. M. Cooley, *A Treatise on the Constitutional Limitations which Rest upon the Legislative Power of the States of the American Union* 124 (Carrington's 8th ed. 1927) (n.p. 1868). See also South Carolina v. United States, 199 U.S. 437, 448 (1895) (Brewer, J.) ("The Constitution is a written instrument. As such, its meaning does not alter. That which it meant when adopted it means now").

One could imagine a version of textualism that incorporates at least evolutionary changes in the meaning of a provision. This approach would typically produce applications consistent with the adopters' intentions on a relatively broad or abstract, rather than a particularistic level. See pp. 236–37 infra. But unless an interpreter were a priori committed to incorporating all such changes, she would need to know both the original meaning of the provision and the history of its evolution, to assure that the present meaning has a "legitimate" genealogy. Without elaborating on the criteria for legitimacy, it might matter who bears primary responsibility for the evolution. For example, assume that "freedom of speech" had a much narrower meaning in the late eighteenth century than it does today, and that "due process" originally dealt solely with the fairness of adjudicatory procedures but now also evokes the notion of so-called "substantive due process." Perhaps a better case can be made for incorporating the former change, which likely reflects a more general change in social and political attitudes, than the change of meaning in a term of art that has been largely (albeit not exclusively) in the control of an elite professional group. Having said this, however, I think that an originalist interpreter would reject evolutionary changes of any sort.

22. See Carter v. Carter Coal Co., 298 U.S. 238 (1936); United States v. E.C. Knight Co., 156 U.S. 1 (1895); Kidd v. Pearson, 128 U.S. 1 (1888).

23. See Champion v. Ames, 188 U.S. 321 (1903). Cf. Ratner, Congressional Power over the Appellate Jurisdiction of the Supreme Court, 109 *U. Pa. L. Rev.* 157, 168–71 (1960) (discussing the eighteenth-century meanings of "exception" and "regulation").

24. See Stern, That Commerce Which Concerns More States Than One, 47 *Harv. L. Rev.* 1335 (1934).

25. See B. Wright, *The Contract Clause of the Constitution* 3–27 (1938).

26. See Note, The Speech and Press Clause of the First Amendment as Ordinary Language, 87 *Harv. L. Rev.* 374 (1973).

27. See Murray v. Hoboken Land & Improvement Co., 59 U.S. (18 How.) 272 (1855); H. Graham, *Everyman's Constitution* 152, 295 (1968); Shattuck, The True Meaning of the Term "Liberty" in Those Clauses in the Federal and State Constitutions Which Protect "Life, Liberty, and Property," 4 *Harv. L. Rev.* 365 (1890); Warren, The New "Liberty" under the Fourteenth Amendment, 39 *Harv. L. Rev.* 431 (1926).

28. Indeed, for an intentionalist, the main function of a written provision is that its adoption provides a moment in time for locating the adopters' intentions: The formalities that enact a particular text into law simultaneously enact the adopters' intentions.

29. The last point may seem incorrect at least with respect to the white 1975 Chevy, which is about as standard as cars can get. But put yourself in the mayor's position and ask just what vehicles you adverted to in the course of adopting the regulation. Did the images of any particular cars pass through your mind? If so, did they include a white '75 Chevy? (After all, it was a blue '73 Ford that you saw at the scene of the accident.) If by chance you imagined a 1975 Chevy, was it the particular car belonging to this citizen? If none of these, then in what sense did you advert to his car?

30. Legal codes commonly stipulate canons for their interpretation. See, e.g., *Pa. Stat. Ann.* tit. 46, sect. 503–601 (Purdon 1969); *National Conference of Commissioners on Uniform State Law, Uniform Statutory Construction Act* (1965).

31. There is nothing paradoxical in these instructions so long as the adopter distinguishes between his interpretive and substantive intentions and intends the interpretive instructions to apply only to the latter.

32. It is possible for a provision to be enacted without a majority of intention-votes either for or against a controverted application. For example, two members of the city council may intend to prohibit mopeds; two may intend not to prohibit them; and the fifth may be utterly indifferent. An intentionalist interpreter should probably treat this as an instance of "intent-not-to": The textual analogue is a proposed text that fails to be adopted for want of a majority.

The institutional intention of a multimember body is fraught with other complexities. For example:

(1) Except for evidentiary purposes, it does not matter whether the fifth council member explicitly withholds his vote in exchange for the other proponents' agreement to his limitations or harbors his limitations in private: There simply are not enough intention-votes for the more far-reaching measure. However, the fact that an intention was not expressed might sometimes cast doubt on the meaning of the other votes, for in some sense nobody knew precisely what issue was being voted on.

(2) Suppose a textualist legal system, in which the city council is divided over the moped issue. When the fifth member threatens to withhold his vote, the two proponents follow either of two strategies: (a) Believing that the fifth member desires some regulation more than he opposes a regulation that prohibits mopeds, they refuse to compromise on a less inclusive regulation. (b) Alternatively, they remind the fifth member that he needs their support on an unrelated measure that means a lot to him. He accedes, and the regulation as adopted prohibits mopeds from using the park. This is a common occurrence in multimember law-making bodies. A textualist judge should—and judges usually do—apply the law as it is written.

Suppose that the identical political dealings occur within an intentionalist legal system, where the issue is not the language of the regulation—in either case it will simply say "no vehicles"—but rather what intentions it will incorporate. By analogy, the intentionalist interpreter must apply the regulation to prohibit mopeds. Although the fifth council member desired to permit mopeds in the park, he alienated his intention-vote in the same way that the lawmaker in a textualist system alienated his actual vote. That is, moved by whatever considerations, he agreed to intend, and hence for these purposes intended, that mopeds be prohibited from the park.

33. But see C. Beard, *An Economic Interpretation of the Constitution of the United States* 73–151 (2d ed. 1935).

34. See S. Padover, *The Living U.S. Constitution* 37–43 (1953).

35. The Twenty-first Amendment was ratified by state conventions.

36. See MacCallum, Legislative Intent, 75 *Yale L. J.* 754, 780–84 (1966).

37. The municipal court judge in our earlier example does not confront the same task. For the mayor probably lacks the authority to determine how his enactments will be interpreted, and is bound by established conventions of interpretations. Not so the adopters of the Constitution. Whether or not they assumed that certain conventions would govern the interpretation of their document, they were not bound by them. A contrary view at least poses serious difficulties for originalist political theory and interpretation.

38. See generally tenBroek, Use by the United States Supreme Court of Extrinsic Aids in Constitutional Construction, 26 *Calif. L. Rev.* 437, 441–43, 448 (1933).

39. G. Endlich, *A Commentary on the Interpretation of Statutes*, sect. 27 (1888); T. Sedgwick, *A Treatise on the Rules Which Govern the Interpretation and Construction of Statutory and Constitutional Law* 194 (1874). See p. 206 supra.

40. But see note 87 infra.

41. On a rather restrictive view, "would have found" means that, although the adopters did not advert to a punishment, they nonetheless intended that it be prohibited.

42. R. Dworkin, *Taking Rights Seriously* 135 (1977).

43. See id. at 134.

44. If you and I purport to agree that "punishment must not be excessive and degrading" but we cannot agree on any applications of this principle, then our agreement probably is illusory.

45. C. Black, *Structure and Relationship in Constitutional Law* 7 (1969).

46. 17 U.S. (4 Wheat.) 316 (1819).

47. C. Black, supra note 45, at 14.

48. 73 U.S. (6 Wall.) 35 (1868).

49. Id. at 44.

50. C. Black, supra note 45, at 29.

51. See generally, G. Gunther, *John Marshall's Defense of McCulloch v. Maryland* (1969).

52. Skinner, Meaning and Understanding in the History of Ideas, 8 *Hist. & Theory* 3 (1969). Skinner is one of several scholars whose work has focused on historiographical problems in political theory. See also J. G. A. Pocock, *Politics, Language, and Time* (1973); Political Thought and Political Action—A Symposium on Quentin Skinner, 2 *Political Theory* 251 (1974). Although these historians are concerned with the intentions of individual theorists rather than with the meaning of a text having thousands of adopters, the originalist constitutional interpreter confronts many of the same difficulties.

53. Skinner, supra note 52, at 6. J. G. A. Pocock has similarly written: "It is part of normal experience to find our thought conditioned by assumptions and paradigms so deep-seated that we did not know they were there until something brought them to the surface; we suspect, if we are historians, that there are others present and operative of which we shall never be aware because they will only be visible from the vantage-points provided by historical moments in the future." J. G. A. Pocock, supra note 52, at 32.

54. See, e.g., C. Fairman, *Reconstruction and Reunion, 1864–88*, pt. 1 (1971); L. Levy, *Origins of the Fifth Amendment* (1968); L. Levy, *Legacy of Suppression* (1960). See also 1 Brant, *The Life of James Madison* (1941–61); G. Wood, *The Creation of the American Republic, 1776–1787* (1969).

55. A recent example is Raoul Berger's *Government by Judiciary: The Transformation of the Fourteenth Amendment* (1977), which argues that almost all of the Supreme Court's decisions under the Fourteenth Amendment are incorrect. See, e.g., Kutler, Raoul Berger's Fourteenth Amendment: A History or Ahistorical, 6 *Hastings Const. L.Q.* 511 (1979); Murphy, Book Review, 87 *Yale L. J.* 1752 (1978); Soifer, Review Essay, 54 *N.Y.U. L. Rev.* 651 (1979). But see Perry, Book Review, 78 *Colum. L. Rev.* 685 (1978).

A somewhat older example is William Winslow Crosskey's two-volume *Politics and the Constitution in the History of the United States* (1953). Based on massive research in eighteenth-century lexicography and politics, Crosskey argued that the received interpretations of various constitutional provisions were incorrect. He urged, for example, that Article I granted Congress plenary power to regulate commerce without regard to whether it was inter- or intra-state; that the Supreme Court was to have general common law-making authority binding on state courts, but that the Court lacked any general authority to review the constitutionality of congressional legislation; and that the "ex post facto" clause included retroactive civil as well as criminal legislation. Although *Politics and the Constitution* received some favorable reviews, see, e.g., Corbin, Book Review, 62 *Yale L. J.* 137 (1953); Sharp, Book Review, 54 *Colum. L. Rev.* 439 (1954); Sholley, Book Review, 49 *Nw.U. L. Rev.* 114 (1954), the dominant reaction was highly critical of Crosskey's historiographic assumptions and methods, see, e.g., Brown, Book Review, 67 *Harv. L. Rev.* 1439 (1954); Goebel, *Ex Parte Clio*, 54 *Colum. L. Rev.* 450 (1954); Hart, Book Review, 67 *Harv. L. Rev.* 1456 (1954).

56. See pp. 236–37, supra.

57. In any case, the adopters' sense of time and change—of the relationship between present and future—was almost certainly not the same as ours, which has been affected by such phenomena as the industrial revolution, theories of evolution, relativity and quantum mechanics, and the possibility of annihilation.

58. See note 87 infra.

59. Or so one might assume from the practice of the time and from the casual references to the practice in the Fifth Amendment. See McGautha v. California, 402 U.S. 183, 226 (1971) (separate opinion of Black, J.).

60. See P. Ariès, *Western Attitudes toward Death* 11–13 (1974); D. Stannard, *The Puritan Way of Death* 93 (1977).

61. See *Death in American Experience* 102 (A. Mack ed. 1973); P. Ariès, supra note 60, at 85–86.

62. See Granucci, "Nor Cruel and Unusual Punishment Inflicted": The Original Meaning, 57 *Calif. L. Rev.* 839 (1969).

63. The First Amendment issue would not be resolved by the (unlikely) conclusion that the adopters intended the free speech clause to apply "absolutely"—unless (equally unlikely) they intended it to apply absolutely to circumstances they could not have envisioned.

64. The problems with coherence lie in the indeterminacy of the level of abstraction on which one characterizes the "event" or "transactions" arguably familiar to the adopters. See p. 231 supra.

65. See Hans-Georg Gadamer, *Truth and Method* (Eng. trans. 1975). See also P. Winch, *The Idea of a Social Science and Its Relation to Philosophy* (1958); Taylor, Interpretation and the Sciences of Man, 25 *Rev. of Metaphysics* 3 (1971). For a sharply critical review of Gadamer's work, see E. D. Hirsch, *Validity in Interpretation* 245 (1967).

66. See p. 242 infra.

67. Compare Roth v. United States, 354 U.S. 476, 508 (Douglas, J. dissenting) with Bork, Neutral Principles and Some First Amendment Problems, 47 *Ind. L. J.* 1 (1971) reprinted in this volume.

68. See, e.g., L. Fuller, supra note 7, at 86–87; Frankfurter, Some Reflections on the Reading of Statutes, 47 *Colum. L. Rev.* 527, 538–39 (1947); Fuller, supra note 19, at 661–66. See also *Processes*, supra note 19, at 41–43.

69. See Moore, The Semantics of Judging (1980) (unpublished manuscript on file at the Boston University Law Review).

70. See J. H. Ely, supra note 1, at chs. 4–6. See also Mills v. Alabama, 384 U.S. 214, 218–20 (1966); Bork, supra note 67, at 212–24.

71. See, e.g., J. S. Mill, *On Liberty* (1859); Richards, Free Speech and Obscenity Law: Toward a Moral Theory of the First Amendment, 123 *U. Pa. L. Rev.* 45 (1974); Scanlon, A Theory of Free Expression, 1 *Phil. & Pub. Affairs* 204 (1972).

72. See generally, *Processes*, supra note 19, at 809–93; Gunther, In Search of Evolving Doctrine on a Changing Court: A Model for a Newer Equal Protection, 86 *Harv. L. Rev.* 1 (1972).

73. See, e.g., Frontiero v. Richardson, 411 U.S. 677 (1973); Bolling v. Sharpe, 347 U.S. 497 (1954); Linde, Judges, Critics, and the Realist Tradition, 82 *Yale L. J.* 227, 233–34 (1972).

74. Compare Justice Black's and Justice Frankfurter's views in Adamson v. California, 332 U.S. 46 (1947). See also L. Levy, The Fourteenth Amendment and the Bill of Rights, in *Judgments: Essays on American Constitutional History* 64 (1972); Fairman, Does the Fourteenth Amendment Incorporate the Bill of Rights? The Original Understanding, 2 *Stan. L. Rev.* 5 (1949); Morrison, Does the Fourteenth Amendment Incorporate the Bill of Rights? The Judicial Interpretation, 2 *Stan. L. Rev.* 140 (1949).

75. See, e.g., R. Berger, supra note 55; C. Fairman, supra note 54, at 1207; H. Graham, supra note 27; Corwin, The Doctrine of Due Process of Law before the Civil War, 24 *Harv. L. Rev.* 366, 460 (1911); Shattuck, supra note 27, at 365 (1891); Warren, supra note 27.

76. See L. Boudin, *Government by Judiciary* (1932); A. Westin, Introduction and Historical Bibliography to C. Beard, *The Supreme Court and the Constitution* (1912); *Judicial Review and the Supreme Court* 1–12 (Levy ed. 1967). But see R. Berger, *Congress v. the Supreme Court* (1969); E. Corwin, *Court over Constitution* (1938); Corwin, Marbury v. Madison and the Doctrine of Judicial Review, 12 *Mich. L. Rev.* 538 (1914); Hart, supra note 55, at 1456. See generally Van Alstyne, A Critical Guide to Marbury v. Madison, 1969 *Duke L. J.* 1.

77. See pp. 248–50 infra.

78. See generally Friedrich, Constitutions and Constitutionalism, in 3 *Ency. Soc. Sci.* 318 (1966); Grey, Constitutionalism: An Analytic Framework, in *Constitutionalism: Nomos* XX 189 (J. R. Pennock and J. W. Chapman eds. 1979).

79. J. Locke's *Second Treatise* (1690) was the classic theoretical formulation and the Declaration of Independence the major political statement.

80. See D. Hume, Of the Original Contract, in *Philosophical Works* 443 (T. Green and T. Gross eds. 1964).

It might be thought that judges and other officials have expressly consented to be bound by the Constitution by virtue of their oath of office "to support this Constitution." U.S. Const. Art VI, sect. 3. But the oath must be understood in the context of two centuries of constitutional decisionmaking. Cf. also Eakin v. Raub, 12 S. & R. 330, 353 (Pa. 1825) (the oath "is designed rather as a test of the political principles of the man, than to bind the officer in the discharge of his duty").

81. Compare H. L. A. Hart, supra note 12, at ch. 6, with Stampp, The Concept of a Perpetual Union, 65 *J. Am. Hist.* 5 (1978).

82. See J. Tussman, *Obligation and the Body Politic* (1960); D. Hume, supra note 80.

83. See generally R. Flathman, *Political Obligation* (1972); C. Pateman, *The Problem of Political Obligation* (1979); Pitkin, Obligation and Consent, 59 *A.P.S.R.* 990 (1965), 60 *A.P.S.R.* 39 (1966).

84. Fiss, The Supreme Court, 1979 Term—Foreword: The Forms of Justice, 93 *Harv. L. Rev.* 1, 38 (1979).

85. A. Bickel, *The Least Dangerous Branch* 24 (1962).

86. Fiss, supra note 84, at 9, 11.

87. This approach may, indeed, partially extricate the originalist from a bind that a naive theory of political obligation puts her in. We saw earlier that a thoroughgoing originalist must adhere to the adopters' interpretive intent and their intended scope of provisions, even if this requires her to be less strictly originalist than she wishes. However, if she chooses to adhere to the adopters' "substantive" intentions, not because they are binding as such, but rather because this practice conduces to the ends of constitutionalism, she is not necessarily bound to adhere to their interpretive intentions.

There is a catch, however. Even—or perhaps especially—the intentionalist interpreter must recognize a difference between the adopters' views on an issue and their intentions for its constitutional resolution. See p. 239–40 supra.

88. United States v. Carolene Prod. Co., 304 U.S. 144 (1938).

89. See A. Bickel, supra note 85, passim.

90. I shall refer to nonoriginalist strategies of constitutional decisionmaking collectively as adjudication.

91. See generally *Processes*, supra note 19, at ch. 12; L. Fuller, *Anatomy of a Law* 84–112 (1968); Simpson, The Common Law and Legal Theory, in *Oxford Essays in Jurisprudence* (2d ed. 1973); Wellington, Common Law Rules and Constitutional Double Standards: Some Notes on Adjudication, 83 *Yale L. J.* 221 (1973). See also Shapiro, Stability and Change in Judicial Decision-Making: Incrementalism or Stare Decisis? 2 *Law in Tran. Q.* 134 (1968).

92. In real life, adjudication is subject to the vicissitudes of stupidity, prejudice, carelessness, and self-interest. A skeptic might in any case question the judges' ability to discern fundamental public or social values. See, e.g., J. H. Ely, supra note 1, at ch. 3. I am not defending adjudication as an intrinsically desirable mode of constitutional decisionmaking, however, but only arguing that it is better than originalism. Judges who avowedly pursue an originalist strategy are, after all, also susceptible to idiocy, corruption, and bias.

93. It is also the method of much statutory interpretation. See generally G. Calabresi, *A Common Law for the Age of Statutes* (1982).

94. See Williams v. Florida, 399 U.S. 78, 122–29 (1970) (Harlan, J., dissenting); National Mut. Ins. Co. v. Tidewater Transfer Co., 337 U.S. 582, 646–55 (1949) (Frankfurter, J., dissenting); Corwin, Judicial Review in Action, 74 *U. Pa. L. Rev.* 639, 659–60 (1926).

95. See Williams v. Florida, 399 U.S. 78, 122–29 (1970) (Harlan, J., dissenting); National Mut. Ins. Co. v. Tidewater Transfer Co., 337 U.S. 582, 646–55 (1949) (Frankfurter, J., dissenting); Corwin, Judicial Review in Action, 74 *U. Pa. L. Rev.* 639, 659–60 (1926).

96. To be sure, no society's moral principles exist in a vacuum, and courts as well as the drafters of a constitution respond to pragmatic concerns. In the area of individual rights, however, the moral dimension is paramount. Moreover, even if the constitutional protection of individual rights must be tempered by pragmatic constraints, there is no justification for binding the present to the compromises of another age.

97. See C. Beard, note 33 supra 73–151. For a useful survey of the controversy over Beard's thesis, see *The Reinterpretation of the American Revolution, 1763–1789*, at 59–67 (J. P. Greene ed. 1968).

98. See R. Berger, supra note 55, at 222–29. The act only prohibited discrimination with respect to the imposition of punishments and the rights to own property, enter into contracts, sue and be sued, and testify in court.

99. See generally G. Myrdal, *An American Dilemma* (1944); C. V. Woodward, *The Strange Career of Jim Crow* (1957); Kelly, The School Desegregation Case, in *Quarrels That Have Shaped the Constitution* 243, 247–49 (Garraty ed. 1964).

100. Brown v. Board of Educ., 347 U.S. 483, 492 (1954).

101. Home Bldg. & Loan Assoc. v. Blaisdell, 290 U.S. 398, 442 (1934).

102. See note 55 supra.

103. E.g., Craig v. Boren, 429 U.S. 190 (1976).

104. E.g., Harper v. Va. Bd. of Elections, 383 U.S. 663 (1966).

105. See Brown v. Board of Educ., 347 U.S. 483, 489–91 (1954); Bickel, The Original Understanding and the Segregation Decision, 69 *Harv. L. Rev.* 1 (1955); Kelly, The Fourteenth Amendment Reconsidered: The Segregation Question, 54 *Mich. L. Rev.* 1049 (1956).

106. Cf. U.S. Const. Amend. XV ("The right of citizens of the United States to vote shall not be denied or abridged . . . on account of race. . . .").

107. See R. Berger, supra note 55.

108. An originalist may wish to insulate a longstanding constitutional doctrine, untenable under originalist canons, by invoking a sort of statute of limitations. For example, Raoul Berger, after arguing that almost every twentieth-century equal protection clause decision is inconsistent with the original understanding of the Fourteenth Amendment, writes: "It would . . . be utterly unrealistic and probably impossible to undo the past in the face of the expectations that the segregation decisions, for example, have aroused in our black citizenry. . . . That is more than the courts should undertake and more, I believe, than the American people would desire." R. Berger, supra note 55, 412–13.

This qualified version of originalism is quite different from nonoriginalism. The nonoriginalist purposely departs from the text and original understanding; the very endurance of deviant doctrine is evidence that it reflects contemporary norms and hence becomes an independent basis for its legitimacy. By contrast, the originalist regrets that the erroneous doctrine ever came into existence and treats it as a burden that must be borne because of the mistakes or willful infidelities of her predecessors. Even if she acknowledges the doctrine, she must not encourage its growth or even strive officiously to sustain it. The originalist program of dealing with an illegitimate doctrine is one of minimum maintenance and, if possible, gradual death. Thus Berger continues: "But to accept thus far accomplished ends is not to condone the continued employment of the unlawful means. . . . [T]he difficulty of a rollback cannot excuse the continuation of such unconstitutional practices. This is not the place to essay the massive task of furnishing a blueprint for a rollback. But the judges might begin by. . . ." Id. at 413.

109. Bolling v. Sharpe, 347 U.S. 497, 500 (1954) (footnotes omitted).

110. See Linde, supra note 73, 233–34.

111. For a brief review of the history of incorporation, see Duncan v. Louisiana, 391 U.S. 145, 147–58 (1968).

112. 418 U.S. 24 (1974).

113. Id. at 43.

114. See Harper v. Virginia Bd. of Elections, 383 U.S. 663 (1966); Reynolds v. Sims, 377 U.S. 533 (1964).

115. Arguably, a moderate originalist would not have had to reach this result. As Justice Marshall wrote in dissent, "Section 2 provides a special remedy . . . to cure a particular form of electoral abuse—the disenfranchisement of the Negro. There is no indication that the framers of the provisions intended that special penalty to be the exclusive remedy for all forms of electoral discrimination. This Court has repeatedly rejected that rationale." 418 U.S. at 74. True, but this presents the greater embarrassment that the adopters of the equal protection clause probably intended it not to encompass voting discrimination at all. See Reynolds v. Sims, 377 U.S. 533, 589–625 (1964) (Harlan, J., dissenting). But see Van Alstyne, The Fourteenth Amendment, the "Right" to Vote, and the Understanding of the Thirty-ninth Congress, 1965 *Sup. Ct. Rev.* 33.

116. Levinson, "The Constitution" in American Civil Religion, 1979 *Sup. Ct. Rev.* 123. See also Lerner, Constitution and Court as Symbols, 46 *Yale L. J.* 1290 (1937).

117. See, e.g., Harper v. Virginia Bd. of Elections, 383 U.S. 663 (1966); Brown v. Board of Educ. 347 U.S. 483 (1954); Home Bldg. & Loan Assoc. v. Blaisdell, 290 U.S. 398 (1934); Weems v. United States, 217 U.S. 349 (1910).

118. Cf. M. Kadish and S. Kadish, *Discretion To Disobey* 45–66, 138–40 (1973) (arguing that in order to keep the jury's power to nullify laws within its proper scope, the jury must not be instructed that it has the power).

This position is not inconsistent with the radical hermeneutic notion that an interpreter can never grasp the original meaning but can only interpret the intervening tradition of changing meanings—the tradition of interpretations of prior interpretations—and that her own interpretation is inextricably bound up with her preconceptions. See pp. 240–41 supra. One might accept this and yet conclude that the best constitutional decisions will emerge from a process in which the interpreter self-consciously focuses on the original sources.

119. See, e.g., R. Wasserstrom, *The Judicial Decision* 25–30 (1961). See generally *Processes*, supra note 19, at 1086–98.

120. Home Bldg. & Loan Assoc. v. Blaisdell, 290 U.S. 398 (1934).

121. Factors besides perceived changes in social values—such as stability, continuity, and respect for democratic decisions—bear on the circumstances in which the presumption may be overcome. See G. Calabresi, supra note 93.

122. Of course, the broader one's view of what is fairly encompassed by the text and original understanding, the more change moderate originalism can accommodate and the less persuasive this point becomes as an argument for nonoriginalist adjudication.

123. Proposals for an equal rights amendment were unsuccessfully introduced as early as 1923. See Brown, Emerson, Falk, and Friedman, The Equal Rights Amendment: A Constitutional Basis for Equal Rights for Women, 80 *Yale L. J.* 871, 886–87 (1971).

124. I have focused on constitutional adjudication designed to protect individual rights and the integrity of majoritarian processes. These are not the only ends of constitutionalism, however, and adjudication is not the only method of constitutional decisionmaking. The bulk of the written Constitution, as its name implies, is constitutive—establishing and marking the boundaries of government entities and determining how the branches of the federal government shall be staffed. And if the judiciary has borne primary responsibility for the development of constitutional liberties, their protection—as well as the implementation of other constitutional norms—is no less the business of other agencies. How, then, does the thesis of this article bear on these different sorts of constitutional decisionmaking?

As a descriptive matter, constitutional decisionmaking concerning the allocation of powers within the national government and between nation and states has not been particularly faithful to the text and original understanding of the Constitution. Changes in the relations between the federal Executive and Congress, and between national and state governments, have occurred primarily through the assertion of power followed by counterassertion or acquiescence, with political factors serving a function somewhat akin to the constraints of adjudication. Analytically and normatively, I see no essential differences among the various areas of constitutional concern that would automatically insulate any of them from the possibility of nonoriginalist decision-making. This is not to say that interests such as certainty and stability do not make some deviations from the text almost unthinkable: It is hard to imagine Congress or the Court changing the number of Senators allocated to each State other than by constitutional amendment. But even this cannot be determined a priori by any timeless principle. It seems both simpler and more accurate to say that there are some instances in which the nonoriginalist presumption of fidelity to the text and original understanding is very unlikely to be rebutted.

Stare Decisis
and Constitutional Adjudication

◆

═══
═══

◆

HENRY PAUL MONAGHAN

DESPITE ENDLESS LITERATURE urging that constitutional adjudication be severed from explorations into the understandings at the creation of the Constitution, original understanding continues to play a prominent role in the Supreme Court's jurisprudence.[1] For the Court, originalism[2] seemingly provides a legitimate ground for decisionmaking; for the people, it provides assurances against judicial usurpation of power properly belonging to other branches of government, or retained by the people themselves.

But difficulties with originalism emerge once the existing constitutional order is actually examined. The Supreme Court's repeated invocations of the Framers' understanding notwithstanding, a significant portion of our constitutional order cannot reasonably be reconciled with original understanding. For example, it is now increasingly acknowledged "that those who wrote and ratified the Fourteenth Amendment believed that it would permit racial segregation in public schools."[3] Consequently, unless they are willing to see it overruled, *Brown* v. *Board of Education*[4] presents deep difficulties for those who insist upon original understanding as the only legitimate canon for constitutional adjudication.

Brown will not be overruled, just as the New Deal and the administrative state, both developments whose constitutionality—from an originalist's perspective—is also highly questionable, will not be declared unlawful. Thus, the originalist confronts a fundamental difficulty. Can originalism make sense out of a constitutional order that varies significantly from its core legitimating principle but that cannot be judicially overruled in the name of a return to original understanding? This essay considers whether stare decisis can provide an acceptable ground for preserving the existing constitutional edifice without simultaneously licensing further departures from original understanding.

Part I of this essay defends the claim that there have been significant and irreversible departures from original understanding. In Part II, the essay begins exploring stare decisis as a way of resolving the normative implications of originalism's inability to provide a descriptively plausible account of much of the present constitutional order. Part II argues that originalists must acknowledge that in the process of constitutional adjudication stare decisis plays a very large role. Next, Parts III and IV examine the possible sources and content of a principle that would privilege precedent above original understanding as a rule of decision in constitutional adjudication. Finally, in Parts V and VI, the essay returns to originalism. These parts ask what remains of originalism's normative appeal if stare decisis is invoked to explain and legitimate so much constitutional change. Indeed, what remains of the fundamental idea of a written constitution? In sum, does our Bicentennial Constitution require that we rethink the very meaning of a written constitution? I am forced to conclude that the original understanding must give way in the face of transformative or longstanding precedent, a conclusion that in turn may make inevitable the unsettling acknowledgment that originalism and stare decisis themselves are but two among several means of maintaining political stability and continuity in society.

I. Originalism and Its Descriptive Inadequacy

A. A Brief Exegesis of Originalism[5]

Originalism insists that at a given point in time "We the People of the United States" can "ordain and establish" a fundamental and lasting framework of government and that the crucial task in any system of constitutional adjudication is to maintain that fundamental law. For originalists, the Constitution is the supreme law; as such, it must bind judges as well as other government officials.[6] Thus, a necessary bond exists between legitimate judicial decision-making and maintaining the original understanding.

The most frequent attacks on originalism maintain that the theory fails because, as applied to a two hundred year old document, the concept lacks a coherent methodology.[7] Such an attack raises the problem of whose intent is relevant and asks if it is realistic to hope to divine an accurate and helpful version of that intent. This is a powerful criticism, and at a minimum makes clear that originalists should not seek any subjective understanding of original intent, such as attempting to aggregate the subjective preferences held by the

Framers at the Constitutional Convention. Such "intentionalist" views, apparently held by some originalists,[8] are an easy mark for most critics of originalism.[9] But the Framers themselves did not intend that their secret deliberations at the Constitutional Convention would provide authoritative guidance;[10] moreover, the goal of accurately aggregating the preferences of so many persons is an unrealistic one.[11] But the critics are wrong in believing that in discrediting intentionalism, they discredit originalism.[12] The relevant inquiry must focus on the *public* understanding of the language when the Constitution was developed.[13] Hamilton put it well: "whatever may have been the intention of the framers of a constitution, or of a law, that intention is to be sought for in the instrument itself, according to the usual & established rules of construction."[14] Thus, while the term original intent is commonly used, original understanding better conveys the public dimensions of originalism.

The level at which the original understanding is generalized is decisive in any theory of originalism. If it is not to be vacuous, originalism must refer to an understanding concrete enough to provide a real and constraining guidance. Moreover, if we want the American Constitution—not some other constitution[15]—to perform the function that the Founders envisaged, the original understanding must be understood in a certain way: the American Constitution was not designed to contain a plethora of dynamic provisions whose meanings evolve and change over time.[16] Likewise, we must recognize that in interpreting the original understanding we cannot ignore the background assumptions as to how the constitutional system would work in practice. Judge Frank Easterbrook thoughtfully insists that "maintaining the line between the expected consequences of a rule and the contents of the rule itself is one of the most delicate tasks of the judicial system."[17] While this general distinction may apply to the Constitution, the crucial point is that Judge Easterbrook's distinction is far softer than he supposes if one recognizes that "purpose" plays an important role in defining the content of the enacted norm. To know what the norm "means," one must resort to inquiries about purpose and expected consequences.

Of course, arguments of this nature necessarily are anchored in a belief that we can know a good deal—not everything, but a good deal that counts—about the original understanding of those who ratified the 1789 Constitution (and the Civil War amendments). Naturally, in any effort to reclaim it, we necessarily "reshap[e] the past [because] no recognized vestige is devoid of present intentions."[18] But even in this era of deconstruction and other reader-centered theories of literary interpretation, observations of that character seem to me to have little purchase in the context of constitutional adjudication. To say that we must necessarily reshape the past does not establish a very different type of claim: that in trying to understand the past we must inexorably, totally, or even substantially reshape it.

B. *The Descriptive Inadequacies of Originalism*

My interest in stare decisis is driven by an important descriptive claim: insistence upon original intent as the only legitimate standard for judicial decisionmaking entails a massive repudiation of the present constitutional order. This claim needs defense. Perhaps no reader will find persuasive all the claims of original understanding here tendered, and I confess to being of two minds about several of the examples cited. The relevant concern, however, is the weight of the general argument, not the validity of each supporting item. And the general argument is that much of the existing constitutional order is at variance with what we know of the original understanding.

In some areas, the Court itself can be said to have been the immediate cause of the departure from original understanding. *Brown* and *Roe* v. *Wade*[19] are salient examples. More frequently, the Court has simply validated departures from original understanding initiated by the political branches. Nonetheless, these two situations possess an important commonality: the Court has not deemed the subjects under consideration to be beyond judicial cognizance.[20] Rather, the Court has purported to legitimate the changes; and with some notable exceptions,[21] this legitimation has been cast in terms of consistency with original understanding.[22]

1. *Civil Liberties*

For most commentators, the civil liberties area has been the battleground on which the original understanding debate has been fought. *Bowers* v. *Hardwick*[23] can be understood to reassert some limitations of the constitutional text against further judicial creation of nontextual rights. Even so, no substantial argument is needed to show that major decisional lines are vulnerable to serious original understanding challenge.

Perhaps the most noteworthy claim concerns the school desegregation cases. For me, originalism's difficulties are intractable here: no satisfying conception of originalism seems capable of accounting for *Brown*. *Brown*'s discussion of the differences between education in 1868 and in 1954[24] is unpersuasive; public schooling was a practice clearly understood at the time and it is conceded that the claim that the practice was invalid would have been *rejected* by those who framed/ratified the Fourteenth Amendment.[25] In such a case, the practice does not become constitutionally invalid with the passage of time on the premise that its significance or meaning, not the meaning of the amendment, has changed over time.[26] And the argument that the Framers had two relevant and contradictory sets of intentions[27] lacks any historical foundation.

In addition to *Brown*, it seems evident that the abortion cases,[28] the reapportionment cases,[29] and the sex discrimination cases[30] are also inconsistent with any constrained conception of the original understanding.[31]

Nor is that the end of the difficulties. Even on the assumption, itself controversial, that the Fourteenth Amendment was intended to make the Bill of Rights applicable to the states,[32] much of the actual judicial development of the Bill of Rights has taken very little from original understanding. Here in particular, "the focus of professional and judicial attention [has shifted] from the . . . text and history to the . . . norm[s] to be derived by analysis and synthesis of the judicial precedents."[33] The result has been the adoption of the substance, as well as the method, of common-law adjudication: some form of interest balancing, with the constitutional guarantees treated simply as one of the interests at stake and assessed in functional rather than historical terms.[34] "The fact is," as the Court put it very recently, "that, regardless of the terminology used, the precise content of most of the Constitution's civil-liberties guarantees rests upon an assessment of what accommodation between governmental need and individual freedom is reasonable. . . ."[35] It may be, as Dean Harry Wellington says, that "the universal practice of courts, when engaged in adjudication, is to acknowledge the power of the relevant text."[36] Yet, given existing interpretations of our civil liberties guarantees, precisely what does it mean to assert that there is a textual Bill of Rights, apart from fixing some outer perimeter limiting judicial decisionmaking?

2. Structure and Relationship

Originalism's major inability to account persuasively for much that is central in the current constitutional order reappears when attention is focused upon the central structural aspects of the Constitution. Here, "it has become increasingly difficult to relate governmental structures and powers to the original Constitution."[37] For our purpose, the central institutional arrangements of the 1789 Constitution were state-centered federalism[38] and congressionally centered national government.[39] The New Deal transformed this entire system by putting pressure on a wide range of constitutional provisions that embodied the assumptions of the old order. Because they seldom have occasion to consider the changes in their entirety, lawyers often fail to appreciate that in virtually every instance the imperatives of the new administrative state triumphed over the apparently limiting constitutional provisions.

a. Federalism. An introduction to the constitutional status of the modern administrative state begins with the problem of federalism. Here the received doctrine is to deny that any transformation has occurred.[40] The scope of national regulatory power finally sustained by the Supreme Court in the late 1930s is said to find firm roots in 1789 understandings and early Marshall Court decisions construing the necessary and proper and commerce clauses, and the contrary intervening case law is dismissed as in error.[41] Indeed, this proposition unites constitutional theorists who otherwise have little in common. For example, Attorney General Meese states: "Similarly, the decisions of the New Deal and beyond that freed Congress to regulate commerce and enact a plethora of social legislation were not judicial adaptations of the

Constitution to new realities. They were in fact removals of encrustations of earlier courts that had strayed from the original intent of the Framers regarding the power of the legislature to make policy."[42] These views are completely endorsed by leading nonoriginalist commentators.[43]

This originalist justification for the New Deal is unconvincing.[44] Admittedly, the Framers were nationally oriented, particularly in foreign affairs. But it is vital not to exaggerate their nationalism, a common mistake caused by focusing on a few Framers such as Hamilton and Washington, and assuming not only that they would be right at home in the modern administrative state but, more important, that they were representative of the majority of those who ratified the Constitution.[45] Circa 1789, the internal orientation of the American people was state-centered to a degree completely lost to modern constitutional law scholars. There is no historical basis for the proposition that the founding generation understood the power to regulate commerce "among the several states" to grant Congress unlimited power to regulate everything and anything it wished.[46] The core idea of a national government of limited powers is completely inconsistent with this idea.

Nor is the foregoing analysis altered if Chief Justice Marshall is thought to have substantially embodied the views of the ratifying generation. In 1824, in *Gibbons* v. *Ogden*, Chief Justice Marshall stated that Congress could regulate what "affected commerce."[47] We may assume that this standard was meant in an economic sense and that it reflected the original understanding,[48] although it is not clear that Congress was intended to have power to do much more than to prevent parochial and restrictive state trade barriers.[49] But it is beyond dispute that this generation did *not* believe that everything affected commerce in a constitutionally relevant sense. Indeed, *Gibbons* itself referred to the "purely internal commerce"[50] of the states, and it cannot be asserted credibly that in 1789 (or in 1824) anyone thought that the "affecting commerce" rationale authorized direct federal regulation of the employer-employee relationship or of agricultural production. Certainly one *could* intend "affecting commerce" to have the limitless scope of its present construction, but a historically centered version of originalism demands that we look beyond *possible* constructions to the understanding—including the intended effects—at the creation.

I doubt whether any acceptable conception of original understanding can provide a satisfactory account of the New Deal. Moreover, in principle the question whether courts should keep out of federalism controversies given the "political safeguards of federalism,"[51] is quite different from whether the Court should have pronounced these exercises of national regulatory authority consistent with original understanding. At most, the political safeguards argument makes a case for judicial declarations of nonjusticiability.[52] It does not support affirmative judicial declarations that congressional legislation is consistent with the original constitutional design.[53]

The Supreme Court decisions sustaining New Deal regulatory claims[54] constitute an important phase in the final victory of nation-centered federalism against the nineteenth-century paradigms[55] of state-centered federalism. The modern exercises of the national taxing and spending powers cement that victory.[56] These include not simply Congress's well-known ability to extract state compliance with national policy objectives through conditional spending,[57] but also the various objects and expansive scale of modern federal spending "for the . . . general welfare."[58] For example, federal spending has resulted in extensive federally financed, regulated, or operated programs in education, medicine and public health, local law enforcement, crop control, social security, and welfare.[59] The scale of this spending reflects a fundamental transformation in the federal/state balance.[60] Moreover, the very transfer of money from the national government to state governments and their political subdivisions[61] undercuts the historical fiscal premises of 1789 federalism, which presupposed a "clear separation between state and federal governments, with each provided with the sources of public revenue for the support of functions assigned to it."[62]

The eclipse of the constitutional theory of "Our Federalism"[63] circa 1789 can be viewed in two ways.[64] One can emphasize the collapse of the eighteenth-century concept of a national government of limited powers. Madison's assurance that the powers of the new national government would be "few and defined [while] [t]hose which are to remain in the State governments are numerous and indefinite"[65] no longer casts even a faint shadow, and originalists cannot ignore the current legal hegemony of the national government.[66] An alternative approach is to see the new federalism not in terms of enlarged national powers, but of enlarged national responsibilities. The Constitution of 1789 emerged toward the end of an agricultural age, at only the very beginning of a manufacturing one. One could ask: In 1789, what internal tasks were contemplated for the new national government? As already described, they included only the regulation of commerce "among the several States" and other commerce-centered activities in a largely nonindustrial economy. While no one foresaw the massive scale of federal intervention, or the various federal attempts to alleviate the market and nonmarket consequences of the new industrial and postindustrial order, perhaps all this national activity can be squared with original understanding through a "changed circumstances" argument.[67] Such an argument differs from the one that must be rejected in *Brown* because the fundamental premise here—the structure of the nation's economy—had changed. But what is the content of a theory of original understanding that warrants national concern with social welfare, education, health and medical research, and local political corruption, all matters understood by the Framers, but probably not included as objectives within the federal government's spending powers?[68] Defense of the national *regulatory* state through a changed circumstances argument is one thing; defense of the national *welfare state* quite another.[69]

b. Separation of Powers. More striking than the transformation in Our Federalism is the extent to which the 1789 version of separation of powers gave way to the necessities of the new administrative and bureaucratic order.[70] The best-known casualty here is the Lockean axiom that the grant of legislative power is only to make laws, not to make other legislators,[71] and thus Congress cannot delegate legislative power.[72] Likewise, the President's executive power and his corresponding duty to "take care that the laws be faithfully executed"[73] were weakened in principle by the rise of the independent regulatory agencies.[74] Perhaps even more important, though little appreciated, is the demise of the apparent premise of several constitutional provisions—Article III, the due process clause, and the jury trial provisions of the Sixth and Seventh Amendments—that most adjudication implementing national regulatory policy would occur before judicial tribunals.[75] This premise failed to prevent extensive administrative determination of the rights and duties created by the modern state.[76] Finally, the transformation extends to the administrative state's enormous and insatiable appetite for information. The appetite rages unrestrained by the constitutional prohibitions against unreasonable searches and seizures and self-incrimination.[77]

c. The Presidency. The transformation of the Constitution of 1789 is seen nowhere more clearly than in the modern Presidency. One hundred years ago, Woodrow Wilson published *Congressional Government*,[78] and the title made the centrally relevant point: national government was congressional government, or more precisely, government by the chairmen of the standing committees of Congress.[79] Wilson put aside the President with the dismissive observation that his "business . . . occasionally great, is usually not much above routine."[80] Such a description of the federal government at least could be defended until the New Deal. But crucial and irrevocable changes began at that point: the consolidation of power in the national government served as the predicate for the consolidation of power within the Presidency. And with national governmental hegemony came the Executive Office of the President, now a significant bureaucracy and an institution that itself marks the vast gulf between 1789 and 1988.[81] Of course, this institutional change was an administrative imperative if the President (or, more accurately, the Executive Office) was to exercise effectively vast new powers. Presidential power was further enhanced as the result of the Second World War and the emergence of the United States as a world leader.[82]

There is no need to labor the familiar: the President today plays a dominant role in the national government completely beyond the understanding in 1789. Perhaps modern Presidents are bound to fail in their ambitious new role; perhaps of necessity they generate unfulfillable expectations.[83] But for us it is the very existence of the new presidential role that is of interest. Even acknowledging that the President's veto power contemplated some policy-making role for the Chief Executive,[84] the current "imperial"

Presidency is characterized by its "appropriation . . . of powers reserved by the Constitution and by long historical practice to Congress."[85] The Constitution invests the President with "the executive Power,"[86] but modern presidents are judged by the success of their "legislative" programs. Indeed, so deeply ingrained is this feature that constantly we hear worries about this or that incident impairing the President's—not Congress's—power to govern.[87] Wholly unnoticed by such commentary is the fact that the Constitution of 1789 did not give governing power to the President.[88]

Presidential ascendancy has been assisted by a series of fundamental, and still ongoing, changes in the mode of Presidential selection. The commonplace observation that, from its inception, the electoral system failed to function as intended has uncommon consequences for originalists.[89] For many, the 1789 design reflected the then still powerful belief that political leadership was properly a function of character, and the process specified in Article II was designed to implement that view.[90] Others believed that (after Washington) the electoral vote would seldom succeed in such an effort; for them, the electoral vote would simply mark the end of the nomination process, with the actual election taking place in the House.[91] But in both views the election of the President was not designed to vest him with any popular mandate. By contrast, the modern Presidency draws powerful support from the President's claim that by virtue of his election he has received precisely such a mandate. With the decline of the role of political parties in the national election, the advent of the direct primary, and the ever increasing impact of television, we are now firmly in the grip of the plebiscitary presidency.[92] Indeed, "the president [has] finally approached an unmediated relationship with the masses,"[93] precisely what was not intended by the 1789 Constitution. And as a result of this transformation the congressional role in the process of government has been rendered so problematic that Presidents feel free to appeal to the people (not to mention foreign governments) to fund foreign policy initiatives that Congress has refused to fund.[94]

The Court has yet to validate explicitly the Presidency's expansive accumulation of power. Frequently, the Court has declared challenges to the scope of presidential power nonjusticiable,[95] and on occasion it even has decided cases on the merits against the President.[96] The Court has, however, affirmatively contributed to enlarged presidential powers: the Presidency has been a major beneficiary of the legitimation of the vast, open-ended delegations of legislative power,[97] and the Court has employed broad language to describe presidential authority in foreign affairs.[98] Moreover, the Court has recently indicated that it can be quite deferential when considering presidential interpretations of law and consequent exercises of power.[99] If ever forced to take a stand, it seems unlikely that the Court would act to constrain the powers of the Presidency in any significant way.

The transfer of power to the Presidency may be important to the originalist in yet another way. The tripartite framework for the federal government created by the Framers contemplated a Presidency balanced, if not dominated, by Congress. This intended distribution of power infuses important principles of separation of power with the imprimatur of the Framers. But it may be critical to understand that these principles of separation of power are premised on a conception of the interaction between the Presidency and Congress that is no longer descriptively accurate. With the failure of the fundamental premise, the originalist must ask if the principles derived from that premise must fail as well.[100] And if they do, what is the source and content of any new principles that should be substituted?

In sum, no acceptable version of original understanding theory can yield a convincing descriptive account of the major features of our "Bicentennial Constitution": nontextual guarantees of civil liberties; a powerful, presidentially centered national government; a huge administrative apparatus: and national responsibility for what had long been conceived of either as local responsibilities or as not the responsibility of government at all. Together these features necessarily pose a formidable challenge to originalists, who cannot reasonably argue that these transformative changes should now be judicially overthrown.

II. *Stare Decisis and Constitutional Change*

ONE COULD respond to this originalist critique of our present constitutional order, and legitimate the transformative changes experienced by that order, with a number of arguments. For example, an originalist could treat any one—or all—of the developments described above as entirely unproblematic by formulating the relevant original understanding at a very high degree of generality.[101] In question-begging fashion one might even point to the changes themselves as requiring precisely that approach. This approach does have the appealing advantage of dissolving at least most of the supposed conflict between the original understanding and our existing constitutional order.[102]

Alternatively, one could deny that original understanding should play any decisive role in constitutional adjudication. Typically, this claim has been advanced to support judicial supplements to textually based civil liberties.[103] If invoked to validate the massive transformations heretofore described, this approach can only mean that original understanding rightly plays only a marginal role in constitutional adjudication. Yet again, one could acknowledge that some of these developments, such as the rise of the New Deal, did fundamentally transform the constitutional order, but attempt to justify them as legitimate constitutional "amendments," even though the amendments occurred outside the framework prescribed by Article V.[104]

For me, each of these approaches presents intractable difficulties, the development of which are beyond my purpose in this essay. But if one accepts the argument that none of the approaches legitimates our constitutional order, one must consider a different inquiry. While most, if not all, of the Supreme Court's decisions noted above are highly suspect, it seems almost unquestionable that these decisions are now beyond judicial recall. This raises questions about whether anything meaningful can be said for—and about—a principled role for stare decisis in constitutional adjudication. Should the Court adhere to a prior controlling decision even though a majority of the Court now believes the precedent to be inconsistent with original understanding (or wrong on some other theory of what constitutes appropriate criteria for constitutional adjudication)? Put differently, for judges concerned with the process of constitutional adjudication, can stare decisis properly provide a sufficient justification for a result?[105] In addition, if stare decisis can legitimately be invoked to insulate the major underpinnings of the existing order, what is now appropriately left for the role of original understanding?

A. *The Apparent Failure of Stare Decisis*

Resort to stare decisis presents formidable problems. In the common law area, the doctrine has been the target of unremitting attack throughout this century.[106] These attacks have generated an attitude that the law must be argued for, with the inevitable result that any simple justificatory appeal to authority possesses little innate attractiveness.[107] If stare decisis cannot maintain a powerful grip on the common-law system that spawned it, it is not surprising that it appears to have fared still worse in the highly charged atmosphere of constitutional adjudication.[108] There the conventional wisdom is that stare decisis should and does have only limited application.[109] The prescriptive side of this claim is usually rested on the Brandeisian assertion that "correction through legislative action is practically impossible."[110] But the argument that judicial change is the only possible means to achieve social improvement is badly overstated. Its undifferentiating character is apparent—no distinction is made among constitutional provisions, and certain applications of some are plainly less important than those of others.[111] More significantly, the argument's central factual premise is overdrawn, at least regarding the decisions to which current commentators seem most anxious to deny binding authority: those *rejecting* autonomy or equality claims. In almost every instance, the results (if not the decisions) can be "overruled" by statute.[112]

Descriptively, however, the conventional wisdom seems to rest on firmer ground.[113] *Garcia* v. *San Antonio Metropolitan Transit Authority*[114] is only the most dramatic illustration of the view held by some commentators[115] that the Supreme Court is largely unconstrained by its own precedents. In *Garcia*, a five-to-four majority overruled its well-known five-to-four majority decision rendered one decade earlier in *National League of Cities* v. *Usery*,[116] which in turn had overruled a six-to-two decision itself only eight years old.[117] The *Garcia* majority brushed aside any supposed precedential compulsion in the penultimate paragraph of a lengthy opinion,[118] and at least two dissenting justices said that *Garcia* should be overruled at the first opportunity.[119] Decisions like *Garcia* have led thoughtful commentators to assert that constitutional law would be better off rid of any formal legal concept of stare decisis.[120] To these commentators it would come as no surprise that in four cases during the last few days of its 1986 Term the Court overruled prior decisions,[121] and in only one of these did it purport to give any serious attention to the question of stare decisis.[122]

Nonetheless, some important and controversial civil liberties cases are still decided on the basis of prior authority and, perhaps, secure acceptance on that basis.[123] But this fact further diminishes the appeal of decisions resting on stare decisis. Because a coherent rationale for the intermittent invocation of stare decisis has not been forthcoming, the impression is created that the doctrine is invoked only as a mask hiding other considerations. As a result, stare decisis seemingly operates with the randomness of a lightning bolt: on occasion it may strike, but when and where can be known only after the fact. A satisfactory theory of constitutional adjudication requires more than that.

B. The Strengths of Stare Decisis

1. Agenda Limitation

Closer examination of the descriptive side of the conventional wisdom shows that, at least from an originalist's perspective, it is deeply wrong: *stare decisis plays a very large role in constitutional law.* Many constitutional issues are so far settled that they are simply off the agenda. For example, it seems clear that under the 1789 Constitution only metal could constitute legal tender.[124] In fact, until driven to do so by the exigencies of the Civil War, the national government never attempted to impart that quality to paper. When the government did take this step the result was a series of post–Civil War decisions, collectively known as the Legal Tender Cases.[125] While they "have [now] disappeared below the surface of American constitutional law . . . [m]easured by the intensity of the public debate at the time, [these cases raised] one of the leading constitutional controversies in American history."[126] Following this painful conflict and one of the most widely criticized overrulings of precedent,[127] use of paper money as legal tender was sustained.[128] Over one hundred years later, in our age of checks, credit cards, and electronic banking, the issue is off the agenda: no Supreme Court would now reexamine the merits, no matter how closely wedded it was to original intent theory and no matter how certain it was of its predecessor's error.

The Fourteenth Amendment provides other examples. Could the Court now be persuaded even to consider the view that section 1 of the Fourteenth

Amendment was intended to reach only "civil"[129]—not social and political—rights and therefore that *Brown* and the reapportionment decisions must be repudiated? What of the objection that the Fourteenth Amendment is itself not law at all? Professor Bruce Ackerman argues that this amendment was adopted in an extra-constitutional manner.[130] If the rebellious states possessed sufficient political capacity to ratify the Thirteenth Amendment, how could they legitimately be excluded from the process of formulating the Fourteenth Amendment, asks Professor Ackerman? For many (though not for Professor Ackerman) the force of this reasoning, if accepted, would necessarily mean that the amendment is not validly part of the Constitution. Can it seriously be thought that the Supreme Court would fairly consider such a claim?

Finally, many of the fundamental transformations in our governmental structure legitimated by the Supreme Court in this century are unquestionably above challenge. Is it conceivable that the Court would outlaw the administrative state? Certainly administrative legislation, in some substantial form, is a permanent feature of our constitutional order. And while the Court may or may not honor *Garcia* in the future, it cannot be doubted that as a constitutional matter the federal government's regulatory power is more aptly described as limitless than limited. The constitutional law, if not the political dimensions of the New Deal, is here to stay.

The operation of stare decisis in these contexts is agenda limiting in nature. The Court could not fairly look at these issues *res nova*. Regardless of whether the Court thought these issues rightly decided, consciously or unconsciously any challenge would be screened out *in limine*. History counts.[131] The only significant question is how.

Were the official theory that stare decisis has no formal role to play in constitutional adjudication, the pressure on originalism would be unremitting—and distorting. Standing alone, originalism can absorb transforming historical reality in only two ways: original understanding simply could be misstated, or it can be stated at such a level of generality that it becomes operationally empty. Either approach drains originalism of integrity. Thus, the important question is how stare decisis is to count, not so much in understanding the present, but in guiding action in the future.

2. Contested Matters

Many constitutional issues currently remain contested despite relevant, if not definitive, Supreme Court pronouncements regarding the subject. In the absence of those factors that coalesce to remove an issue from the agenda, judicial closure seems impossible. Sometimes the Court's continuing divisions simply mirror deep public rifts (abortion, busing), sometimes not (*National League of Cities* and *Garcia*, search and seizure). Of course, as the history of racial segregation itself shows, no sharp distinction can be made between the agenda-limitation and contested-matters categories: the categories are only relatively stable points on a continuum, issues move between them, and many matters not only fall in between the two points but at different times can be at different ends of the continuum.[132] Nonetheless, certain issues clearly fall within the contested category.[133]

At this juncture the pertinent question is whether stare decisis should have any substantial role in cases where the issues remain contested. Here originalists are divided, but many seem to assume that a negative answer is required.[134] Recently, however, interest has surfaced for a potentially stronger role for stare decisis in this area. This interest has been spurred on by the possibility that the Court might soon be composed of a majority who are of the view that *Roe* v. *Wade*,[135] considered *res nova*, is insupportable. The very problematic congressional efforts to "overrule" that decision have now visibly waned. But what of an attack from within the Court itself? One decade after *Roe*, a majority of the Court invoked stare decisis to reject such a challenge: "And arguments continue to be made, in these cases as well, that we erred in interpreting the Constitution. Nonetheless, the doctrine of *stare decisis*, while perhaps never entirely persuasive on a constitutional question, is a doctrine that demands respect in a society governed by the rule of law. We respect it today, and reaffirm *Roe* v. Wade."[136] Quite plainly, the Court does not purport simply to reexamine and revalidate *Roe*. Rather, stare decisis is invoked as a powerful justification for adherence to the decision. This is made even clearer by an accompanying footnote in which the Court adds two "especially compelling reasons": first, "that case was considered with special care," and second, "the Court repeatedly and consistently has accepted [*Roe*'s] basic principle."[137] Three dissenting justices discounted the importance of stare decisis, but they stopped short of calling for *Roe*'s overruling.[138] More recently, however, while the Court rejected efforts by the Solicitor General to have *Roe* overruled, Justice White and Chief Justice Rehnquist expressly issued such a call.[139]

Suppose that the Court were composed of a solid majority who believe that *Roe* was incorrectly decided. What *should* happen? Whether *Roe* should be overruled is a question not reducible to whether *Roe* was decided correctly.[140] One can imagine the Court drawing precisely such a distinction and refusing to overrule *Roe*. Of course, to make this distinction one needs a general theory of constitutional interpretation that includes some account of precedent. Why, for example, is it proper to overrule *National League of Cities*, *Kentucky* v. *Dennison*,[141] and *General Motors Corp.* v. *Washington*,[142] but not *Roe*?[143] Once we acknowledge *some* role for stare decisis in constitutional adjudication—in the agenda-limitation context—it becomes more plausible for an originalist to consider a more generalized role for stare decisis in constitutional adjudication. The problem then becomes explicating that role.

III. Notes Toward a Theory of Stare Decisis: Justification

PRECEDENT IS, of course, part of our understanding of what law is. But that acknowledgment does not resolve the question why it plays such an important role. Generally, judicial adherence to precedent is defended by pointing to the important values in decisionmaking that are promoted thereby: consistency, coherence, fairness, equality, predictability and efficiency.[144] Perhaps, as is sometimes suggested, these values are largely obtainable without any formal doctrine of stare decisis.[145] Be that as it may, I believe that any meaningful role for stare decisis in constitutional adjudication must draw on more powerful considerations, weighty enough to predominate even when the constitutional issues involved are of the first order. For us, those considerations are bottomed upon the concept of legitimation.

John Rawls writes that "in a constitutional democracy one of [political theory's] most important aims is presenting a political conception of justice that can not only provide a shared basis for the justification of political and social institutions but also helps ensure stability from one generation to the next."[146] For Rawls, these are especially vital needs given the ineradicable pluralism of American society. Such a society faces seemingly perpetual centrifugal forces undermining the socially necessary stability. Rawls's analysis is also pertinent to constitutional theory. Stability and continuity of political institutions (and of shared values) are important goals of the process of constitutional adjudication, particularly "in a constitution intended to endure for ages to come, and consequently to be adapted to the various *crises* of human affairs."[147] Moreover, these values are in part at least among the values that the new constitutional order was specifically designed to secure, as the Preamble to the Constitution itself makes plain. Indeed, *The Federalist* No. 49 even decried appeals to the people in order to "maintain the constitutional equilibrium of government."[148]

Achievement of these values depends at least in part upon ideology, particularly the idea of legitimate government. From the very beginning—indeed from pre-Revolutionary days— Americans have been deeply concerned with the question of the legitimacy of their political institutions.[149] Although considerable controversy exists over both the content and utility of "legitimacy" theory as a way of understanding the legal order,[150] legitimation ideology can make certain modest claims as a valid and important construct,[151] particularly given my narrow focus: I am not concerned with the relationship between legitimation ideology and popular culture,[152] but only at the narrower level of elite groups, such as lawyers, public officials, and judges. For these members of the "reasoning class,"[153] the Supreme Court functions as the central means "for bringing about a consensus on the legitimacy of important governmental measures."[154]

A. *System Legitimacy*

At its most general level, stare decisis operates to promote system-wide stability and continuity by ensuring the survival of governmental norms that have achieved unsurpassed importance in American society. Such norms include the freedom from racial discrimination by the government, the general reach of the commerce clause, and even the legality of paper money. Expectations, tangible and symbolic, have developed around the critical decisions; the massive destabilization following a successful attack on any of these would threaten the functioning of the federal government, if not the viability of the constitutional order itself.[155]

But the question of criteria remains. For the Court to invoke a system-legitimacy justification to explain its use of stare decisis in any given instance, it must feel that the consequences of overruling settled precedent are quite serious. Of course, the nation's stability need not be imminently threatened every time such a system-legitimacy justification is appropriate. But this justification supports the use of stare decisis only to prevent disruption of practices and expectations so settled, or to avoid the revitalization of a public debate so divisive, that departure from the precedent would contribute in some perceptible way to a failure of confidence in the lawfulness of fundamental features of the political order.[156]

Because credible justification in system-legitimacy terms for adherence to precedent is so restricted, it seems likely that this justification will roughly correspond to those issues where stare decisis performs an agenda-limitation function. Such issues are too central to our society to overrule, if not simply to question. To permit or vindicate challenges to these traditions would "incite radical and even revolutionary attacks on the legal status quo."[157] Consequently, the Court must remove the issue of constitutional validity from public debate and keep the book closed on the questions. Stare decisis performs that office: to the extent that it restricts judicial reconsideration of legitimacy questions, stare decisis operates to keep issues off the constitutional, if not the political agenda, thereby leaving open for debate only less threatening issues. Accordingly, in part at least, it seems fair to say that the stability of our legal system depends on the doctrine of stare decisis.

The agenda-limiting phenomenon could be viewed in purely Bickelian terms: agenda-limiting stare decisis is a "passive virtue," entirely political in nature.[158] Believing that in the popular mind Supreme Court decisions legitimated governmental decisions not only as valid, but as desirable public policy, Professor Bickel argued that the Court might properly manipulate jurisdictional doctrines to avoid principled merit holdings that would uphold and thereby legitimate undesirable legislation.[159] However, the central function of agenda-limiting stare decisis is different. Its office is not to maintain principles politically favored by the Court, but to avoid delegitimation of deeply entrenched governmental arrangements.[160]

Of course, even when expectations or practices are not deeply entrenched, if serious public debate still surrounds an issue, departure from precedent may sometimes threaten the stability and continuity of the political order and should therefore be avoided:[161] *Roe* provides a ready example. However, the contested area will include few cases with *Roe*'s significance. More typically the public will not be sufficiently concerned that the Court is of two minds about the matter.

Stability and continuity, however, are not the only important constitutional values, and sometimes even these values cannot be achieved without change. Thus, even this argument cannot establish the absolute priority of precedent over text. But constitutional law is in the end a matter of government, and the Court is a part of that government.[162] Although *Brown* will forever remind us that the Supreme Court can occasionally act as a catalyst in generating profound social change,[163] the Court also plays an important role in our government by conserving and perpetuating shared values. In that respect, the very existence of a body of precedent is a conservative, stabilizing force, as Ronald Dworkin observes.[164] A practice of judicial adherence to this body of precedent will further foster conservative values.[165] In the end, therefore, stare decisis reflects a political conception of the nature of our constitutional government, and it must be defended in those terms.

B. Legitimating Judicial Review

Focus on system legitimation convincingly underpins only some aspects of stare decisis. For example, the wisdom of judicial reconsideration of a whole series of "small" constitutional questions—such as whether jeopardy attaches when a jury is sworn rather than when it actually hears evidence, or whether remittitur is consistent with the common-law trial by jury—is not determined by system-maintenance concerns. Of greater note, it seems that most issues one would consider "currently contested"[166] are not easily disposed of by appeals to system legitimacy. There is, however, a second, and perhaps more universal justification for the application of stare decisis to contested matters, one that also arises from a rationale concerned with stability and continuity. Namely, the Court must strive to demonstrate—at least to elites—the continuing legitimacy of judicial review. A general judicial adherence to constitutional precedent supports a consensus about the rule of law, specifically the belief that all organs of government, including the Court, are bound by the law. At first blush it may seem perverse to defend the idea that the Court maintains its subservience to the fundamental law by upholding decisions that depart from that law. But this difficulty is not insurmountable. What the Constitution requires is often a matter for debate, and once having been adequately canvassed and resolved by the Court, an issue might presumptively remain at rest. Even when the prior judicial resolution seems plainly wrong to a majority of the present Court, adherence to precedent can contribute to the important notion that the law is impersonal in character, that the Court believes itself to be following a "law which binds [it] as well as the litigants."[167] In listing "the weighty considerations" supporting adherence to precedent, Justice Harlan included "the necessity of maintaining public faith in the judiciary as a source of impersonal and reasoned judgments."[168]

While it is quite clear to any observer that the Court has no coherent or stable conception of the appropriate role of precedent in constitutional adjudication, Justice Harlan's theme is something of a decorative favorite, especially among dissenters who object to an overruling decision[169] —and it is certain the theme is sensible beyond mere decoration.

To my mind, this rule of law argument does not suffer from criticism that the man in the street is unaware of the overruling of "small" precedents and that, in any event, he would expect the Constitution and not the Court's precedents to control adjudication.[170] For me, the real focus of rule of law theories about the Supreme Court in the main is elites, at least "the reasoning classes." The concern is to contain, if not minimize, the existing cynicism that constitutional law is nothing more than politics carried on in a different forum.[171] In a recent work, Professor Archibald Cox states that the future of judicial review turns largely on whether law is seen by the profession as only judicial policymaking, or "whether room is left for the older belief that judges are truly bound by law both as a confining force and as an ideal search for justice."[172] Perhaps it goes too far to tie the whole future of judicial review to this distinction, but Professor Cox's point does have merit. My submission is that the Court's institutional position would be weakened were it generally perceived that the Court itself views its own decisions as little more than "a restricted railroad ticket, good for this day and train only."[173] If courts are viewed as unbound by precedent, and the law as no more than what the last Court said, considerable efforts would be expended to get control of such an institution—with judicial independence and public confidence greatly weakened.[174]

C. The Uncertain Constitutional Source of Stare Decisis

Once it is acknowledged that stare decisis should play a role in constitutional adjudication, the intriguing question arises as to the constitutional source of this doctrine. Presumably there are two leading possibilities. One could argue that the principle of stare decisis inheres in the "judicial power" of Article III. Alternatively, stare decisis could possess the nature of constitutional common law: not a constitutional imperative, but simply the natural result of judicial powers and duties established in the text and ultimately subject to the control of Congress.[175]

While in most circumstances identification of the precise source of stare decisis is not critical, in one important category of cases the difference could be crucial. If stare decisis is part of the judicial power of Article III, it is an inalienable command binding the Court;[176] its demands remain authoritative in the face of competing demands by the other branches. Constitutional common law, however, is subject to congressional control.[177] Thus, the question arises whether Congress could demand that the Court reconsider its precedents, free of any supposed compulsion introduced by stare decisis.

The general issue might be sharpened by considering the following hypothetical. While Congress cannot "overrule" *Roe* and its companion, *Doe* v. *Bolton*,[178] could it require the Court to reconsider the rule laid down in those cases *res nova*?[179] Is such a statutory directive valid?[180] Indeed, isn't such a precedent-reconsidering demand implicit in any congressional statute: Congress wishes its enactment to stand unless the Court finds that something in the Constitution bars it? Surely, if there is a reasonable chance that the Court would reverse itself on the merits, Congress is not disregarding its duty to obey the law in enacting a new abortion statute.[181] Yet one can anticipate the reaction: many who have never uttered a kind word for stare decisis would rise against the congressional "usurpation" of judicial authority. Apparently, for them stare decisis resides in the judicial power: the Court may act entirely free of any constraint from its precedents, but Congress cannot insist that it do so. But even if such an argument is correct and Congress cannot "require" judicial reappraisal, do the small-letter working assumptions of our constitutional order presuppose that the Court will reexamine controversial and contested precedents when requested to do so by Congress?[182] Putting the issue in these ways is a matter of great significance for judges who would adhere to *Roe* but would not have decided it the same way initially.

IV. Notes Toward a Theory of Stare Decisis

THIS SECTION explores some possible aspects of a theory of stare decisis, starting from the proposition that stare decisis must require more of a court than simply exploring the precedents as possible models for current decision-making.[183] In some sense, the second court must feel *bound* by the *precedent*.[184] Quite plainly, a good deal turns on the content of the italicized words. But these concepts do not possess fixed and immutable essences that, like Platonic form, can be apprehended in their universal states. Binding authority and precedent are simply constructs fashioned from and designed to make sense of our legal order. Moreover, while the content of binding authority seems more readily derivable from the underlying legitimacy justifications for stare decisis than from the content of precedent, the two concepts are closely intertwined. The compulsive aspect of precedent is itself in part a function of what constitutes a precedent, and vice versa. For clarity, however, each term is examined separately.

A. Binding Authority

Professor Arthur Goodhart insisted that for the English courts precedents constituted judge-made statutes: "The prior case, being directly in point, is no longer one which *may* be used as a pattern; it is one which *must* be followed in the subsequent case. It is more than a model; it has become a fixed and binding rule."[185] The view that a judicial precedent is the equivalent of a legislative act has never existed in American law,[186] and no one has proposed that it should. Yet in a well-known essay Max Radin invoked this rigid conception in order to attack the doctrine root and branch. For him the strict view of stare decisis means adherence to precedent simply because the precedent exists. Thus, he excluded from stare decisis following a previous case "because it accords with the weight of authority, because it has been generally accepted and acted on."[187] Indeed, for Radin, if the court is bound by precedent, "it is bound by one decision. A second decision adds nothing."[188] Accordingly, judicial adherence to a long line of decisional authority was not an example of stare decisis, but rather of "estoppel or the force of custom."[189]

Radin's attack was designed to make palatable what he claimed was the more liberal (and progressive) theory of American precedent. According to Radin, stare decisis in America is nothing more than "a matter of technique" requiring of courts only that they "place the situation they are judging within the generalized class of some existing decision."[190] But Radin presents us with a false choice. Stare decisis need not be viewed as either a theory about judge-made statutes or as simply a matter concerning the expository style of judicial opinions.[191]

In the American common law, stare decisis states a conditional obligation: precedent binds absent a showing of substantial countervailing considerations.[192] This formulation is not vacuous, or rather, it need not be. Nearly one-half century ago, Dean Roscoe Pound wrote: "Just how binding is 'binding authority' in our common-law technique? A single decision has never been regarded as absolutely binding at all events. But, on the other hand, it had become established that nothing less than an overriding conviction that a precept fixed by a prior decision was contrary to the principles of the law so that it had an ill effect upon the process of determining new questions by analogical reasoning and was, as Blackstone puts it, 'flatly' unjust in its results, could justify judicial rejection of it."[193]

A similar formulation seems appropriate for constitutional adjudication. Even an "overriding conviction" of prior error is not enough;[194] the precedent must have some palpable adverse consequences beyond its existence.[195] Thus, stare decisis is not simply a tiebreaker, such that the precedent need be followed only if matters otherwise stand evenly in balance. While a distinction must be made between rules and standards as against the principles and reasonings given in a case, at least as to the former stare decisis requires a more solid justification for ignoring a precedent.[196]

Pound mentions two such general factors bearing on adverse consequences: the importance of the decision for determining new questions by analogical reasoning and "flatly unjust" results. These factors are not of equal weight in constitutional adjudication. The first has a scope more limited than in the common-law area.

1. Analogical Reasoning

This aspect of precedent is concerned not so much with the judicially formulated rule or standard in a given case as with the grounds of the decision—the underlying reasoning or principles that generated the rule or standard. It reflects the fact that the still-dominant mode of judicial reasoning is analogical:[197] the reasoning of the precedent is extended until interests sufficiently powerful cluster to halt further expansion.[198] This phenomenon is true of constitutional no less than common law, as the case law under the First and Fourth Amendments amply illustrates. Thus *Bowers* v. *Hardwick* is a hard case for any Court committed not only to *Roe* and its progeny but also to the standard mode of analogical elaboration.[199] Doctrinally it is difficult to reconcile *Roe* and *Bowers*, and doctrinal inconsistency is no more desirable in constitutional adjudication than elsewhere.[200]

But here, as elsewhere, doctrinal consistency is only one value, not the ultimate value.[201] The precedential status of the Court's reasoning need not be equivalent to that of the Court's rule or standard. Surely some measure of doctrinal inconsistency is tolerable in the name of larger interests, particularly in the name of a document that itself is a "bundle of compromises."[202] Accordingly, even if *Roe*'s rule is preserved, the question of whether its reasoning should be extended or is rightly halted in the name of the original understanding presents a quite different issue.[203]

2. Harmful Results

Inevitably, the actual consequences of a prior decision will play a major part in any American theory of stare decisis. Here some concession may perhaps be given to those who insist that stare decisis in constitutional adjudication should be relaxed because of the difficulty of amendment. By replacing Pound's "flatly unjust" criterion with that of "substantial" or "significantly" harmful effect, this factor can be accommodated.

The most difficult question in identifying the harmful effects due to a wrongly decided controlling precedent is whether this criterion can be rendered sufficiently principled so that it is not simply a euphemism describing decisions that a Court majority very much dislikes.[204] Some may insist that any use of stare decisis is necessarily "contentless and subjective"—it is a "discretionary" doctrine inevitably employed "as a means of selectively leaving in place just those decisions which [the commentators] think wrong but whose overruling even they find unthinkable."[205] This challenge is confused. To be sure, the fact that overruling a precedent is "unthinkable" involves judgments concerning the need for stability and continuity that possess, if not subjective, certainly unquantifiable dimensions. Necessarily, the fundamental reference points for these determinations will be legislative in their grounds. But that does not mean that such determinations are thereby "contentless," "discretionary," or unprincipled. Determinations of this nature inhere in the judicial process, as Judge Cardozo long ago reminded us.[206]

Many, if not all the off-the-agenda illustrations previously discussed should be protected by stare decisis simply because (in stability and continuity terms) it is "unthinkable" that they be overruled. The effects of the precedents are not harmful, and overruling the precedents would produce exceptionally harmful effects. Moreover, a significant number of decisions exist that should not be overruled, even though their overruling is entirely thinkable. For example, no reason exists for disturbing a controlling decision that the practice of remittitur is consistent with the constitutional guarantee of trial by jury,[207] or that jeopardy attaches when the jury is sworn rather than when it begins to hear evidence.[208] The results of these precedents are not significantly harmful (and neither decision seems to carry much significance for the process of analogical reasoning).

But some wrongly decided precedents should be subject to recall. Two important illustrations come to mind. If the Court came to believe (as it did in 1937) that the commerce clause justified direct federal regulatory control over manufacturing, mining, and agriculture, contrary decisions should not stand in the way, even if those decisions reinforced the Court's private judgment about the social undesirability of national regulatory controls.[209] The human cost stemming from the lack of national regulatory controls was very great, and few could pretend that the desirability *vel non* of national controls was a consideration constitutionally assigned to the determination of judges. Likewise, when the Court became convinced that the Fourteenth Amendment was intended to prohibit racial segregation generally, stare decisis should not have saved the practice. Indeed, it did not. In *Brown*, John W. Davis, representing South Carolina, placed great weight on stare decisis to protect the institution of racial segregation. He argued that a whole social order rested on this institution.[210] But other overriding considerations eviscerated the strength of this claim: judged by developing national standards (strongly held, at least among elite groups), segregation was perceived to be the gravest of moral wrongs, a national tragedy of the first order.[211] Moreover, it seems doubtful that stare decisis is ever properly invoked to bar the claims of any group prevented from constructing the political and social rules of which they complain.[212]

My central problem here is this: I do not believe that a "substantially harmful" criterion can be fairly reduced to simply the majority's personal views of the desirability *vel non* of a given practice. Furthermore, the judgments called for by the criterion need not be unprincipled. But it may not be possible to go further and formulate relatively determinate implementing criteria, however general, that would guide, if not constrain, judgment. The circumstances seem simply too varied and fact-dependent to make feasible helpful criteria as to what appropriately counts as a sufficiently "substantial" harmful effect justifying overruling.[213] For example, beyond simply inventorying differences, how does one differentiate between *Lochner* and *Brown* (assuming both are inconsistent with the original understanding)? And what of other, less significant precedents? Many decisions fall into the category of nonfoundational matters, such as a governor's duty to honor a fugitive extradition warrant,[214] or the validity of a tax on interstate commerce.[215] How does one add specificity to the general justifications for overruling the controlling precedents in these cases?

3. Clearly Wrong

It is sometimes said that a factor to be taken into account is whether the precedent is clearly wrong. For example, Judge J. Clifford Wallace presents this factor as an additional limitation on overruling a precedent: "a justice should consider overturning a prior decision only when the decision is clearly wrong, has significant effects, and would otherwise be difficult to remedy."[216] I do not believe that this factor should receive much independent weight. Whether a precedent is seen as clearly wrong is often a function of the judge's self-confidence more than of any objective fact. More important, my arguments above[217] are tantamount to advocating a general presumption against overruling wrongly decided precedents. That is, clear departure from the original understanding is not alone enough to merit overruling a precedent. For example, the "ordered liberty" standard of *Palko* v. *Connecticut*[218] and the "evolving standards of decency" standard of *Trop* v. *Dulles*[219] seem clearly wrong as a matter of original understanding. But both have been repeatedly accepted by the Court and are now deeply ingrained in our constitutional jurisprudence. It should take a great deal more than a judgment of clear error to overthrow them.

4. Judicial Self-Protection

One additional important question is whether judicial self-protection is a legitimate criterion that should be taken into account in deciding whether to adhere to a challenged precedent. Consider, for example, the Reagan administration's well-publicized assault on *Miranda*.[220] How should the Court evaluate the following argument; "*Miranda* was wrongly decided. But the Supreme Court should adhere to the decision because it is not clear that it works real harm in the interrogation context (it is not substantially harmful). More important, *Miranda*'s repudiation would make the Court look like a tool of the incumbent administration and thus weaken the Court's position in the American constitutional order." I suspect that these latter "political" considerations would enter into the Court's judgment, and I am reluctant to develop any theory that excludes what must be. Besides, it is not clear where the line is drawn between institutional self-protection and striving to maintain the legitimacy of judicial review, and the latter interest plays an important role in justifying stare decisis. But if institutional self-protection is to play some significant role in legitimation theory, difficult issues must be confronted. Despite arguable examples to the contrary, the general belief has been that decisions on the merits are not to be avoided simply because in the long run the Court would be better off if it could wash its hands of the controversy.[221]

B. Precedent

The meaning of precedent—the definitional problem—assumed obvious importance in English law given the long refusal of the House of Lords to overrule its precedents.[222] And not surprisingly, in the common-law context widely divergent concepts have been advanced. The precedent has been viewed as limited to the "decision" on the "material facts" as seen by the precedent court,[223] or the same as seen by the nonprecedent court;[224] for others, the term means the "rules" formulated by the precedent court;[225] for still others, the term includes the reasons given for the rules formulated.[226]

There is, of course, no necessary right answer here, and English common-law discussions cannot automatically be transplanted to American constitutional law. Still, for us some answers seem better than others. Little is appealing in the Legal Realist claim[227] that stare decisis is concerned only with what the Court *decided* on the material facts, not with what it said. The relevant facts do not identify and classify themselves; criteria are needed to determine what the legally relevant facts are and at what level of generality they are to be specified.[228] More important, stare decisis is invoked to justify subsequent decisions. Necessarily, what the Supreme Court *said* assumes paramount importance.

What the Court said must include the Court's rule or standard.[229] This constitutes the "enactment force of precedent,"[230] in Dworkin's phrase, or the "precept," in Pound's.[231] This is the core of the precedent. The compelling state interest test in cases involving racial discrimination, or the obscenity criteria in First Amendment case law, are examples.

The real issue is whether more should be included, specifically whether the precedent should also include the grounds for the decision—that is, the reasoning or principles behind the rule or standard. The general view in this country has been to deny this. The Legal Realists were emphatic on this score, of course.[232] But even Dean Pound wrote that "it cannot be insisted upon too often that our common-law technique does not make the language authoritative, much less binding authority. It is the result that passes into the law."[233] I disagree, and my disagreement follows from a conception of the judicial opinion as a reasoned elaboration of principle.[234] By the time they get to the Supreme Court, few, if any, cases are exactly alike. The Court necessarily will be required to consult the reasoning elaborated in the prior decision, once any seemingly plausible limitation on extension of the precedent is proffered.[235] In effect, the Court is asked to measure the scope of the rule or standard by the reasoning behind it. Of course, the reasoning must be set in the context of the facts, and some notion of obiter dicta is necessary.[236] Nonetheless, there seems to me no reason to exclude the underlying reasoning from the concept of the precedent. The compulsion behind any precedent is not an inexorable or uniform one,[237] and the compulsion behind judicial reasoning may be taken to be less than the compulsion behind the rule or standard announced.[238] Moreover, fair leeway must be accorded for reexamination of the prior reasoning.[239] But, having recognized all that, there seems to be no advantage in absolutely divorcing the precedent-setting Court's reason for deciding from the precedent it has sought to establish, particularly when the reasoning necessarily helps frame the scope of the rule or standard. In his well-known work, Professor Rupert Cross defines the *ratio decidendi* in a way that is generally satisfactory: "The *ratio decidendi* of a case is any rule of law expressly or impliedly treated by the judge as a necessary step in reaching his conclusion, having regard to the line of reasoning adopted by him, or a necessary part of his direction to the jury."[240]

Of course, there will be argument about what constitutes the precedent, particularly in the case of a single decision.[241] As Justice Brandeis put it, "the process of inclusion and exclusion, so often applied in developing a rule, cannot end with its first enunciation."[242] Definition of a precedent will often take time. Moreover, a reading of any precedent will often be value infused.[243] Even more important, as Neil MacCormick correctly emphasizes, a precedent may be open enough so that it is fairly read to possess more than one *ratio decidendi*.[244]

But no theory of precedent assumes *ex ante* that all precedents are clear.[245] Accordingly, the difficulties described, and they are real ones, seem simply to point to the limits of written communication. However, they do not establish that the entire concept of precedent is without content. They do not establish that the doctrine is incoherent, excessively, indeterminate, unprincipled, or infinitely manipulable.[246] Every court and every lawyer knows that there are precedents that simply cannot be distinguished: they must be either followed or overturned. As Professor Frederick Schauer observes, "precedent rests on similarity, and some determinations of similarity are incontestable within particular cultures or subcultures."[247] Every term of court bears witness to the fact.

V. *The Written Constitution of 1789*

AT FIRST GLANCE it appears that a viable theory of stare decisis could preserve a significant role for originalism. While much of the past would be taken as beyond recall, future decisions would be governed by original understanding, at least in those areas not dominated by precedent. But before accepting such a role for precedent in constitutional adjudication, it is necessary to reexamine the relationship between the written text and judicial precedents. After all, if a significant part of the current constitutional order cannot be squared with any acceptable conception of the original understanding of the written Constitution, the normative force of any further appeal to originalism is not obvious. Put differently, the central problem for originalism is whether the cost of embracing stare decisis is too high—whether, in the end, the embrace destroys originalism's bedrock assumption that, until formally amended, the Constitution establishes a permanent ordering binding on all organs of the government, including the courts.

A. Text Over Case Law

From the beginning of our political and legal tradition, we have differentiated between text and its interpretation. The implicit premise has been to privilege the text over its interpreted gloss.[248] This general phenomenon is no doubt of interest to literary critics, but in the legal tradition this step has been taken in order to permit us to understand and express important elements of our legal order. For example, in constitutional adjudication, this distinction was used to express the once dominant view that a court passed on constitutional issues only as a necessary incident to deciding the concrete rights of actual litigants. Accordingly, the Court did "not pass a statute calling for obedience by all within the purview of the rule that is declared."[249] *Cooper* v. *Aaron*'s[250] well-known identification of judicial interpretations of the Fourteenth Amendment with "the supreme Law of the Land" was widely perceived as an attack on this established tradition,[251] an attack that, *inter alia*, threatened to collapse any distinction between text and interpretation.[252]

Cooper v. *Aaron* notwithstanding, the distinction between text and interpretation has been an important part of our constitutional tradition. Charles Warren long ago wrote that "however the Court may interpret the provisions of the Constitution, it is still the Constitution which is the law and not the decision of the Court."[253] Professor Charles Black echoes a similar claim: "this text, however widely it may be departed from in fact, always stays there." [254] Statements of this nature could readily take the form of a claim that judicial interpretations should have no stare decisis effect whatever; that their status is only evidence of what the text means, with their capacity to persuade entirely a function of the "force of the[ir] reasoning."[255] For many, this position is self-evident.[256]

The obvious breadth of such a position assumes an even more persuasive character when understood in light of the idea of a "written constitution."[257] One can acknowledge not only that the idea of a written constitution is unclear (case-law rules are also written), but also that in theory it would seem to be a meaningless circumstance.[258] Nonetheless, history asserts a powerful claim here, and in that light the written quality of the Constitution counted a great deal. The American Constitution was a watershed in the evolution of thinking about the meaning of a constitution: it culminated a shift from viewing a constitution as simply a description of the fundamental political arrangements of the society to a conception that the constitution stood behind, or grounded and legitimated, those arrangements—and of course constrained them.[259] In this development, the "writtenness" of the American Constitution was crucial.[260] For example, in a 1793 opinion attacking the doctrine of legislative sovereignty, Judge St. George Tucker wrote that the English judges "having no written Constitution to refer to, were obliged to receive whatever exposition of it the legislature might think proper to make."[261] But, he said, "with us, the Constitution is not an 'ideal thing, but a real existence: it can be produced in a visible form': its principles can be ascertained from the living letter, not from obscure reasoning or deductions only."[262] And of course, *Marbury* v. *Madison* itself placed considerable emphasis upon the written nature of the Constitution, stating that the Constitution must be enforced by the courts, otherwise the result would "reduce to nothing what we have deemed the greatest improvement on political institutions—a written constitution."[263]

In the interpretation of this written Constitution, we may assume that the founding generation was much attached to the original, publicly shared understanding of the document.[264] Thus, one can make a good case that, as historically understood, the written Constitution was intended to trump not only statutes but case law. This argument is reinforced if one recalls that to the founding generation it was not clear that judicial opinions would need to play such a dominant role in establishing the meaning of the Constitution.[265]

B. Case Law Over Text

But in the end, the written Constitution argument cannot sustain the absolute primacy of text over gloss. First, a written text is not logically inconsistent with the idea of stare decisis.[266] Second, in fact we cannot know the Framers' original understanding on the subject under discussion: deeply ingrained transformative change. The Framers simply did not comprehend our central factual premise. Moreover, to say that the founding generation expected that there was a metaprinciple always requiring a return to original understanding adds little to the general argument that the founding generation did not intend any departures from original understanding in the first place.[267] The importance of original understanding to the Framers, and their desire that courts should adhere to it may be conceded; our task is to make sense out of a nonoriginalist universe.

In such a universe, the relationship between text and judicial gloss cannot be taken as obvious—at least in the process of constitutional adjudication. Thus, when Attorney General Meese reminds us that "there is the necessary distinction between the Constitution and constitutional law. The two are not synonymous,"[268] he fails to see that this very distinction can be employed to privilege not the text but the case law. The Supreme Court is concerned not with the Constitution, but with constitutional law, which consists largely (albeit not entirely) of case law. As John Chipman Gray insisted long ago, "in truth, all the law is judge-made law," and accordingly, texts are not themselves law, but only sources of the law.[269] This view of constitutional adjudication comports with reality. Judges and lawyers (and even law professors) are centrally concerned with judicial decisions, not with the text. After examining the Court's work at the end of the 1981 Term, Professor Harry Jones wrote:

> What methodological phenomena strike us, or should strike us, as we
> proceed in our reading from case to case?
>   What is certainly most striking, or would be if familiarity had not
> made us take it for granted, is that two-thirds or more of the discussion in the opinions is about past Supreme Court cases, that is, about
> what these past cases arguably "held" and what was said in the
> opinions of the Court justifying the results reached in them . . . . The
> constitutional text is down there somewhere under this massive overlay
> of case law development and refinement, but the usual contest between
> advocates in the Supreme Court, and more often than not between or
> among the justices, is the kind of contest that has characterized the
> common law judicial process at least since the days of Sir Edward
> Coke, a battle over cases and what they should be taken to stand for.[270]

Recognition that in actual process of constitutional adjudication the constitutional text plays only a role, and an increasingly subordinate one at that, has important consequences for originalism. Originalism must confront a constitutional adjudicatory process in which, after two centuries, the original understanding of the text is simply a factor in the process of decisionmaking, a factor to be considered and balanced against other factors. Indeed, frequently the text operates as little more than a boundary marker restraining judicial law-making. In each instance, the case law overwhelms the text and historical understanding. The latter play no directive role in determining most issues. Thus, in the arena of constitutional adjudication it is quite possible to see the case law and not the text as of central importance. A recent opinion for the Court by Justice Stevens illustrates this point: "The State's argument is supported by the plain language of the [Compulsory Process] Clause . . . by the historical evidence that it was intended to provide defendants with subpoena power that they lacked at common law, by some scholarly comment, and by a brief excerpt from the legislative history of the Clause. We have, however, consistently given the Clause the broader reading reflected in contemporaneous state constitutional provisions."[271]

VI. *Conclusion*

THE MORE that stare decisis is used to rationalize the existing order, the more problematic becomes originalism's insistence upon the crucial importance of the written Constitution, at least in the context of constitutional adjudication. The central problem is this: to accord status to stare decisis requires an acknowledgment that originalism plays a purely instrumental role by contributing to the establishment of legitimate government, which in turn promotes stability and continuity. Neither originalism nor the constitutional text has mystical qualities that compel a return to the fold in the face of transforming departures from the original understanding. At this point in our history, when adherence to stare decisis promotes the underlying values of stability and continuity better than does adherence to the original understanding, the latter cannot prevail.

But if the Court legitimately may prevent inquiry into original understanding in order to *maintain* transformative change, does this concession also license prospective disregard of original understanding when the Court is satisfied that change is necessary to maintain systemic equilibrium? Moreover, should the Court reject the precedent itself in favor of still further change when to do so will achieve the important values?

While I certainly have no theory with which to answer these questions, I must tentatively conclude that under some circumstances the answers must be in the affirmative. *Brown*'s departure from the original understanding is not only defensible, but was probably the Supreme Court's only legitimate response to the nation's escalating moral and social turmoil. But does all this mean we should view the Constitution in significant measure as simply a symbolic expression of national continuity and unity?[272] If so, is the political order the ground of the constitutional order rather than vice versa?[273]

But in the end any temptation to dismiss the Constitution of 1789 from our view seems to be a mistake. Paul Brest is surely right in stating that "the written Constitution lies at the core of the American 'civil religion.' "[274] So too is Professor Richard Kay in asserting that "notwithstanding evidence that the document itself is often no more than a peripheral feature of judicial decisionmaking, a constitutional law or a constitutional scholarship without a Constitution will be unthinkable for a long time to come."[275] One can say, however, that no incontrovertible showing can be made that the Court must always adhere to the original understanding of the constitutional text. But this concession leaves originalism with the even larger problem of giving precise content to a theory of constitutional adjudication that includes original understanding, precedent, political equilibrium, and the need for change.[276] Fortunately, that is the topic of another essay, not this one.

Notes

1. I quite agree with Judge Easterbrook that we "cannot simply assume [judicial] review and then argue about [the Constitution's] meaning." Easterbrook, The Influence of Judicial Review on Constitutional Theory," in *A Workable Government?* 170, 175 (B. Marshall ed. 1987). Judge Easterbrook argues that, by ignoring text, structure, and history, much modern constitutional theory is incompatible with a system of judicial review.

2. In this essay, I use interchangeably the terms original understanding, originalism, and original intent.

3. Tribe, How Relevant Is "Original Intent" Doctrine? The Legal Times, Dec. 22, 1986, at 12, col. 1; see R. Dworkin, *Law's Empire* 360–61 (1986); H. Hyman and W. Wiecek, *Equal Justice Under Law: Constitutional Development 1835–1875*, 395–97 (1982). Professor Bickel's well-known effort to construct an originalism account for Brown v. Board of Educ., 347 U.S. 483 (1954), in Bickel, The Original Understanding and the Segregation Decision, 69 *Harv. L. Rev.* 1, 59–60 (1955) is quite unpersuasive as a historical matter. See R. Berger, *Government by Judiciary* 100–110, 117–33 (1977). For further discussion of *Brown* and original understanding, see infra notes 24–27 and accompanying text.

4. 347 U.S. 483 (1954).

5. What follows is intended only as a sketch of originalism's foundational principles; with regard to specific components of my own view of the ideal form of originalism, I am largely exclusive. I have yet to develop fully my own description and defense of originalism.

6. The "framers of the Constitution contemplated that instrument as a rule for the government of *courts* as well as of the legislature." Marbury v. Madison, 5 U.S. (1 Cranch) 137, 179–80 (1803). Originalists also emphasize the difficulties for current democratic theory if judicial control of the political branches lacks a clear textual warrant. See, e.g., Address by Judge Robert Bork, University of San Diego Law School (Nov. 18, 1985) reprinted in *The Great Debate: Interpreting Our Written Constitution* 43, 49–50 (Occasional Paper No. 2, Federalist Society 1986); Address by Attorney General Edwin Meese, American Bar Association (July 9, 1985) reprinted in *The Great Debate*, supra at 1, 9–10.

7. See, e.g., Brest, The Misconceived Quest for the Original Understanding, 60 *B. U. L. Rev.* (1980) (reprinted in this volume); Tushnet, Following the Rules Laid Down: A Critique of Interpretivism and Neutral Principles, 96 *Harv. L. Rev.* 781, 793–804 (1983).

8. See e.g., R. Berger, *Federalism: The Founders' Design* 15–17 (1987).

9. See, e.g., S. Macedo, *The New Right v. the Constitution* 11–16 (1986).

10. See C. Warren, *The Making of the Constitution* 783–804 (1928): Powell, The Modern Misunderstanding of Original Intent, 54 *Univ. Chicago L. Rev.* 1513, 1531–42 (1987).

11. See R. Dworkin, supra note 3 at 320–21.

12. This is a common error. See, e.g., R. Dworkin, supra note 3, at 359–63; S. Macedo, supra note 9, at 13; Bernstein, Charting the Bicentennial (Review Essay), 87 *Colum. L. Rev.* 1565, 1602–7 (1987); Powell, The Original Understanding of Original Intent, 98 *Harv. L. Rev.* (reprinted in this volume, 87–88) 948 (1985).

13. At least some of the Framers, including Madison, understood this point quite clearly by pointing to the State ratifying conventions for authoritative guidance beyond the text itself. C. Warren, supra note 10, at 793–801. Professor Clinton seems to me unconvincing in arguing that "the interpretive line between subjective and objective historical approaches to text appears illusory." Clinton, Original Understanding, Legal Realism, and the Interpretation of "This Constitution," 72 *Iowa L. Rev.* 1177, 1180 n.4 (1987).

14. A. Hamilton, Opinion on the Constitutionality of an Act to Establish a Bank (1791), reprinted in 8 *Papers of Alexander Hamilton* 97, 111 (H. Syrett ed. 1965); see also J. Story, 3 *Commentaries on the Constitution of the United States* ch. 5 (1987) (1st ed. 1833) (discussing the rules for interpreting the Constitution; published prior to Madison's Notes).

15. See Van Alstyne, Notes on a Bicentennial Constitution: Part II, Antinomial Choices and the Role of the Supreme Court, 72 *Iowa L. Rev.* 1281, 1289 and n.16 (1987) (the theory of justice contained in the U.S. Constitution, not some ideal theory of justice, furnishes the supreme law of the land).

16. Monaghan, Our Perfect Constitution, 56 *N.Y.U. L. Rev.* 353, 366–67 (1981). I recognize this is not a universally held assumption. See, e.g., Sherry, The Founders' Unwritten Constitution, 54 *Univ. Chicago L. Rev.* 1127, 1164 (1987).

17. Premier Elec. Constr. Co. v. National Elec. Contractors Assoc. 814 F.2d 358, 364 (7th Cir. 1987); see also American Jewish Congress v. City of Chicago, 827 F.2d 120, 137–39 (7th Cir. 1987) (Easterbrook, J., dissenting) (identification of the level of generality at which to interpret a text is a difficult judicial task); McConnell, Book Review, 54 *Univ. Chicago L. Rev.* 1484, 1490–91 (1987) (meaning of the words of the Constitution is not subordinate to the Founders' intentions). For a related approach, though one that can yield results that Judge Easterbrook would reject, see Richards, Constitutional Legitimacy and Constitutional Privacy, 61 *N.Y.U. L. Rev.* 800, 825–27 (1986) (Framers and Chief Justice Marshall intended the connotative or propositional form of the constitutional language to prevail over the denotative). For a discussion of the view advanced by Richards, see Monaghan, supra note 16, at 378–81.

18. D. Lowenthal, *The Past Is a Foreign Country* 411 (1985). See Nelson, History and Neutrality in Constitutional Adjudication, 72 *Va. L. Rev.* 1237, 1243–44 (1986) (a contextualist approach to history claims that historical inquiry is shaped by the historian's value system or worldview).

19. 410 U.S. 113 (1973).

20. The expanded power of the Presidency is one possible exception to this point. See infra notes 78–100 and accompanying text.

21. See, e.g., Harper v. Virginia Bd. of Elections, 383 U.S. 663, 669 (1966) (Court not "confined to historic notions of equality" in applying Fourteenth Amendment); Missouri v. Holland, 252 U.S. 416, 433 (1920) (constitutional issues must be decided in light of country's whole experience, not simply Framers' intent).

22. Wickard v. Filburn, 317 U.S. 111 (1942) (regulation of production of wheat that never enters the market is within the commerce power of Congress and is consistent with early interpretation of the commerce clause), is perhaps the *locus classicus*. Sometimes the implausible efforts at reconciliation of the result with original understanding are painfully strained See, e.g., Williams v. Florida, 399 U.S. 78, 98–100 (1970) (six-person jury not inconsistent with original intent).

23. 106 S. Ct. 2841 (1986).

24. Brown v. Board of Educ., 347 U.S. 483, 489–90 (1954).

25. This conclusion is frequently denied by people most identified with originalism. For example, Attorney General Meese recently stated: "When the Supreme Court . . . sounded the death knell for official segregation in the country, it earned all the plaudits it received. But the Supreme Court in that case was not giving new life to old words, or adapting a 'living,' 'flexible' Constitution to new reality. It was restoring the original principle of the Constitution to constitutional law. The *Brown* Court was correcting the damage done 50 years earlier, when in *Plessy* v. *Ferguson* [163 U.S. 537] (1896), an earlier Supreme Court had disregarded the clear intent of the Framers of the Civil War amendments to eliminate the legal degradation of blacks, and had contrived a theory of the Constitution to support the charade of 'separate but equal' discrimination." Address by Attorney General Edwin Meese, D.C. Chapter of the Federalist Society Lawyers Division (Nov. 15, 1985) (hereafter cited as Meese [D.C.]), reprinted in *The Great Debate*, supra note 6, at 31, 37–38.

26. Contra G. Jacobsohn, *The Supreme Court and the Decline of Constitutional Aspiration* 52–53 (1986) (segregation is invalid since it is currently viewed as incompatible with Framers' specific goal of guaranteeing blacks the status of full citizenship). For a critical analysis of this general problem, one that is sympathetic to but nonetheless challenges the views expressed in the text, see C. Bradley, *Church-State Relationships in America* 135–47 (1987).

27. See R. Dworkin, supra note 3, at 359–63 (contrasting "the Framers' concrete opinion about segregation . . . with their more abstract convictions about equality").

28. See, e.g., Roe v. Wade, 410 U.S. 113 (1973).

29. See, e.g., Reynolds v. Sims, 377 U.S. 533 (1964).

30. See, e.g., Frontiero v. Richardson, 411 U.S. 677 (1973).

31. See generally R. Berger, supra note 3, 20–245; Monaghan, Comment on Professor Van Alstyne's Paper, 72 *Iowa L. Rev.* 1309, 1310–11 (1987).

32. Compare R. Berger, supra note 3, at 134–156 (no intention to incorporate the Bill of Rights) with M. Curtis, *No State Shall Abridge: The Fourteenth Amendment and the Bill of Rights* 113 (1986) (drafters of the Fourteenth Amendment did intend to incorporate the Bill of Rights).

33. Jones, The Brooding Omnipresence of Constitutional Law, 4 *Vt. L. Rev.* 1, 28 (1979).

34. Monaghan, supra note 16, at 393; see also Brest, supra note 7, at 245–46. For a striking example, see Williams v. Florida, 399 U.S. 78, 102 (1970) (six-member jury consistent with functional view of jury). See generally Aleinikoff, Constitutional Law in the Age of Balancing, 96 *Yale L. J.* 943 (1987) (prevalence and dangers of interest balancing).

35. Anderson v. Creighton, 107 S. Ct. 3034, 3041 (1987).

36. Wellington, Revisiting *The People and the Court*, 95 *Yale L. J.* 1565, 1569 (1986).

37. Palmer, The Federal Common Law of Crime, 4 *Law and Hist. Rev.* 267, 269 (1986).

38. T. Lowi, *The Personal President* 23–28 (1985). This consensus was not materially altered by the Reconstruction amendments, even conceding their nationalistic implications. Even in the area of race, these features limited national regulatory authority. See B. Bailyn, D. Davis, D. Donald, J. Thomas, R. Wiebe and G. Wood, *The Great Republic* 735–41 (1977); Schmidt, Juries, Jurisdiction, and Race Discrimination: The Lost Promise of Strauder v. West Virginia, 61 *Tex. L. Rev.* 1401, 1491–92 (1983) (state orientation prevented development of national institutions necessary to overcome racism). Contra Kaczorowski, Revolutionary Constitutionalism in the Era of the Civil War and Reconstruction, 61 *N.Y.U. L. Rev.* 863, 877–78 (1986) (Republicans' creation of federal law, displacing state law, aided civil rights enforcement).

39. T. Lowi, supra note 38 at 28. Along a somewhat different plane, it bears noting that the emergence of the New Deal worked to destroy not only the once widely shared view of limited or passive government, but also its corollary assumption, that private property was a prepolitical institution that marked the boundary of legitimate governmental authority. The takings, contract, and due process clauses have almost completely failed to prevent redistributive national (and state) legislation. While at the time of the adoption of the Constitution redistributive legislation existed at the state level, see F. McDonald, *Novus Ordo Seclorum: The Intellectual Origins of the Constitution* 155–57 (1985), as the nineteenth century wore on, the institution of private property was seen as a substantial limit on all governmental power. Lochner v. New York, 198 U.S. 45 (1905), is the culmination of that view. Sunstein, Lochner's Legacy, 87 *Colum. L. Rev.* 873, 876–83 (1987).

40. See, e.g., Black, On Worrying about the Constitution, 55 *U. Colo. L. Rev.* 469, 472–76 (1984) ("Under the commerce power . . . the United States has acquired, by a process . . . infrequently and then very little checked since our beginnings, a national government."). On the issue of federalism, Professor Preyer's statement that there were "many 'original understandings,'" Preyer, Jurisdiction to Punish: Federal Authority, Federalism and the Common Law of Crimes in the Early Republic, 4 *Law and Hist. Rev.* 223, (1986), is a vast overstatement, at least if applied to the topics I am considering.

41. See, e.g., Wickard v. Filburn, 317 U.S. 111, 120 (1942) ("at the beginning Chief Justice Marshall described the federal commerce power with a breadth never yet exceeded") (citing Gibbons v. Ogden, 22 U.S. [9 Wheat.] 1, 194–95 [1824]). See generally Currie, The Constitution in the Supreme Court: The New Deal, 1931–1940. 54 *Univ. Chicago L. Rev.* 504 (1987) (reviewing New Deal cases confirming expansive federal power).

42. Meese (D.C.), supra note 25, reprinted in *The Great Debate*, supra note 6, at 38.

43. See e.g., Black, supra note 40, at 472–76.

44. See T. Lowi, supra note 38, at 44–50.

45. See Powell, How Does the Constitution Structure Government? in *A Workable Government?* supra note 1, at 29–33 (nationalists were not the majority).

46. Professor Palmer writes, "The most striking instance [of federal government acting beyond constitutional bounds] is the extension of the interstate commerce power to the conditions of manufacturing. While the appropriate boundaries of commerce are hard to define, ordinary usage would never include everything now regulated as commerce." Palmer, supra note 37, at 269 n.13.

47. 22 U.S. (9 Wheat.) 1, 194 (1824).

48. But see R. Berger, supra note 8, at 133–36 (Marshall's interpretation of commerce clause departed from Framers' intent). Referring to Marshall's opinion in McCulloch v. Maryland, 17 U.S. (4 Wheat.) 316 (1819), another instance where the Court validated an expansive view of the federal government's powers, Marshall's biographer wrote that "in effect [he] rewrote the fundamental law of the Nation." A. Beveridge, 4 *The Life of John Marshall* 308 (1919).

49. See Abel, The Commerce Clause in the Constitutional Convention and in Contemporary Comment, 25 *Minn. L. Rev.* 432, 468–81 (1941); see also R. Berger, supra note 8, at 120–57 (Framers intended restrictive construction of commerce clause); Brown, Book Review, 67 *Harv. L. Rev.* 1439, 1446–55 (1954) (rebutting contention of unlimited federal regulatory power under commerce clause); Epstein, The Proper Scope of the Commerce Power, 73 *Va. L. Rev.* 1387 (1987) (an expansive construction of the commerce clause is "clearly wrong").

50. 22 U.S. (9 Wheat.) at 194–95.

51. Compare Wechsler, The Political Safeguards of Federalism, 54 *Colum. L. Rev.* 543, 559–60 (1954) (states can protect their constitutional prerogatives in the political process) with Oregon v. Mitchell, 400 U.S. 112, 152 (1970) (Harlan, J., concurring in part and dissenting in part) (existence of amendment process presupposes some judicial limitation in name of federalism). But see Merritt, The Guarantee Clause and State Autonomy: Federalism for a Third Century, 88 *Colum. L. Rev.* 1, 15–22 (1988) (criticizing political safeguards argument).

52. See J. Choper, *Judicial Review and the National Political Process* 175–90 (1980). Professor Wechsler's initial formulation of the argument is to the contrary: "This is not to say that the Court can decline to measure national enactment by the Constitution when it is called upon to face the question in the course of ordinary litigation; the supremacy clause governs there as well." Wechsler, supra note 51, at 559. Wechsler advocates limited review, but seems unable to formulate any measurable limit. Dean Choper seems to me to carry the political safeguards argument to its ultimate conclusion: nonjusticiability.

53. This distinction is frequently denied, at least implicitly, see Garcia v. San Antonio Metro. Auth., 469 U.S. 528, 555–57 (1985) (claiming that the political safeguards of federalism argument suggests an expansive view of the commerce clause), or ignored, see Scheiber, Federalism and the Constitution: The Original Understanding, in *American Law and the Constitutional Order* 85, 89 (L. Friedman and H. Scheiber eds. 1978).

54. E.g., Wickard v. Filburn, 317 U.S. 111 (1942); NLRB v. Jones & Laughlin Steel Corp., 301 U.S. 1 (1937).

55. See J. Calhoun, A Discourse on the Constitution and Government of the United States (1853) reprinted in *A Disquisition on Government and Selections from the Discourse* 85, 86 (C. G. Post ed. 1953) (emphasizing "federal" in contrast to "national" nature of U.S. government).

56. See Monaghan, The Burger Court and "Our Federalism," 43 *Law & Contemp. Probs.* 39, 41–42 (1980).

57. See generally Rosenthal, Conditional Federal Spending and the Constitution, 39 *Stan. L. Rev.* 1103 (1987) (describing increased imposition of conditions on federal funds recipients and arguing that Congress should not be able to coerce indirectly what it cannot require directly).

58. U.S. Const. Art. 1, sect. 8, cl. 1. The Court has said that "the level of deference to the congressional decision is such that the Court has more recently questioned whether 'general welfare' is a judicially enforceable restriction at all." South Dakota v. Dole, 107 S. Ct. 2793, 2796 n.2 (1987).

59. For a striking recent example of federal regulation in a traditional state domain, see Honig v. Doe, 108 S. Ct. 592 (1988) (considering federal spending statute's prescribed standards for state schools' treatment of handicapped children).

60. As late as 1928 Charles Warren argued that the spending power was intended to be confined to "carrying out those enumerated and limited powers vested in Congress—and no others." C. Warren, supra note 10, at 475. He thought it peculiar to argue that Congress could fund—and thereby create and control—activity that it could not reach directly under its regulatory authority. Raoul Berger reiterates this argument in R. Berger, supra note 8, at 100–119. But Warren's view did not wholly reflect the early practice of government spending, which at times at least, reflected spending for objects not defended as within national regulatory competence. See 1 *Corwin on the Constitution* 255–70 (R. Loss ed. 1981); Currie, supra note 41, at 535–36 n.148. In any event, Warren himself recognized that it was too late for his view, see C. Warren, supra note 10, at 475–79, thereby correctly anticipating United States v. Butler, 297 U.S. 1, 64–66 (1936).

61. See T. Lowi, supra note 38, at 24.

62. Hamilton, On Nonconstitutional Management of a Constitutional Problem, *Pub. Interest*, Winter 1978, at 111, 113; see also Monaghan, supra note 56, at 41.

63. For a discussion of the term "Our Federalism," see Younger v. Harris, 401 U.S. 37, 44–45 (1971).

64. I emphasize here constitutional theory. Politically, federalism is by no means dead.

65. *Federalist* No. 15, at 313 (J. Madison) (J. Cooke ed. 1961); see R. Berger, supra note 3, at 59–76.

66. At bottom, the non-judicially discredited doctrine of "dual federalism," see, e.g., United States v. Butler. 297 U.S. 1, 63 (1936): Hammer v. Dagenhart, 247 U.S. 251, 275–76 (1918), represented efforts at attempting to prevent federal power from wholly displacing state regulatory power. See R. Berger, supra note 8, at 49–76; Epstein, supra note 49, at 1427–28.

67. The political existence of state-centered federalism during the nineteenth century is not logically inconsistent with the existence of a constitutional design that contemplated the appearance of an omnicompetent national regulatory authority should such a need arise. But as I have said, I doubt that this design reflects the original understanding.

68. The relevant history is untidy here, and the issue is complicated. It may be that responsibility is a term with significance for what Congress can regulate, but not relevant for spending (at least noncoercive spending). The fact that some early exercises of the federal power, fairly read, go beyond the understood reach of national regulatory authority or of national "responsibility." See supra note 60. Yet these early illustrations cannot fairly be seen to prefigure the existing order, given its present scale.

69. But see Black, Further Reflections on the Constitutional Justice of Livelihood, 86 *Colum. L. Rev.* 1103, 1114–15 (1986) (Ninth Amendment now imposes welfare responsibilities on the national government).

70. For a recent and exhaustive analysis of the emergence and possible decline of the New Deal ideal of an autonomous administration, see Sunstein, Constitutionalism after the New Deal, 101

Harv. L. Rev. 421 (1987); see also Lowi, Two Roads to Serfdom: Liberalism, Conservatism and Administrative Power, 36 *Am. U. L. Rev.* 295, 309–14 (1987) (discussing Reagan administration's approach to administrative agencies).

71. J. Locke, *Of Civil Government, Second Treatise* sect. 141, at 118 (Gateway ed. 1955).

72. See Monaghan, *Marbury* and the Administrative State, 83 *Colum. L. Rev.* 1, 25–26 (1983) (collecting sources).

73. U.S. Const. Art. II, sect. 3, cl. 4.

74. See Humphrey's Ex'r v. United States, 295 U.S. 602 (1935). Moreover, the unitary executive concept of Myers v. United States, 272 U.S. 52 (1926), is a problematic idea when asserted as a limit on congressional power to determine how the laws should be implemented. See Grundstein, Presidential Power, Administration and Administrative Law, 18 *Geo. Wash. L. Rev.* 285, 302–4 (1950).

75. Monaghan, Constitutional Fact Review, 85 *Colum. L. Rev.* 229, 247–59 (1985); see also Fallon, Of Legislative Courts, Administrative Agencies, and Article III, 101 *Harv. L. Rev.* 915, 937–43 (1988).

76. Id. For a more recent example, see Commodity Future Trading Comm. v. Schor, 106 S. Ct. 3245, 3259–61 (1986) (Commodity Future Trading Commission's assumption of jurisdiction over state law counterclaims does not violate Article III). See also Currie, The Distribution of Powers after Bowsher, 1986 *Sup. Ct. Rev.* 19, 37–40. Displacement of judicial adjudication by the administrative process coincided with the collapse of substantive constitutional protection against redistributive legislation. It should be noted that the administrative process is not confined to adjudication. Important individual interests are determined by licenses, inspections, testing, etc., and of course by standards set out in administrative codes.

77. See K. Davis, 1 *Administrative Law* sect. 4.7, 4.16 (2d ed. 1978) (summarizing cases).

78. W. Wilson, *Congressional Government* (1956) (1st ed. 1885).

79. Id. at 82.

80. Id. at 176.

81. For a trenchant analysis of the evolution of the Executive Office "at the sacrifice of its fundamental principles," see D. Price, *America's Unwritten Constitution* 99–128 (1983).

82. A. Schlesinger, *The Imperial Presidency* 100–26 (1973).

83. T. Lowi, supra note 38, at 11. But see Schlesinger, After the Imperial Presidency, 47 *Md. L. Rev.* 54, 68–72 (1987) ("bound to fail" thesis is unpersuasive as applied to foreign policy).

84. See L. Fisher, *Constitutional Conflicts Between Congress and the President* 140–47 (1985).

85. A. Schlesinger, supra note 82, at viii. Cf. Black, The Presidency and Congress, 32 *Wash. & Lee L. Rev.* 841, 842 (1975) (except for presidential veto, Constitution could have ended after Article I). This shift in historical understanding is ignored in Feld, Separation of Political Powers: Boundaries or Balance? 21 *Ga. L. Rev.* 171, 172 (1987), which proffers a strained reading of the basic constitutional language and ignores original understanding in positing shared decisionmaking rather than division of power.

86. U.S. Const. Art. II, sect. 1.

87. But D. Price, supra note 81, is a valuable antidote against exaggerating the demise of the congressional role in government. He recognizes that presidential government need not necessarily mean "strong" government. Id. at 124–28. More important, he describes just how much power Congress has to impede coherent, centralized government. "Congress is a collective noun, not a disciplined entity." Id. at 92. Price argues that the defects in American government are subconstitutional in nature. Id. at 9.

88. Whether this decision was or is a good or bad idea is a different inquiry. See Sargentich,

The Contemporary Debate about Legislative-Executive Separation of Powers, 72 *Cornell L. Rev.* 430, 437–38 (1987); Wilson, Does the Separation of Powers Still Work? 86 *Pub. Interest* 36 (1987); see also *Reforming American Government: The Bicentennial Papers of the Committee on the Constitution* (D. Robinson ed. 1987); D. Robinson, *"To the Best of My Ability"* 267–81 (1987) (advocating constitutional reform focusing on powers of President).

89. For the best account of the quick collapse of the Framers' design, see R. McCormick, *The Presidential Game* 16–70 (1982).

90. See G. Wood, *The Creation of the American Republic, 1776–1787*, at 506–18 (1969).

91. *Federalist* No. 39, at 252 (J. Madison) (J. Cooke ed. 1961), hints at this. See T. Lowi, supra note 38, at 33–35.

92. J. Ceasar, *Presidential Selection* 5–6 (1979). For an illuminating analysis, see J. Tulis, *The Rhetorical Presidency* 118–32 (1987) (popular presidential leadership involves a fundamental transformation of original constitutional design).

93. T. Lowi, supra note 38, at 121.

94. For example, Assistant Attorney General Elliott Abrams asked, "Is there something wrong with the Administration, having lost the vote in Congress, appealing directly to the American people?" N.Y. Times, Jan. 20, 1987, at A1. col. 4; see also N.Y. Times, Aug. 27, 1987, at A1, col. 2 (Reagan administration used $2 million in private funds to gain the release of two U.S. hostages in Lebanon). On the related issue of presidential use of "private armies" in covert actions, see generally Lobel, Covert War and Congressional Authority: Hidden War and Forgotten Power, 134 *U. Pa. L. Rev.* 1035 (1986) (covert war should be subject to congressional control via letters of marque and reprisal—authorized by Art. 1, sect. 8—rather than executive control).

95. See, e.g., Burke v. Barnes, 107 S. Ct. 734 (1987) (mootness of challenge to pocket veto); Goldwater v. Carter, 444 U.S. 996, 1002–4 (1979) (Rehnquist, J., plurality opinion) (congressional challenge to president's cancellation of treaty is a nonjusticiable political question).

96. The most important, at least theoretically, is Youngstown Sheet & Tube Co. v. Sawyer, 343 U.S. 579 (1952) (invalidating President Truman's seizure of steel mills to prevent strike during Korean War).

97. See supra notes 71–72 and accompanying text.

98. See e.g., United States v. Curtiss-Wright Export Corp. 299 U.S. 304, 319 (1936) ("In this vast external realm . . . the President alone has the power to speak or listen as a representative of the nation").

99. See Dames & Moore v. Regan, 453 U.S. 654 (1981) (construing presidential action as authorized by statute); AFL-CIO v. Kahn, 618 F.2d 784 (D.C. Cir.) (*en banc*) (same), cert. denied, 443 U.S. 915 (1979) (three justices dissenting); cf. Chrysler Corp. v. Brown, 441 U.S. 281 (1979) (declining to invalidate affirmative action executive order or questionable legality). Furthermore, the practical effect of judgments of nonjusticiability, see supra note 95 and accompanying text, is to enhance presidential power.

100. The question of the constitutionality of the War Powers Resolution, Pub. L. No. 93.148, 87 Stat. 555 (1973), provides a good example of this problem. Even if one assumes the resolution is unconstitutional as a matter of original intent, the Presidency's accumulation of power and the consequent deterioration of Congress's ability to check the President's warmaking powers may suggest that the resolution should now be upheld by the Supreme Court.
Another example can be found in I.N.S. v. Chadha, 462 U.S. 919 (1983). There the Court's sweeping condemnation of legislative vetoes surely reflects original understanding. But how can the Court apply original intent theory to legislative vetoes while continuing to sustain open-ended delegations of legislative power to executive and administrative agencies to which the legislative veto is a response? The decisions sanctioning such delegations are surely inconsistent

with original understanding. If the latter decisions are protected from reexamination by stare decisis, what is the content of a theory that applies original understanding to one set of concerns but stare decisis to a set of closely related concerns?

Finally, in re Sealed Case, Nos. 87.5261, 87.5264, 87.5265, Misc. Nos. 87.00197, 87.00205, 87.00215 (D.C. Cir. Jan. 22, 1988), the recent decision by a panel of the D.C. Circuit striking down the independent counsel provisions of the Ethics in Government Act of 1978, 28 U.S.C. sect. 49, 591–598 (1982 and Supp. III 1985), can be criticized on the same grounds.

101. This I take is the crux of R. Dworkin, supra note 3, at 355–99, and Richards, supra note 17, at 822–25. A variant of the high level of abstraction approach is the argument that, advertently or inadvertently, the Framers delegated open-ended decisionmaking power to future judges. See, e.g.. Komesar, Back to the Future—An Institutional View of Making and Interpreting Constitutions, 81 *Nw. U. L. Rev.* 191, 203 (1987). Closely related to these approaches, even if analytically distinguishable, are those theories which insist that the Framers contemplated shifting interpretations based on social change. See Richards, A Theory of Free Speech, 34 *UCLA L. Rev.* 1837, 1858 (1987).

102. But see Monaghan, supra note 16, at 378–81 (criticizing those who conceptualize original intent at such a level of abstraction that for all practical purposes it is removed as an interpretive constraint).

103. E.g., Brest, supra note 7, at 244–45.

104. Ackerman, The Storrs Lectures: Discovering the Constitution, 93 *Yale L. J.* 1013, 1053–57 (1984). Professor Ackerman will more fully develop this theme in a forthcoming book.

105. See Schauer, Precedent, 39 *Stan. L. Rev.* 571, 591–95 (1987).

106. This attack antedates the Realists. E.g., Whitney, The Doctrine of Stare Decisis, 3 *Mich. L. Rev.* 89, 94 (1904) (doctrine of stare decisis "must disappear through the inevitable course of human progress"). The attack reflects more than the need perceived by the courts to respond effectively to rapidly accelerating social and economic change; it also reflects a centuries old and accelerating decline in beliefs of permanent ordering with respect to any form of social or intellectual activity. See F. Baumer, *Modern European Thought, Continuity and Change in Ideas, 1600–1950,* at 20–23 (1977). In the United States, this decline has been sharply reinforced by the emergence and dominance of pragmatism in philosophy and instrumentalism in legal thinking. "Pragmatic instrumentalism'" has been described as America's dominant philosophy of law. Summers, Professor Fuller's Jurisprudence and America's Dominant Philosophy of Law, 92 *Harv. L. Rev.* 433, 435–36 (1978). See generally Aleinikoff, supra note 34, at 955–58 (discussing growth and tenets of pragmatic instrumentalism).

107. Rather, precedent will only prevail after there has been analysis of the "disadvantages of making the particular change." Schaefer, Precedent and Policy, 34 *Univ. Chicago L. Rev.* 3, 12 (1966).

108. In my view, the currently disfavored status of precedent in constitutional adjudication is also strongly reinforced by the fundamental premises of what I have elsewhere described as "perfectionist" constitutional theory. Monaghan, supra note 16, at 356. But, it must be noted, the disfavored status of precedent is not confined to perfectionists, as the attitude of Chief Justice Rehnquist toward precedent illustrates. See, e.g., Garcia v. San Antonio Metro. Auth., 469 U.S. 528, 580 (1985) (Rehnquist, J., dissenting) (advocating future reversal of the case). Some writers have thought that the background of members of the Court has contributed importantly to attitudes toward precedent. Armstrong, Mr. Justice Douglas on Stare Decisis: A Condensation of the Eighth Cardozo Lecture, 35 *A.B.A.J.* 541, 543 (1949). My own belief is that stare decisis is undercut by law teachers and their deep-rooted belief that lawyers are social engineers.

109. See, e.g., United States v. Scott, 437 U.S. 82 (1978), which contains the canonical reference: "[I]n cases involving the Federal Constitution, where correction through legislative action is practically impossible, this court has often overruled its earlier decisions. The Court bows to the lessons of experience and the force of better reasoning, recognizing that the process of trial and error, so fruitful in the physical sciences, is appropriate also in the judicial function." Id. at 101 (quoting Burnet v. Coronado Oil & Gas Co., 285 U.S. 393, 406–8 [1932]) (Brandeis, J., dissenting).

110. Burnet, 285 U.S. at 406 (Brandeis, J. dissenting).

111. For example, the fact that legislative action cannot shift the point at which double jeopardy attaches from the impanelment of the jury to presentation of evidence, Crist v. Bretz, 437 U.S. 28, 38 (1978), does not support the argument for a dilution of stare decisis in constitutional adjudication. The issue is simply not important enough.

112. Were the Court to sustain, after a Fourteenth Amendment challenge, discrimination against women or illegitimates, nothing would prevent the states from passing corrective legislation to secure the claimed rights. Congress possesses similar competence by virtue of its regulatory authority under the commerce clause and the Fourteenth Amendment, to say nothing of its power to extract adherence to nationally formulated norms through conditional spending. See, e.g., Honig v. Doe, 108 S. Ct. 592 (1988). Much civil rights law is statutory in character, and these statutes impose norms not required by the Constitution standing alone. Affirmative action might be an exception to this argument.

113. Maltz, Some Thoughts on the Death of Stare Decisis in Constitutional Law, 1980 *Wis. L. Rev.* 467, 467 ("It seems fair to say that if a majority of the Warren or Burger Court has considered a case wrongly decided, no constitutional precedent—new or old—has been safe."); see also id. at 494–96 (listing cases from 1960 to 1979 in which the Supreme Court overruled itself). This fact is apparent not only from the freedom with which the Supreme Court overruled precedents, but in the often cavalier way in which they are "distinguished." Monaghan, Taking Supreme Court Opinions Seriously, 39 *Md. L. Rev.* 1, 2–3 (1979).

114. 469 U.S. 528 (1985).

115. See, e.g., Frickey, A Further Comment on Stare Decisis and the Overruling of National League of Cities, 2 *Const. Comment.* 341, 345 (1985); Maltz, supra note 113, at 467.

116. 426 U.S. 833 (1976).

117. Maryland v. Wirtz, 392 U.S. 183 (1968).

118. *Garcia*, 469 U.S. at 557.

119. Id. at 580 (Rehnquist, J., dissenting); id. at 589 (O'Connor, J., dissenting).

120. See Note, The Power That Shall Be Vested in a Precedent: Stare Decisis, the Constitution and the Supreme Court, 66 *B.U. L. Rev.* 345, 371–75 (1986); Giraudo, Realism, Positivism and Adherence to Stare Decisis: Has the Doctrine Outlived Its Usefulness? 37–39 (on file at *Columbia Law Review*).

121. See Welch v. Texas Dept. of Highways and Pub. Transp., 107 S. Ct. 2941 (1987) (overruling the "quasi-constitutional" holding in Parden v. Terminal Ry., 377 U.S. 184 [1964]); Solorio v. United States, 107 S. Ct. 2924 (1987) (overruling O'Callahan v. Parker, 395 U.S. 258 [1969]); Tyler Pipe Indus. v. Washington Dept. of Revenue, 107 S. Ct. 2810 (1987) (overruling General Motors Corp. v. Washington, 377 U.S. 136 [1964]); Puerto Rico v. Branstad, 107 S. Ct. 2802, 2807–10 (1987) (overruling Kentucky v. Dennison, 65 U.S. (24 How.) 66 [1861]).

122. In *Branstad*, the Court elaborated how *Dennison* was "fundamentally incompatible with more than a century of constitutional development." *Branstad*, 107 S. Ct. at 2809. While the Court in *Welch* did not address issues of stare decisis in its decision to overrule *Parden*, it was quick to rely on the force of precedent to refuse to overrule Hans v. Louisiana, 134 U.S. 1 (1890). *Welch*, 107 S. Ct. at 2948–49. Such selective reliance does little to enhance the Court's reputation as an objective or principled arbiter.

123. See, e.g., Vasquez v. Hillery, 474 U.S. 254, 260–64 (1986) (refusing to abandon rule that discriminatory selection of grand jurors cannot be harmless error); Harris v. McRae, 448 U.S. 297, 316–18 (1980) (holding, on basis of Maher v. Roe, 432 U.S. 464 [1977], that states participating in Medicaid program are not obligated under the Social Security Act to continue to fund medically necessary abortions for which federal reimbursements are unavailable); Wolman v. Walter, 433 U.S. 229, 251 n. 18 (1977) (refusing on grounds of stare decisis to presume that state-supported educational materials for private schools would not be used for religious purposes); City of Akron v. Akron Center for Reproductive Health, Inc., 462 U.S. 416 (1983), discussed infra notes 136–38 and accompanying text. A cognate, but not identical problem arises in the area of statutorily based civil liberties. See Johnson v. Transportation Agency, 107 S. Ct. 1442, 1458–60 (1987) (Stevens, J., concurring) (Title VII of Civil Rights Act. 42 U.S.C. sect. 2000e-2[a]); id. at 1460–61 (O'Connor, J., concurring) (same); Runyon v. McCrary, 427 U.S. 160, 189–92 (1976) (Stevens, J., concurring) (sect. 1981 of Civil Rights Act, 42 U.S.C. 1981).

124. See Dam, The Legal Tender Cases, 1981 *Sup. Ct. Rev.* 367, 389 ("In short, although it may have been inconvenient to the proponents and constitutional defenders of legal tender paper money, it is difficult to escape the conclusion that the Framers intended to prohibit its use."). Dam points out that the Framers intended to prohibit paper money altogether, but by the time of the Legal Tender Cases only the issue of investing paper with the quality of legal tender was effectively open. Id. at 390: see also B. Siegan, *The Supreme Court's Constitution* 30 (1987) (reaching similar conclusions).

125. See Dam, supra note 124, at 367 n. 1 (collecting cases).

126. Id. at 367.

127. See Knox v. Lee, 79 U.S. (12 Wall.) 45 (1871) (overruling Hepburn v. Griswold, 75 U.S. [8 Wall.] 603 [1870]). In *Knox*, the Court described *Hepburn* as a case that "was decided by a divided court, and by a court having a less number of judges than the law . . . provided this court shall have." *Knox*, 79 U.S. (12 Wall.) at 553–54. Moreover, overruling was not "unprecedented," and this was not a case of "private right," but one that involved "far-reaching consequences." Id. at 554. Concurring, Justice Bradley said: "On a question relating to the power of the government, where I am perfectly satisfied that it has the power, I can never consent to abide by a decision denying it, unless made with reasonable unanimity and acquiesced in by the country. Where the decision is recent, and is only made by a bare majority of the court, and during a time of public excitement on the subject, when the question has largely entered into the political discussions of the day, I consider it our right and duty to subject it to a further examination, if a majority of the court are dissatisfied with the former decision." Id. at 569–70.

128. This line of decision culminated in Julliard v. Greenman, 110 U.S. 421 (1884), and generated the first law review essay on stare decisis in constitutional law. See Chamberlain, The Doctrine of Stare Decisis as Applied to Decisions of Constitutional Questions, 3 *Harv. L. Rev.* 125 (1889).

129. While a distinction between civil rights and social and political rights cannot be maintained today, to the Framers of the Fourteenth Amendment the distinction was all-important. The amendment was intended to apply only to "civil" rights: personal security, personal liberty (freedom from bodily restraint), and private property. R. Berger, supra note 3, at 20–36.

130. Ackerman, supra note 104, at 1063–70.

131. As Justice Holmes put it, "With regard to that we may add that when we are dealing with words that also are a constituent act, like the Constitution . . . we must realize that they have called into life a being the development of which could not have been foreseen completely by the most gifted of its begetters. . . . The case before us must be considered in the light of our whole experience and not merely in that of what was said a hundred years ago." Missouri v. Holland, 252 U.S. 416, 433 (1920).

132. Perhaps there is still a third category: weak precedents—not really controversial, but not strong enough to hold their own once reexamined. At present, this category, if it exists, seems to add nothing distinctive beyond the contested category, and I subsume it there.

133. There is a separate group of agenda limitation cases not directly dealt with in this essay. These cases are off the agenda not because of their importance but because they involve issues about which there is no current interest. The constitutionality of the remittitur practice may be one example. I have treated these as raising issues not different from the contested area.

134. Typical is the attitude of Attorney General Meese. Apparently he has endorsed a 128-page report urging that Miranda v. Arizona, 384 U.S. 436 (1966), be overruled. So far as presently appears, no attention is given to the systemic implications of overruling well-known decisions. Instead, the focus is solely on the obnoxious precedent and on the assumed immediate need to set right the constitutional law. See Shennon, Meese Seen as Ready to Challenge Rule on Telling Suspects of Rights, N.Y. Times. Jan. 22. 1987, at A1, col. 2 ("'The interesting question is not whether Miranda should go, but how we should facilitate its demise, and what we should replace it with. . . . We regard a challenge to Miranda as essential'") (quoting report).

135. 410 U.S. 113 (1973).

136. City of Akron v. Akron Center for Reproductive Health, Inc., 462 U.S. 416, 419–20 (1983).

137. See id. at 420 n. 1.

138. See id. at 458 (O'Connor, J., dissenting).

139. See Thornburgh v. American College of Obstetricians and Gynecologists, 106 S. Ct. 2169, 2193 (1986) (White, Rehnquist, JJ., dissenting); see also Myers, Prolife Litigation and Civil Liberties, in *Abortion and the Constitution: Reversing* Roe v. Wade *Through the Courts* 32 (D. Horan, E. Grant and P. Cunningham eds. 1987) (discussing Justice White's opinion in *Thornburgh*).

140. See Schauer, supra note 105, at 587.

141. 65 U.S. (24 How.) 66 (1861) (overruled by Puerto Rico v. Branstad, 107 S. Ct. 2802, 2809–2810 [1987]).

142. 377 U.S. 436 (1964) (overruled by Tyler Pipe Indus. v. Washington State Dept. of Revenue, 107 S. Ct. 2810, 2817 [1987]).

143. The need for a theory is true even were one to posit stare decisis as a wholly discretionary political doctrine, permitting the Court to maintain past decisions that it likes. That, of course, is a theory, but it is a theory about the judicial process that would make many people uncomfortable, at least those who believe that the Court is something other than a power organ and that doctrine is not simply a rhetorical mask obscuring this reality.

144. For an evaluation of how well these values are achieved by judicial adherence to precedent, see R. Wasserstrom, *The Judicial Decision: Toward a Theory of Legal Justification* 60–81 (1961).

145. See Giraudo, supra note 120, at 57–67; Note, supra note 120, at 371–75.
    Code countries operate without any formal doctrine of precedent. Moreover, for judges who would overrule precedent, any significant reliance claims can be substantially accommodated through the now common device of prospective overruling. Justice O'Connor overlooked that possibility in American Trucking Assoc. v. Scheiner, 107 S. Ct. 2829, 2849 (1987) (dissenting opinion) ("reliance interest sought to be protected by the doctrine of *stare decisis* has grown up around the settled rule. . . . [when the state] has collected some $300 million in axle taxes").

146. Rawls, The Idea of an Overlapping Consensus, 7 *Oxford J. Legal Stud.* 1, 1 (1987).

147. McCulloch v. Maryland, 17 U.S. (4 Wheat.) 316, 415 (1819). Of course, I do not claim that the values identified are unique to constitutional law, but only that they have greater purchase there.

148. *Federalist* No. 49, at 341 (J. Madison) (J. Cooke ed. 1961). *Federalist* No. 50, at 343–47 (J. Madison) (J. Cooke ed. 1961), also discourages periodic appeals to the people.

149. See J. Greene, *Peripheries and Center* 65–68 (1986) (describing disputes on the nature of the imperial constitution as distinguished from the Constitution of Great Britain); 2 J. Reid, *Constitutional History of the American Revolution* (1987) (describing colonists' perception of the sources and nature of their rights to refuse taxation by British); see also Kay, The Illegality of the Constitution, 4 *Const. Comment.* 57, 71 (1987) ("The political actors who brought the Constitution into effect were well aware of the need for political, non-legal justifications for their actions").

150. See Chase, Toward a Legal Theory of Popular Culture, 1986 *Wis. L. Rev.* 527, 528–29 ("quotidian experience of law and lawyers [is] an appropriate, indeed central, subject of radical and systematic contemporary legal theory" if the legal theory is to be culturally legitimate); Hyde, The Concept of Legitimation in the Sociology of Law, 1983 *Wis. L. Rev.* 379, 419 (current legitimacy theory "explain[s] neither obedience, revolt, nor legal behavior").

151. See M. Kelman, *A Guide to Critical Legal Studies* 262–68 (1987).

152. See Chase, supra note 150, at 543–45 (no adequate reception theory exists for popular culture).

153. J. Ely, *Democracy and Distrust* 59 n** (1980).

154. C. Black, *The People and the Court* 38, 51 (1960). The Supreme Court is not the exclusive mechanism. The amendment process is another. Professor Ackerman's constitutional moments would also qualify. See also Rawls, supra note 146, at 13–20 (an "overlapping consensus" on a political conception of justice controls the public agenda by establishing common ground and placing certain issues outside public debate).

155. This result cannot be avoided simply by saying that the Court could stay any particular judgment until an amendment were passed and that corrective amendments would be enacted. See, e.g., Northern Pipeline Constr. Co. v. Marathon Pipe Line Co. 458 U.S. 50, 87–89 (1982) (giving only prospective effect to holding that bankruptcy courts established by Congress were unconstitutional). Perhaps that would suffice, perhaps not. But I am concerned with a different order of magnitude.

156. Moreover, while my general inclination is to think about legitimation theory within the framework of elite theories of democracy, see Monaghan, Book Review, 94 *Harv. L. Rev.* 296, 308 n.42 (1980), judicial repudiation of any fundamental feature of current constitutional order would extend my concern about the legitimation crisis to the general public.

157. Powell, Parchment Matters: A Meditation on the Constitution as Text, 71 *Iowa L. Rev.* 1127, 1433 (1986).

158. A. Bickel, *The Least Dangerous Branch* 200–1 (1962).

159. Id. at 204–7. In this regard Bickel followed C. Black, supra note 154, at 56–86 (judicial review legitimates governmental action among the general public).

160. Rather than declining jurisdiction, the Court ordinarily uses precedent to avoid delegitimation by refusing to hear cases, or by considering the merits without adverting to any lower court challenge to foundational principles. See, e.g., Wallace v. Jaffree, 472 U.S. 38, 48–50 (1985) (summarily rejecting the district court's "remarkable conclusion" that the establishment clause does not restrict the states).

161. Rawls, supra note 146, at 12–15.

162. "No sound assessment of our Supreme Court can treat it as an isolated, self-sustaining, or self-sufficient institution. It is a unit of a complex, interdependent scheme of government from which it cannot be severed. Nor can it be regarded merely as another law court. The Court's place in the combination was determined by principles drawn from a philosophy broader than mere law." R. Jackson, *The Supreme Court in the American System of Government* 2 (1963); see also O. Holmes, *The Common Law* 36 (M. Howe ed. 1963) ("The first requirement of a sound body of law is, that it should correspond with the actual feelings and demands of the community, whether right or wrong").

163. But it bears emphasis that it acted as a catalyst only. The case-by-case method was ultimately replaced by political action. See South Carolina v. Katzenbach, 383 U.S. 301, 313–15 (1966) (describing the limits of the case-by-case method as a vehicle for eliminating voting discrimination).

164. Dworkin, supra note 3, at 88.

165. A. Cox, *The Court and Constitution* 69–71 (1987). This is an avowedly conservative conception of the judicial office—conservative in a Burkean, not libertarian sense. There is an important and wide difference between the two. See, e.g., S. Macedo, supra note 9, at 21–31 (a libertarian criticism of Judge Bork's "New Right" belief that the animating principle of the Constitution is majority rule).

166. See supra notes 132–33 and accompanying text.

167. A. Cox, *The Role of the Supreme Court in American Government* 50 (1976). Nearly fifty years ago, Roscoe Pound argued that some conception of stare decisis was vital to the concept of limited government and the rule of law by restricting judicial "absolutism." Pound, What of Stare Decisis? 10 *Fordham L. Rev.* 1, 5 (1941). For the—to my mind doubtful—suggestion that the lack of effective stare decisis in constitutional cases blurs any distinction between a written and unwritten Constitution, see Brown, Construing the Constitution: A Trial Lawyer's Plea for Stare Decisis, 44 *A.B.A.J.* 742, 743 (1958).

168. Moragne v. States Marine Lines, 398 U.S. 375, 403 (1970).

169. E.g., Solorio v. United States, 107 S. Ct. 2924, 2941 (1987) (Marshall, J., dissenting) ("bedrock principles are founded in law rather than in the proclivities of individuals") (quoting Vasquez v. Hillery, 474 U.S. 254, 265 [1986]).

170. Note, supra note 120, at 353–56; see also Haltom and Silverstein, The Scholarly Tradition Revisited: Alexander Bickel, Herbert Wechsler, and the Legitimacy of Judicial Review, 4 *Const. Comment.* 25, 32–40 (1987) (person in the street generally unaware of basis of Court's decisions). Recently, Judge Posner expressed his opinion that a general failure to adhere to precedent in constitutional cases would weaken the legitimacy of the federal judiciary by weakening the popular acceptance of judicial decisions. *Harv. L. Record*, Nov. 21, 1986, at 5, col. 3; at 13, col. 1.

171. Professor Cox speculates about the possibility of the "reformist" Warren Court decisions being overruled by a future "reformist" Court and ponders the "effect of a succession of reforms and re-reforms upon the position of the Court and the idea of law." A. Cox, supra note 167, at 111.

172. A. Cox, supra note 165, at 377.

173. Smith v. Allwright, 321 U.S. 649, 669 (1944) (Roberts, J., dissenting).

174. See A. Cox, supra note 165, at 364.

175. See generally Monaghan, The Supreme Court 1974 Term—Foreword: Constitutional Common Law, 89 *Harv. L. Rev.* 1 (1975).

176. Of course, to say that stare decisis is binding on the Court does not specify the content of the command.

177. Monaghan, supra note 175, at 29.

178. 410 U.S. 179 (1973).

179. For example, suppose that Congress enacted a comprehensive criminal code for the District of Columbia enforceable in the United States District Court, in which Congress restricted abortions in a manner similar to that done in the Model Penal Code sect. 230.3 (1985). Substantially such a statute was struck down in *Doe*, 410 U.S. at 193–200, and the new congressional statute would thus be subject to similar condemnation. Even if the new statute were accompanied by a congressional finding of constitutionality, that would be of no avail, since Marbury v. Madison, 5 U.S. (1 Cranch) 137, 177 (1803), makes plain the judicial duty of independent judgment in these circumstances. See Monaghan, supra note 72, at 12. Nor could *Doe*'s authority be avoided by denying the district court "jurisdiction" to consider the constitutionality of the statute. So long as a federal court is called upon to enforce a statute, the federal court system cannot be foreclosed from examining its validity. P. Bator, P. Mishkin, D. Shapiro and H. Wechsler, *Hart and Wechsler's The Federal Courts and the Federal System* 336–41 (2d ed. 1973) (hereafter Hart and Wechsler). Accordingly, unless *Doe* were overruled, the new statute would be invalid. See generally Brest, Congress as Constitutional Decisionmaker and Its Power to Counter Judicial Doctrine, 21 *Ga. L. Rev.* 57, 98–101 (1986) (Congress not presently structured to make challenges to judicially declared constitutional government).

180. Such a statutory directive does not purport to dictate the outcome of the reconsideration; it simply directs the Court to consider the issue *res nova*. Thus, United States v. Klein, 80 U.S. (13 Wall.) 128 (1871), which held that legislation aimed at dictating a court's rule of decision is unconstitutional, is-not on point. See United States v. Sioux Nation of Indians, 448 U.S. 371, 402–5 (1980) (*Klein* not applicable when "Congress was [not] attempting to decide the controversy at issue in the Government's own favor" and when Congress does not attempt to dictate a rule of decision). Moreover, if traditional requirements of justiciability have a textual source, such requirements would also have to be met before the Supreme Court would grant review on the merits.

181. See Wechsler, The Courts and the Constitution, 65 *Colum. L. Rev.* 1001, 1008 (1965).

182. This point seems to me to be ignored by those who rather peremptorily dismiss congressional expressions on the meaning of the Constitution. See, e.g., Carter, The *Morgan* "Power" and the Forced Reconsideration of Constitutional Decisions, 53 *Univ. Chicago L. Rev.* 819, 853–56 (1986).

183. See Radin, Case Law and Stare Decisis: Concerning *Prajudizienrecht in Amerika*, 33 *Colum. L. Rev.* 199, 200–201 (1933).

184. This discussion focuses on stare decisis in terms of the Court rather than in terms of the obligation of an individual member of the Court toward precedent. The latter may well present quite different issues. My own view is that justices are members of a Court, a collective body designed to reach collective judgment, not individual monads that collide only in the process of voting. See Monaghan, supra note 113, at 12–25. I quite agree with Justice Powell that individual justices "have an institutional responsibility not only to respect *stare decisis* but also to make every reasonable effort to harmonize our views on constitutional questions of broad practical application." Robbins v. California, 453 U.S. 420, 436 n.4 (1981) (Powell, J., concurring). The increasing tendency to submit individual views on the merits is, I think, quite deplorable. See also Cox, The Supreme Court, 1979 Term—Foreword: Freedom of Expression in the Burger Court, 94 *Harv. L. Rev.* 1, 72 (1980) ("Continuous fragmentation could well diminish not only the influence of the Court but the ideal of the rule of law"). As both a theoretical and a practical matter his view may improperly discount the individuality of each member of the Court. See Kelman, The Forked Path of Dissent, 1985 *Sup. Ct. Rev.* 227, 228–29 ("In none of the highest courts . . . have the obligations of collegiality or the limits of individuality ever been precisely defined"); see also Douglas, Stare Decisis, 49 *Colum. L. Rev.* 735, 736 (1949) ("personal matter for each judge"). Be that as it may, my emphasis on the Court suggests there are limits imposed on individual dissents based upon original understanding (or any other basis). These limits seem to follow not from stare decisis but from the ongoing commitments one assumes in becoming a member of an institution. For this reason, Justice Harlan's dissenting opinion in

Oregon v. Mitchell, 400 U.S. 112, 152 (1970) (Harlan, J., concurring in part and dissenting in part), has always struck me as among the most troubling in constitutional law. Justice Harlan cast a fifth vote against a congressional act lowering the voting age in state elections to eighteen. Most of his elaborate opinion was designed to show that voting was not an interest intended to be protected by section 1 of the Fourteenth Amendment, a position which I think is historically correct, but which seemed foreclosed by a long and unbroken line of Supreme Court authority. Justice Harlan conceded that were he to have followed the precedents he would have upheld the federal legislation. Id. at 152. Nonetheless, he devoted but a few paragraphs to the claims of stare decisis, ultimately rejecting it on this fundamental matter. Id. at 218–19. I think he was mistaken on this point. I have grave doubt that a judge should cast a deciding vote on the basis of a theory, however historically correct, that is unacceptable to his own colleagues, has long been unacceptable to his colleagues, and that has no reasonable likelihood of being acceptable to any future justice. By contrast, Justices Brennan and Marshall's continuous refusal to be bound by the Court's holding that the death penalty is not per se invalid seems more defensible. See, e.g., McCleskey v. Kemp, 107 S. Ct. 1756, 1781 (1987) (Brennan, J., dissenting). Though I disagree with them on the merits, their institutional commitments as members of the Court cannot yet be invoked to silence their dissents, because it cannot clearly be said that within some reasonable future their view will not commend itself to some future court.

185. Goodhart, Precedent in English and Continental Law, 50 *Law Q. Rev.* 40, 41 (1934).

186. See, e.g., Hudson v. Guestier, 10 U.S. (6 Cranch) 281, 285 (1810) (overruling in part Rose v. Himely, 8 U.S. [4 Cranch] 241 [1808]).

187. Radin, supra note 183, at 200. I agree with Radin's assertion that stare decisis is not involved if the court "follows a previous decision . . . because it is the right decision, because it is logical, because it is just." Id.

188. Id. at 201.

189. Id. On this view, Radin would certainly deny that my agenda-limitation illustrations, see supra notes 124–31 and accompanying text, are examples of stare decisis at all.

190. Radin, supra note 183, at 212. Obviously this conception could—and did—serve as a predicate for a powerful criticism that the doctrine of stare decisis was an absurd way of decisionmaking because it meant that courts "are principally engaged in doing things they know to be irrational for no better reason than that they have seen some one else do them." Id. at 199.

191. It seems more accurate to say that in the American experience "the institution of precedent is not a single doctrine but a whole cluster of doctrines which, taken together, leaves far more room than is commonly supposed for development and change." Jones, Precedent and Policy in Constitutional Law, 4 *Pace L. Rev.* 11, 19 (1983).

192. See generally Schauer, supra note 105, at 591–95 (discussing strength and breadth of precedents).

193. Pound, supra note 167, at 6.

194. I assume that the precedent-setting court is itself "fully committed to [the] principle [of the decision]." Jackson, Decisional Law and Stare Decisis, 30 *A.B.A.J.* 334, 335 (1944). If this assumption does not hold true in any specific instance, a precedent's force may be less binding. See, e.g., Puerto Rico v. Branstad, 107 S. Ct. 2802, 2806, 2809 (1987) (rejecting Kentucky v. Dennison, 65 U.S. [24 How.] 66 [1861]), and suggesting that *Dennison* itself was a decision significantly explicable by the political pressures on the Court).

195. See Fitzleet Estates Ltd. v. Cherry, 3 All E.R. 996, 1000 (H.L. 1977) (Viscount Dilhorne) ("If the decision . . . was wrong, it certainly was not so clearly wrong and productive of injustice as to make it right for the House to depart from it"); Israel, Gideon v. Wainwright: The "Art" of Overruling, 1963 *Sup. Ct. Rev.* 211, 219–26 (precedent is generally overruled on the basis of changed conditions, the lessons of experience, or the existence of inconsistent precedent). On the current attitude of the House of Lords toward overruling precedent, see A. Paterson, *The Law Lords* 156–57 (1982).

196. Perry, Judicial Obligation: Precedent and the Common Law, 7 *Oxford J. Legal Stud.* 215, 221–22 (1987) (comparing strong and weak forms of stare decisis); see infra notes 202–203, 238 and accompanying text.

197. Some constitutional decisions seem to have little analogical impact—whether, for example, the double jeopardy protection commences when the jury is sworn or when evidence is heard.

198. The importance of reasoning by analogy was clear to Bracton in the thirteenth century. "If like matters arise let them be decided by like, since the occasion is a good one for proceeding *a similibus ad similia.*" 2 Bracton, On the Laws and Customs of England 21 (G. Woodbine ed. 1968).

199. Lord Devlin remarked of the common law that it "is tolerant of much illogicality, especially on the surface; but no system of law can be workable if it has not got logic at the root of it." Hedley Byrne & Co. v. Heller & Partners Ltd., 1964 App Cas. 465, 516.

200. See R. Dworkin, supra note 3, at 217–21. Precedents that, for one reason or another, are inconsistent with wider principles are vulnerable to overruling. See, e.g., Puerto Rico v. Branstad, 107 S. Ct. 2802, 2808 (1987) (overruling Kentucky v. Dennison, 65 U.S. [24 How.] 66 [1861], because "basic constitutional principles now point as clearly the other way," and thus the "fundamental premise of the holding in *Dennison* . . . is not representative of the law today").

201. See R. Dworkin, supra note 3, at 219–24 (consistency may sometimes be required to give way to integrity or even pragmatic concerns); Coons, Consistency, 75 *Calif. L. Rev.* 59, 98–113 (1987) (discussing problems with consistency and finding utility in inconsistency).

202. M. Farrand, *The Framing of the Constitution* 201 (1913).

203. In a different context, Justice Scalia put a similar distinction well: "The Board's approach is the product of a familiar phenomenon. Once having succeeded, by benefit of excessive judicial deference, in expanding the scope of a statute beyond a reasonable interpretation of its language, the emboldened agency presses the rationale of that expansion to the limits of its logic. And the Court, having already sanctioned a point of departure that is genuinely not to be found within the language of the statute, finds itself cut off from that authoritative source of the law, and ends up construing not the statute but its own construction. Applied to an erroneous point of departure, the logical reasoning that is ordinarily the mechanism of judicial adherence to the rule of law perversely carries the Court further and further from the meaning of that statute. Some distance down that path, however, there comes a point at which a later incremental step, again rational in itself, leads to a result so far removed from the statute that obedience to text must overcome fidelity to logic." NLRB v. International Brotherhood of Elec. Workers, Local 340, 107 S. Ct. 2002, 2016 (1987) (Scalia, J., concurring).

204. Compare, for example, the efforts by former Justice Goldberg, who viewed the key clauses as open textured, to protect the expansive holdings of the Warren Court with a strong theory of stare decisis. A. Goldberg, *Equal Justice: The Warren Era of the Supreme Court* 74, 80–81 (1971).

205. L. Tribe, *American Constitutional Law* 2 (Supp. 1979).

206. B. Cardozo, *The Nature of the Judicial Process* (1921).

207. See Dimick v. Schiedt, 293 U.S. 474, 482–85 (1935) (remittitur practice probably unconstitutional as a matter of original understanding but followed as a matter of stare decisis).

208. See Crist v. Bretz, 437 U.S. 28, 38 (1978).

209. At least this is so if the decisions do not represent an unbroken line of authority over a long period of time. Carter v. Carter Coal Co., 298 U.S. 238 (1936), in fact rested upon the choice of one conflicting line of authority over another. See Stern, The Commerce Clause and the National Economy, 1933–1946, 59 *Harv. L. Rev.* 645, 647 (1946) ("there was ample authority in the Supreme Court opinions looking both ways").

210. Brief for Appellees on Reargument at 59–60, Briggs v. Elliott, 347 U.S. 483 (1954).

211. It can be argued that the government should never be able to rely on stare decisis to protect its reliance interest; such a principle may have disposed of the stare decisis claim. But this limitation on stare decisis should not often prove important in constitutional adjudication, see supra text accompanying note 145, at least so long as the precedent affected private persons.

212. See J. Ely, supra note 153, at 136–81.

213. See Jones, supra note 191, at 591–93; Pound, supra note 167, at 6. Of course, this formulation is prone to the danger of vacuousness: precedents should be followed unless they shouldn't be. See R. Wasserstrom, supra note 144, at 39–55.

214. See Puerto Rico v. Branstad, 107 S. Ct. 2802 (overruling Kentucky v. Dennison, 65 U.S. [24. How.] 66 [1861]).

215. Tyler Pipe Indus. v. Washington Dept. of Revenue, 107 S. CL. 2810 (1987) (overruling General Motors Corp. v. Washington, 377 U.S. 436 [1964]).

216. Wallace, Whose Constitution? in *Still the Law of the Land?* 10 (C. Roche ed. 1987). See Frickey, supra note 115, at 342 (factors that the Court properly relied on in overruling *National League of Cities* include the fact that the case was wrongly decided, that its precedential value was weak because of an uncertain fifth vote, and that it was unworkable in practice). Chief Justice Rehnquist's readiness to overrule precedent suggests an even less deferential attitude toward stare decisis.

217. See the discussion of the justifications for according stare decisis a role in constitutional adjudication, supra notes 144–74 and accompanying text, especially the discussion of maintaining the legitimacy of judicial review, supra notes 166–74 and accompanying text, which is applicable to all cases; see also the adoption of Dean Pound's formulation of stare decisis, supra note 193 and accompanying text.

218. 302 U.S. 319, 325 (1937).

219. 356 U.S. 86, 101 (1958).

220. See, e.g., Shennon, supra note 134, at A1, col. 2.

221. See Hart and Wechsler, supra note 179, at 660–62.

222. See generally C. Allen, *Law in the Making* 183–258 (6th ed. 1958) (precedent in the English system). We are concerned with "precedent" as it appears to the Supreme Court, not to lower courts. In the latter respect, it may look quite different. Schauer, Book Review, 53 *Univ. Chicago L. Rev.* 682, 682–84 (1986).

223. See Goodhart, Determining the Ratio Decidendi of a Case, 40 *Yale L. J.* 161, 169, 182 (1930).

224. See E. Levi, *An Introduction to Legal Reasoning* 2 (1949).

225. See Simpson, The *Ratio Decidendi* of a Case, 21 *Mod. L. Rev.* 155 (1958); cf. Montrose, Ratio Decidendi and the House of Lords, 20 *Mod. L. Rev.* 124, 125 (1957) (difficulties of applying precedent when defined as articulated legal rules). But see Goodhart, The Ratio Decidendi of a Case, 22 *Mod. L. Rev.* 117, 121 (1959) (criticizing the "classical" theory that the binding precedent is the rule invoked).

226. See Summers, Two Types of Substantive Reasons: The Core of a Theory of Common-Law Justification, 63 *Cornell L. Rev.* 707, 730–32 (1978) (The precedent consists of "nothing less than facts, issues, ruling, and substantive reasons for those rulings.").

227. See J. Frank, *Courts on Trial* 262–89 (1949); Oliphant, A Return to Stare Decisis, 14 *A.B.A.J.* 71, 159 (1928). For a modern statement of this view, see Jones, supra note 191, at 22 ("It is the court's *decision* that is the precedent, not what the court says in the judicial opinion justifying that decision").

228. See, e.g., N. MacCormick, *Legal Reasoning* 117–19 (1978); J. Stone, *The Province and Function of Law* 187–88 (1950).

229. What the Court "said" may be ascertained by implication in some cases. What the Court "said" in a given summary affirmance, for example, may be incontestable even though entirely inferential.

230. R. Dworkin, *Taking Rights Seriously* 111 (1978).

231. Pound, supra note 167, at 9–10.

232. See infra note 246.

233. Pound, supra note 167, at 8.

234. See Monaghan, supra note 113, at 1625. If the Court was simply to announce one summary disposition after another, one would be required to rethink precedent. See Perry, supra note 196, at 235 (jurisprudential analysis of stare decisis which, inter alia, insists that judicial reasoning is part of the precedent).

235. Statements such as those asserting that the prior decision "is not strictly controlling, in the sense that no holding can be broader than the facts before the court," U.S. v. Stanley, 107 S. Ct. 3054, 3062 (1987), are unpersuasive.

236. I do not think we can—or should—dispense with some distinction between holding and dicta. E.g., Crawford Fitting Co. v. J. T. Gibbons, Inc., 107 S. Ct. 2494, 2498 (1987). Some distinction along this line seems to be particularly necessary with respect to often sprawling, undisciplined, heavily footnoted opinions issued by the Supreme Court. Closely analogous is recognition that important holdings are not made in passing in footnotes. E.g., Perry v. Thomas, 107 S. Ct. 2520, 2526 (1987) (oblique reference in footnote to Merrill Lynch, Pierce, Fenner & Smith, Inc. v. Ware, 414 U.S. 117 [1973], cannot fairly be read as a binding holding).

237. See, e.g., R. Dworkin, supra note 3, at 240–50 (suggesting variety of principles that can be drawn from a line of precedents).

238. See Pound, supra note 167:. "Then, too, we must distinguish subsequent judicial rejection of the reasoning by which the result was reached in a prior case and substitution of different reasoning leading to the same result, from a changed course of decision requiring a different result. It ought not to be necessary to say this. But one encounters constantly statements that a line of prior decisions has been overruled and a new line of decisions has been inaugurated, when all that has been done is to announce a better or more all embracing line of reasoning which will sustain the old decisions and lead to better results in new ones which have come up for the first time."

239. As Karl Llewellyn noted, a distinction exists between "the ratio decidendi, the court's own version of the rule of the case, and the *true* rule of the case, to wit, what it *will be made to stand for by another court*." K. Llewellyn, *The Bramble Bush* 52 (1960).

240. This statement is said to be a "tolerably accurate" description of the English understanding. R. Cross, *Precedent in English Law* 76 (3d ed. 1977); cf. N. MacCormick, supra note 228, at 86, 215 (propositions of law included in the holding).

241. "Courts do not accord to their predecessors an unlimited power of laying down wide rules." G. Williams, *Learning the Law* 75 (11th ed. 1982).

242. Washington v. W. C. Dawson & Co., 264 U.S. 219, 236 (1924) (Brandeis, J., dissenting). Max Radin long ago showed this in the common law context. See Radin, supra note 183, at 209; see also E. Levi, supra note 224, at 3 (rules evolve by focusing on important similarities and differences among cases over time).

243. Fallon, A Constructivist Coherence Theory of Constitutional Interpretation, 100 *Harv. L. Rev.* 1189, 1204–9 (1987).

244. N. MacCormick, supra note 228, at 83–84, 215. This point seems nicely illustrated by the various opinions in United States v. Stanley, 107 S. Ct. 3054 (1987) (construing Chappell v. Wallace, 462 U.S. 296 [1983]) (suits by servicemen for service-connected injuries).

245. Professor Schauer gives careful treatment to the difficulties of formulating categories of relevance without succumbing to the belief that "all characterizations of a past event are always up for grabs." Schauer, supra note 105, at 587; see also N. MacCormick, supra note 228, at 219–28 (pointing to similarities between interpretation of statutes and precedents).

246. One of Max Radin's most important criticisms was that the concept of precedent suffers, if not from incoherence, from indeterminacy. Radin, supra note 183, at 206–9. Other Legal Realists carried this criticism much further. Karl Llewellyn insisted that there are two concepts of precedent, one for those decisions that the court favors, another for those it doesn't. K. Llewellyn, supra note 239, at 67–69. See Llewellyn's iconoclastic list of sixty-four different ways to handle precedent, K. Llewellyn, *The Common Law Tradition* 77–91 (1960). Llewellyn's list has been summarized as comprising "eight ways to follow but constrict a precedent, eight to stand by it, thirty-two to expand it, twelve ways to avoid it and four to kill it." Wise, The Doctrine of *Stare Decisis*, 21 *Wayne L. Rev.* 1043, 1051 (1975). No doubt this brand of Realism captures much of the contemporary reality. But in principle this conception seems unacceptable, unless one is willing to reduce adjudication to rhetoric or to the function of simply masking the exercise of political power. Professor Shapiro, in Shapiro, In Defense of Judicial Candor, 100 *Harv. L. Rev.* 731, 734 (1987), seems to me to have overlooked this point when he accepted Llewellyn's model of precedents.

   While Edward Levi never embraced this cynicism, his own views are open to the same criticism. Levi insisted that the American doctrine permits courts unrestrained authority to realign prior cases in terms of the material facts as they see them: the precedent-setting court's own view of the material facts, the controlling rules and the operative theories are not part of the precedent. E. Levi, supra note 224, at 1–4. No doubt one can assign some type of interpretive leverage to the court called upon to apply the precedent. But Levi's view of the second court's function has a dangerous tendency to empty the concept of precedent of any meaning. Stare decisis becomes simply a matter of an expository style or technique, one that impels a second court, so far as practicable, to "place the situation they are judging within the generalized class of some existing decision." Radin, supra note 183, at 212. Moreover, recognition of unconstrained rerationalization readily induces cynicism. The Supreme Court's well known effort in Paul v. Davis, 424 U.S. 693, 701–710 (1976), to distinguish the apparently decisive holding in Wisconsin v. Constantineau, 400 U.S. 433 (1971), on the issue of whether reputation was part of the "liberty" protected by the due process clause seems to meet Levi's specifications. It also drew widespread condemnation as bordering on cynicism.

247. Schauer, supra note 105, at 587. Alas! Even this statement is not without exceptions. See Keystone Bituminous Coal Assoc. v. DeBenedictis, 107 S. Ct. 1232, 1240–50 (1987) ("distinguishing" Pennsylvania Coal Co. v. Mahon, 260 U.S. 393 [1922]); see also Oliphant, supra note 227, at 73 (each case and each precedent "rests at the center of a vast and empty stadium. The angle and distance from which that case is to be viewed involves the choice of a seat").

248. The very idea of a text is itself not straightforward; it is visible only through an interpretive lens. Accordingly, any concept of a constitutional text must subsume ideas about a constitutional language and grammar, which govern how the text is to be interpreted. And it is now commonplace that language is not a neutral mirror of reality, but is constitutive in character. Language helps shape, structure and define reality. E.g., B. Whorf, *Language, Thought and Reality* 246–56 (1956): Joseph and Walker, A Theory of Constitutional Change, 7 *Oxford J. Legal Stud.* 155, 175–78 (1987).

   For recent explorations of the contention that the Framers had such a grammar in the then existing common-law rules for interpreting documents, compare C. Wolfe, *The Rise of Modern Judicial Review: From Constitutional Interpretation to Judge-Made Law* 17–38 (1986) (widespread acceptance among the Framers of certain rules for interpreting laws and legal documents, all designed to ascertain the will of the legislator) with Powell, Book Review, 65 *Tex. L. Rev.* 859, 872 (1987) (Framers may not have shared a common understanding of constitutional interpretation); see also Jacobsohn, supra note 26, at 50–52.

249. Wechsler, supra note 181, at 1008.

250. 358 U.S. 1, 18 (1958).

251. See Hart and Wechsler, supra note 179, at 83–85. See generally Meese, The Law of the Constitution, 61 *Tul. L. Rev.* 979, 986–87 (1987) (Court's dictum in *Cooper* conflicts with the basic principles of democratic government and the very meaning of the rule of law); Perspectives on the Authoritativeness of Supreme Court Decisions, 61 *Tul. L. Rev.* 977, 991–1095 (1987) (symposium).

252. Meese, supra note 251, at 987.

253. C. Warren, *The Supreme Court in United States History* 470–71 (1922). For modern statements, see, e.g., S. Barber, *On What the Constitution Means* 5–6 (1984); Meese, supra note 251, at 985.

254. B. Eckhardt & C. Black, *The Tides of Power* 6 (1976). The same assumption inheres in such statements as "The paradigm of constitutional adjudication . . . is clearly distinguishable from traditional common law adjudication. In common law adjudication a new rule does replace an old one; the new rule's legitimacy is not dependent on its predecessor, or on any other collateral source of law." Note, supra note 120, at 368.

255. The Passenger Cases, 48 U.S. (7 How.) 282, 470 (1849) (Taney, C.J. dissenting).

256. See, e.g., Douglas, supra note 184, at 736 (the oath clause makes irrelevant the "gloss which [the judges'] predecessors may have put on it"); Note, supra note 120, at 365–66 (emphasizing the "writtenness" of the Constitution).

257. Grey, The Constitution as Scripture, 37 *Stan. L. Rev.* 1, 13–17 (1984) (emphasizing that Constitution is written).

258. See Black, supra note 154, at 26.

259. E.g., Vanhorne's Lessee v. Dorrance, 2 U.S. (2 Dall.) 304, 308 (1795). This conception emerged in the debates over the nature of the imperial constitution. J. Greene, supra note 149, at 71–72.

260. See G. Wood, supra note 90, at 536–43; Powell, supra note 45, at 39–43, 45.

261. Kamper v. Hawkins, Virginia (1793), quoted in Jacobsohn, supra note 26, at 83–84.

262. Id.

263. Marbury v. Madison, 5 U.S. (1 Cranch) 137, 178 (1803). Marshall added "in America . . . written constitutions have been viewed with so much reverence . . ." Id. at 178. In his posthumously published essays on the Constitution, Justice Miller wrote, "A constitution, in the American sense of the word, is a written instrument by which the fundamental powers of the government are established, limited, and defined." S. Miller, *Lectures on the Constitution of the United States* 71 (1891).

264. E.g., R. Berger, supra note 3, at 3, 363–67 (collecting sources): C. Warren, supra note 10, at 793–801. It cannot be overemphasized that we are concerned with public understanding. See supra notes 7–14 and accompanying text.

265. Interestingly, as late as 1890 Justice Miller seemed surprised at the emergence of a significant body of case law and that the Court was only then "completing a construction of our Constitution." S. Miller, supra note 263, at 100.

266. Dean Levi long ago made this clear with respect to statutory interpretation. E. Levi, supra note 224, at 31–33. The historic underpinnings of the written constitution argume᷉ ...forecloses treating the Constitution simply as a superstatute. Indeed, Justice Stevens is willing to accord stare decisis weight to the uniform decisions of lower courts in construing federal statutes. See McNally v. United States, 107 S. Ct. 2875, 2890 (1987) (Stevens, J., dissenting). But the superstatute approach has the advantage of reminding us not to view the Constitution as a document produced by a philosophy seminar. See Monaghan, supra note 16, at 390.

267. The Framers were familiar with the idea of precedent. See *Federalist* No. 78, at 529 (A. Hamilton) (J. Cooke ed. 1961). But there is no historical basis for asserting that they intended to accord a privileged position to precedent over text. The whole idea of just what precedent entailed was unclear. See Wise, supra note 246, at 1049 (because doctrine of stare decisis did not become firmly established in England until nineteenth century, colonial and early American courts had no such doctrine to incorporate); see also Kempin, Precedent and Stare Decisis: The Critical Years, 1800–1850, 3 *Am. J. Legal Hist.* 28, 33 (1959) (material from colonial period, although scanty, tends to suggest American courts had no firm doctrine of stare decisis); Powell, supra note 10, at 1536–37 (exploring the Framers' understanding of precedent in construing texts). The relative uncertainty over precedent in 1789 also reflects the fact that "many state courts were manned by laymen, and state law and procedure were frequently in unsettled condition. The colonial and state courts did not enjoy high prestige, and their opinions were not even deemed worthy of publication." R. Jackson, supra note 162, at 33. Moreover, during this time juries asserted power to determine the law as well as the facts.

268. Meese, supra note 251, at 981.

269. J. Gray, *The Nature and Sources of the Law* 125 (2d ed. 1963); see also id. at 283 (law is what the judges declare). Gray was referring to statutory texts, but the same argument may be made in regard to constitutional texts; cf. 1 W. Blackstone. *Commentaries* *71 ("the decisions of courts of justice are the evidence of what is common law"); see generally, Dane, Vested Rights, "Vestedness," and Choice of Law, 96 *Yale L. J.* 1191, 1216–12 (1987) (exploring differences between decision-based and norm-based legal theories).

270. Jones, supra note 191, at 12–13.

271. Taylor v. Illinois, 108 S. Ct. 646, 651–52 (1988).

272. See A. Bickel, supra note 158, at 31. At still another level, it might be asked whether in this view the judicial function is designed simply to create a false consciousness among members of the polity by closing off authoritative arguments about departure from principle. See M. Douglas, *How Organizations Think* 112 (1986) (a successful institution must control the memory and sense of reality of its members).

273. At least for the purposes of constitutional adjudication, have we in effect reformulated our notion of what a constitution is, returning to the pre–Revolutionary War idea that (symbolism aside) a constitution is essentially a description of the fundamental political arrangements?

274. Brest, supra note 7, at 250 (quoting Levinson, "The Constitution" in *American Civil Religion*, 1979 *Sup. Ct. Rev.* 123).

275. Kay, The Illegality of the Constitution, 4 *Const. Comment.* 57 (1987).

276. I owe strong insistence on these points to my colleagues at a faculty workshop, particularly Kent Greenawalt, Lou Henkin, and Jerry Lynch.

Expert Witnesses,
Rational Choice,
and the Search for Intent

J. MORGAN KOUSSER

STUDENTS OF THE INDIVIDUAL personality have been serving as expert witnesses since at least the seventeenth century, when Sir Thomas Browne assured an English jury that witches existed and that, in his opinion, the defendants in the instant case were, indeed, witches. Historians, psychologists, anthropologists, and sociologists only took on a like duty in the 1940s and 1950s with the preparation of the school segregation cases.[1] In *Brown* v. *Board of Education*, the Supreme Court and the litigants were concerned with the question of intent in two very different ways: they asked historians whether the framers of the Fourteenth Amendment had meant to ban racial segregation in schools or not; and they asked other social scientists, in effect, whether segregation was so harmful to black people that a discriminatory motive could be inferred.[2]

In the 1970s and 1980s, the discussion of what became known as *de facto* and *de jure* school segregation turned on the question of motivation, as did those of the legality of various housing laws and employment practices.[3] This stream of decisions perhaps reached its high-water mark in the 1980 voting rights case of *Mobile* v. *Bolden*, which brought historical expert witness testimony to the fore again.[4] In his plurality opinion in *Bolden*, Justice Stewart ruled that it was not enough to show that the at-large election feature of the Mobile City Commission had the *effect* of discriminating against blacks. Instead, it was necessary to demonstrate that the creators of the arrangement had adopted it with an *intent* to discriminate. For the next two years, debates over the renewal of the Voting Rights Act centered on whether an effect standard should replace what Stewart believed was the existing intent standard.[5]

Likewise, issues of intent were also central to the great brouhaha among historians in 1986 over the testimony of Professors Rosalind Rosenberg and Alice Kessler-Harris in the Sears sex discrimination case.[6] Rosenberg was asked to testify on the question of whether the apparent pattern of sex discrimination shown by employment statistics proved that Sears intended to discriminate against women in commission sales hires or whether women's allegedly different motives in seeking employment could explain the statistical results away. The EEOC employed Kessler-Harris to criticize Rosenberg's account of women's purposes. In the ensuing extrajudicial controversy, each of the combatants attacked the other's motives in testifying as she did. Moreover, the emerging strategy of the defendants in both voting rights and affirmative action litigation has concentrated on the use of statistics to prove or disprove intent.[7]

Determining the intent of Congress or other policymaking bodies continues to be crucial in courts as well as in other forums. *Weber*, the affirmative action case, turned on the legislative history of Title VII of the 1964 Civil Rights Acts. Whether the framers of the 1866 and 1870 Civil Rights Acts meant to protect whites of various non-British ethnic and nationality groups was crucial in two 1987 Supreme Court cases.[8] Two major confrontations between Congress and the Reagan administration have involved intent: Did the 1972 SALT I Treaty prohibit tests of beam weapons or other technologically advanced ballistic missile defense system components outside the laboratory?[9] Did the Boland Amendment prohibit the president and employees of the National Security Council from helping to provide military assistance to those seeking to overthrow the Nicaraguan government during 1985? Finally, in a series of nineteenth- and early twentieth-century commerce clause cases, and perhaps most memorably in the 1952 Steel Seizure Case, court decisions depended on judges' interpretations of the reasons why Congress *failed* to pass laws. However difficult it may be to discern the motives for inaction, the problem underlines the importance of discovering intent in statutory and constitutional law.[10]

Although they continually attribute motives to their subjects, historians have published very little on the concept of intention. Legal scholars have expressed themselves more systematically, distinguishing three varieties of motives: the subjective intentions of individuals, which are evidenced by what people say they meant to do and why they meant to do it; foreseeability, or the consequences that "objective" observers think could reasonably have been expected to follow from a particular behavior; and institutional intention, or the effect of a sum of a series of decisions by different officials.[11]

In this article, I shall argue that historians, political scientists, and judges unconsciously do employ all three notions of intent, and that none of the three should be discarded. To rely wholly on direct expressions of people's thoughts is to undermine a proper skepticism about misrepresentations, and, in the many instances in which there are few or no statements at all, to risk abandoning the search intent altogether. To concentrate exclusively on foreseeability is to invite nonterminating disputes between observers who differ on what various actors should have expected, as well as to disregard more straightforward evidence of motives. Finally, institutions do not act in the simple way that vectors do in physics. Institutional intent is often a useful conceit, but it may, like other figures of speech, embellish rather than clarify. The inevitable intermixture of all three notions of intent and the difficulties and advantages of each will be illustrated through an examination of these paradigmatic instances: statistical cases about differential treatment, laws, and a general constitutional provision, the Fourteenth Amendment.

I

EVEN WHEN white male Americans have openly admitted their desires to treat others differently, they have usually disavowed any hostile purposes. When they excluded blacks from common or "white" schools in the 1840s, for instance, the members of the Boston School Committee claimed that they were acting "in the best interests" of blacks. Similarly, southern whites and men everywhere purported to be protecting Afro-Americans and women by denying them the vote. It has never been easy to find sworn, public expressions of ethnic or gender discrimination that would satisfy an antipathetic judge.[12] As a consequence, both jurists and historians have generally turned to circumstantial evidence of intent, which has always included evidence drawn from effects.

It is misleading to mark too bright a line between "intent" and "effect," or "differential treatment" and "adverse impact." Evidence that the goals of certain policies were impermissible has almost always been a matter of inference, rather than of direct statement.[13] Thus, even where nineteenth-century judges ruled school segregation constitutional, they still gauged the motives of school boards by requiring that the education offered blacks had to be "substantially equal" to that given whites.[14] Those effects were often judged by evidence which was at least in principle quantifiable, such as per capita appropriations, teachers' credentials, the quality of school buildings, the distance children had to walk to school, and so on. There is nothing new in using statistics about effects to judge whether discrimination has taken place.

No reasonable person would expect Sears executives or southern legislators or city fathers to admit on the record that they intended to promote sex or race discrimination. Not even the disfranchisers of the late nineteenth century wrote race explicitly into their qualifications. Instead, they skillfully found correlates of race—literacy, property, conviction for such crimes as petty theft or miscegenation—and debarred people with those traits, maintaining that they wanted educated, honest electors who had a "stake in society." They then left it to minor administrators to carry out their actual and obvious purposes.[15] Similarly, present-day employers claim that they want only an aggressive, experienced, unreservedly dedicated work force, and framers of at-large election schemes desire cosmopolitan, rather than locally oriented commissioners, councilmen, or school board members.

The correlation gambit is also used when their practices are challenged in court. The strategy is to find correlates of race or gender and then to use them as explanatory variables, or if they cannot be measured, as explanations in principle. Past discrimination thus becomes an excuse for present and future discrimination. If Sears and other employers rarely hired women to sell consumer durables before 1973, it is not difficult to see why they had such trouble finding experienced women for such lines after that date. Throw in "experience" on the right-hand side of a regression equation, and the likelihood of finding a statistically significant effect for gender is reduced.[16] Likewise, individual Latinos and southern blacks have only recently attained much political visibility, they usually have difficulty raising as much money as white candidates do, and nearly all are Democrats, whereas most southern whites are now at least occasional presidential Republicans. Add such independent variables, and the effect of race on electoral success or polarization tends to wash out.[17] Likewise, in dismissing the most extensive statistical study of the death penalty ever made, the federal district court in the 1987 case of *McCleskey* v. *Kemp* emphasized possible excluded variables and the reduction in the effects of race when twenty additional independent variables were added to the regression equation.[18] But what do such equations really tell us about causation? What picture of the world do they represent?

The portrait is an unreal, idealized one, in which men and women have exactly the same employment histories, express a determination to sell in precisely the same fashion, have equal knowledge of what has heretofore been considered by employers to be a separate male sphere. It is a universe where blacks are just as educated and wealthy as whites, in which partisanship and race are unrelated, and in which the effects of past discrimination all disappeared at the stroke of Lyndon Johnson's pen on the Voting Rights Act. It is a state in which race has no judicially cognizable effect on prosecutors or juries, even though the chances of receiving the death penalty just happen to be seven times as high for blacks who kill whites as for whites who kill blacks.[19] It is a dream world concocted in a computer or a witness's or judge's head for the transparent purpose of preventing those egalitarian fables from becoming realities, a set of tautological creations in which discrimination-free utopias are assumed in order to prove that no discrimination took place.

II

THE DETERMINATION of the intent of the proponents of a law is always uncertain because of the indefiniteness of language, sloppy drafting, the complexity of the legislative process, the paucity of data on legislators' motives, imperfections in the correlations between attitudes and behavior, and multiple purposes of the actors. Sometimes, as Supreme Court Justice John H. Clarke once noted about the language of a particular statute, "it is so plain that to argue it would obscure it."[20] Yet even here, the difficulty of answering a question about motivation depends crucially on how broadly the question is phrased. If the law says that the speed limit shall not exceed fifty-five miles per hour, or that persons who use a gun during the commission of a felony must serve at least some time in prison, or that performing or conspiring to arrange an abortion is illegal, it is easy to identify criminal acts, but not so simple to discover why the legislators voted for the laws. Some may have desired to conserve energy, others, to prevent auto accidents; some, to inhibit violent crimes, others, to punish those who committed them; some, to protect the lives of fetuses, others, merely to avoid electoral challenges from the anti-abortionists or as part of a logrolling agreement.[21] Even an unambiguous statute may not provide unambiguous testimony on motives. The deeper motives of the legislators may be important when a judge is trying to mete out punishment or assign rights in cases brought under such laws, or when a plainly stated law fails to cover unforeseen contingencies. Judges in such instances often rest their interpretations on the lawmakers' broad purposes or on well-known legal principles with which they assume the legislators were familiar. Thus, in construing the law of wills in 1889, New York Appeals Court Judge Robert Earl stated that "a thing which is within the intention of the makers of a statute is as much within the statute as if it were within the letter; and a thing which is within the letter of the statute is not within the statute, unless it be within the intention of the makers."[22]

Inquiry into purpose may or may not be necessary to clarify a statute's meaning. But when a legislative or administrative body adopts a regulation which has the effect of treating groups of people differently, and the reasonableness of the distinction or disadvantage is called into question, courts usually have no alternative but to search for motives. Those who would confine judges entirely to the examination of a statute's language and effects not only needlessly ignore relevant information but they also launch judges on even less clearly demarcated, less certain seas of inquiry.[23] Unless their robes confer mystic powers, judges must look beyond statutory language and to complementary documents produced by members or employees of the relevant official body, to extrinsic materials bearing on the context in which the action took place, and to appropriate case law to determine why the officials behaved as they did.[24] How can this be done systematically?

A law may provide clues to its purpose and genesis on the face of its text, and a knowledge of other related events and of the legislature's standard operating procedures may yield interpretive hints. In 1901, for instance, the Alabama legislature passed a law changing the Dallas County Commission from an appointive to an elective body.[25] Each commissioner had to reside in one of four electoral districts, but all the voters in the county could cast ballots for every commissioner. As of 1981, when I testified in the Justice Department's challenge to this law in Selma—I was sixteen years late for the march, but things had not changed much, anyway—no black person had served on that black belt county's commission for over a century.

I began my testimony by noting that the at-large feature of that local law was added to the end of the statute in a fashion that was barely grammatical and wholly illogical.[26] In the penultimate clause of section 6 of the law, the winner was required to receive a plurality in the district, but the last clause provided that every voter in the county could vote for each commissioner, while remaining silent on what proportion of the whole electorate was necessary for election and what would happen if a commissioner carried the county but lost his district. When I read this to Judge W. Brevard Hand, who had in 1981 been considering the Dallas County voting case for five years, he remarked that the law was so unclear that someone ought to bring a legal challenge to it. The lawyer for Justice deadpanned that he thought that was what we were there for. Why would someone stick on an at-large voting scheme?

The historical context helped. Dallas County had been over 80 percent black since the early antebellum period, and its elected officials during Reconstruction had been either black or white radical Republicans. In the late 1870s, after Alabama had been "redeemed," the state legislature simply abolished local elections in this and several other similar counties, obviating the need for violence or ballot-box stuffing to maintain white Democratic supremacy locally. In 1901, the Populists had been at least temporarily defeated and a constitutional convention to disfranchise blacks and poor whites had been authorized, but not yet convened. Selma Democrats felt confident enough of their ability to control elections to have a bill on the subject introduced. Since Alabama legislators customarily deferred to their colleagues on local legislation (unless, of course, those colleagues happened to be Republicans or Populists), the bill sailed through without reported discussion, amendment, or any adverse votes. Whatever it was these locals wanted, they got. The legislative journals and even hometown newspapers were silent as to the reasons for the suspicious at-large section.[27]

Could the local notables in Selma have had anything to fear from blacks at the time? I concluded that they could have. Suppose that the constitutional convention were to adopt a literacy test as the whole disfranchising device. Despite egregious educational discrimination, the black density in the county was so overwhelming that a small majority of the literate voters, as measured by the 1900 census, would still be nonwhite. By mapping the electoral districts into census districts and sampling from the manuscript census returns, I was able to show that two of the four county commission districts would have had substantial black majorities in 1900, and a third would have had a bare black majority, if the electorate were confined to literate voters. In a district system, then, with anything like a fairly administered literacy qualification, blacks would control half the seats. In an at-large setting, however, it would take only minor skulduggery, compared to what Dallas County voting officials had perpetrated for the last generation in state elections, to segregate the courthouse completely.

It therefore seemed to me that the most plausible reason for the adoption of the 1901 at-large system was a racist one.[28] The at-large system provided insurance in case the convention only disfranchised illiterates or a widely expected lawsuit forced equitable enforcement of voting laws.[29] That is to say, lacking plausible direct evidence, I was forced to try to reconstruct what the crucial actors could have foreseen, and, by adding evidence of their purposes in taking other actions, to determine their motives in this instance. Judge Hand disagreed with me, suggesting during the trial that white Selmans could not have had a racist motive in passing the law, because they could always have stuffed the ballot box or killed their opponents. What motivated them, announced the judge—who has more recently attracted widespread attention by banning school textbooks that propagate what he terms "the religion of secular humanism"—was what he considered the fundamental human drive—greed. It was not so much that they opposed blacks, as that these whites wanted all the offices for themselves. The court of appeals somehow managed to produce a printable response to this reasoning, curtly overturning Judge Hand.[30]

Reflection on this example suggests two preliminary general rules for investigating legislative intent. First, knowing how the body operated in a particular instance—who wrote the bill, how was it changed in committee or on the floor, whether there was a partisan or sectional division on it, etc.—and how the body conventionally proceeded on analogous bills may indicate the importance of various actors in its framing. In this case, since the bill was passed without dissent as written by Selmans, and since the Alabama legislature in this period usually deferred on purely local bills unless they posed some danger to white Democratic supremacy, the intentions that counted most were those of the Dallas county delegation. Although in some circumstances, the weighting will be obvious and uncontroversial, in others, it will not be, and there, it must be justified openly and self-consciously.[31] Second, even if more evidence had been available, it would still have been obviously fallacious to ignore the social and political context of the times and any available evidence about the philosophies and motives of the key participants.

Few state legislatures have kept formal records of debates, newspaper coverage of legislative proceedings is sketchy (although generally less so in the

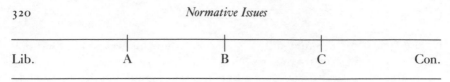

FIGURE 1
One Issue Dimension

nineteenth than in the twentieth century) and committee hearings and reports have rarely been extensive until rather recently. Thus, the amount of
data available for uncovering the motives of state legislators is usually less
than for an Act of Congress. Having less information makes it easier to come
to a conclusion, but harder to be sure of it. On major controversial bills, if
the historian is lucky, there will be a few partially reported speeches, some
frustratingly vague newspaper stories and editorials, a roll call vote or two on
amendments, and perhaps the text of the bill reported out by the relevant
committee. If the object of attention is a bill in Congress, one will almost
surely have this information, plus hearings and reports and maybe a few
mentions in private paper collections. For obscure or local bills, like the Dallas County local government act, the information will usually be much less
plentiful. Even in the best cases, however, inference may not be straightforward.[32]

To see why, it is useful to introduce the concept of an issue space.[33] To
start simply, suppose that we can scale an issue from the most liberal to the
most conservative position, or from spending nothing to spending, say, $1
million, or some other dimension that makes sense in a particular instance.
Suppose that every legislator has an "ideal point" or "bliss point" that represents the bill or provision that she would like to see adopted. Legislator one
prefers point A, two prefers B, and so on. Then if there are enough legislators and enough roll calls, we may be able to determine statistically not only
who ends up on the winning side of each, but where each legislator ranks on
the continuum. By relating speeches to votes, we may be able to nail down
these positions pretty precisely. Yet there are several difficulties and several
hidden assumptions in our analysis. Most importantly, we have assumed, in
effect, that everyone votes and speaks "sincerely," that no strategic behavior
or vote trading takes place.

Suppose that I am one of the 25 percent of the legislators who takes position C, while 30 percent are at about A, and 45 percent are close to B. (See
Figure 1.) Suppose I expect a sequence of votes in which B is the committee
position reported out, and it is matched first against A and then against C.
How should I vote on A versus B?

If I vote for the alternative nearest to my ideal point, I will favor B over A,
and B will win by 70–30. But on the next vote, B will defeat C, which I
prefer, by 75–25, so I end up with my second choice. (See Figure 2.) If I vote

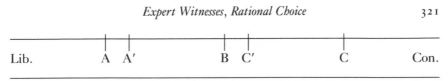

FIGURE 2

Strategic Voting in One Dimension

strategically on the first ballot, A will defeat B, and then C will defeat A, because the people at B are closer to it than they are to A. So, if I vote strategically and no one else does, I will get an outcome (in this example) more to my liking than if I vote my true preferences. If everyone votes strategically, and if the agenda itself can be voted on, the situation immediately becomes vastly more complicated and the outcome may be theoretically indeterminate. Since legislators understood the importance of not being earnest long before the invention of game theory or spatial models, the bare record will often reflect strategic maneuvering and speaking rather than "real" intent.[34]

Legislators may have incentives not only to vote against their own preferences, but also to distort what they think is the content of each proposal. If Group A can convince Group B that A is actually closer to B than C is, then A may win in a sequence of roll calls. Group A may fool not only Group B, but may also confuse later judges or historians. While the bill on its face may appear to be close to position A, the debate may imply the contrary. What should one conclude in this circumstance?

Two simplifying assumptions are often implicitly employed to solve this difficulty. One is that the majority's intent is concentrated at the position of the swing voter. We may refer to this as the "swing voter assumption." If C is the position finally adopted, then, according to this assumption, that is what the whole majority favored, even though we may have reason to believe that most of the members of the majority preferred, say, B to C. The majority of the majority may have been inept, or the rules may have been stacked against it, or its members may have been so risk-averse or so desirous of a consensus solution that they voted for their second choice. Another simplifying assumption is that the members of the assembly said what they believed and acted as they spoke. This I will term the "sincere voting and speaking postulate." Legislators did not contend that the bill's position was at C and at the same time secretly hope that a future judge would construe the bill to have been at position C.

In some important cases, we know not only that the swing voter and sincerity assumptions were incorrect, but also the direction or directions of the biases. It is often remarked, for instance, that opponents of a bill or argument may posit a "parade of imaginary horribles" perhaps marching down a "slippery slope" as the inevitable direction if the bill is passed or the reasoning accepted.

Let me give an example from the recent history of voting rights legislation. The key question in the renewal of the Voting Rights Act in the early 1980s was whether to alter section two to overrule the *Bolden* decision. To oversimplify, liberals believed that the best indicator of whether blacks and Latinos were disadvantaged by an electoral arrangement was whether the candidates of their choice—usually but not always black or Latino—were elected in proportion to the minority population. On a five-person board in a 40 percent black area, for example, two of the officials should be expected to be black. Conservatives, led by political appointees in the Reagan Justice Department, would have required proof of discriminatory intent or else would have limited the Act to a guarantee that blacks or Latinos could register and vote freely. Moderates wanted blacks and Latinos to have a chance to be elected, but feared that a proportionality test would become too mechanical and absolute, and would discourage the sorts of coalitions that elected people like themselves to office. Everyone wanted credit for the passage of an act which by 1980 had gained almost universal rhetorical support. No one to the left of Senator Jesse Helms wanted to be labeled a racist.

The compromise that was worked out was both ingenious and illustrative of the points that I have been stressing. Senator Robert Dole offered an amendment proclaiming an effect standard, but disavowing the necessity of proportional representation, and the Democrats, particularly the ranking minority member on the Judiciary Committee, Senator Edward Kennedy, allowed Dole to claim the credit for breaking the potential deadlock and pushing the bill toward passage. Since the compromise provision language was ambiguous, ancillary congressional materials assumed a heightened importance. In return for the credit, Dole allowed Kennedy to write the Senate Report on the bill, a task which he delegated to two of the chief civil rights lobbyists on the Act. These men not only wrote a strong effect standard into the report but edged towards proportionality. They also made sure that examples were drawn from all the legal cases that were either known to be pending or expected to be filed shortly. When a judge asked subsequently whether Congress meant the law to apply to a case such as that in Hopewell, Virginia, therefore, civil rights lawyers could simply refer him to the Senate Report, which used exactly that example. Moderates got the credit, liberals, the gloss, but what was the single intent of Congress?

The problem is further complicated by two other facts. Before the Kennedy-Dole compromise was proposed, section two had already passed the House without a specific disavowal of proportional representation, and the House bill had collected more than sixty Senate sponsors—enough to shut off a possible filibuster and nearly enough to override a presidential veto. Since substantial majorities of both houses, then, were willing to support the substitution of an effect for an intent criterion and to stop there, was it Congress's real desire to avoid a proportionality requirement? Moreover, in a characteristic display of chutzpah, the Assistant Attorney General for Civil Rights, William Bradford Reynolds, at least initially required his division to act as though section two had not been amended at all, and not to file cases unless the intent of the shapers of an electoral system could be clearly shown to have been discriminatory.[35] Strategize the agenda, strategize the votes, strategize the glosses, and let some poor judge or historian puzzle out what you wanted done!

To simplify their interpretive tasks, courts have often adopted rules of thumb, but as the 1982 Voting Rights Act example shows, an announcement of such rules can further complicate matters. If legislators know that courts will take statements in debate by major sponsors or the wording of congressional reports as authoritative, then the political game will be extended to include those documents, and "institutional intent" will seem to be more and more an artificial construct. Winning not only means winning the roll calls, but also victory in successive judicial struggles over the interpretation of the act. It is a complicated two-stage game with incentives for misrepresentation in both periods. Interpretation is at the very least a sensitive task, and no announced interpretive scheme is strategy-proof.

These difficulties are further compounded if we model the legislative situation more realistically by relaxing the assumption that there is only one bill, and that the bill's provisions are extremely simple. Suppose that in a 100-person legislature a bill has two provisions, neither of which is supported by a majority of the members. But each section has rather different coalitions for and against each, as in Figure 3, panel A, where majorities actually oppose each provision, or panel B, where a large minority opposes, but decisive minorities are indifferent. It is possible that in each case, skilled political entrepreneurs may be able to put together enough vote swaps, even without amending either section of the bill, to pass both provisions, as in Panel C of Figure 3.

The entrepreneurs' task will be facilitated if, for example, those who are unfavorable or indifferent or negative toward one proposal care more about the proposal that they favor than the one that they dislike. In this case, the swing voter assumption would be generally false, for on both provisions (or on two or more bills, in an obvious extension of the example) many of the swing voters were actually opposed or indifferent. In the presence of logrolling, then, the lawmakers' goals are fundamentally indeterminate.

Naturally, there are negative as well as positive logrolls, and one of the most famous examples is of the negative variety. In 1957–58, the Warren Court came under harsh attack by an uneasy coalition of segregationists and fervent anticommunists. The House passed a bill called H.R. 3, removing the Supreme Court's jurisdiction in a relatively minor class of cases, but seen by both sides as an entering wedge for much more substantial attacks. In a story that then-majority leader Lyndon B. Johnson often repeated in his ef-

Panel A: A Preliminary Lineup with Logrolling Potential

		Provision R	
		Yea	*Nea*
Provision S	*Yea*	35	15
	Nay	10	40

Panel B: A Preliminary Lineup with Decisive Minorities Indifferent

		Provision R		
		Yea	*Indiff.*	*Nay*
Provision S	*Yea*	35	22	05
	Indiff.	02	03	01
	Nay	05	05	40

Panel C: A Logroll Achieved

		Provision R	
		Yea	*Nay*
Provision S	*Yea*	51	05
	Nay	04	40

FIGURE 3
Rolling Logs

fort to court liberals in the contest for the 1960 presidential nomination, the Senate vote on H.R. 3 stood at 40–40, when latecomer Robert Kerr of Oklahoma, who was expected to support it, stepped into the chamber. Johnson grabbed Kerr by the lapels and backed him into the Senate cloakroom, reminded him not only of past debts to LBJ, but also of some pending public works measures affecting Oklahoma that Kerr strongly favored. The great arm-twister thus changed Kerr's mind, thereby, as Johnson put it with his typical humility, singlehandedly saving the Supreme Court.[36]

III

LAWS AND MOST constitutional provisions tend to be relatively specific. Recent constitutional amendments setting out the procedures for presidential succession, banning the poll tax, and allowing eighteen-year-olds to vote come to mind. But what of the broad clauses that give rise to so much constitutional controversy? What is freedom of speech, the press, and religion? What constitutes due process of law? What sorts of punishment are cruel and unusual? What nonenumerated rights are reserved to the people? What actions deprive persons of equal protection of the laws?

In *Government by Judiciary*, a book which provoked bitter controversy in law journals, but which has been largely ignored by historians, Raoul Berger attempted to show that the framers of the Fourteenth Amendment did not intend to outlaw segregated schools or malapportioned legislatures or, by implication, gender-based discrimination or interference in the decision to terminate a pregnancy.[37] Rather, the amendment was a carefully constrained attempt to guarantee the 1866 Civil Rights Act (which he also reads very narrowly) against constitutional challenge or partisan reversal. If Berger is right on the facts, and if constitutional provisions today should be interpreted to mean no more and no less than their framers intended, then the foundations of the major decisions of the Warren and Burger and even Rehnquist Courts are undermined. *Brown*, *Baker* v. *Carr*, *Roe* v. *Wade*, *Johnson* v. *Santa Clara*, and many more decisions represent not good law, but mere judicial overreaching.[38] In a pair of 1985 speeches that attracted widespread attention, Attorney General Edwin Meese, III and Supreme Court Justice William J. Brennan, Jr. engaged in a heated exchange that seems to portend an extended public debate on the issues raised by Berger, his allies, and their critics.[39] President Reagan's unsuccessful nomination to the Supreme Court of Robert H. Bork further underlined the crucial nature of the controversy.

Berger's detractors have taken two basic tacks. The first accepts or side-steps his reading of the intent of the framers, but dismisses his interpretive premise that the meaning of broad constitutional sections should be cabined by the views of men of one or two centuries ago.[40] This view is particularly strong among those who would extend constitutional protections to groups that clearly were not envisaged by Reconstruction legislators, such as gays, women, and welfare recipients.[41] The second, and less traveled, path is to question Berger's account of the framers' intentions.[42] By closely analyzing Berger's account, however, I shall attempt to show that the two strategies do not differ as much as might be imagined.

Berger adopts at least eight rules or empirical generalizations to simplify his interpretive task, none of which is uncontroversial and all of which bias his conclusions. Every interpretation, as Ronald Dworkin points out, rests on value-laden principles. The Constitution nowhere states that judges, executives, or legislators must discover and abide by the applications of broad principles to specific situations that the framers may (or may not) have had in mind a century or two ago.[43]

The first of Berger's principles I will call the "floor of Congress" rule— only recorded debates in Congress are probative.[44] This, of course, conven-

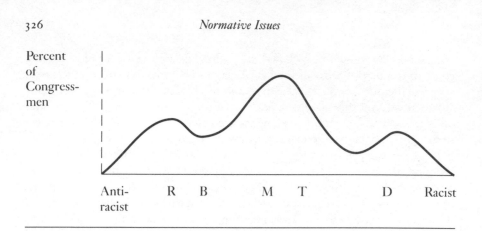

FIGURE 4
Extremists Can Be Swing Voters

iently limits the evidence that one has to examine, but it leaves out contemporary letters, newspaper stories, speeches, and ratification debates in state legislatures, as well as previous documents of all kinds that may illuminate doctrinal developments that led to the amendment, and actions or statements after 1866 that cast reflected light on the motives and meanings of the sponsors.[45] Even if Berger had not read silence as acquiescence and quoted from speeches very selectively, the rule would bias conclusions unless floor comments are a representative sample of all opinions, whether those opinions are officially expressed or not. Since large numbers of congressmen, state legislators, and campaigners, especially the more radical among them, said very little about section one during the debates, it seems unlikely that the *Congressional Record* is representative.[46]

Berger's second rule is what I have called above the "swing voter assumption"—Congress is taken to have enacted the bliss point of that legislator who is just on the margin between voting for or against the proposal. All members whose ideal points are to his right, say, vote "nay," while others would prefer more leftist proposals, but capitulate because without the swing person or group they would lose.

Closely related is Berger's third assumption, sincere behavior.[47] If some legislators vote or abstain strategically, then no single person or group is pivotal, and therefore no position in an issue space is. Suppose that there is a minimal majority rule in effect, for instance, a provision that a constitutional amendment must obtain two-thirds of the votes in both houses of Congress, and that opinion is distributed as in Figure 4.

In this graph, the vertical axis measures the number of people taking a certain position, and the three clumps of people have modes at R (for Radical Republicans), M (for Moderate Republicans), and D (for Democrats). There are more moderates than anything else, and Berger assumes, therefore, that the final position adopted will be at about M or even to the right, at T (for two-thirds). But suppose that the Rs indicate in public or private that they will either vote against M and T or abstain. Then they may be able to convince the other Republicans to favor B (for John A. Bingham, who is usually considered the most important framer), as against D, which amounts to no change at all. Since abstention and strategic voting were rife in the Thirty-ninth Congress, any political entrepreneur would anticipate the possibility and frame his proposals to minimize strategic defections.[48] Since most of the drafting of section one necessarily went on mostly in private, and since much of the floor strategy was thrashed out in private Republican caucuses, the possibility that the meaning of the amendment did not coincide with the moderate swing voters' position certainly cannot be ruled out.[49]

While he assumes that the proponents of the amendment were simple-mindedly sincere, Berger considers the Democrats strategic liars. He views as buncombe their claims that the measure would force the abrogation of school segregation and antimiscegenation laws and would empower the central government to protect all the rights of persons against the states.[50] Not only are Berger's remarks about each side's craftiness incongruous, but his characterization also implies a breadth and vagueness in the amendment that was necessary for the Democratic charges to have any credibility whatsoever. Yet such breadth would go counter to a fifth Berger predisposition—to consider the Fourteenth Amendment a point estimate, or, to put it in Dworkin's terms, an effort to legislate a "concrete," rather than a less specific "abstract" intent.[51] Scholars have often frustratedly remarked that most of the debate by advocates of section one was conducted in sonorous references to Magna Carta, the Declaration of Independence, and the protection of freedmen and southern white loyalists.[52] But should a debate about the most expansively phrased constitutional provision after 1791 have been focused on details of the moment, as if Congress were discussing petty and easily altered regulations, such as a tariff list, a rivers and harbors appropriation bill, or retiring greenbacks? Additionally, in a more practical sense, one of the chief tactics employed to hold any coalition together is ambiguity. If the amendment and the discussion on it were deliberately kept broad and vague in order to hold the Republicans together against a defecting president and a still possibly potent, unreconstructedly racist Democratic opposition, does it make sense to treat the amendment as a shorthand for a specific laundry list of positions on schools, suffrage, etc.?[53]

Berger also assumes attitude stability in three senses: First, the white northern public was, in his eyes, ineradicably and deeply racist and opposed to the centralization of power in the national government. This allows him to use statements from the antebellum era as evidence about feelings in 1866, to shove the abolitionists and their heirs offstage as a tiny minority, and to contend that all Republican politicians must have been terrified of taking liberal positions on racial matters, so that the Civil Rights Bill of 1866 and the Fourteenth Amendment must have been "conservative" measures.[54] Second, because he presumes that individuals never change, statements at any time in their careers evidence their views in 1866, and none of the events of that "critical year" moved them.[55] Third, he assumes that a "moderate" or a "conservative" position is constant in relation to some timeless scale. If the scale itself is in motion—if, for instance, black suffrage was a "radical" measure for Republicans in 1866, but a "mainstream" one by 1869, or if people shifted from faction to faction—then Berger's general argument, which identifies issue positions by their factional sponsorship, is undermined.[56] The argument is also both vague and circular. His strategy is to identify people with factions by informally and unsystematically lining them up on crucial issues, and then to denominate any proposal made by a member of one of these "factions" with that position in some eternal issue space. Thus, a "moderate" is someone who votes with other "moderates," and anything that he proposes or votes for is, by definition, "moderate."[57] Furthermore, Berger's assumption of individual and societal stasis, if ever an appropriate simplification, is surely inapplicable to the years of the growth of antislavery sentiment, the Civil War, emancipation, and the brutal ideological and social conflicts of the Reconstruction period.

A seventh postulate is that key words and phrases had temporally constant, knife-edge sharp, universally recognized definitions.[58] "Liberty" meant only what Blackstone had said it was—freedom of locomotion—a hundred years earlier.[59] All the patriotic and campaign oratory and all the antislavery campaign's books, pamphlets, and newspaper articles did not, in Berger's view, encrust the word with any additional significance.[60] By "due process," the Fourteenth Amendment's sponsors referred only to procedure, not substance, according to Berger, as though there were a "bright line" between the two and as though no antebellum natural rights-substantive due process tradition existed.[61] By "privileges or immunities," they signaled only their adherence to Justice Bushrod Washington's 1823 musings on the Article IV privileges or immunities clause, even though in almost the only mention of the point during the printed debates, the Fourteenth Amendment's Senate manager, Jacob Howard, specifically disavowed any intention to limit the clause to Justice Washington's enumeration.[62] By "equal protection," they evinced a desire to protect only those particular rights that they had enumerated in the 1866 Civil Rights Act, an act that Berger, unlike the Supreme Court and other scholars, reads very narrowly.[63] All of these presumptions serve Berger's evident purpose—to eliminate national protection of the rights of the disadvantaged—and there is little or no evidence for any of them.

Finally, Berger believes that white racial attitudes form a temporally stable Guttman-type scale, from allowing racial intermarriage on one end through school and jury integration, black suffrage, the right to hold office, and pro-

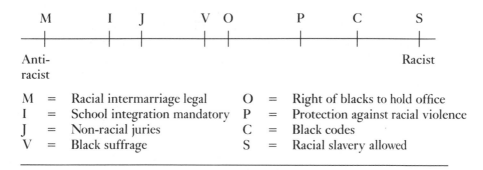

M   =   Racial intermarriage legal   O   =   Right of blacks to hold office
I   =   School integration mandatory   P   =   Protection against racial violence
J   =   Non-racial juries   C   =   Black codes
V   =   Black suffrage   S   =   Racial slavery allowed

FIGURE 5

A Hypothetical Guttman Scale of White Racial Attitudes

tection against racially-motivated violence, all the way to the "Black codes" and slavery on the other end.[64] In such a hierarchical scale, anyone who disavowed black suffrage, for example, must, to be consistent, also have opposed any policy to its left—for instance, school integration, as in Figure 5. If attitudes did form such a scale, if he has properly ordered it, and if no other factors affected people's votes on these issues, then Berger is justified in using evidence that Republicans did not force the suffrage issue in 1866 as support for his view that they did not intend to mandate school integration, outlaw antimiscegenation statutes, etc.

All three of these conditionals seem to me wrong. People may be much more willing to allow such private, voluntary, nonexternality producing acts as the choice of a marriage partner to be free of restrictions than they are to favor obligatory racial contacts that might directly involve everyone in schools or stores. Democrats with few expectations of capturing black votes might more vehemently oppose impartial suffrage than school segregation. Since other attitudes and interests affect white positions on racial matters, and everyone may not order the scales similarly, this last Berger assumption is just as dubious as its predecessors.[65]

The determination of intent will never be either easy or uncontroversial, but historians will be stuck with the problem so long as we keep asking "why?" and judges and lawyers, so long as there are statutes and constitutions to be construed. So far as I know, there is no general algorithm for discovering purposes, but the quest need not be an "unfocused hunting expedition."[66] Uninstructed "common sense" is frequently misleading. In this as in other instances, perhaps the best guidance is the most basic: do not assume that your subjects are simple or stupid; be conscious of your methods and biases; put your thesis at risk; and do not unwittingly adopt theoretical or evidentiary rules that decide the case for you. However obvious, these rules are too seldom strictly adhered to, and it never hurts to remind oneself and others of them—so that we may all live up to our good intentions.

Notes

1. The (Sir Thomas) Browne case is recounted in Garfinkel, Social Science Evidence and the School Segregation Cases, 21 *Journal of Politics* 37, 46–47 (1959). The literature on the use of social scientists and historians as expert witnesses is wider than it is deep, but for convenient introductions and references, see B. Levin and W. Hawley, *The Courts, Social Science, and School Desegregation* (1977); Bourgeois, The Role of the Historian in the Litigation Process, 67 *Canadian Historical Review* 195 (1986); Clark, The Social Scientist as an Expert Witness in Civil Rights Litigation, 1 *Social Problems* 5 (1953); Rosen, The Anthropologist as Expert Witness, 79 *American Anthropologist* 555 (1977); P. McCrary and J. Hebert, Keeping the Courts Honest: Expert Witnesses in Voting Rights and School Desegregation Cases (1986) (unpublished paper delivered at Southern Historical Association Convention).

2. Brown v. Board of Education, 347 U.S. 483 (1954). See, e.g., Rosen, supra note 1, at 557–62, and references cited therein.

3. Village of Arlington Heights v. Metropolitan Housing Dev. Corp., 429 U.S. 252 (1977); Washington v. Davis, 426 U.S. 1229 (1976); L. Tribe, *The Constitutional Protection of Individual Rights: Limits on Governmental Authority*, 1028–32 (1978); Binion, Intent and Equal Protection: A Reconsideration, 1983 *Sup. Ct. Rev.* 397, 398–403; Sellers, The Impact of Intent on Equal Protection Jurisprudence, 84 *Dickinson L. Rev.* 363 (1980); Simon, Racially Prejudiced Governmental Actions: A Motivation Theory of the Constitutional Ban against Racial Discrimination, 15 *San Diego L. Rev.* 1041 (1978).

4. City of Mobile v. Bolden, 446 U.S. 55 (1980). In *Brown,* historians had not actually testified, but had served as consultants to the NAACP, being asked to supply evidence to support that organization's contention that the Fourteenth Amendment was meant to ban school segregation. The responsibilities of private advisers and those who testify under oath are quite different.

5. See, e.g., Thornburgh v. Gingles, 478 U.S. 30 (1986); Sen. Rep. No. 417, 97th Cong., 2d sess. 2 (1982).

6. The U.S. Court of Appeals for the Seventh Circuit has decided the case, upholding the decision of the district court. In a 2–1 vote, Judges Wood and Eschbach made up the majority while Judge Cudahy filed a vigorous dissent. The court denied rehearing *en banc* on March 15, 1988. EEOC v. Sears, Roebuck & Co., 839 F.2d 302 (7th Cir. 1988). On the controversy in the historical profession, see Wiener, Women Fall One Step Back in Sears Case, *In These Times*, July 9–22, 1986; Wiener, Women's History on Trial, 241 *The Nation* 61 (Sept. 7, 1985); Winkler, 2 Scholars' Conflict in Sears Sex-Bias Case Sets Off War in Women's History, *Chronicle of Higher Education*, Feb. 5, 1986; Women's History and EEOC v. Sears, Roebuck and Co., *New Perspectives,* summer 1986, at 21.

7. For introductions to the issues involved in using statistics in employment discrimination cases, see Boardman and Vining, The Role of Probative Statistics in Employment Discrimination Cases, 46 *Law and Contemp. Probs.* 189 (1983); Shoben, The Use of Statistics to Prove Intentional Employment Discrimination, *id.,* 219.

8. St. Francis College v. Al-Khazraji, 107 S. Ct. 2022 (1987); Shaare Tefila Congregation v. Cobb, 107 S. Ct. 2019 (1987); United Steelworkers of America v. Weber, 443 U.S. 193 (1979).

9. See R. Garthoff, *Policy versus the Law: The Reinterpretation of the ABM Treaty,* (1987) (pamphlet published by the Brookings Institution); Chayes and Chayes, Testing and Development of

"Exotic" Systems Under the ABM Treaty: The Great Reinterpretation Caper, 99 *Harv. L. Rev.* 1956 (1986); Sofaer, The ABM Treaty and the Strategic Defense Initiative, *id.*, 1972.

10. Youngstown Sheet and Tube Co. v. Sawyer, 343 U.S. 579 (1952). Laurence H. Tribe argues persuasively that courts must interpret legislative and constitutional silence in L. Tribe, *Constitutional Choices* 29–44 (1985). For a contrary argument, see R. Dickerson, *The Interpretation and Application of Statutes* (1975). One might begin systematic thinking about how to interpret silence by distinguishing between active and inactive silence. The former is more probative, because the legislature is known to have been aware of a possible action and refused to take it—e.g., it refused to prohibit local governments from regulating ship pilots. The passivity of a legislature that is not known to have considered a particular provision obviously provides courts with less guidance. Even in the first case, however, the intentions of the body may be subject to differing interpretations. For example, in 1875 the House turned down amendments to that year's Civil Rights Act that would have allowed school segregation and that would have required at least equal, even if separate schools. Supporters of integration apparently preferred not to enshrine segregation, even if it meant failing to mandate equal racial expenditures, equal school buildings, equal term lengths, etc.

11. Note, Reading the Mind of the School Board: Segregative Intent and the De Facto/De Jure Distinction, 86 *Yale L. J.* 317 (1976) [hereafter cited as Note, Segregative Intent].

12. J. Kousser, *Dead End: The Development of Nineteenth-century Litigation on Racial Discrimination in Schools* (1986) (hereafter cited as J. Kousser, *Dead End*); Kousser, "The Supremacy of Equal Rights": The Struggle against Racial Discrimination in Antebellum Massachusetts and the Foundations of the Fourteenth Amendment, *Nw. U. L. Rev.* 941–1010 (1988).

13. Boardman and Vining, supra note 7, at 191–93; Note, Legislative Purpose, Rationality and Equal Protection, 82 *Yale L. J.* 123, 139–46 (1972) (hereafter cited as Note, Legislative Purposes).

14. Bertonneau v. Board of Directors of New Orleans City Schools. 3 F. Cas. 294 (C.C.D. La. 1878) (No. 1,361); U.S. v. Buntin, 10 F. 730 (C.C.S.D. Oh. 1882).

15. J. Kousser, *The Shaping of Southern Politics: Suffrage Restriction and the Establishment of the One-party South, 1880–1910* (1974); Kousser, Suffrage, in 3 *Encyclopedia of American Political History* 1236 (J. Greene ed. 1984).

16. Essentially, the variance of the estimate of the coefficient for gender will be increased if variables such as experience are entered into the regression equation, if gender and experience are correlated. And as the variance of the estimate rises, an analyst's confidence that the coefficient is not zero will fall. This confidence is what the concept of statistical significance usually refers to in such cases. This will hold for any two (or more) variables. For the mathematics of the statement, see E. Hanushek and J. Jackson, *Statistical Methods for Social Scientists* 87 (1977). For unstated reasons, Judge Nordberg accepted the unusually stringent standard of a "t" value of above 3.0 for statistical significance in the Sears case. If there were no difference in hires or salaries by sex, one would find one in a sample, using this criterion, only 0.27% of the time. The combination of including variables correlated with sex and making it so difficult to find a statistically significant effect for sex reduces almost to zero the chance of concluding that Sears was guilty of discrimination. For a good commonsensical discussion of the issues involved, see Note, Title VII, Multiple Linear Regression Models, and the Courts: An Analysis, 46 *Law and Contemp. Probs.*, 283, 286–88 (1983).

17. This strategy, pioneered in voting rights cases by Professor Charles Bullock of the University of Georgia, has been rejected by the U.S. Supreme Court in *Gingles*, and by Judge Harold A. Boker of the Central Illinois U.S. District Court in Frank McNeil v. City of Springfield, Ill., 658 F. Supp. 1015 (C.D. Ill. 1987).

18. McCleskey v. Kemp, 107 S. Ct. 1756, 1764 n.6 (1987).

19. Id. at 1770 n. 20.

20. Motion Picture Co. v. Universal Film Co., 243 U.S. 502 (1917), quoted in A. Bickel and B. Schmidt, Jr., *The Judiciary and Responsible Government 1910–21*, at 713 (1984).

21. Long recognized by scholars, these difficulties have aroused considerable skepticism about the possibility of determining legislative intent at all. See Note, Legislative Purposes, supra note 13, at 142.

22. Riggs v. Palmer, 22 N.E. 188, 189 (1819), quoted in R. Dworkin, *Law's Empire* 18 (1986). See Wofford, The Blinding Light: The Uses of History in Constitutional Interpretation, 31 *Univ. Chicago L. Rev.* 502, 526 (1964).

23. Clark, Legislative Motivation and Fundamental Rights in Constitutional Law, 15 *San Diego L. Rev.* 953, 974–75 (1978).

24. Thus, much of the legal scholarship on statutory interpretation, which concentrates on ascertaining meaning, is irrelevant to discovering purposes that may go beyond or even controvert apparent statutory intent. In particular, Dickerson's witty diatribe against the systematic use of most legislative documents, in R. Dickerson, supra note 10, at 137–97, is here beside the point.

25. Act of Feb. 8. 1901, No. 328, 1900–1901 Ala. Acts 890.

26. That such a potent inconsistency contradicts the usual presumptions about reading statutes (R. Dickerson, supra note 10, at 223–25) is one of many instances that underline the differences in inquiries directed at meaning and those focusing on purpose.

27. Reports in the *Selma Journal*, a local newspaper, indicate that the at-large section was in the text of the bill as it was first introduced into the legislature, so the provision was added by the bill's initiators, and not to conform to some statewide standard imposed by other legislators.

28. For an analysis of recent equal protection doctrine that focuses on how central impermissible purposes were to an action, see Meyers, Impermissible Purposes and the Equal Protection Clause, 86 *Colum. L. Rev.* 1184, 1208 (1986).

29. No one knew precisely what plan the convention would adopt at the time that the bill was proposed. Two lawsuits growing out of the convention's malpractices reached the U.S. Supreme Court in 1903–4. Giles v. Teasley, 193 U.S. 146 (1904); Giles v. Harris, 189 U.S. 475 (1903).

30. U.S. v. Dallas County Commissioner. 548 F. Supp. 875, 913–14 (S.D. Ala. 1982). rev'd in part and remanded, 739 F.2d 1529 (11th Cir. 1984). For fuller descriptions of Judge Hand's antics, see Caplan, A Good Ol' Boy Sitting on the Federal Bench, L.A. Times, March 29, 1987, at V–3.

31. Compare the unfortunately offhanded justification of weights in the case of the Fourteenth Amendment in Maltz, The Failure of Attacks on Constitutional Originalism, 4 *Const. Comm.* 43, 49–50 (1987).

32. It is easy to sympathize with Dickerson's remarks on "the frustrations, interminable prolixities, blind alleys, and dismal uncertainties of the prevailing patterns of legislative history." R. Dickerson, supra note 10, at 168. For the historian or judge concerned with intent, however, it is impossible to take Dickerson's advice about legislative history: ignore it.

33. A convenient introduction to the literature of "rational choice" is R. Abrams, *Foundations of Political Analysis* (1980). I have drawn freely and without attribution on the standard literature on spatial models and other aspects of rational choice below.

It might be contended that to attempt to determine the intent of a multi-member body is to conduct such an elementary fallacy of composition that it should simply be dismissed as ridiculous. If this were not enough, Kenneth Arrow's famous impossibility theorem about aggregating preferences provides a more formal proof of the absurdity of the effort. Nonetheless, lawyers and judges must construe legislative intent to do their jobs. If we are not to view their effort as merely an elaborate hoax, to cloak their own policy choices, then it is worth trying to understand how they muddle through in a non ideal world.

34. For game theoretic discussions of sincere and sophisticated or strategic voting, see Enelow, Saving Amendments, Killer Amendments, and an Expected Utility Theory of Sophisticated Voting, 43 *J. Pol.* 1062 (1981): Enelow and Koehler, The Amendment in Legislative Strategy: Sophisticated Voting in the U.S. Congress, 42 *J. Pol.* 396 (1980).

35. N.Y. Times, May 12, 1984, at A–9; N.Y. Times, July 27, 1985, at A–29; N.Y. Times, Sept. 6. 1985, at A–22; Voting Rights Review, Jan. 1987, at 2–3; Editorial, Boston Globe, April 13, 1987.

36. Most details of this story appear in W. Murphy, *Congress and the Court* 193–223 (1962). As the example implies, logrolling may not involve simple vote trading, but also trade-offs with more general goals, such as friendship or indebtedness to a leader or party loyalty. In a parliamentary system, backbenchers or even cabinet ministers may support statutes that they actually oppose out of loyalty or a disinclination to force a dissolution of the government. In such cases, the "true" intent behind the law cannot really be determined.

37. R. Berger, *Government by Judiciary: The Transformation of the Fourteenth Amendment* (1977). See Avins, De Facto and De Jure Segregation: Some Reflected Light on the Fourteenth Amendment from the Civil Rights Act of 1875, 38 *Miss. L. J.* 179, 246–47 (1967).

38. Johnson v. Santa Clara, 107 S. Ct. 1442 (1987); Roe v. Wade, 410 U.S. 113 (1973); Baker v. Carr, 369 U.S. 186 (1962); Brown v. Board of Education, 347 U.S. 483 (1954).

39. W. Brennan, Speech at Georgetown University 4–5 (Oct. 12, 1985) (reprinted in this volume); E. Meese, Speech before American Bar Association, 13–17 (July 9, 1985).

40. E.g., R. Dworkin, supra note 22, at 360–63; Alfange, On Judicial Policymaking and Constitutional Change: Another Look at the "Original Intent" Theory of Constitutional Interpretation, 5 *Hast. Const. L. Q.* 603 (1978); Bridwell, Book Review, 1978 *Duke L. J.* 907; Gangi, Judicial Expansionism: An Evaluation of the Ongoing Debate, 8 *Ohio N.U. L. Rev.* 1 (1981); Lynch, Book Review, 63 *Cornell L. Rev.* 1091 (1978); Munzer and Nickel, Does The Constitution Mean What It Always Meant? 77 *Colum. L. Rev.* 1029, 1032 (1977); Perry, Interpretivism, Freedom of Expression, and Equal Protection, *Ohio St. L. J.* 261, 270, 285, 292–97 (1981); Simon, The Authority of the Framers of the Constitution: Can Originalist Interpretation Be Sustained? 73 *Calif. L. Rev.* 1482 (1985); Tushnet, Following the Rules Laid Down: A Critique of Interpretivism and Neutral Principles, 96 *Harv. L. Rev.* 781, 800–01 (1983). The clearest and most persuasive statement is Brest, The Misconceived Quest for the Original Understanding, 60 *B.U. L. Rev.* 204 (1980) (reprinted in this volume).

41. Whether these critics seek other criteria because they find Berger's arguments convincing, or accept Berger too casually (in my view) because they want to argue for using other modes of interpretation is unclear, at least to me. Whatever the critics' intentions, I think they have failed to realize the weaknesses of Berger's specific arguments about the original understanding of the Fourteenth Amendment.

42. See Curtis, The Fourteenth Amendment and the Bill of Rights, 14 *Conn. L. Rev.* 237 (1982); Curtis, The Bill of Rights as a Limitation on State Authority: A Reply to Professor Berger, 16 *Wake Forest L. Rev.* 45 (1980): Kutler, Raoul Berger's 14th Amendment: A History or Ahistorical? 6 *Hastings Const. L. Q.* 511 (1979); Mendelson, A Note on the Cause and Cure of the 14th Amendment, 43 *J. Pol.* 152 (1981): Murphy, Constitutional Interpretation: The Art of the Historian, Magician, or Statesman? 87 *Yale L. J.* 1752 (1978); Soifer, Protecting Civil Rights: A Critique of Raoul Berger's History, 54 *N.Y.U. L. Rev.* 651 (1979).

43. R. Dworkin, *A Matter of Principle* 52–55, 165 (1985). See also Tushnet, supra note 40, at 784–96. Legal commentators such as Berger who urge the adoption of certain maxims of constitutional exegesis and conventions for determining intent do not eliminate normative behavior by judges or historians, as they claim to do. Lyons, Constitutional Interpretation and Original Meaning, 4 *Soc. Phil. and Policy* 75 (1986). Those theorists merely believe that choices should be made at the level of interpretive principles, rather than on matters of substantive policy, and they implicitly assert that those standards are neutral, and that they are chosen independently of substantive outcomes, as though they took place behind a Rawlsian "veil of ignorance." J. Rawls, *A Theory of Justice* 136–42 (1971).

If they do not, if the implications of adhering to a particular rule or interpretive formula can be largely if perhaps imperfectly foreseen, then any rigid distinction between choosing rules and choosing policies dissolves. In the instance before us, it is hard to imagine that Berger's muddled, often self-contradictory, law-office history was cooked up without a consideration of its present-day consequences, and utterly ludicrous to maintain that endorsements of his position by such persons as Attorney General Edwin Meese were.

44. R. Berger, supra note 37, at 6–7.

45. J. Kousser, *Dead End*, supra note 12; R. Dworkin, supra note 43, at 43–48; J. tenBroek, *Equal under Law* (1965); Bennett, "Mere" Rationality in Constitutional Law: Judicial Review and Democratic Theory, 67 *Calif. L. Rev.* 1049, 1091 (1979); Murphy, supra note 42, at 1755.

46. Soifer, supra note 42, at 682.

47. R. Berger, supra note 37, at 116, 241.

48. As Earl M. Maltz points out, radicals joined Democrats to defeat an early version of the reduction-of-representation section of the Fourteenth Amendment. Thus, uncompromising supporters and uncompromising opponents of black suffrage refused to accept a middle way. Maltz, The Fourteenth Amendment as Political Compromise—Section One in the Joint Committee on Reconstruction, 45 *Ohio St. L. J.* 933, 942 (1984). For further examples of such behavior, see D. Donald, *The Politics of Reconstruction, 1863–1867* (1965).

49. Mendelson, supra note 42, at 154–56; Farber and Muench, The Ideological Origins of the Fourteenth Amendment, 1 *Const. Comm.* 235, 273–74 (1984).

50. For a discussion of Representative Andrew Rogers's (D., N.J.) statement charging that both the 1866 Civil Rights bill and the Fourteenth Amendment would outlaw segregated schools, see Kelly, The Fourteenth Amendment Reconsidered: The Segregation Question, 54 *Mich. L. Rev.* 1049, 1066–67, 1074 (1956). For Berger's views on the untrustworthiness of Democratic statements, see R. Berger, supra note 37, at 157–65.

51. R. Dworkin, supra note 42, at 48–57.

52. Bickel, The Original Understanding and the Segregation Decision, 69 *Harv. L. Rev.* 1, 56–59 (1955): Farber and Muench, supra note 49, at 269: Kelly, supra note 50, at 1077.

53. Kelly, supra note 50, at 1071, 1084; Bickel, supra note 52, at 61–63. Charles Sumner, the protégé of Supreme Court Justice Joseph Story who succeeded Story as Professor at Harvard Law, and George F. Edmunds, for twenty years head of the Senate Judiciary Committee, stated in 1869 that the Fourteenth Amendment by itself enfranchised blacks. See 1 J. Story, *Commentaries on the Constitution* 686 (T. Cooley 4th ed. 1873).

54. R. Berger, supra note 37, at 10–16, 56–57, 85, 161, 407.

55. Mendelson, supra note 42, 158 n.34; R. Berger, supra note 37, at 91.

56. For evidence of the shift of the issue space see Kaczorowski, To Begin the Nation Anew: Congress, Citizenship, and Civil Rights after the Civil War, 92 *Am. Hist. Rev.* 45, 49 (1987). For evidence of factional fluidity, see A. Bogue, *The Earnest Men: Republicans of the Civil War Senate* 104–5 (1981).

57. Maltz, who also argues for a relatively conservative reading of the Fourteenth Amendment, provides a particularly succinct example of such reasoning: "The voting pattern on the Bingham substitute clearly reflects the Moderate origin of the current language of section one [of the Fourteenth Amendment]. The more Moderate and Conservative elements of the Joint Committee [on Reconstruction] were virtually unanimous in their support of the proposal. Among this group only Grimes dissented. One would hardly expect such near unanimity unless the proposal softened the language of section one." Maltz, supra note 48, at 963. The capitalization of factional labels presumably heightens the reader's sense of their reality.

58. R. Berger, supra note 37, at 134–56, 194–95, 200, 243. Cf. Bickel, supra note 52, at 34–35 ("Sir, I defy any man upon the other side of the House to name to me any right of the citizen which is not included in the words 'life, liberty, privileges, and immunities,' unless it should be the right of suffrage" [quoting the statement of A. J. Rogers, {D., N.J.}]).

59. R. Berger, supra note 37, at 2021, 34–35, 243, 270.

60. In an 1844 pamphlet, for instance, the abolitionist William Godell had defined the "liberty" of the Fifth Amendment due process clause as "the power of acting as one thinks fit, without restraint or control except from the laws of nature." Quoted in J. tenBroek, supra note 45, at 75. For a summary of the use of the term "liberty" in the debates over the Thirteenth Amendment, see id. at 167–68.

61. R. Berger, supra note 34, at 139–40, 193–214. Cf. Dred Scott v. Sanford, 60 U.S. 393 (1856); Wynehamer v. The People, 13 N.Y. 378 (1856); J. tenBroek, supra note 45. For an excellent critique of the substance/process distinction, see L. Tribe, supra note 10, at 9–20.

62. Mendelson, supra note 42, at 154–55; Farber and Muench, supra note 49, at 274.

63. R. Berger, supra note 37, at 171. For a much broader, and, I think, more convincing reading, see J. tenBroek, supra note 45, at 179–81.

64. R. Berger, supra note 37, at 123, 174, 239, 243 n.54, 412.

65. Maltz, supra note 48, at 947, 950 n. 75, 961, contends that Reconstruction Republican congressmen's votes did not always reflect their true preferences because of "political expediency," "the pressures" of "events," or "the need to preserve this newly found unity."

66. Note, Segregative Intent, supra note 11, at 325.

Select Bibliography

◆

──
──

◆

THERE IS AN IMMENSE body of scholarly literature on the history of the Constitution and all the questions—legal *and* historical—that its interpretation poses. This bibliography includes only items that bear directly on the contents of this volume or specific analyses of the original meaning of particular clauses.

The Public Debate

Berns, Walter. *Taking the Constitution Seriously*. New York: Simon and Schuster, 1987.

Bork, Robert H. "Original Intent and the Constitution." *Humanities* 7 (1986): 22, 26–27.

────. *The Tempting of America: The Political Seduction of the Law*. New York: The Free Press, 1990.

[Federalist Society]. *The Great Debate: Interpreting Our Written Constitution*. Washington, D.C.: Federalist Society, 1986.

Gabel, Peter. "Founding Father Knows Best: A Response to Tushnet." *Tikkun* 1, no. 2 (n.d. [1986]): 41–45.

Levinson, Sanford. "Clashes of Taste in Constitutional Interpretation." *Dissent*, Summer 1988, 301–12.

Kammen, Michael G. *Sovereignty and Liberty: Constitutional Discourse in American Culture*. Madison: University of Wisconsin Press, 1988. Chapter 7: "Constitutional Pluralism: Conflicting Interpretations of the Founders' Intentions."

────

Macedo, Stephen. *The New Right v. the Constitution.* Washington, D.C.: Cato Institute, 1987.

McNamara, Joseph S., ed. *Still the Law of the Land?: Essays on Changing Interpretations of the Constitution.* Hillsdale, Mich.: Hillsdale College Press, 1987.

Posner, Richard A. "What Am I? A Potted Plant?" *New Republic,* September 28 (1987): 23-25.

Taylor, Stuart, Jr. "Meese v. Brennan." *New Republic,* January 6, 13 (1986): 17–21.

Tribe, Laurence H. "The Holy Grail of Original Intent." *Humanities* 7 (1986): 23–25.

Tushnet, Mark. "The U.S. Constitution and the Intent of the Framers." *Tikkun* 1, no. 2 (n.d. [1986]): 35–40.

Historical Approaches

Belz, Herman. "The Civil War Amendments to the Constitution: The Relevance of Original Intent." *Constitutional Commentary* 5 (1988): 115–141.

Berger, Raoul. *Federalism: The Founders' Design.* Norman: University of Oklahoma Press, 1987.

―――. *Government by Judiciary: The Transformation of the Fourteenth Amendment.* Cambridge, Mass.: Harvard University Press, 1977.

―――. "'Original Intention' in Historical Perspective." *George Washington Law Review* 54 (1986): 296–337.

Bestor, Arthur, "Respective Roles of Senate and President in the Making and Abrogation of Treaties: The Original Intent of the Framers Historically Examined." *Washington Law Review* 55 (1979): 1–136.

―――. "Separation of Powers in the Domain of Foreign Affairs: The Intent of the Constitution Historically Examined." *Seton Hall Law Review* 5 (1974): 527–666.

Bickel, Alexander. "The Original Understanding and the Segregation Decision." *Harvard Law Review* 69 (1955): 1–43.

Cuddihy, William, and B. Carmon Hardy. "A Man's House Was Not His Castle: Origins of the Fourth Amendment." *William and Mary Quarterly* 3d ser., 37 (1980): 371–400.

Curry, Thomas. *The First Freedoms: Church and State in America to the Passage of the First Amendment.* New York: Oxford University Press, 1986.

Fairman, Charles. "Does the Fourteenth Amendment Incorporate the Bill of Rights? The Original Understanding." *Stanford Law Review* 2 (1949): 5–139.

Finkelman, Paul. "The Constitution and the Intentions of the Framers: The Limits of Historical Analysis." *University of Pittsburgh Law Review* 50 (1988–89): 349–98.

Grey, Thomas C. "Do We Have an Unwritten Constitution?" *Stanford Law Review* 27 (1975): 703–18.

―――. "Origins of the Unwritten Constitution: Fundamental Law in American Revolutionary Thought." *Stanford Law Review* 30 (1978): 843–96.

Hoffer, Peter C., and N.E.H. Hull. *Impeachment in America, 1635–1805*. New Haven: Yale University Press, 1980.

Kahn, Paul W. "Reason and Will in the Origins of American Constitutionalism." *Yale Law Journal* 98 (1988–89): 449–517.

Kelly, Alfred H. "Clio and the Court: An Illicit Love Affair." *Supreme Court Review: 1965*: 117–58.

Levy, Leonard W. *Emergence of a Free Press*. New York: Oxford University Press, 1985.

———. *Original Intent and the Framers' Constitution*. New York: Macmillan, 1988.

———. *Origins of the Fifth Amendment: The Right Against Self-Incrimination*. New York: Oxford University Press, 1968.

Lofgren, Charles A. *"Government from Reflection and Choice": Constitutional Essays on War, Foreign Relations, and Federalism*. New York: Oxford University Press, 1986.

Miller, Charles. *The Supreme Court and the Uses of History*. Cambridge, Mass: Harvard University Press, 1969.

Nelson, William E. *The Fourteenth Amendment: From Political Principle to Judicial Doctrine*. Cambridge, Mass.: Harvard University Press, 1988.

Rakove, Jack N. "Solving a Constitutional Puzzle: The Treatymaking Clause as a Case Study." *Perspectives in American History*, n.s., 1 (1984): 233–81.

———. [Comment]. *Maryland Law Review* 47 (1987–88), 226–33.

Shalhope, Robert E. "The Ideological Origins of the Second Amendment." *Journal of American History* 69 (1982): 599–614.

Sherry, Suzanne. "The Founders' Unwritten Constitution." *University of Chicago Law Review* 54 (1987): 1127–77.

Legal and Normative Issues

Anderson, William. "The Intention of the Framers: A Note on Constitutional Interpretation." *American Political Science Review* 49 (1955): 340–352.

Bittker, Boris I. "The Bicentennial of the Jurisprudence of Original Intent: The Recent Past." *California Law Review* 77 (1989): 235–82.

Clinton, Robert N. "Original Understanding, Legal Realism, and the Interpretation of 'This Constitution.' " *Iowa Law Review* 72 (1986–87): 1179–1279.

Dworkin, Ronald. *Law's Empire*. Cambridge, Mass.: Harvard University Press, 1986, chapters 9–10.

Farber, Daniel A. "The Originalism Debate: A Guide for the Perplexed." *Ohio State Law Journal* 49 (1988–89): 1085–1106.

Kay, Richard S. "Adherence to the Original Intentions in Constitutional Adjudication: Three Objections and Responses." *Northwestern University Law Review* 82 (1988): 226–92.

Maltz, Earl. "Some New Thoughts on an Old Problem: The Role of the Intent of the Framers in Constitutional History." *Boston University Law Review* 63 (1983): 811–51.

Monaghan, Henry P. "Our Perfect Constitution." *New York University Law Review* 56 (1981): 353–77.

Nelson, William E. "History and Neutrality in Constitutional Adjudication." *Virginia Law Review* 72 (1986): 1237–96.

Perry, Michael J. "Interpreting the Constitution." *Brigham Young University Law Review* (1987): 1157–1238.

Powell, H. Jefferson. "Rules for Originalists." *Virginia Law Review* 73 (1987): 659–99.

Sandalow, Terrance. "Constitutional Interpretation." *Michigan Law Review* 79 (1981): 1033–72.

Simon, Larry G. "The Authority of the Framers of the Constitution: Can Originalist Interpretation Ever Be Justified?" *California Law Review* 73 (1985): 1482–1539.

Tushnet, Mark V. "Following the Rules Laid Down: A Critique of Interpretivism and Neutral Principles." *Harvard Law Review* 96 (1983): 781–827.

White, James Boyd. "Constructing a Constitution: 'Original Intention' in the Slave Cases." *Maryland Law Review* 47 (1987–88): 239–70.

Contributors

◆

＝＝＝

◆

ROBERT H. BORK, formerly Professor of Law at Yale University and Judge of the United States Court of Appeals for the District of Columbia, is now a fellow at the American Enterprise Institute.

WILLIAM J. BRENNAN, JR., served as the senior Associate Justice of the United States Supreme Court until his retirement in 1990.

PAUL BREST is Dean of the Stanford Law School.

LINO GRAGLIA is the A. Dalton Cross Professor of Law at the University of Texas at Austin.

JAMES H. HUTSON is Chief of the Manuscript Division at the Library of Congress.

J. MORGAN KOUSSER is Professor of History and Social Science at the California Institute of Technology.

CHARLES A. LOFGREN is the Roy P. Crocker Professor of American History and Politics at Claremont McKenna College.

EDWIN MEESE III, formerly Attorney General of the United States, is a fellow at the Heritage Foundation.

HENRY PAUL MONAGHAN is the Harlan Fiske Stone Professor of Constitutional Law at Columbia University.

H. JEFFERSON POWELL is Professor of Law and Divinity at Duke University.

JACK N. RAKOVE is Professor of History at Stanford University.

Index of Cases

◆

═══

◆

General Index

✦

⸻
⸻
⸻

✦

Abortion, 36, 41, 180, 266–67

Abrams, Elliot, 298*n*94

Accuracy: of Convention journals, 154–56; of Madison's Convention notes, 162–68; of records of ratification debates, 158–62; of Yates's notes, 156–58

Ackerman, Bruce, 275, 303*n*154

Adams, John, 54, 75, 186

Adams, John Quincy, 58, 108*n*246, 154–55, 159, 165

Adjudication: defects of, 259*n*92; moderate originalism and, 245–46, 252–53

Administrative state, 270, 275

Adopters: consent of, as binding on later generations, 243; identity of, 234; perspective of, 238–39. *See also* Framers; Ratifier intent

Agenda limitation, and stare decisis, 274–75, 278, 302*n*133

Alabama, intent of voting statute in, 318–19

Alien and Sedition Acts, 75–77, 103*n*202

Alien Enemies Act, 104*n*213. *See also* Alien and Sedition Acts

Ambiguity: identity of originators and, 118; of institutional intent, 235–36; interpreta-

tion and, 60, 68–69; in language, 322; sovereignty issue and, 107*n*238

Amendment process, 111*n*287, 303*n*154; as challenge to nonoriginalist adjudication, 251–52; early views of interpretation and, 133–34; ratifier intent and, 127

Ames, Fisher, 101*n*150

Analogical reasoning, 217–18, 283, 307*n*198

Anglican Book of Common Prayer, 89*n*19

Annals of Congress, 168–69

Anti-Federalists. *See under* Ratification

Anti-interpretive tradition, 56–58

Arrow, Kenneth, 332*n*33

Articles of Confederation: contractual model and, 63; Madison's role in, 184; origin of Constitution and, 14, 42, 77–78, 98*n*112

Atherton, Joshua, 160

Attitude stability, 327–29

Bacon, Francis, 60

Baldwin, Abraham, 100*n*149, 132, 134

Bass, Andrew, 98*n*107

Bassett, Richard (Justice), 96*n*83

Beccaria, Cesare, 57

References to cases may be found in Index of Cases

⸻

347